Natural Enemies

Natural Enemies

The United States and the Soviet Union in the Cold War, 1917-1991

Robert C. Grogin

LEXINGTON BOOKS
Lanham • Boulder • New York • Oxford

LEXINGTON BOOKS

Published in the United States of America
by Lexington Books
4720 Boston Way, Lanham, Maryland 20706

12 Hid's Copse Road
Cumnor Hill, Oxford OX2 9JJ, England

British Library Cataloguing in Publication Information Available

Library of Congress Cataloging-in-Publication Data

Grogin, R. C. (Robert C.), 1935-
    Natural enemies : the United States and the Soviet Union in the Cold War, 1917-
1991 / Robert C. Grogin.
        p. cm.
    Includes bibliographical references and index.
    ISBN 0-7391-0139-0 (cloth: alk. paper)—ISBN 0-7391-0160-9 (paper : alk. paper)
        1. United States—Foreign relations—Soviet Union. 2. Soviet Union—Foreign
relations—United States. 3. Cold War. I. Title.

E183.8.S65 G756 2000
327.73047—dc21   00-030979

Printed in the United States of America

♾™ The paper used in this publication meets the minimum requirements of American
National Standard for Information Sciences—Permanence of Paper for Printed Library
Materials, ANSI/NISO Z39.48–1992.

for my children:
William
Daniel
Rebecca

Contents

Acknowledgments

I am deeply grateful to a number of people from whose advice and support I have benefited in the preparation of this book. I would like to thank Professor Larry Stewart, Chairman of the History Department, University of Saskatchewan, for reading the manuscript and improving it immeasurably. I would also like to thank Professor Jene Porter of the Department of Political Studies, University of Saskatchewan, who gave me solid encouragement in this project and who offered thoughtful criticism of the interpretation underpinning it. Long conversations with him during the course of many years helped me clarify the ideas in this book. His insights have affected me in more ways than he can know.

A special appreciation goes to Jean Horosko who typed the manuscript, and to Joni Mazer whose valuable expertise contributed to the final revisions of the book.

Finally, I owe a substantial debt to my wife, Esther, who has shared my life for the last thirty-three years and whose enduring encouragement I acknowledge with deep appreciation.

Introduction

This book is about the emergence and development of one of the key power struggles of modern times. It spans the entire history of the Cold War from the emergence of Leninism in the Russian Revolution of 1917 to the disintegration of communism in the 1980s and the lowering of the Red Flag in Moscow in 1991.

Natural Enemies argues the thesis that the Cold War arose out of the clash of two ideologically motivated political systems—between a United States that projected a Wilsonian-inspired traditional power politics and the radical nature of the Soviet regime. This book demonstrates that through the course of time there developed on both sides a belief in the essential incompatibility of their separate views of the international system—one Leninist, the other Wilsonian—and of the great powers in it. The historical struggle between them, the book argues, was irreconcilable and bound to lead to conflict. Because it was, there was bred in each country the sense of being natural enemies.

Natural Enemies explores the widening gulf between the superpowers arising out of their wartime alliance and examines the consequences of the key conferences: Teheran, Yalta, and Potsdam. It covers the postwar crises during which the Iron Curtain arose and the Cold War hardened into its permanent form. The middle chapters therefore deal with the creation of the Soviet Bloc; the crisis of 1946 in Iran, Turkey, and Greece; the Truman Doctrine and the Marshall Plan; the Berlin Blockade and the formation of NATO. Chapters eleven to twenty deal with those crises that sharpened the conflict in the Third World: the Korean War, the Suez Crisis, the Cuban Missile Crisis, the Vietnam War, etc., and the various attempts at détente. The final chapters examine at great length the collapse of communist power in Eastern Europe, both within the U.S.S.R. and within the Soviet Bloc.

1

Background to the Conflict

In his justifiably famous book, *Democracy in America* (1835), Alexis de Tocqueville prophetically anticipated the impending geo-strategic power shifts of the modern era.

> There are now two great nations in the world which, starting from different points, seem to be advancing toward the same goal . . . All other peoples seem to have nearly reached their natural limits and to need nothing but to preserve them; but these two are growing. All the others have halted or advanced only through great exertions; they alone march easily and quickly forward along a path whose end no eye can yet see . . . Their point of departure is different and their paths diverse; nevertheless, each seems called by some recent design of Providence one day to hold in its hands the destinies of half the world.[1]

What de Tocqueville was saying in early anticipation of Sir Halford Mackinder's seminal lecture on geo-politics (1904) was that certain states that were uniquely endowed by their size and their industrial and agricultural potential could and would take advantage of their interior lines of communication and their steadily expanding frontiers and populations to eventually build empires of the future. And since power was shifting to the vast, continent-wide states it was clearly inevitable, according to de Tocqueville, that the United States and Russia would try and shape the international environment in their own images. Twelve years later, in 1847, the literary critic and historian Charles-Augustin Saint-Beuve, claimed that "the future of the world lies between these two masters. One day they will collide . . ." Saint-Beuve was acknowledging something very basic in the international political system; that great power rivalry is integral to that system of world politics and that if history teaches us anything it is that great states traditionally distrust each other and that sooner or later they become adversarial. What reinforced this in the case of the United States and Russia was a shared belief in the natural superiority of a particular system. The American political tradition was democratic and invited immigrants to share in a society that set strict limits to governmental intervention. Tsarist Russia, on the other hand, had always been a closed society under a monarchy as absolute as any in Europe, where the state played the leading role in

1

Chapter One

national life. Despite the obvious differences between the two systems, it is clear
that Ralph Waldo Emerson's claim for America in 1844 that "she should speak for
the human race" is the same assertion that most Russians had been making since
the sixteenth century. In that century Ivan IV assumed the title of Tsar and led the
first of many Russian wars of conquest resulting in the extensive Russification of
foreign peoples, as well as occasional forced resettlements of them. Beginning in
1500, every seven years Russia added as much territory to its empire as that
occupied by the kingdom of Norway.² Mobilized in this "messianic" drive were the
services of the Orthodox Church. Since Ivan's day, despite the invidious
comparisons between backward Russia and the always more advanced West, the
Russians have claimed superiority, arguing that Holy Russia, "The Third Rome,"
that unique mixture of autocracy, orthodoxy, and nationality, and not the Catholic
west represented true Christianity. Both the United States and Russia, as different
as they obviously were, and situated at opposite ends of the globe, felt called by
their histories and by a divine Providence to special civilizing missions and
destinies.

Nevertheless, if Russia was locked in a great power struggle at all by the
nineteenth century, it was with Great Britain and not the United States. For most
of the century relations between the United States and Russia were distant and
tranquil.³ Until the end of the century Americans sought to preserve their unique
experiment of keeping the country aloof from the sordid quarrels of the rest of the
world.

Relations between the United States and Russia began to deteriorate in the last
third of the nineteenth century. During this generation both countries consolidated
their frontiers, attracted huge investments from abroad, began an accelerated
program of railway construction and industrialization, and moved forcefully from
the nationalist to the imperialist state of expansion. Certainly by the Spanish-
American War in 1898—which was America's debut as a great power—and the
subsequent administration of Theodore Roosevelt, the United States had become
the world's leading industrial power. By 1900 it was reaching out for colonies and
exercising a strong and independent influence in international affairs commensurate with that power. Along with other major states, especially Great Britain and
Japan, the United States sought to expand commercially into the power vacuum left
by the political decline of Manchu China. That expansion brought them into
contact with the Russian sphere of influence in North East Asia. The American
Open Door Policy grew out of this new power constellation. The policy, itself a
consequence of the recent rapprochement in Anglo-American relations, was
designed both to open up the China market to the trade of all the world (and
specifically the United States), and, at the same time, to guarantee the territorial
integrity of China. The new Anglo-American relationship and the British alliance
with Japan in 1902 for a time left Russia as isolated as she had been in the Crimean
War of the 1850s.

A further reason for the growing suspicion and hostility between the two states,
especially on the American side, was the changing American perceptions of Tsarist

Russia. Once reasonably neutral about conditions in Russia and unwilling to link the domestic arrangements of any country with its foreign policy, Americans began to view autocracy (and not just the Tsarist variant) in a new light. What had been traditionally regarded as virtues in Russia were now seen as serious defects in the United States. Driven by the emergence of a new, informed public opinion and the expansion of public education and literacy, and led at times by the large and often truculent press, Americans for the first time took a more than passing interest in the internal systems of both great and small states. Americans had not done this before, remaining curiously silent even during the Latin American wars of independence in the 1820s. Now in the 1880s and especially following the assassination of Tsar Alexander II in 1881, the American view of the world became more politically pointed. That this was so was due not only to the major economic changes in the country but also to the dramatic social changes in American society. The period 1880-1910 witnessed an enormous tide of immigration into the United States, much of it coming from the Russian empire. It helped make Americans aware of the appalling conditions in Eastern Europe. The American people were increasingly informed about the prison camp system of Tsarist Russia and about the mass persecution of that country's minorities, especially its Jewish population. Two incidents in the early part of the twentieth century served to focus American hostility on the Tsarist regime: one was the pogrom in Kishinev in 1903 in which hundreds of Jews were killed; the other was the Mendel Beilis case of 1911, a ritual murder charge brought against a Russian Jew.

With the news of the Kishinev pogrom there was a massive outpouring of moral indignation in the United States against the Tsarist government, and not only from the country's Jewish minority; from thousands of clergymen, publicists, and politicians was heard praise for Jews as champions of the oppressed and supporters of democracy.[4] No one did this more dramatically than President Theodore Roosevelt himself who that same year lashed out at the Tsarist government and condemned the pogroms. In 1911 during the Beilis Trial the Taft administration saw fit to abrogate an old commercial treaty between the two countries dating from 1832. In both cases American protests were ignored. Russia was as insular and as impervious to outside criticism as it would be in the later Cold War.

There was more here in these two episodes than mere deference to pressure groups protesting the repression of co-religionists abroad and seeking a linkage between the political nature of a country and its foreign policy. To be sure, these incidents produced banquet speeches, mass rallies, petitions, a torrent of newsprint, and, of course, pressure on Washington to do something. (Irish-Americans had tried in a similar way to alter Washington's foreign policy vis-à-vis Great Britain all through the nineteenth century.) But there was also in the United States a more general tendency to see in the ideas and deeds of the Tsarist authorities not only the dead hand of the past but the complete bankruptcy of the old order. At the same time, Americans seemed to be trumpeting their own modernity and, of course, their own exceptionalism. Their motives in trying to reshape foreign policy toward Russia were basically humanitarian. The moral and legal outrage was genuine as was the feeling that the special dispensation that had blessed the country should be converted into the service of all mankind. This need to extend the American political and economic system to the rest of the world and especially to backward Russia has remained a staple of America's relationship with Russia and later the Soviet Union, ever since. As John Lewis Gaddis has pointed out, there was a connection between the progressive reform movement in the United States and the increasing hostility toward Tsarist Russia. The progressives, he argues, emphasized the virtues of efficiency, honesty, and social justice—the very qualities Americans thought missing in Russia, and the very things that Theodore Roosevelt indicated as defining qualities in national life when he privately denounced the Russians during the negotiations ending the Russo-Japanese War.[5]

In other words, what originally created the jaundiced American view of Tsarist Russia was a combination of things: the vicious and backward nature of the regime now revealed in the light of day, the demands of pressure groups for redress of grievances in an attempt to reshape their country's foreign policy toward that regime, and at the same time, the unrealistic power of morality and legality as it was embodied in the American experience to remake certain despotisms after the American example, and, finally, the growing belief in the beneficent impact of world opinion, which would in a more rational world soon replace power politics as the major force in international affairs. What Americans could not see was that the Tsarist despotism, moribund as it was on the eve of the Great War, was still able to generate in many of its people a sense of being on virtue's side. The American attempt to create a better world in 1903 and 1911 was as disconnected from the hard facts of political life as it proved to be in 1919.

All of this in the generation before the Great War does not by any stretch of the imagination constitute conflict. There was a publicly declared contempt and outrage and certainly irritation and friction, but nothing approaching conflict. Standing in 1900 it would have been easy to ignore the warnings that de Tocqueville and Saint-Beuve made so long before. The majority of people in 1900 viewed the prospects for the new century in extremely optimistic terms. People everywhere placed their hopes for a peaceful and progressive future on the general acceptance of a more rational behavior among the major states of the world. Even Tsarist Russia, despite its periodical lapses into cruelty and repression, introduced a fledgling parliament in 1906 (admittedly under the impetus of revolution) and helped to initiate the Hague conferences of 1899 and 1907.

The meetings at the Hague were envisaged as steps toward a more adequate organization of the state system. In fact, by the second conference in 1907, which included representatives of forty-four states, one could conclude that the world by that year achieved its first General Assembly. The Russian government, sensing its own fragility and concerned about the costs of the contemporary arms race, helped to reintroduce at the Hague the old concert of Europe concept of regular, periodic international conferences, along with agencies like the Permanent Court of Arbitration and various international commissions of inquiry that would be at the permanent disposal of concerned states. It is not hard to see why so many people clung to the belief that the new century would be better than the old one and would in short order realize the liberal ideal in international relations.

As the clouds of war gathered on the eve of 1914 relations between the United States and Russia remained, on the whole, as stable and as correct as they had been in the nineteenth century. The fact that Russia belonged to an alliance system that included Great Britain and France and that the United States remained in isolation was responsible for this. There was as yet no belief between them in the necessity of a struggle for survival so characteristic of the later Cold War, nor was there even a basic incompatibility between their views of the international system and of the great powers in it, and there was no sense of a conflict between living and dying nations so endemic in Europe during the imperial epoch. The United States held itself aloof from the arms race and the alliance systems of the day, while Russia was about to place its very life as a state in jeopardy. No one in 1913, the last full year of peace, could foresee the collapse of European monarchies and empires, the rise of communism in Russia and Nazism in Germany, or the war and superpower conflict that would follow from all the history that would be made after 1914. What few could picture, let alone predict, was the seminal event of twentieth-century history—the First World War.

Notes

1. Alexis de Tocqueville, *Democracy in America,* trans. George Lawrence (New York: Harper and Row, 1966), I, 378-79.

2. According to the analysis of Fridtjof Nansen, cited in Elena Klepikova and Vladimir Solovyov, "Russia's Geographic Imperialism," *The Guardian,* 30 March 1980, 17-18.

3. Norman Saul, *Distant Friends. The United States and Russia, 1763-1867* (Lawrence: University Press of Kansas, 1991).

4. Albert S. Lindemann, *Three Anti-Semitic Affairs (Dreyfus, Beilis, Frank) 1894-1915* (Cambridge: Cambridge University Press, 1991), 204-9.

5. John Lewis Gaddis, *The Long Peace. Inquiries into the History of the Cold War* (New York: Oxford University Press, 1987), 9.

2

The United States,
the Soviet Union, and World Revolution

Alongside the glorification of war so prevalent in the period leading up to 1914 went premonitions of catastrophe. While it was true that one could find groups in the brittle empires of Austria-Hungary and Russia that tended to view war as an enormous antidote to the domestic revolutionary movement, there were others who inclined to the view that a general European war would only serve to finish off the monarchies permanently and increase the potential for radical social and political change. It seems clear that the Tsar, Nicholas II, belonged to the latter group.

Ascending to the throne of Russia in 1896 in an atmosphere of decline and continually beset by what he felt were mounting spectres of doom, Nicholas represented a curious blend of hope and fatalism. He was hopeful that a clever diplomacy could hold off the approaching catastrophe and his initiatives in calling for the Hague conferences certainly point in that direction, as did his letters to his cousin, Wilhelm II of Germany—the so-called Willi-Nikki correspondence. Sensing the fragility of his regime as the internal revolutionary crisis grew, and hearing the mounting drum beat for war, the Tsar remained fatalistic about his country's chances of averting the collision.

It is a commonplace that Imperial Russia was doomed to collapse, if not through war then through natural attrition. The Russian decision for war in 1914 was made when there were no less than one hundred thousand men on strike in St. Petersburg alone, many from the important weapons factories. Moreover, the decision was made despite the fact that by the first half of 1914 strikes were breaking out at a rate of sixteen new ones a day. This was a mounting revolutionary crisis and clearly it was not in the national interest to declare war. All the chief executives of 1914—Nicholas II, Wilhelm II, and Francis Joseph of Austria-Hungary—who initially hesitated and wished to draw back from the brink—could ultimately neither stand up to the pressures of the crisis nor resist the appetite for action of their general staffs. Disregarding the mounting revolutionary storm Nicholas took his country to war and doomed his regime.

War serves many a harsh notice on civilizations and social orders. The perceptive few in Europe could see that the catalyst of war's battlefields could serve as so many burial grounds for outworn institutions and, at the same time, could provide laboratories for new ideas and new institutions.

Russia summoned fourteen million men to the colors in 1914 and gave them few modern weapons to fight with and a feudal aristocracy to lead them. Russia was completely unprepared for modern warfare. By the end of 1916 there were already five million Russians killed or wounded and by January 1917 there were more than a million deserters on the loose in the rear of the army. According to the French historian, Elie Halèvy, 1916-1917 was the First World War's turning point. It was the moment when the war crisis began to melt into the twentieth-century revolutionary crisis.[1] One crisis began to usher in the other when the great battles at Verdun and the Somme were fought to horrendous casualties and not even a modest gain in territory. By September 1916 there were already seven million casualties on the western front and yet the stalemate seemed complete. With the disaster of the Nivelle offensive in early 1917 and the collapse at Caporetto a bit later, the cracks produced by the futility and carnage began to appear: strikes and bread riots all over Europe and a mutiny in the French army. And in the middle of it all the Russian Revolution broke out.

During the first week of March 1917 cracks began to appear in the Russian facade. With the first wave of strikes and bread riots that week it became obvious that the old order in Russia was bankrupt, its leadership discredited, and its Tsarist symbols battered. During the second week of March the demonstrations grew in size as the traditional whips of the autocracy—the Army and the Cossacks—began to falter. On March 12 the military began to fraternize with the crowds and before the day was over three hundred years of Tsarism ceased to exist. On the same day members of the Duma, the Russian parliament, refused to disband when ordered to do so and formed a provisional government.

The United States approached war in 1917 with as much reluctance as had Russia in 1914. Just as it would in 1941 it entered world politics against its will. Until drawn into the conflict that year the Wilson administration was not prepared to take any action since national feeling did not allow for it. The United States seemed too far away from the struggle. Instead, Woodrow Wilson sought to play the role of mediator between the Entente and the Central Powers. In January 1917 in an address before the U.S. Senate, Wilson called for a "peace without victory." Instead of exploring the possibilities of peace through the neutral auspices of Washington, the Germans in February of 1917 declared unrestricted submarine warfare. This, along with the discovery of the Zimmerman Telegram—a cable from Berlin to its minister in Mexico City instructing him to try to bring Mexico into the war should the United States intervene—served to inflame American opinion at precisely that moment when Russia began to totter and the balance of power in Europe was most seriously threatened.

The impending political collapse of Europe was more than apparent to Wilson in early 1917. "The danger of our time," he said, "is nothing less than the unsettlement of the foundations of civilization." For the most part, Americans had been repelled by the autocratic and militaristic character of the Central Powers. The news that Nicholas II had abdicated on March 15, 1917, removed a natural impediment to joining the Allied cause. In fact, Wilson regarded Tsarism's fall as the war's first victory. On March 20, 1917, the United States became the first state to recognize the Provisional Government in Russia.

The American intervention in the First World War helped to tip the balance against the Central Powers. Even though a great American army would not reach the battlefields of France until 1918, the American economic contribution to the war effort was enormous. The United States made available large credits that permitted the Allies to obtain raw materials and munitions in almost unlimited quantities. At the same time, other neutrals, including many in Latin America, followed the American example and fell into the service of the Allied cause.

The Wilson government was at first sympathetic to the March Revolution because it was inspired by the overthrow of one of the oldest autocracies in the world. Wilson could now redefine the war as a struggle between liberal democracy and autocratic militarism. Second, the United States was quick to recognize the Provisional Government because it was composed of moderate leftists like Alexander Kerensky (soon to be its leader) and constitutional democrats like Paul Milyukov, an historian by trade and now minister of foreign affairs. Not a Jacobin among them, these men endeared themselves to the Allies because they appeared willing and able to construct a parliamentary democracy on the ruins of Tsarist Russia, and, at the same time, renew the Russian war effort under more competent leadership. What the Allies failed to understand was that the leaders of the new government had no real contacts with the people and that the people were exhausted by the privations of the war. The Russian people were also basically unconcerned with the legal arrangements and terminology of new constitutions. The key slogan heard in Russia in 1917—"Land, peace, bread"—meant leaving the war and parcelling out the land. Grateful only that the new leadership did not appear radical, the West completely misunderstood the situation in Russia in 1917.

One of history's tragic figures, Alexander Kerensky was a man of some intellectual caliber and not a little charisma, but he was operating within a situation of war, revolution, and anarchy. His greatest mistake was in continuing an unpopular war. If he needed anything in 1917 it was a period of repose and popularity. And to gain favor for the new regime he had to end the war quickly and release millions of soldiers so they could return to their homes and participate in the land distribution that had been underway since March. The Kerensky government seemed powerless to solve the economic crisis, which only increased the general sense of aimless drift. Another error he made was in putting off elections to the Constituent Assembly until November 1917. The assembly would have determined Russia's future form of government and helped to stabilize the situation. Instead of legitimizing a responsible government, the months between March and November saw the gains of the revolution unravel. As Victor Chernov, one of the leaders of the social revolutionaries, said of this period: "power would slip into the streets." The period served to give the far left time to ready itself for the coup that November. Speaking of these same months, Lenin said, "power is in the streets, you only have to pick it up."

Kerensky understood something of this harsh calculus of power and there is some reason to believe that he feared that his regime might be only an interlude between two despotisms. This is what he meant when he warned his over-confident colleagues: "Just you wait, Lenin himself is coming, then the real thing will begin."

Vladimir Ilyich Lenin was a careerist conspirator. His whole life, from the day in 1887 when his older brother was executed for treasonable activities at the University, to the day in 1917 when he seized power, was dedicated to the pursuit of revolution. His life, Louis Fischer has written, is "the greatest evidence of a man's dedication to an idea: revolution."[2] His career initially represented one of the century's first attempts to rejuvenate nineteenth-century Marxism and convert it into a fighting faith better suited to the turbulent conditions of the new era. The original socialist movement in Russia was very western in its character and orientations. Being gradualist in their beliefs, many socialists felt the revolution would work itself out inevitably in stages. Many felt that capitalism was not in an advanced stage of decay and until that situation changed, socialists should subordinate their program to the democratic process.

What Lenin sought to do was adjust socialism's premises and methods. He did this by challenging the Marxist determinism of his day and by de-emphasizing the impersonal economic forces that so preoccupied Marxist theoreticians in 1900. What Lenin succeeded in doing was rescuing the catastrophic tradition of early Marxism by emphasizing the revolutionary will and the political opportunism of seizing power—ideas allowed to lapse in the 1880s and 1890s. At the same time, Lenin extended the definition of the proletariat to include the peasantry and he remained convinced that the red flag could be raised in a backward society. And the engine that would propel the whole movement forward was the small, professional, revolutionary party, hierarchically organized and centrally controlled, a party in which the role of the leader was paramount. Only a dedicated party of revolutionaries ready to sacrifice all for the cause, Lenin argued, could promote a fighting force prepared to take power. Only a party like this, dogmatically assured, intolerant of other parties and views, and violent in deed when it was imperative to be so, could know the interests of the workers better than the workers themselves.[3] Only a party like this could aspire to total power and once it was achieved would have the conviction and ruthlessness to twist society in a preconceived ideological direction. The men that Lenin succeeded in recruiting to his movement between 1903 and 1917, although relatively small in numbers, were certainly clear in their conception of the class struggle. For them it was social warfare with winners and losers, and in that struggle every party member was prepared to take the consequences.

The central organizing myth of Lenin's movement and the key inspirational idea for the revolution was the final victory of the proletariat. After 1917 it would still remain the central myth of Lenin's and Stalin's foreign policy. In other words, Lenin's ideological criticism of Marxism furnished Russia with the intellectual prelude to the revolution. At the same time, the party's extreme and often amoral activism, which subordinated the democratic process to the Bolshevik program, led eventually to the conquest of power.

When Lenin arrived at the Finland Station in April 1917, in a city which would soon bear his name, he found his Bolshevik party divided and curiously moderate. Its right wing talked the language of social democracy and seemed to welcome the idea of rapprochement with the Mensheviks. From Lenin's standpoint such a collaboration was unthinkable, as was a Bolshevik party under another leader. Lenin reestablished his ascendency over the party almost immediately by forcefully reminding its members of their original radical purpose. In a statement of goals he issued that April (the April Theses) he demanded a breach with the Provisional Government, a new citizen army and bureaucracy, the division of land among the peasantry, the socialization of the banks, and the control by the workers of the production in the factories and the distribution of goods. Lenin's sense of urgency in convincing the party to be more bold in its reach for power was prompted by his belief that it was Russia's mission to pave the way for the European revolution. Aware of the strains in both alliance systems, Lenin thought the moment ripe for a universal revolutionary breakthrough. "We stand on the threshold of a worldwide proletarian revolution," he said in October 1917. "If we come out now, we shall have on our side all proletarian Europe."

The other competing vision of 1917 was the one provided by Woodrow Wilson of the United States. Even before the March Revolution, Wilson, in an address to the U. S. Senate (January 1917) had called for a peace without victory, a "community of power" rather than a balance of power, freedom of the seas (which was his proposal for an open, tariff-free world trading system), a moderation of the old arms race, and, above all, a democratic call for a "government by the consent of the governed." The program outlined in this speech constituted a complete repudiation of that system which Wilson felt had brought the world to war. He understood every bit as much as Lenin that the great power diplomacy of the imperial epoch had failed to keep the peace and that as that system declined it would have to be replaced by a new one. What Wilson was trying to do in 1917, again in the Fourteen Points of 1918, and still later in the League of Nations Covenant, was foster a reorganization of international politics along democratic lines. He sincerely believed that democracies, in contrast to the autocracies that caused the war, were inherently peaceful and could be trusted to preserve the peace of the world. Wilson was, of course, assuming that with the general exhaustion of the old world, the age of democracy had arrived.[4] Raised to believe optimistically that every problem had a solution Wilson felt that international conflict could be rationally resolved. He may have appeared naive to many of his more experienced contemporaries, like David Lloyd George and Georges Clemenceau, but he insisted that the old diplomacy of balance of power and sphere of influence guarantees had indeed failed. His call for a community of power was an attempt to create a new system in which competition between states would remain, but in which sovereignty was equalized and security for all was anchored in a world body. And the United States would lead the way not only because it was uniquely endowed politically and economically but because, as he said in 1919, "America is the only idealistic nation in the world." This was probably why his speech of January 1917 provoked such worldwide discussion. Eighty-nine French socialists in the Chamber of Deputies called it "the charter of the civilized universe."

Watching this from the frustration of exile, Lenin grew alarmed at Wilson's program for a new world order. Already by 1917 it was clear to Lenin that neither the present international system nor the one that Wilson was outlining was not and could not be the guardian of working-class interests, and that an alternative system needed to be created. No less a man of destiny than Wilson, Lenin had cast the traditional Russian intellectuals' repudiation of the West into Marxist terms. Hoping for a global revolutionary breakthrough against the western capitalist yoke, Lenin warned the world that Wilson was not really so different from other capitalist statesmen, just more seductive in his attempt to divert the world masses from the revolutionary struggle that was about to crest. As Leon Trotsky once put it, Lenin and Wilson were "the apocalyptic antipodes of our time."

The Wilson administration was indeed aware of the Bolshevik left before November 1917, but thought it a temporary phenomenon, the kind of political debris that is swept onto the stages of history whenever there is a 1789 or an 1848. Although present (as were anarchists to the left of them) and potentially dangerous, they lacked numbers and significant roots among the people; they would sooner or later be relegated to the margins of history. At least this seemed to be the view of Colonel Edward House, Wilson's friend and close advisor, who felt that the rising tide of democracy in Russia would absorb all the thoughtless radicalisms in the country and render them extinct. This differed markedly from the view of Secretary of State Robert Lansing. Lansing recognized how few the Bolsheviks actually were, but he was under no illusions as to how tough and dedicated they were, and how unscrupulous and uncompromising they might prove to be. He also seems to be the first in the And government to sense how truly radical the Bolsheviks were and how irreconcilable their ideology was with liberal, democratic capitalism. Nevertheless, while Kerensky still governed in Russia and Lenin and the Bolsheviks were held at bay, the problem of dealing with a radical fringe did not press to the fore.[5]

There matters stood until Lenin called for an insurrection on October 25, 1917. Organised by the Petrograd Soviet led by Leon Trotsky with Lenin in charge of the higher strategy, Red troops occupied all the strategic points in the country and encountered limited resistance. The Kerensky government capitulated that night. Through the whole period from March to October the Bolsheviks had exercised neither power nor responsibility. The Bolshevik coup surprised everyone. It simply did not draw upon the support of the Russian masses. In fact, most of the urban proletariat would have preferred one of the other left-wing parties and the bulk of the peasantry would have preferred the Social Revolutionaries—a quasi-anarchist party that had promised land to the people.

When Lenin assumed power the financial system had already collapsed and almost all institutional life had ceased functioning. To help generate the popularity that so eluded Kerensky and the breathing spell that would help maintain his party in power, Lenin issued two decrees: a land decree and a peace decree. The land decree called for the immediate distribution of land to the peasants. This was a tactical retreat since the Bolsheviks were opposed to the private ownership of land, but it made good tactical sense since the peasants were seizing land anyway. The second decree called for the termination of hostilities, a separate peace for Russia. This too constituted a retreat from party goals since it meant yielding on Lenin's original plan to obtain peace only through a world revolution. Lenin was turning inward to consolidate the revolution.

Elections to the Constituent Assembly had been fixed by the Provisional Government for November 25, 1917, and the Bolsheviks were committed to it. Almost forty million Russians went to the polls in what would be the most free and democratic election held in Russia until the 1990s. The Bolsheviks lost to the Social Revolutionaries by an almost two to one margin. They only seemed to do well in the areas closest to Petrograd and Moscow. Whether three-fourths of the Russian people preferred other parties did not matter to Lenin in the least. Only one month later, on January 19, 1918, he forced the Central Committee of the Communist Party to dissolve the Assembly. The Assembly had met for one day. In defending his action, Lenin argued that parliamentary democracy had outlived its purpose, and that it was now "incompatible with conceiving socialism." And anyway, he said, national institutions like parliaments were no longer relevant. Only class institutions, like Soviets, were important. Finally, since an assembly would allow the other competing parties to share some power with the Bolsheviks, as an institution it was by definition a counterrevolutionary threat.[6] The Communist Party had obviously begun arrogating to itself the authority to speak for millions of people who regarded them as a small group of usurping terrorists.

In the United States Wilson was clearly alarmed at the destruction of Russian democracy and soon began rethinking his hopes for a more democratic Russia.

On October 4, 1918, the Germans had made an appeal to Wilson for an armistice. Wilson's response to this came with the program he outlined earlier on January 8, 1918, in his famous Fourteen Points. It was the most important statement of American policy made during the First World War and it was made with one eye on the western front and the eventual outcome of the military conflict and one eye on the anti-democratic turn of events in Russia.

Wilson believed the great changes in Russia to be due to a large, ecumenical movement stretching back to the democratic revolutions of the eighteenth century. When he issued his Fourteen Points he understood that the world was entering a new, revolutionary period such as that which followed 1789. It was Wilson's hope that he might control these revolutions and turn them in a liberal democratic direction. At first he underestimated the implacable hostility emanating from the new Russia. Lenin had cast western power in its most demonic light. He envied that power and he wanted to transplant it to Russian soil, but minus the social system that gave rise to it. In other words, Lenin's assault on capitalism, the removal of an entire ruling class, the attack on religion and democracy, and the broader ideological call for a Manichaean conflict between the socialist and capitalist camps represented the greatest challenge the West has ever faced. And it is this challenge and the response to it that has moulded the thinking of the Kremlin and western leaders down to our own day.

Lenin's was a revelatory worldview actualized in a situation of conflict and crisis. In terms of its political and social goals—egalitarianism, the dictatorship of the proletariat, the withering away of the state, etc.—it helped to introduce the utopian phase in modern political history.

Today the Fourteen Points seem rather tame contrasted to the challenge emanating from Moscow. But in 1918 they promised great change and carried great moral weight; the signature of the American president gave them moral authority.

The Fourteen Points formed the heart of Wilson's "New Order." Based on "open covenants openly arrived at," point one followed Wilson's condemnation of the old, secret diplomacy in which the fate of the world's masses was decided without their consent. This and his fourteenth point—the proposal of a League of Nations—were declarations of general principle. The rest of the points dealt with specific questions. For example, points two, three, and four called for an open diplomacy, freedom of the seas and free trade, disarmament and respect for colonial peoples. They were not merely notions that captured the public's enthusiasm; in economic terms Wilson was trying to replace the older nineteenth-century system of national commercial barriers that, he felt, had caused the war. Once this was done, it would clear the way for an inherently peaceful international capitalism—led by the United States and not by Europe—that would bring about universal progress and prosperity. Here you have the translation in twentieth-century terms of the familiar liberal philosophy of the nineteenth-century Anglo-Saxon world. Other points dealt with crucial territorial issues. In point six, for example, Wilson addressed the Russian problem. He called for the evacuation of the German army from Russian soil and he welcomed Russia back into the family of nations "under institutions of her own choosing." At this moment he was still hoping that Russia would return to a more liberal political system. Other points called for a similar evacuation from Belgium and Alsace-Lorraine, an independent Poland, an independent Turkey minus its empire, and new Italian frontiers. Point ten dealt with Austria-Hungary and in 1918 Wilson was opposed to the empire's breakup.[7] His call for the autonomy of subject nationalities of the empire in independent states along democratic lines, but within the Austro-Hungarian Empire, was very much like George Bush's call to the peoples of the Soviet Union from 1989 to 1992.

The Fourteen Points were not nearly as radical or utopian as Marxism-Leninism, rather they carried a high moral tone in endorsing the nineteenth-century trends of democracy and nationalism—the very things that Lenin was denouncing so vehemently in 1918. Wilson's offer to the world of a League and an open prosperous world society free of traditional military alliances succeeded briefly in inspiring and cementing the morale of millions of people around the world.

With the military collapse of the Central Powers in 1918 the German army began its withdrawal from Eastern Europe. The Russian Civil War broke out that summer. With the Red Army doing well in the field against its enemies the danger of the Russian Revolution spreading across Europe was a real one, and one that worried western leaders. Writing in his diary, Colonel House would worry that "Bolshevism is gaining ground everywhere . . . we are sitting on an open powder magazine and some day a spark may ignite it."[8] Lenin, of course, was counting on such a windfall, especially in the industrialized countries, as the best way to insure the success of his own revolution. Already by late 1918 Soviet communism had succeeded in expressing the revolutionary impulse for millions of people in the twentieth century that the French Revolution had expressed for millions in the nineteenth century. For example, in the last month of the war sailors of the German Grand Fleet at Kiel mutinied when ordered out to engage the British fleet in one last decisive battle. They formed sailors' soviets, ran up red flags on board ships, and killed a few officers along the way. In what would become the German Revolution of 1918, the movement spread inland from the ports of northern Germany to the other major cities of the country. At its peak the rebels took over the city of Munich and proclaimed the Bavarian Soviet Republic. At the same time, the Red Army was already on the march in Eastern Europe in a direct attempt to spread the revolution. That same November it marched into Estonia, Latvia, and Lithuania where fighting raged bitterly into 1919.

The revolution coming as it did in the midst of the greatest war in history served to fire the imagination of millions in the western and colonial worlds. The suffering and privations of the war provided the desperate soil for change, but the successful example of overthrowing a powerful autocracy and the humane vision projected by the revolution in its natal hour—however hollow that would later prove to be—inspired people to believe that the world stood poised at the dawn of a new age. The ferment produced by war and revolution was worldwide. It sparked massive strikes and demonstrations in far-flung places like Australia, Canada, and South Africa, as it did in the neutral countries of Switzerland, Holland, and Spain. In the British and French military there were several examples of near mutinies involving thousands of men.

Even before the war ended the world press was calling for a crusade against Bolshevism. In the United States where there were large strikes in some of the larger cities and where, in some cases, bombs were mailed to senators, prominent Americans were moved to speak out and urge President Wilson to do something. Indeed, the Allies were compelled to reassess their whole policy toward the Russian Revolution.

Woodrow Wilson was a student of history and understood that an earlier intervention in France in the 1790s had given that revolution a renewed life and made it swell beyond its borders. A similar intervention in Russia might have a similar effect. On the other hand, if a small group of dedicated activists could seize control of a country like Russia, might not similar groups, taking advantage of the same destitution and misery, do the same in Europe as a whole? The danger seemed real, especially since some of these groups had already come to power in several places, including Munich and Budapest. Wilson felt he had to respond not only to the Bolshevik regime and the revolution in Russia but also to Lenin's persistent attempt to interfere in the internal regimes of other countries.

It has long been an argument of revisionist historians that the intervention in the Russian Civil War was based on the Allied opposition to the radical nature of the Bolshevik regime. I think this is in part true.

The Allied decision in March 1918 to send troops to Russia was made when the war still hung in the balance. The Treaty of Brest-Litovsk, Russia's separate peace with Germany, was signed on March 3, 1918, and the first Anglo-French landing was made at Murmansk six days later. Further landings took place at Vladivostok in April and Archangel in the summer—all before the Russian civil war broke out. Roughly 15,000 American troops were sent to Siberia in 1918. The general idea behind it all was to somehow prop up a Russia sliding into chaos, and one that might very well become a German satellite.[9] More specifically, the Allies sought to protect the oilfields of southern Russia from a German-Turkish invasion and to keep the large stores of arms in northern Russia from falling into the hands of the Reds. In other words, the intervention was initially dictated by the immediate needs of the war but soon became political. At first the Allies responded to the war's challenge and then responded to the revolution's challenge and the attempt to export it. There is certainly some evidence that whenever they could, the Allied forces did aid the White armies. Nevertheless, the intervention, whatever its purposes, was half-hearted. At the end of over four years of trench warfare the West had neither the manpower, money, nor will to do anything about the direction of events in Russia. And could anyone seriously expect the revolution to be crushed from Murmansk, Archangel, and Vladivostok? Only a massive intervention, the kind of effort Winston Churchill called for, could accomplish this, and the West lacked the capacity to do it.

The intervention, which lasted only a few years, permanently embittered the Communist Party of the Soviet Union and became a key component of Soviet hostility ever since. It lent substance to the Marxist-Leninist belief that the world was divided into two hostile camps and that between them there was an unrelenting rivalry. Between the socialist and capitalist worlds there could be no peaceful coexistence since the animus between them was a permanent feature of international life—the intervention of 1918 had always been used by the Soviet Regime as proof of the inherent validity of their ideological thesis. To an extent never fully appreciated in the West, the Soviet rulers from Lenin to Andropov never really wavered from this Manichaean interpretation of present and future history. Nor did they weaken in their sense of mission and in their belief that in the global struggle being waged history was on their side. This is not to say that ideology governed Soviet international behavior. This has not been true since the failed attempt to spread the revolution to Eastern Europe under Lenin. But what ideology did was provide an intellectual framework for the leadership—a way of looking at the world. Whatever the nationalist premises of Soviet foreign policy were beginning in the 1920s, the rulers in the Kremlin framed their goals in ideological terms. The danger was twofold: on one hand, it kept people in the West from viewing the Cold War with the Soviet Union in its proper light—as a struggle to alter the balance of power. On the other hand, because the ideology was so uncompromising it only made an inherently negative relationship with the West infinitely worse.

The offensive policy of the military intervention was followed by the more defensive one of *cordon sanitaire*. This represented an attempt to encircle the Soviet Union economically and thereby contain the virus of revolution. Whatever else this policy meant to do, it informed Lenin that the Soviet Union would not soon be invaded, thus allowing the Communist Party time to consolidate the gains of the revolution and build "socialism in one country."

The Russian Civil War was the greatest crisis the Communist Party ever faced. To defeat the White armies and the counterrevolution and to break the power of the previous ruling groups for good, the Communist Party—otherwise inexperienced in the art of ruling—fell back on the only instrument at its disposal for holding power in Russia: the terror. The unique circumstances created by war, revolution, and civil war required special means to master them. Certainly since 1789 revolutionary terror has been justified by a vision of an ideal society. Determined as he was to retain exclusive dictatorial power in the hands of the party, Lenin often used the Jacobin example as justification for his own use of terror. Lenin is clearly central to the modern discussion of the subject. It was what distinguished him from the other socialist leaders. According to R.V. Daniels, the terror followed from what he calls "the moral deficiency of bolshevism"—the belief that any means, however violent and criminal, must be employed in order to achieve and preserve the revolution.[10] In an interview with Lenin in 1920 the philosopher, Bertrand Russell, expressed shock at the thousands being consumed by the fires of the revolution; Russell remembered Lenin's "guffaw at the thought of those massacred," a gesture "which made," Russell said, "his blood run cold." When Molotov was asked in the 1980s whether Lenin or Stalin was the more ruthless, he replied: "Lenin, undoubtedly . . . He could not stand opposition."

In the summer of 1918 two Communist Party leaders were assassinated by Social Revolutionaries, and at the same time an attempt was made on Lenin's life. The party had already created its "sentinel of the revolution," the Cheka, just six weeks after the revolution. This secret police had its own military arm, its own bureaucracy, its own prison camp system, and its own reason for being. It could arrest people, try them, and execute them. The Cheka became the party's organ of absolute power. More than just a permanent feature of Soviet life (later it would become the KGB), it became the model for such organizations in the twentieth century. Under its first leader, Felix Dzerzhinsky, the Cheka became the instrument by which the Communist Party consolidated its grip on the state:

> We stand for organized terror . . . terror is the absolute necessity during times of revolution . . . The Cheka is obliged to defend the revolution and conquer the enemy even if its sword does by chance sometimes fall upon the heads of the innocent."

The terror soon blanketed Russia with tens of thousands of people arrested, tried, and either sent to penal camps in the Soviet East or summarily executed.

Lenin was not just waging war internally against the hidden enemy; he was also striving to stimulate revolution abroad by waging war against external enemies. He had already begun his assault on the European settlement by encouraging every Communist Party, no matter how small, to seize power in its respective country. His instrument for doing this was the Communist International (the Comintern). Woodrow Wilson might think of shoring up the world status quo in a new "community of power" when he was at the peace conference of 1919, but Lenin had always believed in a dynamically changing world order and he wished to create strategies and tactics to fit this view.

From its creation in 1919, the Comintern was structured differently from the previous Internationals of 1864 and 1889. For example, the decisions of its executive committee were binding on all Communist parties making up the membership and through its hold on the committee the Soviet Union dominated the Comintern. The organization had two goals: all members of the Comintern had to regard the defense and strengthening of the Soviet regime as absolutely paramount, and every Communist Party in every country had to work to create support for the revolution. They could do this by forming youth organizations, parties, and trade unions, or at least infiltrate the older groups. Whether the Communist parties worked openly or secretly depended on the conditions prevailing in each state. All of these conditions were stated by Lenin in 1920 in the *Twenty-one Conditions for Admittance to the Third International.*[11] If socialists accepted these conditions they had the right to call themselves communists. If they balked, then they were no longer in the movement. What the conditions succeeded in doing was destroying the unity of the world socialist movement since many socialists could not and would not accept the rigid discipline or even the goals of the movement. Even though the Comintern's record of success was a slim one, it helped create the feeling in the West that there was a sinister communist conspiracy in the world whose tentacles could be found in every nation.

While through the Comintern Lenin tried to interfere in the internal affairs of other countries he also hurled the Red Army into Poland in 1920, in a direct attempt to export the revolution. With the Red Army at the gates of Warsaw American diplomats in Poland were using the domino theory to warn Washington about the impending calamity. If this outpost of Christian civilization should fall to the Reds, they warned, Germany, Austria, and Italy would soon follow suit. One American diplomat even drew a parallel between the siege of Warsaw and the seventeenth-century defense of Vienna against the Turks.[12]

Lenin also turned his attention to the revolution of Asian peoples against the West. In September 1920 he summoned a "Congress of the Peoples of the East" to meet in Baku. The dramatic highlight of the conference came when Zinoviev, the president of the Comintern, shouted:

> The Communist International turns today to the peoples of the east and
> says to them: 'Brothers, we summon you to Holy War first of all against

British Imperialism.'[13]

This was more than a broad attempt to fish in troubled waters. It was at the same time a direct appeal and offer of aid to Kemal Ataturk in his attempt to challenge European supremacy.

By 1920 Turkey, already divested of its empire, was undergoing a national revival. Ataturk, a prominent member of the earlier Young Turk movement, took the lead in trying to establish control over all of Turkey. This brought him into direct conflict with the British, the French, and the Greeks, all of whom had troops in the country. With Turkish nationalism on the march, the Lenin government in 1921 extended military aid to the Turks in the form of weapons and advisors. In fact, the Soviet Union provided the Ataturk government with its only support and helped to insure the rebels' victory.

With Turkish nationalism triumphant, Ataturk then turned to the problem of reforming and modernizing his country. In doing so, he created a one-party government modelled on the Communist Party of the Soviet Union. He also followed the Soviet model of a state-directed economy in which heavy industries were built and operated by the state. On the land, peasant cooperatives were encouraged, and in the 1930s so when the Soviet Union introduced its five-year plans, Turkey did as well.

Here was the Soviet Union's first attempt to fuse communism with a foreign nationalism and identify it with the anti-imperialist cause. It helped to fuel the extension of Soviet prestige in the colonial world as early as the 1920s.

Between 1917 and 1924 (the year Lenin died), both Lenin and Wilson had staked out claims to world leadership. The United States, which had dictated so much of the post-war peace, repudiated Wilson's peacemaking efforts and never even joined the League of Nations. Until 1923 the United States even refused to answer the League's communications. The Soviet Union had nothing to do with the postwar settlement, and, as the world's only revolutionary state, it felt compelled to destroy it.

If one looks at the history made between 1917 and 1924, one can see a pattern emerging where these two states are concerned. On one hand, the United States emerged as a satisfied power seeking to stabilize external relationships in the world and, on the other, the Soviet Union emerged as a have-not power, which at times would assume certain burdens of risk to destroy that same international system. The Soviet Union acts, and the United States contains. These characteristics would govern the relationship between the two states throughout the entire Cold War. Furthermore, the very existence of an independent communist state as large and potentially powerful as the Soviet Union made the whole postwar settlement unsafe. And whenever it could, that state intensified, either directly or inadvertently, the social unrest following the First World War.

Americans were clearly worried about the new Soviet Union and it is not hard to see why. The Soviet Union was a despotism immediately recognizable to Americans. It seemed heir to the longest autocratic and imperial tradition in European history. When Americans viewed events in Moscow they saw the same sort of power-wielding group exploiting and regimenting the same unfortunate masses. Lenin seemed to be the founder of a new Tsarist dynasty. At the same time, the hated Okhrana, the Tsarist secret police, seemed to have spawned an even more vicious successor, which also placed enemies of the state in the same old camps. In fact, the terror seemed even more institutionalized than it was before. Moreover, men like Lenin and Stalin had risen through conspiracy, persecuting and often liquidating their opponents. Compulsion and violence were the political determinants of Soviet life as they had been for Tsarist Russia, even though its leaders persistently invoked the symbols and values of democracy.

Second, the Soviet Union represented a new and dangerous adversarial culture. The Communist Party had declared war on the traditional pillars of the social order—property, religion, and bourgeois morality. Ever since 1917 Soviet communism came nearer than anything else to expressing the revolutionary impulse for our era. Communism won for itself not only an international audience ready to accept the utopian blandishments of Moscow, who took communism's growth for granted, but it also succeeded in gaining the adherence of a large part of the world's intellectual class, who wished to believe that Marxism-Leninism occupied the intellectual and moral highground.

The Soviet Union after 1917 projected an alternative model for change. The massive ideological assault that accompanied this struck at the heart of America's own projected universal model. According to Theodore von Laue, this succeeded in implanting a permanent sense of insecurity and "laid the groundwork for defining the American collective identity in outraged contrast to Soviet Communism."[14] Particularly unnerving for Americans were the Soviet claims to ideological infallibility and the almost religious appeal of communism, which expressed its sacrifices for the faith in utopian terms. "A faith," Arthur Koestler once said, in trying to explain his own conversion to Communism, "is not acquired by reasoning.. . . All true faith involves a revolt against the believer's social environment, the projection into the future of an ideal derived from the remote past."[15]

Two opposed worlds emerged after 1917 and between them there existed a deep ideological suspicion and rivalry. In both countries, over the course of the next generation, there was bred the sense of being natural enemies. The revolution and everything it spawned after 1917 was bound to lead to conflict between the two systems. On the plane of ideas the bases for the Cold War were laid between 1917 and 1924.

Notes

1. Elie Halèvy, *The World Crisis of 1914-1918* (Oxford: Clarendon Press, 1930).
2. Louis Fischer, *The Life of Lenin* (New York: Harper and Row, 1964), 46-47.

3. V. I. Lenin, *What Is to Be Done?* (New York: International Publishers, 1929).

4. N. Gordon Levin, Jr., *Woodrow Wilson and World Politics. America's Response to War and Revolution* (New York: Oxford University Press, 1971).

5. Arno J. Mayer, *Wilson vs. Lenin: Political Origins of the New Diplomacy 1917-1918* (New York: Meridian Books, 1967).

6. R. V. Daniels, *A Documentary History of Communism, Vol. I* (New York: Vintage Books, 1962), 133-35.

7. Thomas G. Barnes and Gerald D. Feldman, eds., *Breakdown and Rebirth, 1914 to the Present* (Boston: Little, Brown and Co., 1972), 40-41.

8. E. H. Carr, *The Bolshevik Revolution* (London: Penguin Books, 1966), III, 135.

9. George Kennan, *The Decision to Intervene* (London: Faber and Faber, 1958).

10. R. V. Daniels, *The Nature of Communism* (New York: Vintage Books, 1962), 92-93.

11. Helmut Gruber, *International Communism in the Era of Lenin. A Documentary History* (New York: Anchor Books, 1972), 241-46.

12. Norman A. Graebner, *America as a World Power. A Realistic Appraisal from Wilson to Reagan* (Wilmington, Del.: Scholarly Resources Inc., 1984), 13.

13. Louis Fischer, *The Soviets in World Affairs* (New York: Vintage Books, 1951), 205.

14. Theodore H. Von Laue, *The World Revolution of Westernization. The Twentieth Century in Global Perspective* (New York: Oxford University Press, 1987), 66.

15. Richard Crossman, ed., *The God That Failed* (New York: Bantam Books, 1959), 12.

3

Prelude to War

The Communist Party leadership emerged from the Russian civil war victorious, but feeling itself in a state of siege and frightened at the prospects of mass discontent. Instead of forcing the pace of nationalization and industrialization and leaping directly into the communist future that Lenin had promised, the party retrenched to preserve the gains of the revolution and maintain itself in power. The practical result of this policy shift was the New Economic Program (N.E.P.).

Created in 1921 to allow the Soviet Union a period in which to recover from the war, N.E.P. allowed private trade to be licensed, handed over many factories to trusts and even at times to individuals, and turned toward the West for its capital resources. The idea of world revolution had been shelved.

By 1928 the economy had been restored to the levels it had attained in 1913. Nevertheless, even with a reasonably liberal economy, the party dictatorship still remained in place and the CHEKA was still as vigilant and ruthless as it always had been.

Emerging from the N.E.P. in 1928 it was clear that all of the West's worst fears for the Soviet Union had come to pass. All the building blocks of liberal democracy were missing in the new Soviet Union: a multiparty system and a parliament to house it; a free press and a politically sophisticated middle class that relied upon it; and a rule of law as the West understands that term. As Lenin put it in 1918 when he liquidated the old Russian legal system, "the dictatorship of the proletariat is unrestricted by law."

Joseph Stalin began his rise to power during the same period of the civil war and N.E.P. Long an agitator in the communist underground he shared Lenin's hatred of anything in the country that embodied Tsarism. Ever distrustful and "sickly suspicious," as Khrushchev once put it, obsessive about secrecy and security, opportunistically following his own star and totally unconcerned about human life ("Death solves all problems," Stalin once said. "No man, no problem."), his personal rudeness and callousness toward comrades had even alarmed Lenin. His daughter once noted that he saw enemies everywhere. When Charles De Gaulle later met him during the Second World War Stalin impressed him as an "Asiatic despot, and quite consciously so." Despite his later attempts to alter the historical record, Stalin's role during the momentous events of 1917 was a consistently moderate one. He had accepted the "bourgeois revolution" of March as he did the Provisional Government and he apparently called for a reunification with the Mensheviks. He held these positions until Lenin returned to Russia in April and convinced him to change his mind. If Stalin understood anything thereafter, it was that stalwart bureaucrats like himself rather than brilliant theoreticians and colorful revolutionaries shape the socioeconomic forces that go into statebuilding. Rising to power within the bureaucracy through his deft ability to manipulate the party machinery in order to create a personal following, Stalin was soon in a good position to reach for power once Lenin's health began to deteriorate in 1923. The titanic struggle for power between Stalin and his strongest competitor, Leon Trotsky, really began in that year. Stalin's success in becoming leader of the Soviet Union followed from ceaseless political maneuvering and a patient, single-minded policy of easing Trotsky and his supporters out of hundreds of key positions and replacing them with Stalin loyalists.

Having won this struggle for power Stalin then revived Lenin's original "Left Communist" program in 1928. From the first Five-Year Plan of that year to 1939 the Communist Party used its dictatorial power to impose sacrifices on workers and peasants alike in a headlong rush to industrialize and collectivize the country. The accelerated pace and the massive use of terror were central to the program, as was the unprecedented intrusion of the state into all branches of economic, social, and cultural life. There had been an intraparty battle over this policy and the party had been warned about the dire consequences of such a policy by one of Stalin's major rivals, Nikolai Bukharin: "If Stalin gets his way, we are left with nothing but a police state." His warning fell on deaf ears. The first Five-Year Plan of 1928 marks the real beginning of Soviet totalitarianism.

Stalin's "Second Russian Revolution," as it is often called, was designed to create forward movement in a substantially backward society. It had always been assumed dialectically by communists directed by an ideological vision that there has to be suffering to advance and that bureaucratic methods are best to achieve socioeconomic goals. Terror and violence in the hands of the party and secret police are integral to such efforts. They are proof of the serious intention of the party to proceed in the group interest no matter what the material or human costs might be. At the same time, the nationalization of the land and resources meant the reblossoming of statism and traditional Russian bureaucracy. In other words, Stalinism, rooted as it was in the worst elements of Russian history, represented a synthesis of the worst aspects of Tsarism (the idolatry of the state and bureaucracy) and Leninism (the Communist Party and the institutionalized terror). The party drew its teachings and institutions from Lenin and its practices from Stalin. Like Lenin, Stalin hated Tsarism and yet acted in ways that helped to resuscitate it in another form. Like its Tsarist predecessor, Stalinism was authority oriented and paternalistic. It was a system that treated its citizens as natives in the modern sense. It was a unique Caesarism that insisted on the infallibility of the leadership, which, along with its use of terror, became an effective mechanism of social control.

The campaign to industrialize and collectivize the Soviet Union was carried out on a scale unparalleled in modern times. The party's massive use of propaganda and terror ultimately succeeded in creating a command society and economy. At the same time it succeeded in traumatizing the country and destroying much of the Soviet peasantry. Estimates of those who died in the camps and in the famine range as high as fourteen million. With the emergence of Stalinism in the 1930s the humane vision of 1917 disappeared. At the same time, the social convulsions of the decade revived all the old western fears of anti-western messianism.

In an interview with Stalin in 1934, the English writer H.G. Wells urged Stalin to abandon the stifling of dissent and the institutionalization of class war that were taking such a high toll. More than appalling losses of humanity were involved, Wells said. The whole effort in the Soviet Union was having a terrible effect upon world opinion, especially opinion in the United States. Stalin dismissed the criticism and based the defense of his policies on a strict ideological appeal to Marx and Lenin. As to Well's hope that one day the United States and the Soviet Union could be partners in creating a better world, Stalin responded that no cooperation or even compromise with that country was possible since Franklin Roosevelt was a lackey of the propertied classes, who controlled the United States. He asserted further that the Rooseveltian New Deal was a fraud designed to mislead the American proletariat. There was in Stalin's response a clear presumption of superiority and the belief that a rival system like the American was of its very nature illegitimate. Stalin was simply saying that the Soviet Union *could not* and *would not* coexist with the United States or any other state like it.[1]

The first Five-Year Plan was meant to reconstruct the collective existence within the national system. The goal was to create "socialism in one country." What Stalin meant by that misunderstood term was that, if left to her own resources and devices, the Communist Party would succeed in attaining socialism and in so doing finally catch up to the West economically. Furthermore, it was meant ultimately to challenge the West, since, like Lenin, Stalin understood that socialism could not flourish for long in one country when it was surrounded by enemies. This belief motivated Stalin's "revolution" as it had Peter the Great's over two hundred years before. Quoting Lenin, Stalin wrote:

> We are living not only in a state but in a system of states, and the existence of the Soviet Republic side by side with imperialist states for a long time is unthinkable. One or the other must triumph in the end. And before the end comes, a series of frightful clashes between the Soviet republic and the bourgeois states is inevitable.

And then writing on his own Stalin added:

> It is a Leninist principle that the final victory of Socialism . . . is only possible on an international scale . . . For what else is our country, 'the country that is building up socialism,' but the base of the world revolution?[2]

Stalin was unmistakably one of Lenin's children.

While the Soviet Union endured civil war, N.E.P., and collectivization, the United States disengaged itself from its commitments to the League of Nations and collective security and withdrew into isolation. This was not the aberrant international behavior it has often been made out to be. The American diplomatic tradition has always run—with a few lapses—to isolationism. Wishing to remain aloof from the political complexities of Europe, the United States returned to the isolationism of the pre-1890 period.

The United States spent the 1920s in an attempt to reduce the size of the world's large navies, in an effort to diminish the prospects of war. This she accomplished, at least in the short run, at the Washington Naval Conference of 1921-1922. She also succeeded in getting the great states of the world to renounce war as an instrument of national policy by getting their signatures on the Kellogg-Briand Pact of 1928. The Americans suggested extending the pact and eventually sixty-three nations signed. The pact on the American side reflected the optimistic belief inherited from Woodrow Wilson that if you could only lay a good cause before mankind then international conflicts could indeed be resolved and that through the spread of education in the court of public opinion even bitter rivals would sooner or later abide by the rule of law. The Kellogg-Briand Pact, which lacked any machinery to enforce the peace, was the perfect treaty for an isolationist America that wished to remain aloof and morally superior. It was, writes one historian, the ultimate expression of utopian internationalism. What also underlay the pact was the fact that potentially revisionist states like the Soviet Union and Germany were still recovering from the war and were at their weakest. Moreover, the belief that there was a world interest in peace was seriously flawed. In a matter of months the world depression struck, Hitler began his rise to power, and the Soviet Union was undergoing the convulsions of the first Five-Year Plan. Utopian internationalism willfully ignored the reality that some nations like Germany and the Soviet Union were dissatisfied with the distribution of power, resources, and territory, and therefore that they would challenge the diplomatic status quo.

Hitler came to power in Germany in 1933 and one year later he withdrew his country from a disarmament conference and even more dramatically from the League of Nations. The territorial and military status quo was about to shatter and the world began to live in an atmosphere of universal tension. At Geneva, the home of the League, people began speculating about war, as they did everywhere else in the world. When asked in 1933 by the American publicist, William Randolph Hearst, "How can there be a war between Germany and the Soviet Union when they have no common frontiers?" Stalin replied: "There will be."[3] In the same year that Germany left the League, the Soviet Union joined it.

In the same year that Hitler became chancellor of Germany, Franklin Delano Roosevelt became president of the United States. A member of one of the most prominent families in American history, and the product of an impeccable education, Roosevelt grew up an extremely self-confident son of privilege. During World War I he was an assistant secretary of the navy in the Wilson administration.

An unabashed Wilsonian, Roosevelt had spent the 1920s working hard for international cooperation. He seems to have always been vitally concerned about international affairs. In 1921 he became one of the architects of the Woodrow Wilson Foundation, which rewarded contributions to international harmony. Elsewhere in the 1920s he helped launch the Walter Hines Page School of International Relations at Johns Hopkins University and helped promote international relations courses in universities all over the world. Not surprisingly he remained a committed advocate of the League of Nations. Furthermore, Roosevelt believed that the national welfare, indeed, the survival of individual freedom within the United States depended on a healthy and stable international system.[4] That belief, which underlay the Truman Doctrine and the Marshall Plan twenty years later, was given some thrust when the Great Depression spun out of control. When American money markets seriously weakened after 1929, the repercussions it nearly destroyed the economies of Germany and Japan whose prosperity to a great extent was based on American loans. And as those economies buckled, America's foreign markets all but dried up and the unemployment rate in the United States soared to 25 percent.

Starting in 1933—the same year he extended diplomatic recognition to the Soviet Union—Roosevelt gradually began to restore the American role in world affairs and increasingly turned his attention to developments in Europe. From the spring and summer of 1937 he was urged by various European leaders to use his office to bolster world peace. Roosevelt was worried about the German and Japanese problems but his outlook was also running well-ahead of that of his people. There was, for example, the proposal he made to the British government in 1937 that a conference of great states be called to look seriously at the whole issue of world peace (Stalin would make a bit later a similar proposal). Neville Chamberlain was aware that there was indignation in the United States at German and Japanese behavior but there was also the American Neutrality Act of 1935, which forbade the export of war materials to all belligerents. Moreover, according to public opinion polls taken in February 1937, 95 percent of the American people were opposed to participating in another war.[5] "It is always best and safest," said Chamberlain, "to count on nothing from the Americans but words." And as far as the Soviet Union was concerned, it was for Chamberlain a "half-Asiatic" country that in 1937 purged its own army and which he often referred to privately as "the enemy."[6]

Between 1935 and 1939 the three militarist powers—Germany, Italy, and Japan—had linked up in the Axis, Italy had left the League, the Japanese were trying to conquer China, and there was a civil war raging in Spain. The peace of the world was crumbling. The United States seemed as far away as it had been in 1914 and just as impotent to do anything. At the same time, the Soviet Union was all but ignored in a Europe drifting toward war. Neither country had been invited to the Munich Conference of 1938.

The Munich crisis had broken down the system of collective security between East and West leaving the Soviet Union as isolated as she had ever been between the wars. In a speech at the Eighteenth Communist Party Congress in 1939, Stalin accused the West of predicating its appeasement policy on war between Germany and the Soviet Union. Nevertheless, with the lines between the West and the Axis being increasingly drawn, no country on either side could feel completely secure without an understanding with the Soviet Union. The Soviets, conscious of their own vulnerability (the purge of 1937 had stripped the Red Army of thousands of experienced officers and left the rest thoroughly demoralized), understood this bargaining advantage and began negotiations in the spring of 1939 openly with Great Britain and France and, at the same moment, secretly with Nazi Germany.

It was clear from the beginning of negotiations that the price for a Soviet alliance was going to be a high one. Stalin wanted to occupy what the Tsars always called Russia's "natural ramparts" in the Baltics—Latvia, Estonia, and Lithuania; he also wanted the Red Army to move through Poland and Rumania in the event of war. To the Poles, who rejected the whole idea of a western agreement with the Soviet Union, this was out of the question. As one Polish minister is reported to have said: "With the Germans we lose our liberty, but with the Russians we lose our soul." But even Chamberlain and Edouard Daladier, the French premier, had trouble with Stalin's demands; would it not mean, they felt, converting a large area of Eastern Europe into a Soviet satellite? A Winston Churchill might have met this price but to someone with Neville Chamberlain's track record it was unthinkable. And he reacted this way despite an April 1939 Gallup Poll that showed that 92 per cent of the British people favored an alliance with the Soviet Union. The Soviet terms were rejected and never progressed further.

Villains abound in the diplomatic prelude to the Second World War and Stalin's hands were no cleaner than Chamberlain's or Daladier's. According to Louis Fischer, if Stalin had really wanted an understanding with the West, which after all posed no threat to his country, he could have had one by openly negotiating with Hitler. This would have brought great pressure to bear on Chamberlain and Daladier to yield to Stalin's demands. Instead, openly negotiating with the West pressured Hitler to make the best possible deal with Stalin.[7]

Regardless of the ideological differences and the hate campaigns conducted in both countries, a deal with Nazi Germany seems to have been Stalin's first choice. In fact from 1936 on, even as Popular Fronts in Europe were being encouraged by Stalin in the early struggle against fascism, he was putting out feelers to the Nazis through his personal emissaries. Concerned about the security of his country and anxious to make the best possible deal for it, Stalin proceeded to bring to a head the negotiations with Germany. The practical result of this was the Nazi-Soviet Pact of August 1939.

The Nazi-Soviet Pact was, on the surface at least, a non-aggression pact designed to split any grand alliance from forming against Hitler and that gave the Soviet Union a vitally needed breathing spell before the inevitable struggle with Germany. This pact and the discussions held in November 1940 between Joachim von Ribbentrop and Vyacheslav Molotov tell us a great deal about what Soviet goals were like on the eve of the Second World War.

In a "secret additional protocol" attached to the Nazi-Soviet Pact spheres of influence in Eastern Europe were assigned to both countries in the event of war with Poland, the country Molotov once referred to as "that monster child of the Treaty of Versailles." Under the arrangement that would follow such a conflict the Soviet Union was to have Finland, Estonia, and Latvia on the Baltic, the eastern part of Poland, and the Rumanian province of Bessarabia. Germany was to get Lithuania and the rest of Poland.[8] After the defeat of Poland in 1939 there was another secret agreement between the two countries. It added Lithuania to the Soviet sphere and committed the two to suppress any "Polish agitation" should any arise, as they had previously done during the partitions of that unfortunate country during the 1790s. Partitions, territorial compensations, and sphere of influence settlements were standard practice of European politics in Eastern and Central Europe for centuries. This latter agreement led to mass executions and the deportations of thousands of Poles in the 1940s.

In 1939 Stalin deemed these borderlands of the Soviet Union vital to the security needs of his country and, even after the invasion of his country in 1941, he insisted that his western allies recognize the legitimacy of his demands of 1939. He wanted no less from the United States and Great Britain than what Hitler had promised him in the Nazi-Soviet Pact. As we shall see, these demands and the reluctance of the West to meet them provide the Grand Alliance with some of the friction leading to the Cold War.

If in 1939 Stalin thought of moving westward into Eastern Europe, in 1940 he was encouraged by Germany to think of moving in a middle-eastern direction as well. In the discussions between Molotov and von Ribbentrop of November 1940, held at a time when France had already fallen and when Britain seemed to be on its last legs, the Soviet Union expressed its long-range intention of ousting Britain from its pride of place in the region and moving in the general direction of Iraq, Iran, and the Persian Gulf. Von Ribbentrop seemed willing to encourage this but pulled up short when Molotov also demanded bases on the Dardanelles and garrisons in other districts of Turkey. Disagreement over Soviet designs on Turkey led to the breaking off of the discussions.

Stalin was trying to do several things in 1939 and 1940, an examination of which will shed some light on the growing clash between East and West in the last stage of the Second World War. At the very least, he found himself confronting a set of ad hoc opportunistic responses reacting to what he believed was the impending collapse of western power in a sort of modern Punic War. This historical realignment of power afforded him the opportunity to alter the balance of power in at least Eastern Europe and at the same time create an alternative security system to the one that emerged after the First World War. Trained as a Marxist-Leninist to think in terms of the world correlation of forces he acted as he did because of a certain intuitive grasp of world events at a given moment. Guided by a ruthless realism and a studied contempt for the protests of smaller states (a Tsarist and great power legacy as much as a Leninist one) Stalin sought to alter the balance of power in Europe in two ways: on the territorial level he tried to advance the borders of the Soviet Union westward at the expense of the smaller states of the region. From the Nazi-Soviet Pact of 1939, this aim was pursued tenaciously and single-mindedly through the conferences at Teheran, Yalta, and Potsdam, a calculated bid for as much of European domination as possible. When he justified what he wanted territorially he always used the defensive argument of protecting the physical safety of the Soviet Union. This was why he never kept his territorial ambitions a secret and why he would announce in 1941, when his country was fighting for its very life, that the Soviet Union would keep exactly what Hitler had promised it in 1939. "All we ask for," he told Anthony Eden, "is to restore our country to its former frontiers."

Second, on the ideological level, the communist belief system was almost as important in the formulation of Soviet goals as politics was. Like all Marxist-Leninists Stalin believed that there was an historically dictated right to this dominance on Soviet borders and that communist elements in Europe could be made to serve the Soviet state in the same way as proletarian internationalism served it between the wars. The Soviet leadership was always sensitive to the economic and social developments in all states and certainly in neighboring ones, and it felt that it could exploit the internal polarization in each country between communist and anti-communist forces. In other words, when the time was ripe native communist elements were to be harnessed in a bid to alter the correlation of internal forces in those countries, something Lenin tried and failed to do between 1917 and 1924. This is what Stalin meant when he told Tito in 1945 in what must surely be his most sophisticated remark of the Second World War:

> This war is not like the wars of the past; whoever occupies a territory imposes his own social system on it. Each one imposes his own system as far as his army can advance. It could not be otherwise.[9]

In other words, Ideology represents something more important than what Leszek Kolakowski has called a "rhetorical dressing for the realpolitik of the Soviet Empire." Stalin's foreign policy is one of the clearest expressions we have of the "two camps doctrine" that was followed rather consistently (with the possible exception of the Khrushchev era) throughout Soviet history. With this as his starting point Stalin viewed international affairs predominantly as the political and military rivalry between major states, but also as a competition between differing social systems. When as we shall see the Red Army liberated sections of eastern and central Europe from German occupation, it was not only extending the rule of the Soviet military it was also incrementally communizing those areas. Isaac Deutscher has called this building "socialism in one zone."[10] Although such tactics constituted something less than a blueprint for world conquest, the Soviet leadership under Stalin nevertheless felt that it could plot and gradually alter the curve of history.

If the Soviet leadership was committed to a long-term view of history, the Axis powers, especially Germany and Japan, were not. Between 1937 and 1941 both countries, believing that they faced nothing but weakness and irresolution, decided that they could challenge the world status quo.

The weeks before the attack on the Soviet Union on June 22, 1941, found Hitler extremely ambivalent. On one hand, he felt that the Soviet Union could be defeated in six months—"We have only to kick in the door," he said, "and the whole rotten structure will come crashing down." On the other hand, on the evening of the attack he admitted to a feeling that he was "pushing open the door into a darkroom without knowing what lies beyond it."

Stalin, who most certainly must accept the historical blame for his country's lack of military preparedness in 1941, exhibited the same sense of ambivalence about the impending conflict. On one hand, he had anticipated the approaching war years before and with the implementation of the third Five-Year Plan of 1938 Soviet Russia began to build a new, industrial base in the eastern regions of the country—the Urals and western Siberia—that were secure from enemy attack. Designed to be an alternative arms base, iron and coal mines were opened there as were railways, power plants, and factories. By the German invasion three and a half years later the region was producing roughly one-third of the country's steel, coal, and electricity. On the other hand, Stalin continued selling war material to Germany, including oil, copper, manganese, and chromium. At the same time he ignored all the substantial warnings about Hitler's intentions to invade his country. Appeasing Hitler no less than Neville Chamberlain, Stalin once confessed to Harry Hopkins about the former that "he trusted that man."

In invading the Soviet Union that summer of 1941 the Germans felt that their historical moment had come. Looking like a mismatch from the start, since Germany was much more militarily prepared and more industrially and technologically advanced, the German challenge only succeeded in awakening a country just a few years away from superpowerhood, forcing it to respond to the challenge and hastening its ultimate transition to empire.

Notes

1. Anthony Wells, *H.G. Wells. Aspects of a Life* (New York: Random House, 1984), 134-36.

2. Joseph Stalin, *Problems of Leninism* (Moscow: Foreign Languages Publishing House, 1953), 192-93.

3. André Malraux, *Anti-Memoirs*, trans. Terence Kilmartin (New York: Holt, Rinehart and Winston, 1968), 90.

4. Alexander Dallek, *Franklin D. Roosevelt and American Foreign Policy, 1932-1945* (New York: Oxford University Press, 1979).

5. Hadley Cantril, ed., *Public Opinion, 1935-1946* (Princeton, N.J.: Princeton University Press, 1951), 966.

6. Keith Feiling, *The Life of Neville Chamberlain* (London: MacMillan, 1946).

7. Louis Fischer, *The Life and Death of Stalin* (London: Cape, 1953), 162.

8. Louis L. Snyder, *50 Documents of the 20th Century* (New York: D. Van Nostrand Company, 1964), 176-78.

9. Milovan Djilas, *Conversations with Stalin*, trans. Michael B. Petrovich (New York: Harcourt, Brace and World, Inc., 1962), 114.

10. Isaac Deutscher, *Stalin. A Political Biography* (London: Oxford University Press, 1949), chapter 14.

4

The Big Three and the Grand Alliance

The very thing that Soviet diplomacy in the late 1930s had hoped to avoid, namely, facing a militarized and aggressive Germany alone, came to pass. When the German army invaded the Soviet Union in the summer of 1941 it found an adversary basically ignorant of military tactics and strategy, armed with obsolete planes and tanks, and struggling with a generally archaic transportation and supply system. Judged by western standards, the Red Army was a gigantic but primitive instrument, albeit one that contained millions of tough peasants defending their own country and led by a regime that would stop at nothing to repel the invader. By the end of that summer the Soviet Union had been deprived of roughly one-half of its total industrial capacity, all of her air force, most of her tanks, and had lost at least three and a half million men either killed or captured. Commenting on this performance years later, Nikita Khrushchev claimed that "even the Tsar when he went to war against Germany in 1914, had a larger supply of rifles than we had the day after Hitler invaded."[1]

The West's view of the Soviet Union's ability to withstand the German assault reflected an ambivalence of its own. Western military estimates of the Soviet Union's capacity to wage a modern war had been uniformly critical since the Red Army purge of 1937. Because of that purge roughly half the officers corps was either shot or imprisoned. Until 1943 and the Battle of Stalingrad the West generally felt that the Soviet military was too backward and demoralized, the political system too alien and fragile, and the loyalty of the people to its regime almost nonexistent. To better assess the Soviet will to resist the enemy two separate missions were dispatched to Moscow in 1941. The first took place in July 1941 and was led by Harry Hopkins, President Roosevelt's close advisor and personal emissary. Just a few weeks after the German invasion Hopkins put the question to Stalin directly: did he think his country could hold out, and, if so, how much aid did she need to maintain her war effort? Hopkins was impressed with Stalin's requests. Stalin asked for guns and ammunition and aluminum—the first two for protection, Hopkins concluded, and the aluminum for aeroplanes. On the basis of these requests, Hopkins told Roosevelt that the Soviet Union would not crumble and that Stalin was banking on a protracted war. Roosevelt's positive view of Soviet determination was originally based on a hunch, and it was now reinforced by Hopkins's report, despite the fact that Hopkins was a man of no military experience or expertise and that therefore the opinion he formed in Moscow was a purely subjective one.

The second mission was led by Lord Beaverbrook, one of the great press lords of the day and Britain's minister of aircraft production. Beaverbrook was a strong "help-Russia" man who met with Stalin in September 1941. More than an assessment of Soviet strength and determination, the mission represented an economic conference to determine what the Soviet Union needed in the way of aid to see it through the worst. Both missions, as it turned out, were a prelude to the granting that November of the first Lend-Lease loan to the Soviet Union of one billion dollars. This program was to be extended to any country for its self-defense if that defense was considered necessary to American security. In other words, even before the bombing of Pearl Harbor in December 1941, Washington deemed it in the national interest to maintain the Soviet Union as a potentially valuable ally in what Roosevelt felt was the approaching conflict with Germany.

Roosevelt's view of the Soviet will to resist stood in sharp contrast to that of his secretary of war, Henry Stimson, as well as to that of Winston Churchill. Men such as Churchill and Stimson felt that—despite the reports of Beaverbrook and Hopkins—aid to the struggling Soviet Union represented a waste of vital resources since they believed that even after the successful defense of Moscow in the winter of 1941 Soviet defenses would crumble. Certainly Churchill's sceptical view of Russia as an expendable ally with only a few months of independence left helped to create British strategy in the Second World War. Along with the grim memories of the First World War and Britain's lack of readiness for the second, fear that the Soviet Union would not stay the course prompted Churchill to avoid considering the continent directly in British military planning, at least until 1944. And not considering a second front in France to relieve pressure on the Russian front helped to generate invidious comparisons between the Soviet and western military performances in the war and therefore a great deal of friction within the Grand Alliance at every wartime conference until the summer of 1944.

What leaders in the West failed to see (as did Hitler as well) was Stalin's innovative synthesis of communism with Russian nationalism. His appeal to the Soviet people in the first desperate hours of the German invasion was made in the name of Mother Russia, as he called for a national effort comparable to the one that repelled Napoleon in 1812. In September 1941 he admitted to Averell Harriman, the U.S. ambassador to the Soviet Union (1943-1946), that the Soviet people were fighting "for their homeland, not for us."[2] Communism has triumphed in the twentieth century when it has successfully allied itself with the forces of nationalism in a particular country. The experiences of Communist parties in wartime Yugoslavia and China, and later in Cuba and Vietnam, are further examples of this.

The German army came even closer to Moscow and victory in 1941 than it had to Paris in 1914. However, by December 5, 1941, the German attack had stalled. On the next day General Zhukov launched a major counterattack followed by another one on the day after the Japanese bombed Pearl Harbor. People all across the world now began to talk of "the ring closing on the Axis." A major step had been taken toward the formation of the Grand Alliance.

It is now a commonplace to say that the Grand Alliance was neither grand nor much of an alliance. Certainly there were built-in stresses and suspicions in the coalition, as there were clashes between the Allies over the basic strategies to win the war. Furthermore, there were fears on each side about the other side making a separate peace, and finally, there was serious disagreement over the fate of Eastern Europe and the way the postwar world should be run.

Until June 22, 1941, the day of the German invasion of the Soviet Union, the Soviet Union was considered an enemy of Great Britain and for very sound reasons. As we have seen, the Soviet Union's trade with Germany in vital raw materials undermined a key element of British strategy, which sought to keep those materials from a blockaded Germany. At the same time, the Soviet Union had collaborated with Germany in the destruction and dismemberment of Poland, a country for whom Great Britain went to war in 1939. The Soviet Union had also tried to extend her power into Finland. After months of trying and failing to elicit territorial concessions from the Finns, the Soviet Union invaded that country in late November 1939. Roosevelt called the attack "this dreadful rape of Finland," and for a brief spell the war against Nazi Germany was forgotten as all eyes turned to the brave and futile Finnish resistance. When the League of Nations Council met for the last time in December 1939 Britain was instrumental in getting the organization to expel the Soviet Union. All of these recent events undermined the prospects for a solid alliance.

On the Soviet side Stalin demanded a second front immediately to relieve the relentless pressure on his own forces. The charge that Britain was not doing enough in the war, especially after the Battle of Britain assured that country's security, was raised repeatedly during the war on every level of diplomatic and military liaison between the two countries. Churchill's views toward the Soviet war effort softened as the war progressed but initially he had little sympathy for a country that he had regarded as an enemy since 1917. When Ivan Maisky, the Soviet ambassador to Great Britain, demanded a second front from Churchill in September 1941, Churchill responded, "Remember that only four months ago we in this island did not know whether you were coming in against us on the German side. You of all people have no right to make reproaches to us."[3] On another occasion over the same issue, Churchill demanded to know "why the Soviets hadn't opened a second front in 1940 when the French Army had its back to the wall?"

There was also a tension between the United States and Great Britain over the same issue of what strategy would be best to win the war in the shortest space of time. The U.S. military was certainly critical of the mainlines of the British battle plan. Like Stalin, Roosevelt and his generals argued for a cross-channel invasion launched as soon as possible from the safety of fortress Britain that would secure the early liberation of France and place the Allied forces on the most direct route to the industrial heartland of Germany. Thinking his country not prepared for such an undertaking and haunted by the fear that Britain might once again incur millions of casualties on Europe's battlefields as she had in the previous war Churchill strongly resisted any suggestion for a cross-channel invasion in 1942 or 1943. When General George Marshall, the U.S. chief of staff, argued strongly for such an invasion he was told by Lord Cherwell, Churchill's science and technology advisor, "It's no use—you are arguing against the casualties on the Somme."[4] Instead of invading France in 1942 the Allies compromised and invaded North Africa (Operation Torch). This news was conveyed to Stalin personally by Churchill in August of 1942. "It was," said Churchill, "like carrying a large lump of ice to the North Pole." At first furious about the delay in the second front he wanted, Stalin seemed to come around and wished the project success in a rather uncharacteristic way: "May God prosper this undertaking,"[5] he said. But privately Stalin was still bitter about the lack of a second front in France and extremely suspicious over Operation Torch. "A campaign in Africa," he said, "They want us to bleed white in order to dictate to us their terms later on. . . . They hope that we shall lose Stalingrad and lose the springboard for an offensive."[6] And then in a memorandum handed to Churchill Stalin made it patently clear that the British refusal to establish a second front in 1942 in France "struck a mortal blow at the whole of Soviet society, which had counted on the establishment of a second front."

Roosevelt conveyed a similar message to Stalin in 1943 when he told him that an invasion of France was not possible until at least the spring of 1944. On June 24, 1943, Stalin's bitterness spilled over in an angry reply to Roosevelt: "The Soviet Government cannot become reconciled to this disregard of vital Soviet interests in the war against the common enemy. . . . The point here is not just the disappointment of the Soviet Government, but the preservation of its confidence in its Allies, a confidence which is being subjected to severe stress."[7] Churchill replied quite sharply to this when he read it and soon after Stalin recalled his ambassadors from Washington and London. A meeting between Roosevelt and Stalin was then postponed indefinitely as relations between East and West reached their nadir in the Second World War.

Until the day that the invasion of France (Operation Overlord) took place Stalin remained sceptical that it would ever happen. When he was informed by Churchill the day before, June 5, 1944, that the invasion was on for the following day, Stalin privately made light of it: "Yes, there'll be a landing, if there is no fog. Until now there was always something that interfered. I suspect tomorrow it will be something else. Maybe they'll meet up with some Germans!. . . Maybe there won't be a landing then, but just promises as usual."[8]

It must also be pointed out that the alliance was never a complete one. Churchill waited for months, despite Stalin's urgings, to declare war on Germany's European satellites. On the other hand, Stalin did not declare war on Japan until the summer of 1945, and not before he bargained for many concessions at Yalta for doing so. The United States maintained relations with Finland throughout the war even though she was an enemy of the Soviet Union. And finally the Soviet Union and the West in 1944-1945 recognized two separate Polish governments-in-exile. In other words, the wartime coalition was not the least bit homogeneous nor united on most issues, including how best to defeat Nazi Germany. There was even disagreement over the issue of unconditional surrender.

The idea of unconditional surrender was hatched initially at the Casablanca Conference of January 1943. By that point the German advance, unimpeded since 1939, had been halted in North Africa at El Alamein, and in Eastern Europe at Stalingrad. The myth of German invincibility had been laid to rest and because of it the conference was decidedly optimistic. But in no other sense was it. Russian criticism of the lack of western initiatives on the European continent crested in 1943 and that tension also pervaded the conference—as it would later that year at the Teheran Conference.

Roosevelt and Churchill committed themselves at Casablanca to the policy of unconditional surrender for several reasons: sensing their own growing power in 1943 both leaders sought to express this in a declaration that conveyed to the rest of the coalition the determination that never again would the Axis countries be allowed to threaten the peace.

Roosevelt, rather than Churchill, was the proud architect of this policy. An unabashed Wilsonian he could not allow himself to view the war as a struggle to reerect the balance of power. "There can never be," he said, "a successful compromise between good and evil. Only total victory can reward the champions of tolerance, and decency, and faith." But more than teaching the Axis a lesson was involved in the birth of the new policy. When Roosevelt and Churchill committed themselves to this uncompromising position they were also motivated by fear—the fear that the Soviet Union, which until this point in the war had absorbed most of the struggle's casualties, in totalling up these losses and in estimating its future sacrifices, might decide to seek a separate peace with Nazi Germany.

It was clear that, with the loss of the German Sixth Army at Stalingrad and certainly with the even greater defeat months later at the Kursk Salient, the belief grew in German military circles that a decisive victory in the war was no longer possible. By the end of 1943 the German army had sustained more fatal casualties than the German total for the entire First World War. Nevertheless, the German army was large, powerful, and determined, and it still occupied advanced positions deep in Soviet territory. Its generals knew they could not win the war but they were not yet conceding the inevitability of defeat. The industrial plant of much of Europe was still open to German exploitation, and the aerial bombardment of Germany's cities had not yet begun.

On the Soviet side the projected human and material cost of waging the war to final victory must have appeared overwhelming, especially in view of the fact that there was no second front in sight. According to Vojtech Mastny the situation called for a compromise peace, a trade of military gains for a political compromise.[9] And this was probably why Stalin did not adhere to the policy of unconditional surrender until September 1943.

As early as October 1941, again in December 1942, and at various times following Stalingrad in 1943, contact was made in neutral Stockholm between Soviet intermediaries and representatives of the German Foreign Office. In the meetings before Stalingrad Moscow was prepared to make a serious accommodation with the Nazi regime. In return for a desperately needed breathing space, according to Nikita Khrushchev, Moscow was willing to let the Germans retain everything they had already conquered, including Belorussia and half of the Ukraine.[10] After Stalingrad, with the balance of military forces achieved on the eastern front, Moscow demanded that Germany relinquish its conquests of Soviet soil and return its army to Germany's pre-1941 borders. She also demanded confirmation of the Soviet Union's own territorial gains made in the Nazi-Soviet Pact of 1939. Tracked by agents of British and American military intelligence, the reports of these meetings served to alarm the West. In fact, the possibility of a Russo-German rapprochement was acknowledged publicly by Harry Hopkins in October 1943.[11]

On his side, Stalin was also alarmed at reports of peace probes between the Germans and the West, real and imagined, at least three times during the war. The first occasion came when Rudolf Hess made his dramatic flight to Great Britain in May of 1941, and the next two came when representatives of the Nazi S.S. met with Allen Dulles, head of U.S. intelligence in Switzerland.

It has never been adequately explained whether Hess's flight was the solitary act of a disturbed man or whether his mission was officially sponsored by the Hitler government with the aim of negotiating a favorable peace with Great Britain before the German army swung east and invaded the Soviet Union. Whatever the original intent and even though the Soviet Union was not yet in the war, the "probe" produced genuine concern in Moscow that Great Britain was seeking a separate peace.[12]

The initial contact between a top S.S. officer, Prince Von Hohenlohe, and Allen Dulles took place in Geneva in early 1943. Acting on behalf of Heinrich Himmler, Hohenlohe raised the whole issue of a separate peace with the West. The probe does not appear to have been taken seriously by Washington.

The second and much more important contact between representatives of the S.S. and Dulles occurred in March and April 1945. Like all contacts made between the Germans and the West during the war, whether they were made by diplomats, generals, or resistance groups, they were made without the knowledge of Hitler or his inner circle.

According to the Soviets who knew about the meetings but were excluded from them, the Germans were proposing to negotiate the surrender of a million men on the western front with the purposes of "letting in the West" and allowing western armies to march as rapidly east as possible. The Germans in return were asking for an easing of the policy of unconditional surrender. But according to the Americans, the talks were basically exploratory and when they reached the actual stage of surrender the Soviets would be included.[13] The presence at these discussions of an American general, Lyman Lemnitzer, seemed to lend substance to the Soviet charge that actual surrender negotiations were underway. Indeed, it is hard to avoid this conclusion. In an earlier exchange with Roosevelt Stalin had bitterly complained about what he felt was "the absence of German resistance on the western front." He was referring in part to the episode at the Remagen Bridge on the Rhine River. For some now obscure reason the German army failed to blow up this last bridge on the river and the Allied armies surged across in March 1945. Just five days after this incident, in a growing atmosphere of suspicion and resentment, the Soviets learned that contact had been made with the Germans at Berne and that the U.S. was examining their offer to surrender. In March, Molotov, the Soviet foreign minister, accused the British and the Americans of negotiating "behind the back of the Soviet government," and he insisted that negotiations with the Germans be broken off. In a direct cable to Roosevelt Stalin bitterly complained that on the basis of the Berne discussions the Germans were transferring three divisions from Italy to the Russian front. He refused to accept Roosevelt's assurances about the meetings and went so far as to accuse the West of having already made an agreement with the Germans to open the entire western front to the Allied armies. Stalin was accusing Roosevelt of acting in bad faith and Roosevelt's reply was an angry one:

> "Frankly, I cannot avoid a feeling of bitter resentment toward your
> informers, whoever they are, for such vile misrepresentations of my
> actions or those of my trusted subordinates."[14]

There was either a gross failure in coordination between Washington and its representatives in Berne or Roosevelt was deliberately misleading his eastern ally. Writing in his memoir about this whole episode years later, Allen Dulles admitted that the Germans did, in fact, raise the whole question of surrendering the entire western front, and that he felt at one point that an agreement between the two parties was imminent. To keep the initiative in his own hands he said that he only reported the "bare facts" of the meetings to Washington. At any rate, the talks came to nothing but they did succeed in arousing more suspicion and resentment and helped to weaken an already shaky coalition.

From the Casablanca Conference until the opening of the Teheran Conference in late November 1943 the western allies were occupied with wrapping up the North African campaign, the seizing of Sicily that summer, and the invading of Italy in September. By mid-1943 American forces in the Pacific were on the offensive everywhere. With the tide turning that year the American position with respect to the cross-channel invasion prevailed. Planning the greatest operation of its kind in history required, in the western view, some coordination with the Russian front, and because of this the Teheran Conference was called for November 28, 1943.

Long before they established a foothold in occupied Europe, the Big Three, as they were referred to during the war, turned their efforts to the coming peace. And it was already clear from the summer of 1941 that the American vision for the post-war world clashed strongly with Soviet policy goals. This became evident at the dramatic meeting of Roosevelt and Churchill off the Newfoundland coast in mid-

August 1941, the meeting in which they drew up the Atlantic Charter.

The Atlantic Charter was the initial statement of American and to some extent British war aims for the next four years. It also represented the first enshrinement of Wilsonian universalism in the Second World War. In fact, the charter was strikingly analogous to the Fourteen Points of 1918. The two leaders pledged in a moment of high principle that their countries sought no territorial or any other kind of aggrandizement; that they desired "to see no territorial changes that do not accord with the freely expressed wishes of the peoples concerned;" that the peoples of the world had the right to choose the form of government under which they chose to live; that there should be freedom of the seas and that all states should be given "access, on equal terms, to the trade and to the raw materials of the world;" that the states of the world should disarm and renounce the use of force as an instrument of policy; and finally, that there should be a permanent system of general security.[15] Here again was the second major instalment of Woodrow Wilson's "new order," yet another translation in twentieth-century terms of the familiar liberal philosophy of nineteenth-century America. According to this Wilsonian view the world was to be made over in the American image.

As the war progressed it became clear to Churchill that the charter's provisions were rather utopian and at the Yalta conference in 1945 he told Roosevelt that the charter was "not a law, but a star." But Roosevelt took it seriously as witnessed by the successive reaffirmations of its principles during the war—for example, in the Declaration of the United Nations in 1942 and the Moscow Declaration of 1943. The latter was the first formal call for a United Nations, which produced the first draft of the United Nations Charter. The final enshrinement of the principles of the Atlantic Charter came with the Bretton Woods Agreement of 1944. Signed by forty-four states (but not the Soviet Union) it was here that the United States began to create its postwar strategy based on a growth-oriented international trading system in which all nations could participate on a free and equal basis. The groundwork for a new financial and commercial system, given in outlined form in 1918 and 1941, was carefully laid in 1944. An International Monetary Fund (IMF), an International Bank for Reconstruction and Development (the World Bank), and an International Trade Organization (ITO) were created with the idea of regulating exchange rates to eliminate uncertainty in money markets and removing commercial obstacles to enhance the flow of goods and services globally. Within the new commercial order the U.S. dollar was to be pegged to gold and all other currencies were to be pegged to the dollar. In other words, beginning with the Atlantic Charter the United States pressed for the creation of a new world order that would be free of colonial empires, trading blocs, and protectionist tariffs, in which collective security for the international community was to be grounded in a world organization.

What Roosevelt began to do in 1941 was to restore the lost Wilsonian vision of 1918-1919. But Roosevelt went a step further; the central idea in his approach to international organization and collective security was his concept of big-power domination. If the diplomatic prelude to the Second World War proved anything to him it was that small nations, however well intentioned, simply lacked the wherewithal of power, will, and resources to play a controlling role in maintaining the peace of the world. Only an international police force, "The Four Policemen," as Roosevelt called them—the United States, Great Britain, the Soviet Union, and China—could maintain the peace and prevent the outbreak of war. If any of the aggressor nations of the Second World War began to rearm in the future, the four policemen would blockade the offending country and, as a last resort, they would subject it to a bombardment. The idea of keeping the peace by force in a new version of the Holy Alliance actually represented a significant departure from Wilsonianism. But this particular idea could not have been a well thought out one since, when he came to expound it to Stalin at the Teheran Conference, he had not realized just what the military implications of his idea entailed for his country. When asked by Stalin whether his big power concept implied the use of U.S. forces abroad, Roosevelt replied weakly that he was really thinking of a limited military commitment—just the U.S. Air Force or Navy—and that he hoped that Great Britain and the Soviet Union would use *their* soldiers to keep the peace in Europe. Later in the conference when Stalin pushed the matter for further clarification Roosevelt backed off and gradually abandoned the whole idea.

This episode clearly illustrates Roosevelt's whole approach to diplomacy and the postwar settlement. He was inclined to throw open an idea and then postpone its discussion until the war was over. In the meantime he concentrated on military victory and vague statements about universal peace. This is not to say that Roosevelt was insincere about these ideas, but rather that he was indecisive about promoting them, precisely because they were in embryonic form and still a bit obscure. There may, in fact, be some justice in Adam Ulam's charge that the real target of Roosevelt's diplomacy was the American people and that therefore the Soviet Union had to be presented in its most favorable light to force the American people out of its traditional isolationist habits and into the wider world of international affairs.[16] If this was the case, it certainly worked. By the time the Grand Alliance was formed Roosevelt had succeeded in shaping, and was in turn shaped by, a very important shift in American public opinion.

The isolationist impulse and the popular fear and distaste for the Soviet Union was particularly intense in the United States before 1941. With the coming of the war for Americans and the formation of the Grand Alliance, American views of the world and the Soviet Union took a remarkable turn. Not only was isolationism thoroughly discredited and the American sense of mission rekindled, but the Soviet Union was no longer regarded by Americans as the world's pariah. If Americans now made moral judgments about another country it was Nazi Germany, which drew their contempt and outrage. When, after 1941, Americans talked of a new international system in the future it included the Soviet Union as a member in good standing. Joseph E. Davies, former ambassador to the Soviet Union (1937-1938) and one of the great apologists for that regime, spoke to this issue in 1941. In his best-selling *Mission to Moscow* he argued that the Soviet Union was essentially a peaceful and progressive regime and therefore worthy of American friendship. He continued to argue this point on speaking tours in the United States and Canada. His argument was echoed in the speeches of Vice-President Henry Wallace, who always included the Soviet Union in his definition of "the free world." At the same time Wendell Wilkie, Roosevelt's opponent in the presidential race of 1940, made a similar plea for international cooperation in his book *One World*, which appeared in 1943 and was a runaway best-seller. Along with Henry Luce's essay of 1941 in *Life Magazine*, "The American Century," they became overnight popular examples of American universalism. That the American people were in an internationalist phase was shown in a Gallup Poll held in the summer of 1942. Gallup detected "a profound change in viewpoint on international affairs" among the American people; by the spring of 1943, no less than 74 percent of those polled in the United States endorsed the country's participation in an international peacekeeping force.[17] Finally, their elected representatives in the U.S. Senate and the House of Representatives in 1943 passed the Fulbright and Connally resolutions, which by wide margins endorsed the idea of a postwar organization.

Part of Roosevelt's problem in dealing with the Soviets on the world stage was his emphasis on personal diplomacy. He certainly felt that he was more than equipped by knowledge and experience to be at the helm of a great country at a critical moment in its history. Moreover, he believed that the impact of personal character was a prime determinant in the shaping of contemporary history and that, if given a chance, he could come to terms with Stalin in a series of personal encounters. When William C. Bullitt, a former U.S. ambassador to Moscow, told Roosevelt in 1943 that Stalin's dictatorship was every bit as dangerous and expansive as Hitler's, Roosevelt, at his naive worst, replied, "I just have a hunch that Stalin is not that kind of man. Harry [Hopkins] says he's not and that he doesn't want anything but security for his country, and I think that if I give him everything I possibly can and ask nothing from him in return, *noblesse oblige*, he won't try to annex anything and will work with me for a world of democracy and peace."[18] At the same time, he lacked confidence in his State Department and often excluded it from the war's diplomacy. Writing to Churchill in March 1942, Roosevelt clarified this attitude: "I know you will not mind my being brutally frank when I tell you that I think I can personally handle Stalin better than either your Foreign office or my State Department." If Roosevelt was badly informed during the war, it was clearly his own fault.

There is in Franklin Roosevelt more than any other modern leader the curious mixture of the naive and the realistic, the hopeful and the cynical. His views of the Soviet Union best illustrate the point. In 1940 when he addressed a meeting of the American Youth Congress, a left-wing group that was critical of his extending aid to Finland (he had already condemned the Soviet Union's "dreadful rape of Finland"), he told them that "the Soviet Union, as everybody who has the courage to face the facts knows, is run by a dictatorship as absolute as any other dictatorship in the world."[19] Nevertheless when the Nazi-Soviet Pact was signed the year before, Roosevelt kept the door open to a future relationship with the Soviet Union after shrewdly guessing that the pact wouldn't last. This was probably why he extended only the minimum amount of aid to the Finns, recognizing as he did that the Soviet Union was becoming an increasingly important factor in world affairs and that antagonizing a potential ally might prove to be unwise. All of this was realistic enough, but when the Nazis invaded the Soviet Union Roosevelt told Admiral William Leahy, his military advisor, that Soviet domination in Europe was not something to worry about. In other words, the Soviet Union was a totalitarian system like Nazi Germany but one that was simply not imperialistic and led by a man he felt he could work with. Roosevelt had a realistic sense of Soviet power, but no appreciation of how it could be used.

If Roosevelt was consistent about one thing between 1941 and 1945 it was winning the war. If Stalin was consistently tenacious about anything in that same crucial period, it was not just about pursuing a military victory over Germany, but also about improving his country's relative position when the war was over. While Roosevelt thought constantly of new ways to structure world peace, Stalin single-mindedly pressed his territorial demands on his Allies with the same vigor as he pressed them on Hitler in 1939. In other words, Soviet territorialism stood at the center of Stalin's diplomacy from 1939 to 1945. Communism and its spread, which had for tactical reasons been played down at home during the Soviet war effort, was also deemphasized in the Soviet Union's external relations with the West. Even though revolution and territorialism went together, Stalin and his western allies behaved (at least publicly) as though they did not. This was how Stalin ended his country's diplomatic isolation by disassociating himself, at least outwardly, from world revolution. He therefore not only avoided discussing communism at any meeting with western leaders during the war and carefully avoided the term "export of revolution" (except privately), but he also sought to reassure the West by dissolving the Comintern in 1943. More than an attempt to reassure allies, the dissolution was meant to allow Stalin to deal with the states of Eastern and Central Europe on an individual basis. Unlike Lenin, Stalin did not believe in spreading communism in a great revolutionary breakthrough, but rather incrementally spreading it by military conquest.

The year 1943 is pivotal in understanding the war's turning point in the diplomatic as well as the military sense. From 1943 on the Soviet leadership could view the successes of the Red Army on the battlefield, the industrial power of their state, and their own iron determination as furnishing their country with the basis of eventually revising at least the European status quo. The Soviet leadership since Lenin's day had always felt that theirs was an historically dictated ideological right to world dominion even in the territorial sense. The entire superstructure of the communist program was controlled by an ideological vision. In this sense, communism had been the fulfillment, rather than the negation, of Russian history. It represented the fulfillment of its centralizing tendencies, its statism, and, in the hands of Stalin and the Communist Party, its imperial dreams. Stalin, who was part of the Marxist ideological mainstream, prevailed at all the wartime conferences and was able to make the United States and Great Britain easy accomplices in the achievement of Soviet aims because he knew what he wanted and he knew how to get it. On every occasion of contact with western leaders or their representatives Stalin pressed relentlessly for recognition of his territorial goals that would extend Soviet control after the war. He wanted, he said, the eastern part of Poland, all the Baltic states, and territorial concessions from Finland and Romania.

From the start of the Soviet involvement in the Second World War, Stalin made clear his determination to recover the frontier of 1941. As early as the Beaverbrook Mission of that year he demanded that Great Britain should recognize those frontiers. In September 1941, Ivan Maisky, the Soviet ambassador to Great Britain, endorsed the Atlantic Charter on behalf of his country but added that account had to be taken that "practical application of these principles will necessarily adapt itself to the circumstances, needs, and historic peculiarities of particular countries . . ."[20] The direction of Stalin's thinking then was already clear when Anthony Eden, foreign secretary of Great Britain, travelled to Moscow in December 1941 to discuss the common concerns of the Grand Alliance.

In the December meetings Eden offered a very general resolution on Anglo-Soviet cooperation. Waving this aside almost contemptuously, Stalin proceeded to expand on the Soviet reservation to the Atlantic Charter in September and to spell out his war aims in some detail. Stalin wanted a secret protocol, the kind he got from Hitler in 1939 and one that accomplished the same basic goals: The Soviet Union would take the eastern part of Poland up to the Curzon Line, leaving the Soviets in possession of the western Ukrainian and western Belorussian lands seized from Poland in 1939. Poland would be compensated at Germany's expense. Furthermore, the Soviet Union would secure from Romania Bessarabia and northern Bukovina. As for Latvia, Lithuania, and Estonia, these countries would be restored to the Soviet Union and the frontier with Finland of 1941 would be restored as well. Both Finland and Romania would also have to provide Soviet military bases on their soil. Stalin also raised the questions of postwar reparations as he did the division of Germany, and he tentatively called for a council of victorious powers that would keep the peace after the war. As far as his territorial goals went, Stalin demanded the immediate recognition of them or no agreement at all. When Eden stalled and lamely fell back on the Atlantic Charter, Stalin replied, "I thought that the Atlantic Charter was directed against those people who were trying to establish world dominion. It now looks as if the Charter was directed against the USSR." Referring to Eden's offer and indirectly to the Charter, Stalin said, "A declaration I regard as algebra, but an agreement as practical arithmetic. I do not wish to decry algebra, but I prefer practical arithmetic . . ."[21]

Winston Churchill, who, like Stalin, thought in categories based on a nineteenth-century concept of international relations, was willing by 1942 to approve at least some of Stalin's territorial goals. In the Anglo-Russian Agreement of May 1942 the British recognized the Soviet Union's right to occupy the Baltic states and to acquire the eastern part of Poland. These were, of course, secret clauses and because they violated both the letter and spirit of the Atlantic Charter Roosevelt objected strenuously to them. When he did, both Britain and the Soviet Union backed away from the agreement.

If Stalin liked arithmetic in his understandings with the West, Roosevelt was committed to a Wilsonian approach to international affairs and relied upon the algebra of principles and declarations to hold the alliance together. His gaze was so fixed on crushing Germany's attempt to dominate Europe now and in the future that he failed to give much thought to the Soviet Union's future ability to do the same thing. In Roosevelt's mind peace for the foreseeable future had to be approached militarily and had to be carefully separated from political, social, and economic considerations. This whole approach, of course, clashed with that of Stalin, a man raised in the Marxist tradition whose training prompted him to view these very things as inseparable. Peace and security for the Soviet Union were to be obtained through the extension of its military and socioeconomic system to its neighbors. While Roosevelt was dreaming nobly of a community of nations led by responsible powers, Stalin was planning the domination of whole societies. Being so narrow in his approach Roosevelt failed to come to a political understanding about Europe early in the war when the Soviet Union was still fighting for its life and when the Red Army had not yet crossed its western borders. Instead of either a clear acceptance or a firm rejection of Soviet war aims (or a sensible compromise) between 1941 and 1943, Roosevelt only succeeded in frustrating every British or Soviet attempt to clarify relationships and borders. Not only did he miss a chance of achieving a solid understanding with the Soviet Union when it was at its weakest, but he also relinquished the diplomatic initiative early in the war, leaving the Soviets with a relatively free hand to pursue their own goals in their own ways. And Churchill saw clearly that, if Washington continued to avoid specific agreements, the West's bargaining position would suffer.

If Roosevelt was the consummate politician able to build a domestic consensus by manipulating whole constituencies, Stalin, who was under no domestic restraints except the pull of Russian nationalism, was the shrewd statesman who could go to the heart of a complicated problem quickly and "appreciate all the implications of a situation with a quick and unerring eye."[22] Furthermore, he had an unmatched sense of timing; he knew when to bide his time and hold his counsel, and he knew when to seize the right moment to voice his growing demands for territory and spheres of influence agreements. For example, in December 1941, when he told General Sikorski of the Polish government-in-exile that he wanted "a bite of Germany," he also hinted that his territorial ambitions might grow as the opportunities grew. "There is no need to speak at the present of any Soviet desires, but when the time comes we will speak."[23] In no way the puppet of impersonal forces but rather the master of events, Stalin understood how to translate his power into political gains. Equally important and what made him such a formidable opponent during the war, he came to understand the American reluctance to translate its power into political gains. At the same time, according to Churchill, the spell of Stalin's personality exercised a powerful fascination on both himself and on Roosevelt. To Churchill, Stalin was the "profound Russian statesman" and even the "great revolutionary chief."[24] It is therefore not hard to see why Stalin succeeded in outmaneuvering his western allies at Teheran and Yalta.

Roosevelt's rejection of territorial acquisition as a power requirement precedent to creating a better world was shaped by the dictates of American history and by his own belief that the American people would not tolerate a long military occupation of Europe. And because he was so adamant about creating the conditions for world peace and about holding the wartime coalition together, he was willing to compromise on even his most important principles. This is why he appears so hypocritical to so much of posterity. He saw the weaknesses of the old diplomacy, but like Woodrow Wilson he confidently expected that with time and the experience of working within a world body all problems between nations would be ironed out and the Soviet Union would gradually become integrated into the family of nations. On no account, even for the most important principles on behalf of which war was being waged, would Roosevelt jeopardize the Grand Alliance. Roosevelt made this clear in an interview he granted to Francis Cardinal Spellman of New York on September 3, 1943. Two months before his first meeting with Stalin at Teheran the president who believed so strongly in the self-determination of peoples was pessimistically predicting that Europe in the future would be divided into spheres of influence with the Soviet Union dominating much of it. Included in the spheres were the states of Eastern Europe, as well as Austria, Hungary, and Croatia and even Germany. "The European people," Roosevelt said, "will simply have to endure the Russian domination in the hope that—in ten or twenty years—the European influence would bring the Russians to become less barbarian." Learning to live with the powerful Soviet Union was, he told the cardinal, more important than limiting Soviet expansion in Europe.[25] This was a rare moment of pessimism for Roosevelt during the war and on the face of it seems to contradict his predominant view that the Soviet Union was not as expansionary as Nazi Germany. Nevertheless, he felt that there was a qualitative difference between the two dictatorships and that Soviet control of a foreign country would somehow be benevolent and that the peoples involved need not fear a "long Soviet night." Stalin was no Hitler, Roosevelt told his closest advisors on October 5, 1943, and "when he meets with Stalin" he would "appeal to him on grounds of high morality" to respect the east European's right to self-determination. It should be evident that the Wilsonian image Roosevelt projected was a hollow one. There was in him yet another mixture of resolution and timidity, of high principle and political expediency. Consequently, there was never any serious determination to stand up to Stalin and speak on behalf of the peoples of Eastern and Central Europe despite the hopeful promises of the Atlantic Charter. Nowhere is this more clear than at the Teheran Conference of November 28 to December 1, 1943.

Since 1945 it has been widely and wrongly assumed that the Yalta Conference was the central diplomatic disaster of the Second World War because the division of Europe into spheres of influence was given a legitimacy for the first time. The Yalta Conference has been unrivalled in terms of popular appeal, in part because of the secret agreements signed there by a dying American president, and in part because it was used as an American domestic political football in the ongoing political debate between Democrats and Republicans. When a few years later it was learned that Alger Hiss, a suspected spy, was there as well, it succeeded in making millions of Americans believe that Yalta was some sort of a sellout.

Yet the Teheran Conference deserves far more attention than it has heretofore received. There are a number of reasons for this; first, it was only one of two conferences that brought the Big Three face to face and whose decisions were extremely important in a fundamental sense. Second, Teheran marked the first time that the United States took the lead in dealing with the Soviet Union during the war. In fact the United States came to regard itself as the senior partner in the alliance and Soviet power as its most important problem for the future. At the earlier Quebec Conference of 1943 military planners had prepared an estimate of the Soviet Union's postwar position in Europe:

> Russia's post-war position in Europe will be a dominant one. With Germany crushed, there is no power in Europe to oppose her tremendous military forces. . . . Since Russia is the decisive factor in the war, she must be given every assistance and every effort must be made to obtain her friendship. Likewise, since without question she will dominate Europe on the defeat of the Axis, it is even more essential to develop and maintain the most friendly relations with Russia.[26]

The report concluded that Soviet support was essential in the war against the Japanese Empire. This military estimate was extremely important in helping to shape subsequent decisions at Teheran and Yalta. In other words the slippage of British power was already clear in 1943 as was the rise of Soviet importance, which only grew more obvious as the war neared its end. Harold Macmillan was acknowledging this when he said in 1944, "We are like the Greeks in the late Roman Empire. They ran it because they were so much cleverer than the Romans, but they never told the Romans this. That must be our relation to the Americans."[27] And this is what Sir Alexander Cadogan, a senior British diplomat, meant when he called the Potsdam Conference of 1945 a meeting of the "Big Two and a Half."[28] Third, it was at Teheran that the Big Three finally agreed on Operation Overlord. Since 1942 Churchill had rejected the idea of a cross-channel invasion and argued instead for one through southeastern and Central Europe to liberate whole sections of the Balkans and Eastern Europe from German occupation. Mixing political with military considerations Churchill argued that this was the best way to prevent the extension of Soviet power deep into Central Europe. Like Stalin he viewed international relations predominately as the political and military rivalry between major states but also as a competition between differing social systems. "It would be a measureless disaster," he said in 1942, "if Russian barbarism were to overlay the culture and independence of the ancient states of Europe." He also understood that future sphere of influence claims rested on the preponderance of Allied and Soviet power at a given place. His point all along was that a determined invasion in the right place might carry the Allied armies into areas of Europe that a cross-channel invasion could never reach. For two years he tried to make Roosevelt think territorially and to view the Soviet Union as a future danger to the peace of the world. Roosevelt, however, never accepted the territorial argument. At the earlier Cairo Conference of 1943 he chided Churchill: "You have four-hundred years of acquisitive instinct in your blood and you just don't understand how a country might not want to acquire land somewhere if they can get it."[29] Taking the longer view of the postwar world Churchill complained to Harold Macmillan at Teheran that Roosevelt's view of the future of world politics was impossibly narrow. "Germany is finished," he said, "though it may take some time to clean up the mess. The real problem now is Russia. I can't get the Americans to see it."[30] Churchill's problem, of course, was in trying to get an American president to initiate a major policy change in the middle of the war at a time when, traditionally, Presidents initiate such changes only when the threat to American interests is so clear that it cannot be ignored. For Roosevelt a Balkan front was "back-door warfare," which would only serve British interests. When a similar idea for militarily excluding the Soviets from Eastern Europe was advanced by William Bullitt in 1943 the War and State Departments labelled it as "sheer military fantasy," the sort of thing that smacked of British imperialism and could only steer the Anglo-American armies away from the decisive front in France.[31] Refusing to mix war and politics (except domestically) Roosevelt was more interested in bringing the Soviet Union into the war against the Japanese and in securing their partnership in the future United Nations. Roosevelt's military chiefs generally opposed Churchill's strategy, although there were a few exceptions, like Generals Mark Clark and Walter Bedell Smith, who believed that an operation of that kind was militarily feasible.[32] Be that as it may, the endorsement of Operation Overlord was nevertheless the decision that ultimately led to the deep military division of Europe in 1945 and that set the stage for Soviet political and social hegemony over all of Eastern and most of Central Europe.

What finally made Teheran the real diplomatic disaster of the Second World War was the tacit recognition by the Big Three of a sphere of influence postwar settlement extremely favorable to the Soviet Union. This recognition slowly grew from the beginning of the Grand Alliance despite all the grand phrases about self-determination. Self-determination was indeed subject to practical tests and two examples should illustrate the point, namely, concessions to the Soviet Union over their requested participation in the war against Japan and concessions made over the Polish and Baltic problems.

At the Moscow Foreign Ministers' conference of October 1943 the Soviets agreed to enter the war against Japan some time after the defeat of Nazi Germany. At this point no strings were attached by the Soviets, but at Teheran a month later Stalin indicated his interest in strategic concessions in the Far East. Given Soviet losses in the war thus far and the requirement that even more might be lost in Asia, Stalin felt justified in asking for something in return. What Stalin was asking for was the restoration to the Soviet Union of those rights and possessions that had been taken from her by the Japanese in the war of 1904-1905—namely, the re-establishment of Soviet influence in Manchuria, Mongolia, and Korea, control of southern Sakhalin Island and the Kurile Islands, occupation of Port Arthur and

Dairen on the China coast, and control of the Chinese Eastern and South Manchurian Railways.

These demands were placed on the table at Teheran and thoroughly explored. If no formal agreement on this was signed at the conference it was because Stalin did not push for one and would not until he was much closer to victory in Europe ("When the time comes we will speak"). Nevertheless, it is clear that the Allies not only discussed the Far Eastern concessions but generally agreed to them. It was only left to commit them to paper at the Yalta Conference of 1945. At Yalta, once he formally received these concessions, Stalin affirmed that his country would go to war with Japan no later than three months after victory was secured in Europe.

The other critical issues that were dealt with at Teheran and which became central to the emerging Cold War were the concessions made over the Baltics, Germany, and Poland.

By the time Roosevelt went to Teheran he was convinced that Stalin wanted to annex the Baltic states and that he intended to act unilaterally in Poland and the rest of Eastern Europe. Roosevelt told Stalin that he appreciated the Soviet Union's historic ties with the Baltic states and he "jokingly" assured him that when Soviet forces reoccupied these countries, "he did not intend to go to war with the Soviet Union on this point."[33] The United States here was acknowledging Russia's special interest in the region subject, of course, to vague promises of consultation. Nevertheless, if the reoccupation of the Baltics was to be an accomplished fact, he had to put the best face on it with his own people. This could be done—if Stalin would only agree—through the use of plebiscites, a gesture toward self-determination in the region. Roosevelt assured Stalin that the Baltic peoples would, in such a referendum, vote for incorporation into the Soviet Union. Roosevelt said this to a man who once claimed that "voters decide nothing; people who count votes decide everything." This would account for the Kremlin's surprise when Churchill was ousted in the elections of 1945. Stalin agreed to the plebiscite but only under the auspices of the Soviet constitution and not in any internationally supervised form. Latvia, Lithuania, and Estonia were therefore doomed to another half-century of foreign occupation.

As important as the Baltics were, they did not lie at the center of the split between East and West. If there was a defining political and diplomatic problem by 1945 it was the Polish problem. Poland was a testcase and a problem the solution of which formed a precedent for the way the rest of the region would be dealt with.

From the beginning of the Soviet involvement in the war the Polish government-in-exile, formed after the Nazi-Soviet partition of Poland, made clear its fierce opposition to every Soviet move to recover the frontiers of 1941. Despite the extinction of their sovereignty the Poles remained proud and assertive and easily persuaded that concessions to their Soviet neighbor would have only the worst possible impact on Poland's future. This view was reinforced in the spring of 1943 when a mass grave of thousands of executed Polish officers was discovered by the German army in the Katyn Forest near Smolensk. The London

Poles had tried unsuccessfully to get an accounting from Moscow about the missing men and now, in calling for an investigation, they more or less accused the Soviet government of committing the atrocity. In recent years the Soviet government has acknowledged Stalin's complicity in the massacre, but in 1943 it vehemently denied it. Stalin's reaction was an angry one and he eventually broke off relations with the London Poles, who, he claimed, were in collusion with the Nazis. The episode only served to aggravate an already sensitive issue and provided yet additional freight for all parties to carry into Teheran and Yalta.

The breach between the London Poles and the Soviet Union was an embarrassment for the alliance but the Soviets made it clear that if it was to be healed it would be on Soviet terms. On the eve of Teheran, at the Moscow Conference of Foreign Ministers, Molotov asserted that Poland was largely a Soviet concern and that once Polish independence was restored it had to be led by a government "friendly to Russians."[34] This was the first of many times this phrase was used. The American response to the possibility of Soviet expansion reveals all the inconsistencies of U.S. foreign policy in the Second World War. Speaking to Congress in 1943 Secretary of State Cordell Hull declared that "there will no longer be need for spheres of influence, for alliances, for balances of power, or any other of the special arrangements through which in the unhappy past, nations strove to safeguard their security or to promote their interests."[35] But Hull was speaking out of both sides of his mouth. At all the conferences of 1943 he refused to be drawn into any agreement that might clarify the matter once and for all. Unwilling to antagonize an important ally unnecessarily and thinking more of the postwar foundations of peace to which the Soviets were crucial, the U.S. administration refused to challenge the Soviet Union over Poland and simply deferred the whole matter until Yalta.

Another determinant of U.S. behavior during Teheran and later at Yalta comprised the constraints placed on an American president by domestic political considerations. One year away from the presidential elections of 1944, Roosevelt was reluctant to invite a political backlash from various ethnic minorities in the United States who had a personal interest in the fate of Eastern Europe. Concern over this prompted him to draw Stalin aside at Teheran just before the Polish issue was to be raised. He told Stalin that between six and seven million Poles voted in the United States and that a premature settlement not considerate of their sensibilities would alienate them at election time. Churchill had earlier warned Stalin over the Katyn episode that a "public announcement of a break would do the greatest possible harm in the United States where the Poles are numerous and influential." For this reason Roosevelt told Stalin that he could not take any public position on the matter at *that* conference, although privately he endorsed Churchill's suggestion that the Polish border be shifted westward at the expense of Germany. The new Poland was to lay between the Oder River in the west and the Curzon Line in the east, transferring everything east of that line to the Soviet Union. Once again, the Polish question sets the pattern for what will happen in the rest of Eastern Europe. Roosevelt at Teheran made no real effort to get anything in return for the Poles. Stalin was therefore free to draw the inference that the United States had no serious interest in the Balkans or in Eastern Europe. When Boleslaw Bierut, the Polish Communist leader, asked Stalin, "Will there by any conflict over Poland with the West?" Stalin replied that there would be no conflict at all.[36] It is certainly clear at Teheran that the failure to open a second front earlier (the West only promised one at Teheran) put the diplomatic leverage in Stalin's hands. Informal as the understanding was over Poland, Averell Harriman believed that the Soviets interpreted the American position at Teheran as acquiescence in Soviet territorial expansion. As Anthony Eden recorded in his memoirs: "I began to fear greatly for the Poles." He might have expanded that to include all of Eastern Europe.

The other major problem raised at Teheran and formally dealt with at future conferences was the German question. Long before Roosevelt initialled the Morgenthau Plan, a draconian plan to split Germany into pieces and at the same time to pastoralize it, he advocated the dismemberment of the country. In privately approving the transfer of most of East Prussia to Poland Roosevelt was not only trying to compensate Poland for everything she was to lose east of the Curzon Line, but he was also trying to put an end to the Prussian component in German history. Nazi tyranny and Prussian militarism were linked in Roosevelt's and Churchill's minds. And since this was the source of the war's infection Germany had to be taught a lesson and reeducated. Roosevelt raised the German problem at the conference by saying that the question was either to split it or not. Stalin promptly stated that he favored dismemberment and then Roosevelt submitted a plan to divide Germany into five parts. Nothing specific, however, was agreed upon at Teheran, but the Big Three did agree upon the idea of dismemberment. Nevertheless, no one at the conference envisioned a permanent division of Germany. The British, with time, grew lukewarm to the whole idea anyway. Churchill and Eden thought more of the balance of power to which a divided Germany was inimical. After all, what were the implications of weakening Germany in this way? Would it not leave Soviet power dominant throughout the continent? Roosevelt seemed not to have thought the matter through and, because of it, stood almost passively by and allowed the geographic conditions for the Cold War to be set right before his eyes. Charles Bohlen, who was special assistant to the secretary of state and acted as a liaison officer between the State Department and the White House (the State Department never favored the idea of Germany's division), neatly summarized the implications of this and other results of the Teheran conference.

> Germany is to be broken up and kept broken up. The states of eastern, southeastern and central Europe will not be permitted to group themselves into any federation or association . . . Poland and Italy will remain approximately their present territorial size, but it is doubtful if either will be permitted to maintain any appreciable armed force. The result would be that the Soviet Union would be the only important military and political force on the continent of Europe. The rest of

Europe would be reduced to military and political impotence.[37]

Notes

1. Strobe Talbott, ed., *Khrushchev Remembers* (Boston: Little, Brown and Company, 1970), 159.

2. Averell Harriman, *Peace with Russia?* (New York: Simon and Schuster, 1959), 11.

3. Winston S. Churchill, *The Grand Alliance* (Boston: Houghton Mifflin Company, 1950), 457-58.

4. Robert H. Ferrel, *American Diplomacy. A History* (New York: W.W. Norton and Co., 1969), 643.

5. Winston S. Churchill, *The Hinge of Fate* (Boston: Houghton Mifflin Company, 1950), 475, 481.

6. Isaac Deutscher, *Stalin. A Political Biography* (London: Oxford University Press, 1949), 479.

7. *Stalin's Correspondence with Churchill, Attlee, Roosevelt and Truman* (London: Lawrence and Wishart, 1958), Part II, 70-71.

8. Milovan Djilas, *Conversations with Stalin* (New York: Harcourt, Brace and World, Inc., 1962), 81.

9. Vojtech Mastny, *Russia's Road to the Cold War* (New York: Columbia University Press, 1979), 73.

10. Jerrold L. Schecter, ed., *Khrushchev Remembers. The Glasnost Tapes* (Boston: Little, Brown and Company, 1990), 65.

11. Harry Hopkins, "We Can Win in 1945," *American Magazine* 136, no. 4 (October 1943): 100.

12. Schecter, *Khrushchev Remembers*, 133.

13. Allen Dulles, *The Secret Surrender* (New York: Popular Library, 1966).

14. Winston Churchill, *Triumph and Tragedy* (Boston: Houghton Mifflin Company, 1950), 448.

15. Walter La Feber, *The Origins of the Cold War 1941-1947* (New York: John Wiley and Sons, 1971), 33.

16. Adam Ulam, *The Rivals. America and Russia since World War II* (New York: Viking Press, 1971), 32.

17. Daniel Yergin, *Shattered Peace. The Origins of the Cold War and the National Security State* (Boston: Houghton Mifflin Company, 1977), 46.

18. William C. Bullitt, "How We Won the War and Lost the Peace," *Life* 25 (30 August 1948): 94.

19. Robert Divine, *Roosevelt and World War II* (Baltimore, Md.: Penguin Books, 1970), 78.

20. La Feber, *Origins of the Cold War*, 35.

21. Anthony Eden, *The Reckoning* (Boston: Houghton Mifflin Company, 1965), 334-35.

22. Quoted in Robin Edmonds, *The Big Three. Churchill, Roosevelt and Stalin in Peace and War* (New York: W.W. Norton and Company, 1991), 341.

23. Vojtech Mastny, "Soviet War Aims at the Moscow and Teheran Conferences of 1943," *Journal of Modern History* 47, no. 3 (1975): 500.

24. Churchill, *The Hinge of Fate*, 477.

25. Robert I. Gannon, *The Cardinal Spellman Story* (Garden City, N.Y.: Doubleday and Co., 1962), 223-24.

26. Robert E. Sherwood, *Roosevelt and Hopkins. An Intimate History* (New York: Harper and Brothers, 1948), 748-49.

27. Quoted in Randall B. Woods and Howard Jones, *Dawning of the Cold War. The United States' Quest for Order* (Athens, Ga.: University of Georgia Press, 1991), 12.

28. Edmonds, *The Big Three*, 453.

29. Quoted in Terry Anderson, *The United States and the Cold War, 1944-1947* (New York: Columbia University Press, 1981), 4.

30. Harold Macmillan, *Winds of Change. 1914-1939* (New York: Harper and Row, 1966), 14.

31. Lynn E. Davis, *The Cold War Begins* (Princeton, N.J.: Princeton University Press, 1974), 79-80.

32. Mark W. Clark, *Calculated Risk* (New York: Harper and Row, 1950), 348-49.

33. Robert Dallek, *Franklin D. Roosevelt and American Foreign Policy 1932-1945* (New York: Oxford University Press, 1979), 418, 436.

34. Keith Sainsbury, *The Turning Point* (Oxford: Oxford University Press, 1985), 104.

35. Sainsbury, *The Turning Point*, 117.

36. Jan Novak in Michael Charlton, "On the Origins of the Cold War. The Spectre of Yalta," *Encounter* (June 1983), 20.

37. Charles E. Bohlen, *Witness to History. 1929-1969* (New York: W.W. Norton and Company, 1973), 153.

5

The Yalta Legacy

It has been Poland's geographic misfortune in modern times to occupy the high road between Russia and Germany. Clinging stubbornly and at times desperately to its national identity, Poland was for generations the Russian Empire's trouble spot. By the twentieth century the Polish people easily qualified as the most subversive foreign element in the Tsarist empire.

As we have seen, the long-festering dispute over Poland's future flared up in 1939 and later became the major bone of contention between the partners of the Grand Alliance. Stalin had already in April 1943 withdrawn diplomatic recognition of the London Polish government-in-exile over the Katyn Forest massacre. In July 1944 the Red Army stormed into Poland and advanced rapidly to the Vistula River near Warsaw. Shortly thereafter Stalin sponsored a rival group to the London Polish government called the Polish Committee of National Liberation, which was based in Lublin after that city's capture by the Red Army.

With military events moving so swiftly in Eastern Europe the heady optimism in Washington that followed Teheran was disappearing just as quickly. With the political map of Europe about to be redrawn dramatically, Roosevelt on several occasions during 1944 advised the leaders of the London Polish government to seek reconciliation with the Soviet Union. Roosevelt pointed out to them the obvious lessons of political mathematics when he informed them that there were five times as many Russians as Poles, "and let me tell you now," he added, "the British and the Americans have no intention of fighting Russia."[1] Ignoring these warnings the London Polish government unwisely authorized its Home Army in Warsaw to assert the country's independence by rising against the occupying Germans and liberate its own capital city. With the Red Army only twelve miles from Moscow and encouraged by radio broadcasts beamed in from Moscow, the Home Army launched a general insurrection on August 1, 1944. On the same day the Russian military advance halted "to regroup." For two months the Red Army waited and did nothing while the German S.S. brutally extinguished Polish resistance.

From the beginning of the rising Churchill had appealed to Stalin for permission to fly in relief supplies to the beleaguered city and at the same time make use of Soviet airfields to refuel Allied aircraft. The appeal fell on deaf ears

in the Kremlin. Churchill described the Russians' behavior as "strange and sinister." Churchill, who had brought his country into the war on behalf of the Poles, had even wanted to present Stalin, with a fait accompli and fly Allied aircraft to Warsaw; but Roosevelt, in Churchill's words, "could not bring himself to make a decision." Roosevelt did not think that the fate of the Home Army warranted a clash with Stalin, which might hurt the Grand Alliance. From the beginning Stalin deemed the rising in Warsaw a reckless undertaking and worse, he referred to the Home Army as a "group of criminals." What Stalin really meant was that a Polish victory would obviously run counter to Soviet plans for the political subjection of Poland. More than the Katyn episode of 1943, the fate of the Warsaw Uprising of 1944 brought Churchill and Roosevelt face to face with the grim reality of Stalin's designs for Poland. Stalin had made it abundantly clear that he was prepared to smash those Poles who were not prepared to accept communist authority. Stalin wanted not only territorial security like the Tsars but political security as well. The defeat of the uprising was the crucial turning point in the later emergence of communist Poland. According to Norman Davies, the rising marked the end of the old order in Poland. The Polish government-in-exile lost any control it had over events in Poland, while the Home Army, the one effective challenge to Soviet rule, was soon disbanded and its leaders confined to Soviet jails. One cannot avoid the conclusion that the Nazis had done the Soviet's work for them.[2]

The disillusionment in certain influential quarters of Washington over the way the Warsaw Uprising was handled helped make the episode something of a turning point in East-West relations. Professional diplomats like George F. Kennan and Charles E. Bohlen, ambassadors like Averell Harriman and Joseph Grew, and cabinet members like James V. Forrestal and Edward Stettinius, Jr., now raised doubts about whether the Grand Alliance could be maintained into the postwar period. These were men, furthermore, who were determined to assume control over foreign policy in the near future. All of them had been alarmed at Stalin's behavior during the uprising and all were increasingly inclined to emphasize the national security of the United States in all future dealings with the Soviet Union.

The fluid international environment and the growing Russian presence in Eastern Europe had begun to worry the U.S. State Department as well. By the fall of 1944 this concern prompted Secretary of State Cordell Hull to request the American embassy in Moscow to provide an interpretation of Soviet policy. George Kennan, who was counsellor of the embassy, and Averell Harriman, the American ambassador, filed separate reports that September. Both men were extremely critical of Soviet diplomacy. They both stated that the credibility of Russian pledges was dictated by the military situation and they both warned that Stalin intended to establish a Russian sphere of influence in Eastern Europe. They also stated that Stalin would never allow a refurbished League of Nations to interfere in Russia's dealings with its neighbors. Harriman and Kennan had cabled to Washington in this vein before and had been consistently ignored. Now their reports were read closely and their ideas would soon help to define a new U.S. foreign policy. Kennan had been especially shocked by the Warsaw Uprising. In his view this should have been the moment to stage a showdown with the Russians.[3] As extreme as this idea was, it was somewhat typical of the group generally. Averell Harriman warned Washington with no less intensity that unless the United States confronted Soviet behavior head-on there was "every indication that the Soviet Union will become a bully whenever their interests are involved." And all of them shared Charles Bohlen's view of Stalin. "Historians," he wrote in his memoirs, "will argue whether Stalin was simply a realist with no moral values or a monster whose paranoia led him into senseless crimes. Judged by his actions, I believe he runs high on the list of the world's monsters."[4] It is in this space of time between the Warsaw Uprising and the Yalta Conference that we can begin to speak of the emergence in Washington of "hard liners." Revisionist historians have rejected this notion and have argued instead that there was a clear anti-communist predisposition in Washington that led to the inevitable clash. This is not, strictly speaking, true. The United States was led throughout the war by men who sincerely felt that Soviet and Western ideas about democratic constitutional development could be compatible and that cooperation between the Great Powers could be carried over from war to peacetime. If that leadership grew disillusioned it was Soviet behavior in Poland that provided the wake-up call.

In an interview granted to the American journalist, Edgar Rice Snow, in October 1944, Maxim Litvinov, an early Russian exponent of detente with the West, acknowledged the growing split between East and West and more or less blamed Moscow for it. Diplomacy might have avoided the rift, he said, "if we had made clear the limit of our needs, but now it is too late, suspicions are rife on both sides." Furthermore, Litvinov, who was an expert on the West, put his finger on the problem; it was, he said, the lack of expertise in the Foreign Commissariat (which he had headed in the 1930s). It "is run by three men and none of them understands America or Britain." He was still worried about this in the spring of 1945 when he told Averell Harriman that the "root cause" of the trouble between East and West was the "ideological conception prevailing [in Moscow] that conflict between communism and capitalism is inevitable."[5] Once again he felt that the wrong people were making key decisions in the Kremlin on behalf of a man whose isolation bred a distorted view of the West. It is hard not to agree with the conclusion of William Taubman that Stalin's "own machinations were bringing the future closer, and faster, than he knew."[6]

While the heroic effort in Warsaw was being crushed the Red Army unleashed a series of large offensives through Romania in the direction of Bulgaria and Yugoslavia. In a matter of days Romania accepted Moscow's armistice terms and switched allegiances, and Bulgaria decided on immediate neutrality, although not quick enough to save her from invasion. As the Red Army made tremendous advances, Churchill and Roosevelt became increasingly apprehensive. "Good God," Churchill told Lord Moran, "can't you see that the Russians are spreading across Europe like a tide. There is nothing to prevent them from marching into Turkey and Greece." He also admitted wearily, "I have a strong feeling that my work is done. I have no message, I had a message. Now I only say 'fight the damned socialists.' I do not believe in this brave new world."[7]

In September 1944 with the Red Army poised for an advance into Yugoslavia, Hungary, and Greece, Churchill invited himself to Moscow for an October meeting with Stalin. He was clearly bothered by the developments in Eastern Europe. What Churchill wanted to do was clarify the political orientation of the Balkan nations by quantifying the Soviet and British spheres of influence in the region. At their first meeting Churchill told Stalin:

> Let us settle our affairs in the Balkans. Your armies are in Rumania and Bulgaria. We have interests, missions, and agents there. Don't let us get at cross-purposes in small ways. As far as Britain and Russia are concerned, how would it do for you to have ninety percent predominance in Rumania, for us to have ninety percent of the say in Greece, and go fifty-fifty about Yugoslavia?

He proceeded to suggest that the Soviet Union's interest predominate in seventy-five percent of Bulgaria and that they go "fifty-fifty" in Hungary. At this point Churchill shoved a piece of paper toward Stalin, who promptly indicated his acceptance with a pencil tick next to the suggested ratios. Then Churchill, one of the architects of the Atlantic Charter, hesitated and remarked: "Might it not be thought rather cynical if it seemed we had disposed of these issues, so fateful to millions of people, in such an offhand manner? Let us burn the paper." To this, Stalin replied, "No, you keep it."[8]

What is the meaning of this so-called "Percentages Agreement" in the diplomacy of the Second World War? Churchill later insisted on the temporary nature of such arrangements, which were in any case only to last until the war ended and a final peace settlement was created. It is very doubtful that Stalin appreciated this distinction. Churchill was certainly less than candid about the whole thing. One thing he omitted to say was that discussions of ratios between Molotov and Eden went on after the Churchill-Stalin meeting and the Russians succeeded in obtaining alterations in the percentages favorable to the Soviet Union. In fact the Soviet Union succeeded in raising their share of influence in Hungary by 30 percent and in Bulgaria by 5 percent. The British got nothing more for themselves. In other words, in trying to halt the burgeoning unilateralism of the Soviet Union and deeply concerned with the lack of decisiveness in his American ally, Churchill was in his despair making the best deal for himself and at least salvaging Greece from the Soviet sphere. Nevertheless, in seeking a private advantage Churchill helped to put the stamp of legitimacy on the division of Europe into spheres of influence. And that legitimacy rested on the preponderance of Soviet and Allied power at a given place in late 1944. Western diplomacy was unravelling at the Moscow meeting. Stalin had to be encouraged by Roosevelt's failure to raise major objections to a cynical bargain that violated every diplomatic canon the man had stood for since 1919. From Stalin's standpoint he could not fail to take Roosevelt's silence as a signal of tacit acceptance of the sphere of influence approach to the political future of Eastern Europe, and specifically to the geographical divisions agreed upon at Moscow.

By early 1945 the war in Europe had reached an advanced stage and the defeat of Germany seemed imminent. At the same time, Washington estimated that it would take another eighteen months to subdue Japan and that an invasion of the Japanese home islands might cost upward of one million American casualties. Victory in the Pacific War seemed assured, but no one doubted that a formidable task still lay ahead. Almost as alarmed as Churchill was over the Balkan offensive, Roosevelt asked for a Big Three conference to not only discuss the fate of Eastern Europe but to at the same time plan for the final attack on Germany and enlist the aid of the Soviet Union in the Pacific War.

In February 1945 when the Big Three assembled in Russia's Crimea for the Yalta Conference the military setting offered no diplomatic advantage to the West. In the previous December the Germans had counterattacked in the Ardennes offensive and inflicted heavy casualties on the Allied armies, which were driven back beyond Germany's western borders. By February the Allies had only just succeeded in regaining the line they held in December. At the same time, the Rhine had yet to be forced and worse, there was friction in the Allied camp, which found the British very critical over the way General Eisenhower was running things. While the Allies were struggling to regain the momentum of six weeks before, a Soviet force of seven million was driving across Poland into Germany. By the time the Yalta Conference convened the Red Army was in control of the Silesian industrial complex, just forty miles from Berlin and eighty miles from Vienna.

Roosevelt recognized the new situation when he told a group of senators in January 1945 that the Red Army was in control of much of Eastern and Central Europe, that they were carving for themselves a huge sphere of influence there, and that it would be best for the era that followed to recognize these developments and work with the Russians to ameliorate the situation.[9] As he told his son Elliot, "Britain is in decline, China—still in the eighteenth century. Russia—suspicious of us, and making us suspicious of her. America is the only great power than can make peace in the world stick."[10] And it could do these things, he felt, by acting responsibly, accepting the world as it had become, and cooperating with the Russians by drawing her into a world body like the United Nations. Roosevelt was acknowledging something basic about the balance of power. Only four short years before the Soviet Union had been extremely weak and vulnerable and its leader had tried to appease an unappeasable dictator. In 1945 with his armies swarming all over Eastern and Central Europe Stalin could, if he wished, confront and expand against his democratic allies. Unlike 1878, when Russia had beaten the Turks and been deprived of her gains, no one could now cheat her out of what she regarded as her legitimate spoils of war. A momentous shift in the balance of power had taken place.

Nevertheless, no proper estimates of Soviet material and economic strength were made before Yalta. Roosevelt and Churchill approached the conference table with no real sense of the fragility of the Soviet system. Consequently, given the performance of the Red Army since 1943, Western estimates of Soviet military power were decidedly exaggerated. As Adam Ulam points out, the West should have known that Russia's human and material losses in the war were nothing less than staggering and that she would not be able to draw upon unlimited manpower reserves and keep them mobilized for years on end. Nor was the Soviet Union the internal political monolith she wanted the world to believe she was. To believe otherwise was to ignore the panic and desertions in the first stage of the war, the Kremlin-ordered transfers of politically suspect populations, and the anti-Soviet partisan activity that flickered on throughout various parts of the Soviet empire until well past 1945. According to Ulam the West was over-compensating for the previous low estimate it made of Soviet power in 1941.[11]

At Stalin's suggestion Roosevelt presided over the Yalta Conference. This only served to encourage Roosevelt's exercise of personal diplomacy. This and the exaggerated estimate of Soviet power accounts for the way he opened the conference at Yalta by volunteering that while he would like the Russians to make concessions, he would not insist on any. He also repeated what he had already made clear at Teheran: that the United States would withdraw its forces from Europe within eighteen months of the end of the war. He was thus unilaterally promising to remove the one obstacle to Soviet domination in Eastern Europe. It was for this reason that Churchill pressed for the return of France to the main councils of European history. It was agreed at Yalta to temporarily divide Germany into four zones of occupation each under the administration of one of the Allies: Great Britain, the United States, the Soviet Union, and France. Over Russian protests France was now accorded a seat on the Allied Control Council, which would briefly administer the country. In the long run Roosevelt's incautious remark about troop withdrawals seems to have influenced Stalin's decision in May to declare himself against permanent German dismemberment, thus reversing his position at Teheran. Why split Germany up when a pro-Soviet Fifth Column might just turn the whole country in Russia's direction? According to Milovan Djilas, this was precisely Stalin's plan for Germany, which he presented to Bulgarian and Yugoslavian communists in 1946.[12]

At the same time, there were other ways to ensure Russian security and keep Germany weak. The question of reparations, which also involved the German problem, was raised very forcefully by Stalin at the Yalta Conference. Only the Polish question produced more friction among the Big Three. No doubt misled by the Morgenthau Plan, which Roosevelt and Churchill had briefly initialled, Stalin demanded a decision to deindustrialize Germany and rebuild the Soviet Union with German equipment. Reparations in kind, as it might be called, was a form of economic disarmament in which 80 percent of Germany's heavy industrial equipment was to be removed in a two-year period following its surrender. At the same time the Russians asked for direct capital reparations to the tune of twenty billion dollars with half going to itself and half to those countries that had been victims of German conquest. Both Roosevelt and Churchill protested this figure as being far in excess of what Germany could afford and too redolent of what had been extracted from that country after 1919. Churchill raised the spectre of famine in Germany if this was done and Roosevelt made it clear that the United States would not play the role of banker to Germany as she had in the 1920s. Both statesmen were, of course, afraid of re-creating the conditions that had produced Nazism in the first place. Moreover, they felt that a revived German economy was too central to European recovery and that the Germans, whatever their past sins, must be allowed to earn their own way. Nevertheless, Roosevelt acknowledged the Russian claim to reparations but not in the extreme form in which they had been presented. Stalin however insisted that the figure ten billion be included in the agreement and Roosevelt accepted that figure as the basis for future discussion. When Roosevelt died two months later the Russians erroneously claimed that he had supported that figure, a bone of contention between the two parties for years.

On the question of German reparations the Soviet Union never completely got its way. This was so because the United States and Great Britain shared in the conquest of Germany and were therefore in a stronger position and the Yalta Agreement reflected that fact. Only on the Polish question did Russia enjoy the dominant position and this too was reflected at Yalta.

The long simmering dispute over Poland flared up at Yalta where it was hotly debated for six days and nights. In fact the Polish "problem" became a testcase for what would happen in Eastern Europe—the settlements in the rest of the region followed the precedent it set.

When Yalta convened on February 4, 1945, Russia was already in control of the destiny of most of Eastern Europe and she certainly did not need Western approval to retain it. After all, what Russian power had conquered not even the most determined Great Power diplomacy could get them to relinquish. There is some wisdom in the way James F. Byrnes, one of the American advisors at the conference, summarized the diplomatic predicament at Yalta: "It was not a question of what we would *let* the Russians do, but what we could *get* them to do." It is almost unthinkable, even in hindsight, to argue that at this late date in the war the West could have repudiated Russia and the gains she had made. This is especially true given what the West had already approved eighteen months before at Teheran. At that conference Roosevelt had acknowledged Russia's special interest in Eastern Europe, agreeing to the Curzon Line in the process. He had never made any real effort to get anything in return for the Poles, or for that matter, the Baltic peoples, whom he also allowed to slide quietly into the Soviet sphere. But Churchill, for all his rhetoric at Yalta, had also been a willing accomplice in the creation of that sphere. The "Percentages Agreement" four months before most certainly hampered his protest over what Stalin proposed to do in Poland, and Churchill admitted as much. Showing the usual inadequate connection between its assets and the resolve to use them the West at Yalta ended up pitting the abstract principles of self-determination and international cooperation against the forces of Soviet military occupation.

If the West could not sustain a free and independent Poland, a country on whose behalf it had gone to war in 1939, what could it hope to do for any other country in Europe, especially those states that had associated themselves with the

German war machine. Therein lay the West's dilemma at Yalta: how does one bridge the gap between Wilsonian objectives to foster a reorganization of international politics along democratic lines, and the realities of power politics as practiced by a powerful rival. A policy of trying to force the Red Army to relinquish its hold over vast tracts of Europe and withdraw to its pre-1939 borders was militarily impossible, and the policy of trying to persuade them to do it willingly for the sake of world peace was diplomatically unrealistic. Nevertheless, Roosevelt was an advocate of the generous gesture and he sincerely believed that he could get along with Stalin. He believed enthusiastically in the family of nations and the underlying harmony within it and he explained his whole approach to the problem in his inaugural address in January 1945 by quoting Emerson: "the only way to have a friend is to be one." At Yalta he asked Stalin to recognize the potential effect on American domestic politics of the Polish issue on Polish voters at home and he appealed to Stalin to show some generosity toward the Poles over the matter of their eastern frontiers. However, and this was typical of Roosevelt, he made it clear that he was simply putting forward a suggestion and would not insist upon it. Churchill also hoped for a "gesture of magnaminity" from Stalin, which would be much appreciated. Stalin reacted angrily to this approach and pointed out to his partners in the Grand Alliance that "the Germans were savages and seemed to hate with a sadistic hatred the creative work of human beings." Twice in twenty-five years the Germans had attacked the Soviet Union through Poland waging warfare that resembled "the incursions of Huns." That corridor of invasion had to be closed to the Germans in the future. And as far as the Curzon Line went, that border had been fixed several decades before by Clemenceau and Lord Curzon and tacitly agreed to by the Allies at Teheran. In the end Roosevelt and Churchill accepted Russia's borders of 1941 and agreed to move Poland's western frontier toward the Oder and Neisse rivers. Since there were two Neisse rivers (and Stalin did not know it) the final delineation was left unresolved.

The one course open to the West that might, they thought, break the Soviet monopoly of power in Eastern Europe was the establishment of democratically elected governments all over the region. This was why the debates over Poland centered not so much on drawing boundaries as over the political governance of the country. Recognizing the new Polish frontiers even tacitly was bad enough but, worse, Poland seemed likely to lose its internal autonomy and to be subjected to a Soviet-type police state where members of its government were to be chosen by Stalin. It was this that produced some of Churchill's most forceful remarks at the conference. Great Britain, Churchill had told Stalin, had gone to war to honor its commitment to a free Poland. He said that "we could never accept any settlement which did not leave her free, independent, and sovereign."[13] Stalin replied that for the Soviet Union it was a matter "both of honor and security." He added somewhat sarcastically that the Lublin regime in Poland was "as democratic as De Gaulle." All through the Yalta Conference Roosevelt and Churchill talked the accommodating language of multiparty democracy while Stalin talked the realpolitik language of Russian expansion. And the guiding principle that inspired

Stalin's demands at Yalta was, of course, the extension of the Soviet national interest, but filtered through the emotions of the revolution. Stalin was not only the latest Russian architect of imperial expansion but he was also the first leader after Lenin to lay claim to the ideological leadership of the system it embodied.

After days of lengthy discussion the Big Three agreed on a democratic formula for the Polish government: the Lublin government was to be the dominant core of a new coalition that would include all the democratic forces in Poland, including Polish leaders living abroad. It was also to pledge itself to "free and unfettered elections as soon as possible." Roosevelt had been very eager to get the Polish problem out of the way. He had already come to the conclusion that "when a thing becomes unavoidable, one should adapt oneself to it." There was really too much at stake for him to allow the Polish question to fester and remain a major difference between the Allies. Roosevelt had one eye on the creation of the United Nations and the other on nailing down the war against Japan and he needed Soviet participation in both cases. He did succeed in extracting a promise from Stalin for an election in Poland in one month's time. "I want the election in Poland to be above suspicion," Roosevelt said, "like Caesar's wife." The promised Polish election was so much window-dressing and Roosevelt knew it. He was under no illusions about developments over Poland. He understood that despite the pledges made over the new Polish government the West had no way of assuring the representative nature of the Polish regime. "Mr. President," Admiral Leahy, his military advisor, told him after looking at the report on Poland, "this is so elastic that the Russians can stretch it all the way from Yalta to Washington without ever technically breaking it." "I know, Bill," Roosevelt replied, "I know it. But it's the best I can do for Poland at this time." As a matter of fact, the elections that Stalin had promised were not held until January 1947, and they were far from "free." Moreover, that development contributed directly to the ultimate breach between the Soviet Union and the West.

Besides the agreement over free elections in Poland Roosevelt, ever the consummate politician, sought to assure the U.S. Congress and the American people in one more way that the peace of the world would not be lost as it had been back in 1919. He did this by asking Churchill and Stalin to sign the declaration of Liberated Europe. The declaration had been drafted by the State Department and accepted in toto by the conferees. The document represented another statement of Wilsonian purpose. "By this declaration," the Big Three announced, "we affirm our faith in the principles of the Atlantic Charter, our pledge in the Declaration by the United Nations, and our determination to build in cooperation with other peace loving nations world order under law, dedicated to peace, security, freedom and general well-being of all mankind." The declaration committed the occupying powers to hold free and unsupervised elections and clamp constitutional safeguards on those lands liberated by the Allies from German control. At the same time the exiled governments would in principle return to participate in the democratic process. The declaration echoed the theme that the war was a moral war and according to Robert Dallek, it was part of Roosevelt's strategy to place a "moral burden" on the Russians to act with restraint.[14] But could Roosevelt really expect Stalin, a man who had already telegraphed his intentions during the Warsaw Uprising, to act with moral restraint? And did he really expect Stalin to assign the same meaning to terms like freedom, democracy, and independence as he did himself? Here is yet another example of Roosevelt's love of the algebra of abstract principles. One senses in Roosevelt's diplomatic initiatives the weakness of Wilsonian-inspired theories disconnected from the hard facts of political life, which seems so odd for a first-rate politician.

The Declaration of Liberated Europe had an insidious effect on Soviet zones in the months ahead. The declaration had the immediate result of conferring on the activities of the Soviet occupation authorities in Eastern Europe a certain moral legitimacy. The declaration was posted conspicuously throughout the liberated areas by the Red Army, thus making the task of the occupation easier. Without the Yalta agreement and the declaration there might have been a greater opposition to that occupation. It is clear that Yalta helped to weaken this resistance in advance. More than one critic has pointed to the widespread psychology of resignation in the region—that any resistance to the inevitable would be a useless gesture doomed to inevitable failure. The Soviets could now brandish the text of the declaration throughout the liberated countries and graft upon those regimes their own version of democracy. Viewed in this light it is not hard to see why George Kennan called the declaration the "shabbiest sort of equivocation."

Nevertheless, from Roosevelt's standpoint the conference gave him what he wanted: The Russian adherence to the U.N. with the "Four Policemen" dominating, the Russian entrance into the Pacific war three months after the German surrender, and the promise of democratic elections in Eastern Europe. Indeed, the Yalta conference ended with Roosevelt in a state of what Robert Sherwood called "supreme exaltation." But surely this was hyperbole since Roosevelt told a sceptical Adolph Berle a few weeks later, "Adolf, I didn't say the result was good. I said it was the best I could do."

The immediate reaction to what was accomplished at Yalta resembled in no small way the euphoria that followed the Munich Conference of 1938. Congratulations poured into Washington from all sides, not only from prominent individuals but also from the world press all with nothing less than ecstatic expressions about what had been achieved. The decisions made at Yalta seemed for a time to fire the imaginations of all sorts of commentators with the belief that the world stood poised on the threshold of a new, cooperative era of peace and harmony. Roosevelt himself, of course, helped to stimulate these utopian hopes. Returning to Washington in March he assured a joint session of Congress that Yalta had once and for all ended the old sphere of influence, balance of power system in favor of a genuinely universal organization in which all peace-loving nations could join. None of his listeners had any doubt that he included a trusting and cooperative Soviet Union in that organization. Much of this was echoed by Winston Churchill. Unlike Roosevelt he did believe in balances of power but chose to display to the House of Commons a confidence, which he perhaps did not feel: "The impression

I brought back from the Crimea . . . is that Marshal Stalin and the Soviet leaders wish to live in honourable friendship and equality with the western democracies. I feel also that their word is their bond. I know of no government which stands to its obligations, even in its own despite, more solidly than the Russian Soviet Government."[15] Roosevelt and Churchill were putting the best face on what they had done. Harry Hopkins, speaking with more conviction, went so far as to say that "we were absolutely certain that we had won the first great victory of the peace—and by 'we' I mean *all* of us, the whole civilized human race."[16]

Despite the general euphoria about what had been accomplished at Yalta the criticism, barely heard at first amid the din of enthusiasm, began to mount. The setting in March and April 1945 was important in understanding this shift of opinion. On one hand one heard talk of peace, democracy, and international cooperation, and on the other the behavior of the Russian occupation forces caused second thoughts about Yalta and helped create the feeling that somehow the West had sinned. It was in these weeks there arose among the peoples of Eastern Europe the feeling that Yalta was a betrayal, another Munich, yet another feeble attempt by Western democracies to appease another totalitarian dictator at the expense of their region. This is what made Yalta for so many the "original sin" as one commentator puts it, the founding myth of a divided Europe. Indeed, ever since 1945 official Soviet bloc propaganda consistently referred to the work of the conference to legitimize Soviet domination.[17]

Yalta has become synonymous with Sovietization and the disappearance of anything resembling independent regimes. Between the end of the conference and Roosevelt's death in April Russia proceeded immediately and relentlessly with the final subjugation of Eastern Europe. Soviet methods to Sovietize differed somewhat by country but were fundamentally similar in approach. The object of the strategy was to create communist regimes in Eastern Europe but without going so quickly that it alarmed an already suspicious West. There was to be no revolutionary convulsion like 1919 especially in view of the fact that there were more communists in France and Italy than there were in Eastern Europe. The Russians wanted to incrementally spread communism, first by establishing coalition governments, the so-called "People's Democracies" (the term was originally coined by Tito). The strategy was an extension of the popular front idea of the 1930s. The communist members of the coalition, supported by the Russian military, then infiltrated every position of responsibility in the new government. The Soviet armed presence in Eastern Europe made all the difference. André Malraux once said in drawing the contrast between the coalitions of the 1930s and 1940s: "A weak Russia wants Popular Fronts, a strong Russia wants people's democracies." In some cases the pace was swifter and communist regimes were installed more directly. As early as September 1944, when the Red Army invaded Bulgaria, it instigated a coup that installed a "people's democracy." Romania was even more dramatic. Immediately following Yalta Andrei Vyshinsky proceeded to Bucharest and forced King Michael, under the threat of tank fire, to dismiss his anti-communist prime minister, and appoint a man favorable to the Soviet Union.

When the new prime minister was appointed he turned over the Ministry of the Interior to a communist. In fact, whenever the Russian occupation forces installed themselves a wave of arrests followed that swept up the political leaders of all the bourgeois parties effectively eliminating them from politics. In Poland, for example, the Kremlin ignored its Yalta pledge to expand the Lublin government by including members of the Polish resistance and the London government-in-exile. Instead, sixteen Polish underground leaders were arrested by the Russians after having promised them safe conduct to come to Moscow to discuss broadening the Lublin regime. This was typical of what was happening all over Eastern Europe. Totalitarian regimes were being installed swiftly and inexorably in 1945 in the face of Western passivity and Yalta was becoming a code word for the new Soviet dominated status quo.

Repeated protests from Washington and London accomplished very little. The new regimes in Eastern Europe lacked popular support, but Russian obstructiveness made it difficult to discover what was going on. Ambassador Harriman kept reminding Washington that Soviet behavior in Eastern Europe was a clear and intolerable violation of the Yalta agreement. "The Soviet program," he argued, "is the establishment of totalitarianism, ending personal liberty and democracy as we know it and respect." He pressed Washington to demand Soviet adherence to what had been agreed to at Yalta.

Roosevelt was pressed even more forcefully by Churchill. Even though he later admitted in his memoirs that the "Percentages Agreement" somewhat hampered British protest over what Stalin was doing in Eastern Europe, Churchill was still sufficiently alarmed to counsel "a firm and blunt stand" in the face of expansionism. Writing to Roosevelt on March 13, 1945, Churchill said:

> Poland has lost her frontier. Is she now to lose her freedom? . . . We are in the presence of a great failure and an utter breakdown of what was settled at Yalta . . . I believe that combined dogged pressure . . . would very likely succeed.[18]

It is clear that the events in Poland and elsewhere in Eastern Europe, and the urgent letters of Churchill and Harriman shook Roosevelt's confidence. By April he was convinced that something else besides the "politics of morality" was needed to move Stalin in the right direction. Privately, his view of the Soviet Union was hardening. He told Senator Arthur H. Vandenberg that he was "coming to know the Russians better." On the eve of his death one of Harriman's cables about Soviet duplicity produced anger and he banged the arm of his wheelchair and said, "Averell is right, we can't do business with Stalin. He has broken everyone of the promises he made at Yalta." On April 1, 1945, he sent Stalin a telegram in which he pointed out that "a thinly disguised continuation of the present Warsaw government would be entirely unacceptable, and would cause our people to regard the Yalta agreement as a failure."[19] Stalin replied by claiming that the real problem lay with the misguided efforts of the American and British ambassadors in Moscow to reinterpret the provisions of the Yalta agreement.

On the eve of his death Roosevelt's view of the Soviet Union had obviously hardened and he was convinced that he needed to adopt a more vigilant and firm approach in his dealings with it. "We must not permit anybody to entertain a false impression that we are afraid," he wrote Churchill. "Our armies will in a very few days be in a position that will permit us to become 'tougher' than has heretofore appeared advantageous to the war effort."[20] There was certainly a growing belief in the spring of 1945 in both Washington and Moscow that a struggle between the two states was inevitable and unavoidable. According to Louis Halle, who was then a member of the Policy Planning Staff in the Office of the Secretary of State, the predominant worry in Washington as the war drew to a close "was over the deadly struggle to contain the Soviet Union that could already be foreseen."[21] That the conflict between the two states had irrevocably hardened was noticed on the Russian side by Maxim Litvinov in one of his many off-the-record interviews in which he gave vent to his frustrations. For years a critic of the rigidity of the Soviet system Litvinov expressed his pessimism about the continuance of the Grand Alliance in June 1945 and made a brief diagnosis of the growing crisis. Edgar Rice Snow asked Litvinov if things were better or worse than when they last met in late 1944. "Worse," he replied. "Why did you Americans wait until now to begin opposing us in the Balkans and Eastern Europe? . . . You should have done this three years ago. Now it's too late and your complaints only arouse suspicion here."[22] What Litvinov was acknowledging, in a moment of genuine candor, was something basic about the emerging Cold War. If there was one side that bore the onus for beginning the struggle, it was his own. He was saying that the Soviet Union had grasped for far more in Europe than it really needed to maintain its security and that this was not recognized or resisted early enough by the West. This expansionist policy had led to a struggle that in his eyes was now inevitable. "First the western powers make a mistake and rub us the wrong way," he told Cyrus L. Sulzberger of the *New York Times*. "Then we make a mistake and rub you the wrong way."[23] Nor was Litvinov the only Russian diplomat embarrassed by the clumsy way their government behaved in 1945. Ivan Maisky, the former ambassador to Great Britain, felt the need to explain the Russian striving for power and influence as arising out of the Russian's deep-seated sense of inferiority. At the same time Alexandra M. Kollontai, the former ambassador to Sweden, acknowledged that Russians knew and cared little about the psychology of other peoples and therefore never realized they were offending them. "So the three Soviet officials most knowledgeable about the western world," writes Vojtech Mastny, "were also the most apologetic about these government's policies, indirectly pointing out the real culprit."[24]

Whatever hopes Franklin Roosevelt may have had for dealing with this mounting crisis and whatever beliefs he may have entertained about cooperating with the Russians in the future, they now died with him on April 12, 1945. Only a few short weeks later on May 7, the German military authorities formally surrendered to the Allies.

The collapse of the German state and the disappearance of almost all indigenous political authority in Central Europe left in its wake a giant geopolitical vacuum. To a certain extent this was inevitable given the character of the war just waged and the Allied imposition of the policy of unconditional surrender.

Even before the guns fell silent it was clear that Europe had been partitioned into spheres of influence with each major power reconstructing its zones according to its respective political and economic models and insuring that its foreign policy reflected the larger international goals of the dominating state.

Roosevelt's role in creating this post-Yalta crisis defies easy definition. Like most American presidents he was a politician rather than a statesman by training, although he possessed more historical background than most of them. Roosevelt was a believer in personal diplomacy and he certainly believed in his own ability to exert an influence over Stalin. He felt that in face-to-face encounters he could convince the Soviet dictator that he too had a vested interest in peace. Behind this failed policy lay some very basic assumptions: first, that conflicts do not arise from the nature of a particular regime; second, that there was no calculated Soviet bid for European domination; and third, that there was, as far as Roosevelt was concerned, a "new" Russia at the conference tables of the war, a Russia that was far more democratic and peaceful and less revolutionary in spirit than it had been in Lenin's day; and that furthermore this new Russia would reconcile itself to a creative and peaceful role in the world if treated with generosity. Odd as it was coming from a shrewd politician, there was in his thinking the weakness of theory disconnected from the hard facts of political life. Roosevelt genuinely wanted to lower the barriers between nations and thought that he could bring an otherwise uncompromising Stalin around to his way of thinking. His ideas for a postwar renewal were certainly noble in intent, but fundamentally unsound. As an individual interacting with the historical circumstances of his time he left much to be desired. Had he allowed himself to view the future as Churchill did, in terms of a clash of systems, he might have succeeded in creating a balance of power more amenable to the West.

This is not to say that Roosevelt allowed Stalin to walk all over him as had been alleged by his many critics. After all, he refused to share the secrets of the atomic bomb project with the Russians, he allowed them no effective say over the way Italy was to be run after 1943, nor did he allow them anything like the reconstruction loans or reparations they demanded and felt entitled to. When Roosevelt wanted to he could remain firm.

Part visionary and part pragmatist Roosevelt may have misunderstood the nature of the Soviet threat, but he certainly understood his own people. He knew that Americans believed that they were fighting for self-determination and the principles of the Atlantic Charter. This dedication to universalist principles, which emanated from the very foundations of the country, prevented Roosevelt and his people from viewing the looming Cold War in its proper light—as a struggle to alter the balance of power. With Roosevelt's death the steady barrage of Wilsonian rhetoric which emanated from the White House was replaced (although not completely) by the tough-minded realism of geopolitics.

Stalin's role in creating the post-Yalta crisis allows for a clearer definition. The West went to Yalta believing that Stalin could be persuaded to make a sensible compromise for the sake of a lasting peace. The Stalin they encountered was an uncompromising man, one of the top players of the 1917 revolution who strove not for a rational settlement but for a power and influence far in excess of Russia's security requirements. Instead of a partner in peace they discovered a leader bent on imperial expansion and at the same time determined to promote the communist revolution.

Stalin was led to believe, by what the Allies did and did not do during the war, that they were resigned to the inevitability of Soviet domination in Eastern Europe. He arrived at this conclusion because the United States and Great Britain did not demand a settlement during the war. Had Churchill and especially Roosevelt been less idealistic and as tough-minded as Stalin early in the war when the Soviet Union was in its greatest peril, they might have struck a better bargain than the one they sealed in 1945. Moreover, it would have been a bargain based on Allied aid and the prospects of a second front. Sadly, the attempt was never made. By 1943 the moment was lost when Russia reversed the military balance on the eastern front. By 1945 Stalin demonstrated to what extent he was the diplomatic master of the Grand Alliance. When requested by Roosevelt to open a new front in Asia and enter the war against the Japanese, Stalin insisted on compensation. He demanded the territories and rights Russia enjoyed in Asia prior to the defeat of 1905 because only this would justify fighting the Japanese to the Russian people. The West could have done the same thing on behalf of Eastern Europe in 1942. Russian expansion may have been the prime determinant in causing the rift, but the flaccid diplomacy of the United States helped to inadvertently accelerate the emergence of the Cold War.

The future of whole tracts of Eastern and Central Europe now lay with Stalin and as we shall see the key events of the late 1940s and 1950s bear this out.

Notes

1. Quoted in John Lewis Gaddis, *The United States and the Origins of the Cold War 1941-1947* (New York: Columbia University Press, 1972), 144.

2. Norman Davies, *God's Playground. A History of Poland* (Oxford: Clarendon Press, 1981), II, 479-80.

3. B. Kevrig, *The Myth of Liberation: East-Central Europe in United States Diplomacy and Politics since 1941* (Baltimore, Md.: Johns Hopkins University Press, 1973), 18.

4. Charles E. Bohlen, *Witness to History, 1929-1969* (New York: W.W. Norton and Co., 1973), 338-89.

5. Vojtech Mastny, *Russia's Road to the Cold War. Diplomacy, Warfare, and the Politics of Communism, 1941-1945* (New York: Columbia University Press, 1979), 222-23.

6. William Taubman, *Stalin's American Policy. From Entente to Détente to Cold War* (New York: W.W. Norton and Co., 1982), 94.

7. Lord Moran, *Churchill: The Struggle for Survival* (Boston: Houghton Mifflin, 1966), 173.

8. Winston Churchill, *Triumph and Tragedy* (Boston: Houghton Mifflin Company, 1950), 226-28.

9. Robert Dallek, *Franklin D. Roosevelt and American Foreign Policy 1932-1935* (New York: Oxford University Press, 1979), 507-8.

10. Elliott Roosevelt, *As I Saw It* (New York: Duell, Sloan and Peace, 1946), 130.

11. Adam Ulam, *The Rivals. America and Russia since World War II* (New York: The Viking Press, 1971), 7-9.

12. Milovan Djilas, *Conversations with Stalin* (New York: Harcourt, Brace and World, 1962), 153.

13. Churchill, *Triumph and Tragedy*, 368.

14. Dallek, *Franklin D. Roosevelt*, 516.

15. Churchill, *Triumph and Tragedy*, 400-1.

16. Quoted in Robert E. Sherwood, *Roosevelt and Hopkins. An Intimate History* (New York: Harper and Brothers, 1948), 870.

17. Jacques Rupnik, *The Other Europe* (London: Weidenfeld and Nicolson, 1989), 63.

18. Churchill, *Triumph and Tragedy*, 426.

19. Martin Herz, *Beginnings of the Cold War* (Bloomington: University of Indiana Press, 1966), 90.

20. See Francis L. Loewenheim, Harold D. Langley, and Manfred Jonas, eds., *Roosevelt and Churchill: Their Secret Wartime Correspondence* (New York: E.P. Dutton, 1975).

21. Louis J. Halle, *The Cold War as History* (New York: Harper and Row, 1967), 39.

22. Edgar Rice Snow, *Journey to the Beginning* (London: Gollancz, 1959), 357.

23. Cyrus L. Sulzberger, "Litvinov a Lonely Jeremiah Who Foresaw the 'Cold War,'" *New York Times*, 3 January 1952, 9.

24. Mastny, *Russia's Road to the Cold War*, 266.

6

Potsdam and the Division of Europe

In the spring of 1945 as the Red Army swept across Eastern Europe the West became increasingly alarmed over the spread of Soviet power. Winston Churchill called this advance "one of the most melancholy in history." Added to the anxiety of the moment was the crisis in Western leadership. Franklin Roosevelt died in April 1945 to be replaced by an inexperienced Harry S. Truman, and Churchill was defeated in the British general election of July 1945 to be replaced by Clement Atlee, a man who lacked the prestige of his predecessor.

It had been known for some time among Roosevelt's closest associates that their president was a dying man, and yet they made no attempt to brief Harry Truman on anything of consequence before April 12. It is one of the ironies of this transition that Stalin knew more about the atomic bomb project in the United States than Truman did. Consequently, Truman, politically and emotionally unprepared for high office, became president during a critical moment in his nation's history.

Roosevelt and Truman could not have been more different. Unlike the pedigreed and educated Roosevelt, Truman was a man from the midwest heartland of America, with no real education beyond the secondary school level. He had always been a bit insecure about this and had tried to compensate for it by massive reading, especially in the subject of history. This was why, according to Admiral Leahy, Truman was so extremely well informed in military matters. Although untutored in foreign affairs and holding extremely simplistic and provincial ideas about the world beyond America's borders, Truman at least possessed a natural antagonism toward dictatorships. In 1941, for example, when the Russo-German war was raging and Roosevelt was requesting lend-lease aid, Truman, then a senator, was suggesting, "If we see that Germany is winning the war we ought to help Russia and if Russia is winning we ought to help Germany and that way let them kill as many as possible, although I don't want to see Hitler victorious under any circumstances. Neither of them think anything of their pledged word."[1]

Despite his initial feelings of confusion when sworn in as President, Truman had some personal qualities that would serve him well in his new position. He was a personally tough, no nonsense type of man who did not suffer fools easily. Relatively candid for a politician he had a penchant for plain talking and an innate ability to act decisively when called upon to do so. He also had the pragmatist's contempt for theories and abstractions—what he sneeringly called "professor talk." All of these qualities had helped make him an effective U.S. senator from 1934 to 1944. Because of his qualities of character he was determined to enter the White House in 1945 and assert his authority.

While the United States and Great Britain changed leadership in 1945 the Soviet Union did not. Stalin was very much in control of Russia's destiny and he continued to follow the course he charted when the Red Army crossed the Polish border in 1944: he proceeded to systematically extinguish Eastern Europe's political independence using the heavy hand of the Red Army to do so. At the same time there was scarcely any Western resistance to the gradual satellization of Eastern and Central Europe. A good example of this was the case of Czechoslovakia. The United States chose to honor an earlier agreement with Stalin and withdraw its forces from the country when it could easily have liberated two-thirds of it. Consequently the Czechs, who boasted a genuinely democratic tradition, and who once again felt as abandoned as in 1938, chose to head off Soviet pressure by voluntarily reorganizing their government to include a large communist presence. But Stalin was not merely trying to alter the internal correlation of forces in those countries, he also wanted to be paid in territorial coin. Despite the Czech initiative Stalin demanded Ruthenia, a territory that had never been part of Russia. In appropriating it Stalin could move the Soviet frontier farther west until it bordered on Hungary. He also retained part of the mouth of the Danube River by keeping a piece of Romania and at the same time detached a piece of East Prussia, which included the ice-free port of Königsberg (soon to be called Kaliningrad). All of these acquisitions were supposedly to be administered tentatively, pending a conference and peace treaty. But in fact they became permanent parts of the Soviet empire.

The Soviet drive for territory and influence was not confined to the parts of Europe the Red Army occupied. Greece, Turkey, and Iran were the first states beyond the area of Red Army occupation to feel the expansionist pressure of the Soviet Union.

The first stage of the Greek civil war began in 1944 foreshadowing the major conflict that was to tear Greece apart between 1947 and 1949. The communist wing of the Greek national resistance regarded their rebellion as a means of coming to power themselves and making a social revolution. Fortunately for Greece, Stalin chose to honor his agreement with Churchill (the "Percentages Agreement") and refrained from intervening directly, thus allowing the British army an opportunity to crush the rebels in Athens.

Stalin had no such inhibitions about Turkey. Soviet pressure on Turkey, for example, had begun in March 1945 when Stalin had denounced the treaty of friendship that had existed between the two countries since 1925. In June 1945 Russia announced its terms to Turkey when it demanded the revision of the Montreux Convention of 1936, which had allowed Turkey to militarize the straits and close them in wartime. It also demanded the cession of several districts in eastern Turkey, as well as military bases on the Straits. Stalin made it clear that he wanted a reorientation of Turkish foreign policy toward the Soviet Union. All of this was punctuated by a carefully designed war of nerves; Soviet naval maneuvers were held off Turkey's Black Sea coast while Red Army maneuvers were staged near the borders of Transcaucasia and Bulgaria where the Russians stationed thousands of troops. The campaign that was also carried on in the Soviet radio and press seemed to underline the threat of Soviet invasion. According to Bruce Kuniholm, the war of nerves in the summer of 1945 reminded many diplomats of the Nazi pressures directed against Czechoslovakia in 1938.

The situation was just as ominous in Iran. Soviet designs on that country went back to 1920 when the Red Army had briefly occupied the Iranian province of Gilan in Azerbaijan and set up the so-called Soviet Republic of Gilan. That effort had been supported by Stalin, but Lenin had detached the Russians from the country and renounced Soviet ambitions in Iran. Russia again signalled her imperial interest in the region in 1940 during the Molotov-Ribbentrop discussions. By 1941 the Russians and the British agreed to divide Iran into spheres of influence (as they had in 1907) to last for the duration of the war.

Russia began its effort to intimidate the Iranians as early as 1944 with a massive propaganda campaign in the radio and press and the deliberate attempt to assist separatist movements in Azerbaijan, one of the country's larger provinces. The Red Army succeeded in fomenting huge demonstrations in Teheran and Tabriz and prevented the Iranian police from restoring order. When the Iranian government protested, they were met by very menacing Russian demands for oil concessions. When Washington protested Soviet behavior the Russians insisted that the government in Teheran did not speak for the Iranian people and should therefore be ignored. Instead of backing down the Russians only turned up the heat in 1945 when armed rebels in Tabriz, operating behind a Red Army shield, captured government buildings and proclaimed their autonomy.

While the Russians threatened to expand into the Near and Middle East they also controlled Manchuria and North Korea. By the autumn of 1945, despite a wartime understanding between Roosevelt and Stalin to exercise a joint trusteeship of Korea for upward to thirty years, Soviet troops in North Korea had sealed off the country north of the 38th parallel. This frustrated the American plan of unifying the peninsula under free elections.

In all of these cases Stalin was attempting to define the correlation of forces in strategic parts of the world. With the old balance of power destroyed by the war and power vacuums taking its place, Moscow saw its chance to alter not merely the military balance but also the overall evolution of internal social forces that existed in these regions. The Marxist concept of correlation of forces is a bit vague and allows for a great deal of subjective interpretation, but it seems to pertain to the communist control and direction of anything from armed partisans in Iran, peasant and labor unions in Hungary, coalitions in Czechoslovakia and Poland, "people's committees" in North Korea, to communist electorates in France and Italy. The strategic idea behind all of these activities was that when enough of these geographical, military, and political positions were secured, the balance of power would decisively shift in the Soviet Union's favor.

When Truman entered the White House he inherited the task of winding down the war in Asia, dealing with an aggressive Soviet Union, and building a new international order out of the ashes of the old. At first he adhered to the universal formulas of his predecessor and retained his advisors. This was not surprising in view of the fact that the U.S. Chiefs of Staff clung to the belief that Soviet participation was still vital for the conquest of Japan. Moreover, there was a distinct tolerance among the American people toward the Soviet Union and Gallup Polls taken throughout 1945 bore this out; they indicated that the American public remained confident that American-Soviet cooperation after the war could be sustained. The American tolerance of the Soviet Union and even of domestic communists was an early victim of the Cold War but not in 1945-1946, and Truman had to be cognizant of it.

In his initial survey of the geopolitical terrain Truman assumed, as Roosevelt had, a community of aims between the United States and the Soviet Union. Basically unsophisticated when it came to the world of political ideologies, he felt that the problem the Russians had in international affairs was one of style rather than substance. "They don't know how to behave," Truman said. "They are like bulls in a china shop. They are only twenty-five years old. We are over a hundred and the British are centuries older. We have to teach them how to behave."[2]

Truman therefore began his presidency by trying to reassure the Soviet Union. He did this initially by rejecting any proposal for an Anglo-American alliance. Neither he nor the country was ready for this. Truman was of two minds over the Soviet problem: on one hand, he did not want Stalin to feel that the West was ganging up on Russia, and so he pointedly did not stop off at London to confer with Churchill on the way to the Potsdam Conference. Truman's concern, like his predecessor's, was to avoid the old balance of power solutions of the past which Churchill as much as Stalin represented. Like all new Presidents facing enormously complicated problems, Truman was at the mercy of conflicting counsels. Although personally an admirer of Churchill, he inherited a certain distrust for the prime minister among some of his advisors when he assumed office. Admiral Leahy, Joseph E. Davies, and Harry Hopkins had come to believe that Churchill, in pursuing the British historical quest for a balance in Europe, might easily pervert the universalist policies laid out so clearly by Franklin Roosevelt. This was one of the reasons why Truman rejected Churchill's suggestion not to retreat to the agreed demarcation line in Germany when the Allied armies found that they had liberated areas further east than they had expected, and use what territory was seized as leverage in future negotiations with Stalin. On the other hand, Truman had never really liked or trusted the Russians. They were, he told Henry Wallace, like people from across the tracks whose manners were bad. They seldom kept their word, he felt, and their effort to dominate other peoples was wrong and immoral.[3]

On Truman's second day in office he asked Secretary of State Edward Stettinius for a report on the present state of American-Soviet relations. The report he received back from the State Department the same day claimed that the Soviet government had taken up a "firm and uncompromising" stand on nearly every major question that had arisen in its relations with the United States[4] Truman then closeted himself with his foreign policy advisors, principle among them being Averell Harriman. Harriman, one of the most influential members of the anti-Russian group in Washington, seems to have had the most influence with the new President. To Harriman, the Soviet Union was not a nation-state like Nazi Germany, but a totalitarian empire with a unique and brutal history, whose tentacles now threatened to spread its influence over much of Europe. Wherever the Soviet Union succeeded in imposing its occupation forces, he argued, it also imposed a communist "system"; that is, a foreign policy and economic order subservient to Moscow and, above all, a police state. What the West was faced with, in a line he could have borrowed from Churchill, was the "barbarian invasion" of Europe. Like Churchill, he felt that this domination was intolerable and should be firmly resisted. Roosevelt, he said, had merely coddled and spoiled the Russians and the Russians only interpreted American generosity as a sign of weakness. Along with General John Deane, head of the military mission to Moscow during the Second World War, Harriman argued that the United States had gotten nothing from the Russians in return. It was time to toughen America's whole approach and the way to begin doing this was to dangle before the Russians the economic assistance they so desperately needed to reconstruct their economy.

Truman was then faced with a choice of salvaging the special relationship that Hopkins and others felt existed between Stalin and Roosevelt and fulfilling the latter's policies through negotiations, or taking a harder line as Harriman wanted (as did Churchill), by basing all future policies toward the Soviet Union on considerations of power alone. In just a few short days Truman made up his mind and decided to challenge the Soviet Union's efforts to dominate parts of Europe. He opted for the harder line because he felt that Roosevelt's approach had failed to prevent the extension of Russia's influence. As a matter of fact, Harriman may have been preaching to the converted. When Harriman briefed the President he found that Truman had not only done his homework and read the full documentation of the Yalta Conference, but had come to believe that Stalin had broken most of the promises he had made there. Harriman was amazed to find the President in complete control of the situation. Through Harriman and the "hard-liners" and through his own efforts, Truman came to view the Soviet threat in a more realistic light. He became convinced that Stalin did not want a head-on clash with American power in 1945, and that it had but one major concern going into the Potsdam Conference and that was to keep the United States at bay diplomatically while it kept and digested its principal war aim—control over Central and Eastern Europe. Truman, who came from pioneering stock and who had a solid understanding of his country and its values, would make no concessions from basic principles or traditions in order to win Soviet favor.

The first occasion to test the new hard line came on April 23 when Truman had an interview with the Russian foreign minister, Molotov, who happened to be in the United States for the opening of the U.N. Conference at San Francisco. Stalin had

Molotov stop off in Washington to determine whether Truman contemplated any policy changes. Molotov soon learned that the country most closely watched in Washington and considered the ultimate test of Russia's intentions was Poland. In the now famous interview Truman came quickly and bluntly to the point. To the delight of the foreign policy establishment Truman accused the Soviet Union of violating the Yalta accord. He repeatedly told Molotov that an agreement had been made on Poland and the United States expected Russia to honor that agreement. Molotov, a stubborn and abrasive man, who once succeeded in flustering Hitler, could only protest, "I have never been talked to like that in my life."[5] Truman shot back, "Carry out your agreements and you won't get talked to like that." When Stalin heard of the interview he cabled Washington two days later saying that the West had not taken the interests of the Soviet Union into consideration when it set up the governments of Belgium and Greece, and that Russia understood Western security needs. Why then, Stalin asked, couldn't the West give the Soviet Union the same latitude when it came to areas of Europe vital to Soviet security? There can be no doubt that Stalin viewed the Truman-Molotov confrontation as evidence that the new president had abandoned Roosevelt's policy of cooperation with his country.

On April 25, 1945 the United Nations Conference on International Organization opened in San Francisco. No sooner was Molotov in his seat than he demanded that the representatives of the Lublin regime be seated immediately. Pressed by the official Polish delegation, Secretary of State Stettinius rejected the demand publicly because it would, he felt, destroy any chance of the new U.N. charter being approved in the U.S. Senate. A week later tensions increased when the Soviet Government acknowledged arresting sixteen Polish leaders after inviting them to come to Moscow to help broaden the Lublin regime. This last development produced such outrage that for the first time since the Russo-Finnish War of 1939-1940 the Russians had to endure a widespread and intense attack from the U.S. media.

These developments caused great concern among prominent Republicans like John Foster Dulles, an advisor to the U.S. delegation at San Francisco, and Arthur Vandenberg, the leading Republican at the conference. Through the course of the conference they became extremely pessimistic about the U.N. being able to keep the peace in the postwar world and both were convinced that the only way to negotiate with a dangerous adversary was to assume an absolutely rock-hard position and avoid all compromise. The belief in the inevitability of superpower conflict that came out of San Francisco was shared by elements in both political parties. Acting Secretary of State Joseph Grew went so far as to say privately that the Soviet Union was "the one certain future enemy," and that "a future war with Soviet Russia is as certain as anything in this world."[6]

The strain in U.S.-Soviet relations grew worse when on May 8, 1945, the day the Germans formally surrendered, Truman abruptly cancelled nonmilitary lend-lease aid to Russia. It was done so abruptly that when the order was given many ships on the high seas were ordered to turn around and head immediately back to port. Truman made this move on the ostensible grounds that such aid was to be provided only as long as the war in Europe lasted. The Russians were alarmed at the suddenness of it and, of course, felt betrayed. Public reaction in the United States was very critical of the cut-back and Truman sought to deflect criticism by blaming his foreign economic administration chief, Leo Crowley, for overreacting to the cancellation order. But there can be little doubt today that the President intended to use U.S. aid to regulate Russia's international behavior.

Should the Russians have been surprised? During Molotov's interview with Truman, the president made the point of reminding his guest that the U.S. Congress traditionally approved foreign economic aid, the implication being that any financial assistance to his country would depend on Soviet behavior and the goodwill of the American people. This linkage between U.S. loans and Soviet international behavior was also made and relayed to Molotov a few days later by Stettinius. He advised Molotov that Russia had one more opportunity to prove to the American people that it deserved major economic assistance.

In conjunction with the economic leverage provided by the cancellation of lend-lease aid the United States demanded that the Soviet Union allow the United States and Great Britain a greater say in the political and economic reconstruction of Romania and Bulgaria.

The new change in policy accomplished nothing. What Truman in fact encountered was the unwavering determination of the Soviet Government to establish a security belt of subservient satellite states in Eastern and Central Europe. And no amount of economic or political pressure could alter that.

Truman, who was still pulled in two directions by his advisors, was not willing to risk a military clash with the Soviet Union. This accounts for his somewhat contradictory approach toward the Russians. On one hand, he toughened up diplomatically and economically, but on the other, he continued to cooperate with them militarily. If anything avoided an open break with the Soviet Union in the summer of 1945 it was the American decision to allow the Red Army to occupy Berlin and Prague. Despite the advice of Churchill who wanted to use territory as leverage, Truman instead took the advice of his Joint Chiefs of Staff. They advised him that where the lives of American soldiers were at stake military considerations should get top priority over political policies. "I should be loath to hazard American lives for political purposes," said George Marshall.[7]

On the surface of it, this may have been sound advice for an American general to give his president, but to Winston Churchill war and politics had always proven historically inseparable. He felt that stability in Europe and a permanent understanding with the Soviet Union would elude the West unless the United States could demonstrate its superior economic, and especially military, strength before the armies of democracy melted away. On May 12, four days after V-E Day, Churchill sent a memorable cable to President Truman: "What will be the position in a year or two, when the British and American Armies have melted and the French have not yet been formed on any major scale, when we may have a handful of divisions, mostly French, and when Russia may choose to keep two or three hundred on active service? An iron curtain is drawn down upon their front. We do not know what is going on behind. . . . Surely it is vital now to come to an understanding with Russia, or see where we are with her, before we weaken our armies mortally."[8]

This sound advice from one of the premier statesmen in twentieth-century history went unheeded because Truman was simply not ready for it. And lack of presidential confidence accounts for only part of the reason. If Truman was reluctant to translate power into political gains it was because of his wish not to risk an alliance-shattering confrontation with the Soviet Union. He had not yet reached the point of viewing the Soviet Union as the "aggressor of tomorrow," as Arthur Vandenberg wrote in his diary, and he would not reach this point until the crises of 1946 and 1947 when he would begin to "mobilize the conscience of mankind."[9]

What Truman did do in May 1945 was dispatch Harry Hopkins to Moscow, both to forestall a confrontation with the Russians, and to prepare for a summit meeting between the Big Three.

By sending Roosevelt's trusted advisor to Moscow, Truman sought to breathe some new life into the Grand Alliance. "I want peace and I am willing to work hard for it," the President confided to his diary, and "to have a reasonably lasting peace, the three great powers must be able to trust each other." Truman gave Hopkins wide terms of reference. He instructed Hopkins to "make it clear to Uncle Joe Stalin that I know what I wanted—and that I intended to get—peace for the world for at least 90 years." Truman wanted Hopkins to tell Stalin that the United States had no ulterior motives in Europe, either territorial or economic, it meant to adhere to the letter of its agreements, and it expected the Soviet Union to do the same.[10]

Sending the ailing Hopkins to Moscow was an unfortunate choice. He was known to think power politics an outdated and discredited policy and he was, until his death in January 1946, strongly sympathetic toward the Soviet Union.

Hopkins began his mission, which lasted from May 26 through June 6, 1945, by reassuring Stalin about the abrupt cutoff of lend-lease. It was not an attempt to exploit American economic power for diplomatic advantage, he said, but rather a bureaucratic mix-up by overeager and incompetent underlings. He also asserted that the United States was prepared to rethink its policy of reparations for the Soviet Union.

Stalin and Hopkins sparred for days over a variety of problems that Hopkins claimed had produced a serious deterioration in the American opinion of Russia. Central to American concern, said Hopkins, was the failure of the Soviet Union to carry out the Yalta agreement on Poland. He explained to Stalin that Poland was the acid test whether or not the two countries could work together in the postwar world. Stalin replied that Russia's lines of communication with Germany cut across Poland and that twice in twenty-five years either Polish weakness or hostility had let the German army through. Hopkins assured him that the United States was not interested in reestablishing the old *cordon sanitaire* on Russia's borders; quite the contrary, the United States preferred to see friendly states on all of Russia's borders. Urged by Hopkins to suggest a solution of the quarrel over the Polish regime, Stalin offered four or five of the eighteen or twenty ministries to the non-Lublin Poles. The present Warsaw government would form the basis of the future Polish Provisional Government of National Unity. Stalin also accepted the provision of free elections and the respect of individual rights and liberties. But he would not release the sixteen leaders of the Polish Home Front. All that he would concede in this matter was the principle of a fair trial and lenient sentences.

Stalin was, of course, aided by the willingness of Hopkins and, to a certain extent Truman, to be deceived. Truman who had held out hope for an American solution to the Polish problem decided to accept Stalin's formula in early June, although it was far less than previous Western demands.

In Washington the Stalin-Hopkins agreement was hailed as a great success, and even Churchill reluctantly concurred in the agreement because it was "the best Hopkins can get." It is Henry Kissinger's view that Hopkins could have done a bit better. Indeed, according to Kissinger, Hopkins's mission had the unintended effect of deepening the deadlock over Eastern Europe and in the long run "hastened the onset of the Cold War." Hopkins, Kissinger argues, missed a chance to convey to Stalin the deep feelings of the American people and the intransigence of its leaders about the self-determination of East European peoples. This may be so, but as Kissinger himself points out, "Stalin could have been induced to settle, if at all, only under extreme duress, and even then only at the last moment."[11] With the war in its final stage this was the sort of pressure that Truman, like Roosevelt, felt he could not afford to apply.

Encouraged by the Hopkins mission, officials in Washington kept alive the hope that they could moderate Soviet behavior through gentle coercion and the pressure of world opinion. What made them optimistic about the immediate future was the upcoming conference at Potsdam where Truman and Stalin would meet face to face and the full power of the United States could be brought to bear, economically and militarily.

The final defeat of Nazi Germany made another conference necessary. Churchill proposed that it be held "in some unshattered town in Germany, if such can be found."

The conference finally got underway in Potsdam, near Berlin, on July 17, 1945. President Truman and his new Secretary of State, James F. Byrnes, turned their attention to the reconstruction of Europe in order to terminate American military and political responsibilities there as quickly as possible. This is not to say that either man wanted to resume the threads of interwar isolationism, but rather it meant that, like the politicians of any great democracy, they were sensitive to the public's wish for a return to normalcy. Truman wanted a solid arrangement in Europe before it became necessary to "bring the boys home."

Despite his contempt for political abstractions, Truman went to Potsdam believing in the essential points of Wilsonianism and armed with a State Department briefing paper of Wilsonian content, which delegation members made scriptural allusions to. Truman merely repeated the Rooseveltian patterns of wartime diplomacy. In fact, he proved just as eager as Roosevelt to treat the

Kremlin leadership as fellow politicians with whom he could make a satisfactory deal. This was why he compared Stalin to Tom Pendergast, the old political boss of Kansas City, and then confided to Joseph Davies during the conference, "I wanted to convince him that we are 'on the level' and interested in peace and a decent world, and had no purposes hostile to them; that I wanted nothing for ourselves, but security for our country, and peace with friendship and neighborliness, and that it was our joint job to do that. I 'spread it on thick,' and I think he believes me. I meant every word of it."[12] The assumptions in this remark were naive and tragically wrong as they were earlier in the war when Roosevelt said something similar in his "noblesse oblige" comment to William Bullitt. But the leaders of the Soviet Union were not like American or British politicians. They were Marxist-Leninists who were tested as revolutionaries and raised as such to believe that states not communist were automatically enemies, and no amount of personal assurance could convince them otherwise.

The Potsdam Conference began with lots of talk about the meaning of democracy, as applied to East European elections and the democratization of Germany. On the political future of Europe Stalin was uncompromising, and he placed a completely different interpretation on the term "democracy" than did his allies. When Truman and Churchill used that term they meant an unfettered multiparty democracy and free elections; for Stalin, it meant Communist Party domination of the politics of a given country. At one point during the conference he admitted frankly that "a freely elected government in any of these East European countries would be anti-Soviet, and that we cannot allow."[13]

When Truman went to Potsdam he optimistically felt that a carrot-and-stick approach would prove effective in dealing with the Soviets and produce a fair and equitable settlement for Germany and Eastern Europe. He was led to think this because he was convinced that the Russians needed a reconstruction loan desperately and that once the atomic bomb, which was nearing completion, was tested the dual pressure of both would convince them of the need to cooperate with an American colossus. In other words, the trumpeting of American economic and technological superiority was designed to both tempt the Russians and, at the same time, make them anxious for their safety. Economic diplomacy was a common enough staple of international relations, but "atomic diplomacy" was altogether new. And yet the latter was intended to be the "master card" for American diplomacy, as Henry Stimson was fond of saying, the "badly needed equalizer" which would finally break the deadlock with the Russians.[14] Nevertheless, when Potsdam convened, the bomb had not even been tested.

The decisions made at Potsdam and the failure to resolve the more important issues were almost foreordained. In planning for a postwar Germany, which was the central concern of the conference, the Western allies had for years wavered back and forth between moderation and severity. In 1944 they had agreed to the Morgenthau Plan which would have pastoralized Germany. They actually endorsed a plan which would have made Germany support a twentieth-century population of some seventy million with an eighteenth-century economy. By the time of the

Yalta Conference Churchill had softened and pleaded for humane treatment for Germany, but Roosevelt had not completely relented and seemed just a bit hesitant about it all. All that the Western allies seemed to agree on was the vindication of democratic principles and self-determination in Europe.

Stalin's purpose at Potsdam was clear and consistent, as it had been throughout the war. What he wanted out of Germany, be it a zone or a country, was a client state. This could be swiftly achieved by a social revolution in the Soviet zone which would break the backs of the previous ruling groups and their traditional political parties. Moreover, he wanted to make the Soviet Union the recipient of reparations drawn from Germany as compensation for war damage at home. And finally he wanted to extend the Polish boundary to the Oder-Neisse line. His goals were specific and detailed and he was single-minded in his pursuit of them.

The Big Three were able to agree on a number of less controversial things: they agreed on the level to which German industry would be limited; they pledged to treat Germany as a single economic unit; and they agreed generally on the demilitarization and democratization (subject to interpretation) of German society. Actually these were agreements which dealt with principles and methods rather than substance. Despite Truman's eagerness for quick results (he chaired the proceedings) the conference accomplished little of consequence.

The first clear sign in the conference that Russia was prepared to go its own way in the postwar world came when she admitted to unilaterally assigning Poland a slice of Germany up to the Oder-Neisse line, in compensation for Poland's loss to Russia of the territory east of the Curzon Line. In response to western protests Stalin claimed that these territories were practically all Polish anyway because the local German population had fled before the Red Army had arrived. At this point in the conference, Admiral Leahy whispered to Truman, "of course there are no Germans left. The Bolshies have killed them all."[15] In fact, Stalin's fait accompli caused an exodus into the remainder of Germany of roughly five million displaced Germans. Sacrificing liberty for expediency the Americans and British merely acquiesced in this expulsion and territorial shift and lamely said in the conference's protocol that "the final delineation of the western frontier of Poland should await the peace settlement."

On the reparations problem the Americans took a firmer stand. The Russians felt that they had a good moral claim on this question. They pressed for the twenty billion dollar figure they raised originally at Yalta with half going to the Soviet Union. The Russians even insisted that they be included in the joint administration of the Ruhr Valley, the industrial heart of Germany. If approved, this would have given them a hammerlock on one of the most important economic regions in Europe and coincidentally given them the opportunity to spread Soviet ideological influence throughout the country. Truman was adamant over stopping this. "There was one pitfall I intended to avoid," he recalled in his memoirs, "we did not intend to pay, under any circumstances, the reparations bill for Europe."[16] And as far as installing Russians in the heart of Germany, the idea was never seriously entertained by the West at Potsdam. Nevertheless, the Russians continued to press their claim for reparations and James Byrnes countered each demand with an insistence on the "first charge" principle— "that there will be no reparations until imports in the American zone are paid for. There can be no discussion of this matter." The exchanges over this were acrimonious at best and Byrnes broke the deadlock when he proposed that each occupying power simply take what it wanted from its own zone. Since the American and British zones contained the bulk of German industry, Brynes offered the Russians a certain percentage of what was produced in the Western zones in return for a certain amount of food shipments from the Soviet zone. On the face of it these provisions were in contradiction to the agreed principle of treating Germany as an economic unit. The Russians were unhappy with this compromise, but went along with it, since it was better than getting no reparations at all.

Almost immediately, the Russians went their own way in the economic management of Germany. Even before Potsdam they had begun to strip their zone of heavy industry, rolling stock, and agricultural implements. They now accelerated the process of dismantling factories in Eastern Germany and shipping them to the Soviet Union, and at the same time they began to tap current German production. In other words, they operated their zone as a self-contained economic entity even as they sovietized it. What began to emerge in the process were two Germanys. In a matter of months the American and British zones were merged economically and administratively into what would be the nucleus of the West German state. By the end of 1945 the partition of Germany between East and West was an established fact with the eastern part of Germany and all of Eastern Europe sinking swiftly behind an Iron Curtain. While it was therefore true that the failure to resolve the Polish question poisoned relations between East and West, it was the deadlock over the German question that led to the final break.

One item that was not on the formal agenda at Potsdam, that was destined to haunt the protagonists of the Cold War from the beginning, was the atomic bomb and its diplomatic implications.

Revisionist historians have tended to argue that the atomic bomb was not really needed in the final subjugation of Japan since it was already beaten and ready to surrender anyway. The dropping of the bomb on Hiroshima and Nagasaki was really designed, they argue, both to politically intimidate the Soviets, with whom relations were deteriorating, and to end the Japanese war quickly before the Red Army could get very far in the Far East and claim a role in the postwar military occupation of Japan. To end it quickly, the revisionists conclude, the United States considered the political value of the atomic bomb.[17]

It had always been assumed from the beginning of the Manhattan Project that the bomb would be utilized militarily if and when it was completed. In 1945 there was general agreement in Washington that the bomb was indispensable to ending the war quickly and much earlier than previously estimated.

In the spring of 1945 the American military planners assumed, despite the decline in the Japanese military situation, that the invasion of the Japanese home islands would have to be attempted. The planners predicted victory by November

1946 but estimated that the conquest would produce upward of one million American casualties.

In the period between the Battle of Okinawa and the surrender of Japan the Allies fighting in Asia sustained over seven thousand casualties per week. They also appreciated the fanaticism of the Japanese military and they were aware that their prisoners of war were being systematically starved in Japanese prison camps. All of these were factors taken into consideration by the Truman administration: the saving of Allied lives,which meant bringing the war to an end as quickly as possible. The American people would have demanded no less. As Churchill put it: "The historic fact remains and must be judged in the after-time, that the decision whether or not to use the atomic bomb to compel the surrender of Japan was never an issue. There was unanimous, automatic, unquestioned agreement around our table."

The Russians were performing original research in the nuclear field as early as the mid-1930s. By 1940 they had proved the existence of spontaneous fission in uranium. The German invasion in 1941 brought nuclear research to a temporary halt, but by 1943 the whole effort began again in earnest after the Battle of Stalingrad, the turning point in the country's struggle for national survival. According to Nikita Khrushchev, the Soviet Union had been spying on the Manhattan Project since 1941 and was well-aware of the massive program to construct a bomb at Los Alamos, New Mexico.[18] President Roosevelt knew of the Soviet espionage effort as early as 1943 when his secretary of war, Henry Stimson, informed him that spies "are already getting information about vital secrets and sending them to Russia." Both men were worried about how much the Russians might know about the Manhattan Project. Stimson told Roosevelt that he "believed that it was essential not to take them into our confidence until we were sure to get a real *quid pro quo* from our frankness." Roosevelt agreed to this.[19]

If Harry Truman inherited anything of so-called atomic diplomacy from his predecessor it was a belief in the legitimate military uses of the weapon and a belief that the bomb would impress the Soviets and make them more tractable—and in that order—first a military victory spearheaded by the new weapon, and then its incidental use as a bargaining lever in extracting concessions from the Russians.

At Potsdam Truman received the news that the bomb had been successfully tested in New Mexico. He then informed Stalin almost matter of factly that the United States had developed "a new weapon of unusual destructive force." Stalin cooly replied that he hoped the United States would make good use of it against the Japanese. Members of the American delegation were so surprised at Stalin's reaction that they thought he had not fully grasped the importance of what was told him. We now know that that was not the case.

By Potsdam the Russians had a serious atomic bomb project under way and Stalin knew from his espionage network that the Americans were close to testing the weapon. As far as reacting coldly to Truman's announcement, Stalin was a master of playing his cards close to his vest. Khrushchev would later say that the news of the American test frightened Stalin "to the point of cowardice." Actually, as soon as the conference was over, when Stalin returned to Moscow in August, he assembled his munitions commissar, his deputies, and, most important, Igor Kurchatov, the scientific director of the atomic project in the Soviet Union. "A single demand of you, comrades," said Stalin. "Provide us with atomic weapons in the shortest possible time. You know that Hiroshima has shaken the whole world. The balance has been destroyed. Provide the bomb—it will remove a great danger from us." When asked by Stalin how long it would take to build the bomb, Kurchatov replied, five years.[20] Actually it took the Russians four years to produce the weapon.

All along the "real" Soviet response to the dropping of the bomb on Hiroshima was hidden from public view. If the West grew accustomed to overestimating the Russians militarily, by the same token it underestimated them diplomatically—something the West had done for centuries. At every public event the Russians made a point of trivializing the bomb as a weapon of mass destruction. This tactic was meant to prevent the United States from deriving any military or diplomatic advantage from its monopoly of the weapon. For example, in September 1946, Stalin said that "I do not consider the atomic bomb as serious a force as some politicians are inclined to do. Atomic bombs are meant to frighten those with weak nerves, but they cannot decide the fate of wars since atomic bombs are quite insufficient for that." In reality the Hiroshima explosion came as quite a blow to the Russians. One American journalist, Alexander Werth, who was in Moscow at the time, wrote that the news from Hiroshima had "an acutely depressing effect on everybody."[21]

On at least one occasion, at the London Conference of Foreign Ministers in September 1945, the Russian fears surfaced publicly. At one point during the conference Molotov jokingly asked James Byrnes if he had an atomic bomb in his pocket. "You don't know southerners," Byrnes replied. "We carry our artillery in our hip pocket. If you don't cut out all this stalling and let us get down to work I am going to pull an atomic bomb out of my hip pocket and let you have it." Molotov forced a laugh over this, but a few days later Molotov told Byrnes that he had two advantages over the Russian foreign minister—eloquence and the atomic bomb.[22]

The American leadership did not, as revisionists allege, believe in the "diplomatic omnipotence" of the atomic bomb. It was true that Truman's outward behavior changed at the conference when he learned of the successful text in New Mexico and everyone noticed it. The bomb was psychologically important for an inexperienced president who was meeting Churchill and Stalin for the first time, but not to the exclusion of everything else. The bomb at this point had only been tested. Nevertheless, as early as May 1945 the idea of using the bomb once it was finished as a bargaining chip in postwar negotiations had been raised by Henry Stimson and approved by Truman. There may even be some evidence, as Martin J. Sherwin has suggested, for believing that Truman and Stimson by the summer of 1945 were thinking seriously of taking the Soviet Union into an atomic partnership in return for American participation in the occupation and governing of Poland, Romania, Yugoslavia, and Manchuria.[23] Be that as it may, once Truman initially mentioned the bomb to Stalin, nothing further was said about it at the conference. No attempt had been made at Potsdam or after to threaten the Russians with the bomb. Truman and Byrnes apparently assumed that merely being in possession of the monopoly would make the Russians more pliant and make them see the necessity for concessions. But there is no evidence that the U.S. monopoly of the bomb made them more flexible. Quite the contrary, given what was actually decided there, and how intransigent Stalin was throughout the conference on all important issues, it would seem that "atomic diplomacy" as a foreign policy stratagem was still-born. If the military use of the bomb did anything it was to traumatize the Japanese and shorten the war, and, of course, usher in the nuclear age.

Would sharing the bomb's secret with Moscow have succeeded in heading off the Cold War? Based on documents made available in Russia and on interviews with Andrei Sakharov and other physicists, David Holloway has recently argued that Stalin had decided on a tough postwar course long before Hiroshima. Regardless of whether the bomb was used or not by the United States, the evidence shows that Stalin still would have wanted a bomb of his own.[24]

The atomic bomb therefore did not cause the Cold War, but it certainly in the years to come helped shape the tensions and fears of the struggle. After all, not only had the United States barred the Soviet Union from any knowledge of the project, even though the two countries were allied, but she never informed Russia when and where the bomb was to be dropped. Nor did the United States invite the Russians to join in the postwar control of atomic energy. What is clear is that the atomic assault on Japan was a dramatic demonstration to the Russians that the United States was not only capable of building a bomb and demonstrating to them just how technologically behind they still were but also was willing to use it.

On August 9, 1945, the day Nagasaki was bombed, Truman delivered an address to the nation on the Potsdam meeting. He chose to mask the failure of the conference from the American people. The Grand Alliance, he said, was as closely knit as it ever was and "we shall continue to march together to our objective." Nevertheless, Truman parted the curtain into a more dangerous world to come when he took Russia to task for what she had appropriated in Europe. The Balkan nations, he said "are not to be the spheres of influence of any one power." What had happened at Yalta and Potsdam was not acceptable to the United States. Moreover, Truman gave a clear warning that the United States "would maintain military bases necessary for the complete protection of our interests and of world peace." And as far as the bomb went, there would be no sharing of its secrets until the world ceased being "lawless." Truman's speech was indicative of the fundamental and inescapable trend of world politics toward a permanently divided Europe and, of course, a divided world.

Notes

1. Quoted in *New York Times*, 24 July 1941.

2. John Morton Blum, ed., *The Price of Vision: The Diary of Henry A. Wallace* (Boston: Houghton Mifflin, 1973), 451.

3. Blum, *The Price of Vision*, 451.

4. Harry S. Truman, *Memoirs. Year of Decisions* (Garden City, N.Y.: Doubleday & Company, 1955), 14-15.

5. Truman, *Year of Decisions*, 81-82.

6. Joseph C. Grew, *Turbulent Era: A Diplomatic Record of Forty Years 1904-1945* (Boston: Houghton Mifflin, 1952), Vol. 2, 1446.

7. Quoted in John Wheeler-Bennett and Anthony Nicholls, *The Semblance of Peace. The Political Settlement after the Second World War* (New York: W.W. Norton, 1974), 318.

8. Winston Churchill, *Triumph and Tragedy*, 601.

9. Quoted in John Lewis Gaddis, *The United States and the Origins of the Cold War 1941-1947* (New York: Columbia University Press, 1972), 228.

10. William Hillman, ed., *Mr. President: Personal Diaries, Private Letters, Papers, and Revealing Interviews of Harry S. Truman* (New York: Farrar, Straus and Young, 1952), 99.

11. Henry Kissinger, *Diplomacy* (New York: Simon and Schuster, 1994), 431.

12. Quoted in Robert J. Donovan, *Conflict and Crisis. The Presidency of Harry S. Truman 1945-1948* (New York: W.W. Norton, 1977), 84.

13. Norman A. Graebner, *America as a World Power. A Realist Appraisal from Wilson to Reagan* (Wilmington, Del.: Scholarly Resources Inc., 1984), 122.

14. Henry L. Stimson and McGeorge Bundy, *On Active Service in Peace and War* (New York: Harper and Row, 1947), 617.

15. Truman, *Year of Decisions*, 369.

16. Truman, *Year of Decisions*, 323.

17. Gar Alperovitz, *Atomic Diplomacy: Hiroshima and Potsdam* (London: Secker and Warburg, 1966).

18. David Holloway, *The Soviet Union and the Arms Race*, 2nd ed. (New Haven, Conn.: Yale University Press, 1984).

19. Gregg Herken, *The Winning Weapon. The Atomic Bomb in the Cold War 1945-1950* (New York: Alfred A. Knopf, 1980), 16.

20. McGeorge Bundy, *Danger and Survival. Choices about the Bomb in the First Fifty Years* (New York: Vintage Books, 1990), 177.

21. Alexander Werth, *Russia at War 1941-1945* (New York: E.P. Dutton and Co., 1964), 1037.

22. Quoted in Herken, *The Winning Weapon*, 48.

23. Martin J. Sherwin, *A World Destroyed. The Atomic Bomb and the Grand Alliance* (New York: Alfred Knopf, 1975), 194.

24. David Holloway, *Stalin and the Bomb: The Soviet Union and Atomic Energy, 1939-1956* (New Haven, Conn.: Yale University Press, 1994).

7

Confronting the Soviet Union: The Crisis of 1946

The political and economic chaos following World War II was global in scope and therefore much greater than the distress that followed 1918. This was so because the situation was just as chaotic in the colonial world as it was in Europe. The collapse of Japanese power created yet another power vacuum at a key location in the heartland of the industrialized world. At the same time, the war had succeeded in undermining the foundations of colonial rule everywhere. The French collapse of 1940 and the Japanese victory over the British and Dutch in Southeast Asia in 1942 severely damaged the prestige of the European powers. Hit so badly by the war in Europe, Great Britain and France were on the defensive after 1945 and never able to reestablish their prewar positions in their former colonies. Even before the war ended, the British and French reached the conclusion that colonial authority could never be the same again. Despite their best efforts to delay the end of empire, they eventually had to accept the logic of withdrawing from their colonies.

The great colonial empires were in an advanced state of disintegration with national liberation movements proliferating on almost every continent. To the shock about European devastation was added the fear about revolutionary upheaval in the Third World and the threat that the Soviet Union would exploit the situation. The United States, however nostalgic it was for the settled convictions of the isolationist era, was forced by the unprecedented situation in international relations to shake off its reticence in claiming global and economic leadership and find its proper international voice. It was ultimately able to do this because President Truman and his successors quickly came to appreciate that Western civilization was moving into the eye of a hurricane. Moreover, despite the fact that the American diplomatic tradition ran counter to that of European states (i.e., to neutrality), Washington realized that diplomacy was now global in its reach, that the United States was the world's great colossus, especially in view of the fact that all of its major competitors were then prostrate or close to it, and that how the United States responded to the developments of 1946-1947 would determine the course of world history for the rest of the twentieth century.

The fledgling U.N. was not able to assume a similar burden of stabilizing the postwar situation for reasons that even then were obvious. The Soviet and later Chinese communist impulse toward national and ideological self-assertion kept the world unstable and dynamic and served to undermine the U.N. in the same way that fascist aggression had weakened the League of Nations in the 1930s.

Since 1945 there had been many points of conflict between the victors of the Second World War—like Poland and Germany—but they had been treated as separate problems that could ultimately be resolved through persistent negotiations. Ever since Yalta the United States and the Soviet Union had reacted to each problem as it arose. In 1945 there was, as yet, no idea in Washington of a global ideological conflict between the two. But in 1946 the tensions between the powers evolved into an historical struggle between ideological systems. And the seminal crisis that seemed to clarify the relationship and accelerate what would become a life and death struggle between the two, was their first postwar confrontation in the so-called "Northern Tier" of Turkey, Iran, and Greece.

As we have seen in chapter six the Russians had been pressing their claims in the region because they felt entitled to a territorial and economic interest in the area commensurate with their role in the war, and the traditional dictates of Russian foreign policy.

In Turkey the issue revolved around the Dardanelles, the straits between the Black Sea and the Mediterranean that provided the only access to the ports of southern Europe and North Africa for Russian military and commercial shipping. A confrontation with the West occurred when the Russians, who had been badgering the Turks throughout the last stage of the war, turned up the pressure and demanded a military base on the Dardanelles, guaranteeing herself a voice in the governance of the straits. For centuries the Russians had sought access through the Black Sea to the warm-water ports of the Mediterranean and at Teheran in 1943 Churchill had vaguely promised Stalin such access.

On February 9, 1946, Stalin made a major speech designed to rally his people to the new challenges of the postwar era. In his address Stalin came out fighting. He began by attributing the two world wars to the inner contradictions and absurdities of world capitalism. He predicted that the capitalist system, which was inherently vicious, would lurch from one crisis and catastrophe to another. Stalin was apparently convinced that capitalism was headed for collapse. At the same time capitalist encirclement was a perennial danger guaranteeing continuing friction between the capitalist and socialist camps. As long as this situation continued to fester, he warned, the Russian people could eventually expect another war.

Stalin's speech was not just another restatement of the "two camps doctrine." He also called his people to prepare for a war with the West by girding themselves for three more five-year plans and all the sacrifices inherent in them. He also demanded that a renewed spur be given to scientific research, which on the face of it was interpreted in the West as a renewed call to build an atomic bomb. In this sense the speech hinted at a deep insecurity in Moscow.[1]

Nowhere in Stalin's speech did he threaten war with the West. Nevertheless, the speech produced shock in Washington because of its ideological component and its exhortation to meet the American challenge. This was taken very seriously, especially in view of what was taking place throughout the Mediterranean and the Middle East. It was clear from the speech that Stalin was trying to perpetuate the monolithic shape into which the Soviet Union had been forced since 1928, the year of the first Five-Year Plan. It also indicated that a major crisis was shaping up in the Northern Tier and that only months after the end of the Second World War the Grand Alliance had passed into history.

The crisis in the Northern Tier entered a new stage when the Soviet Union began stationing troops adjacent to Turkish territory. American reaction was immediate and betrayed an extreme view of Soviet intentions. Writing to James Byrnes, Truman said: "There isn't a doubt in my mind that Russia intends an invasion of Turkey and the seizure of the Black Sea Straits to the Mediterranean. . . ." He went on to add that "only one language do they understand—'How many divisions have you?'" Truman made it clear that he was "tired of babying the Soviets."[2] Truman's attempts at accommodation and conciliation were coming to an abrupt end.

Nine days after Stalin's speech the story of the Canadian Spy Case broke in Ottawa. Canada announced the arrest of a large spy ring, which had been trying to steal information on the atomic bomb for the Soviet Union. The dramatic news played into the hands of all those people who had been advocating a hard line toward the Soviets and who were now able to establish a close link between the external Soviet menace and the atomic threat it might one day pose, and the vulnerability caused by the espionage efforts of the internal communist enemy.

Until this point in early 1946 there was no consensus in Washington on the nature of the relationship between the United States and the Soviet Union in the postwar world. Members of the administration had for months reacted viscerally to Soviet initiatives in the world. Most people in Washington understood that what was needed was a more rigorous intellectual appraisal of Soviet behavior and a clear policy recommendation for coping with the Soviet Union in the future. Soon after Stalin's speech the State Department had urgently requested such an analytical interpretation from George Kennan, which would explain the meaning and importance of Stalin's message. On February 22, 1946, an 8,000 word cable arrived at the State Department from Kennan, who at the time was the American chargé d'affaires in Moscow. It helped to fill the policy vacuum in Washington and it served to give focus to the changing attitudes of the administration.

For Kennan this was his chance to educate the well meaning but ignorant policymakers in Washington. He certainly had the credentials for doing so. Educated at Princeton and fluent in Russian and German, Kennan, became an expert on Russian history and civilization and twentieth-century politics. He joined the foreign service in the 1920s and became a member of a very small and select group of Russian experts trained by the State Department to help occupy the American listening post in Riga, Latvia, until the United States formally recognized the Soviet Union. When this recognition came in 1933 he helped to open the United States Embassy in Moscow where he remained for most of the next dozen years. As a member of the embassy he had witnessed the growth of Soviet totalitarianism first-hand and had come to despise the Soviet system and its foreign policy. It was his considered belief, starting well back in the war, that Washington's hopes of collaboration with the Soviets were ill-considered and hopelessly naive.

Kennan's analysis in the so-called Long Telegram[3] began with a detailed exposition of the communist outlook on world affairs. The Soviet leadership, he explained, believed that they were encircled by a capitalism, "with which in the long run there can be no permanent peaceful coexistence." Between the two worlds there was no shared community of interests. Soviet antagonism was innate and its hostility would last until capitalism was destroyed. Behind this hostility to the West lay the deep insecurity of the Soviet leadership. That insecurity was, he said, both traditional and instinctive and determined in part by the lack of protective natural barriers to the recurrent invasions Russia sustained throughout its history; and in part it followed from the conspiratorial nature of the party leadership itself—men raised in a besieged minority position who were both paranoid and obsessed with secrecy and unity. Beneath the Kremlin's "neurotic" view of world affairs lay also the "fear of more competent, more powerful, more highly organized societies." According to Kennan, ideology only made the insecurity worse, reinforcing the traditional and instinctive fears of enemies, both foreign and domestic. As Kennan saw it, the function of ideology was twofold: on one hand, it acted as a stimulus for political action, and on the other hand, it was used to justify the actions the leadership had decided upon. But Kennan made it clear in his analysis, and in the unsigned article he published in *Foreign Affairs* magazine in 1947 ("The Sources of Soviet Conduct"),[4] that politics was the prime determinant of what constituted the Soviet national interest and not, however important it might be, ideology. He even held out the hope that as the Soviet national interest shifted in direction, so too would Soviet communism. Until this happened cooperation with the Soviet Union would be next to impossible, since for the Kremlin leadership there was no real break between war and peace. The leadership believed that it was in a war with the West, but one with no timetable of conquest. Instead, they were content to exert constant pressure to both reduce Western power and to enlarge their own power at the expense of strategic, contiguous areas like Turkey and Iran. The pressure to extend Russia's borders Kennan saw as neither adventuristic or schematic, but as "only the steady advance of uneasy Russian nationalism." The struggle with Russia would, he predicted, be a long one, made that much more difficult because it was "impervious to the logic of reason." Nevertheless, it was also "highly sensitive to the logic of force." Soviet power must therefore be confronted and, in what may be considered a first instalment of the containment policy, he maintained that Soviet power would back off "when strong resistance is encountered at any point." It followed then that the object of containment should be Soviet expansionism, and that the ideology would constitute a threat in-so-far as it helped to fuel that expansionism.

For Kennan power in the world was measured by industrial capacity, together with the geographical access to the raw materials necessary to sustain it. In 1946 and in ensuing years, Kennan wrote in his *Memoirs*, "I expressed in talks and lectures the view that there were only five regions in the world—the United States, the United Kingdom, the Rhine valley with adjacent industrial areas, the Soviet Union, and Japan—where the sinews of modern military strength could be produced in quantity; I pointed out that only one of these was under Communist control; and I defined the main task of containment, accordingly, as one of seeing to it that none of the remaining ones fell under such control."[5] It should therefore be the U.S. strategy to bring hope and comfort to countries in or near those key regions so that their people did not become so demoralized that they ended up believing that Soviet communism was the wave of the future. It should also be the policy of Washington through an extended period of time to try to alter the "thinking" of the Soviet leadership. That is, to make them see, through persuasion mixed with resistance, the futility of their trying to achieve their goals through expansion, and to convince them that they share a community of aims with the United States. The Soviet Union, after all, was not a rigid monolith ruled by a permanently empowered dictatorship (even though it seemed that way to Americans). There were obvious sources of instability built into the system that rendered it fragile and "unproven," and which eventually would contribute to its demise. That system had been shaken to its foundations during the transfer of power following Lenin's death in 1924. Stalin's death, he predicted, would produce a similar period of strain and instability. The other source of constant strain would be the digestion of Russia's recent territorial expansions into Eastern Europe, which had absorbed millions of people who hated Soviet rule. In Kennan's *Foreign Affairs* article he predicted prophetically that if the United States could sustain the struggle with the Soviet Union long enough, without injuring its own economy, the Russian state would undergo a period of immense strain climaxing in "either the break-up or the gradual mellowing of Soviet power."

In order to accomplish its historic task, Kennan urged Washington to begin educating the American people about the Soviet problem and the historical role it would have to play in dealing with it. "Providence," he would say in 1947, provided them with this challenge and dictated that they accept "the responsibilities of moral and political leadership that history plainly intended them to bear."

The effects of Stalin's speech and the Long Telegram were, as Kennan afterward acknowledged, "nothing less than sensational." The cable was sent to virtually all decision makers in the State Department and quickly started a chain reaction of speeches by prominent politicians who had learned a new vocabulary. James Byrnes, John Foster Dulles, and Arthur Vandenberg now spoke out against the Soviet danger using the main themes of Kennan's cable.

The crisis which had already moved to Iran came to a head just after Kennan dispatched his cable, and a few days before Winston Churchill made his Iron Curtain Speech.

The London Foreign Minister's Conference of 1945 had set March 2, 1946, as the date for the withdrawal of all foreign troops from Iran. The Americans pulled out of Iran in January 1946 and the British on March 2, but it was clear when the deadline arrived that the Russians had no intention of withdrawing. Instead, in that same month they initiated heavy movements of troops and armor in the Balkans by rail south into Bulgaria to the Turkish border. It was reported by Allied intelligence that Romanian hospitals were being evacuated in preparation for military casualties. In the same month, there were similar movements of Russian armor and infantry through Azerbaijan into northern Iran.[6]

The picture in Greece was no more encouraging. In 1946 the situation began to deteriorate as the civil war entered a new round. Battles between Greek Communist guerrillas and the Athens government raged all over the northern part of the country with the rebellion aided directly by Albania, Bulgaria, and Yugoslavia. With Eastern Europe already lost to the Russian sphere, and with large Communist parties in war-devastated France and Italy poised to seize power, Soviet initiatives in Turkey and Iran appeared to Washington to be a dramatic test of the American will and a strategic attempt to effect a major breakthrough into the Middle East. Since the region links three continents and is so resource rich it has always had a great geopolitical importance. It has been coveted by almost every would-be world conqueror in modern times.

The events in Greece, Turkey, and Iran produced alarm in Washington. In early 1946, even before the Long Telegram, the Joint Chiefs of Staff warned the president about Soviet threats to American interests in the region. The implications of Soviet control of Turkey and the Aegean, they argued, would bring great pressure to bear upon Great Britain from Suez to Iran. The eventual disintegration of the British Empire, which might ensue was to be avoided at all costs, since it was now clear that the United States needed a great ally in the region.[7]

In an early version of the "domino theory," Dean Acheson, soon to be the secretary of state, warned Truman that the Russians were bent on dominating the key areas of the world beginning with Greece, then Turkey, and then the oil-rich Middle East. This test of the American will should be resisted at all costs. Truman was more teacher in these deliberations than student. According to Acheson, Truman asked the Joint Chiefs and the secretaries of the military services to gather around a map of the Middle East and the eastern Mediterranean and gave them a brief lecture on the geostrategic importance of the area and the lengths to which he was prepared to go to keep it out of Soviet hands.[8]

Revisionist historians like to play the whole thing down and insist that there was no real crisis at all. They argue that Russian demands for positions on the straits and for oil concessions in Iran were legitimate requests given their large role in the Second World War. The argument is an apologetic. Turkey and Iran were neutrals during the war and Russian demands voiced as they were for whatever reason were no reason for provoking a crisis. What Truman understood was that the Russians were doing what they already had done in Eastern Europe: increasing their national strength by pressuring small but strategically important states and trying to bring them into the Soviet sphere of influence. To President Truman this was clear evidence of Soviet expansionism. As far as the Russian program in Iran goes: "There is no justification for it. It is a parallel to the program of Russia in Latvia, Estonia and Lithuania. It is also in line with the high-handed and arbitrary manner in which Russia acted in Poland."[9]

The United States had decided to assume the historical British commitment to block any Soviet penetration into the Middle East. He also understood that this was the first real skirmish between the superpowers in the postwar world. He understood that the United States had to support the Iranians because the region was the first area where Russia imperiled American strategic and economic interests (as they did not in Eastern Europe) notably access to Middle Eastern oil. In Truman's remarks can be found the earliest indication that the United States was prepared to move toward the strategy of containment.

The pressures on president Truman were enormous in 1946 and unprecedented for a peacetime president. While Truman groped his way toward a foreign policy that could help him deal with a new world situation, he was subjected to a growing attack at home from prominent Republicans who for the most part had gone along with Franklin Roosevelt. Because of a certain underlying growth of uneasiness about Russian intentions, a concomitant determination to assert American influence, and a partisan frustration at being forced to relinquish control of the White House and the Congress in 1932, Republicans now demanded that Truman and Secretary Byrnes "get tough" with the Soviets. Republicans like John Foster Dulles, Clare Boothe Luce, and Senator Vandenberg denounced the administration's abandonment of the principles of the Atlantic Charter, as well as its failure to stand up to the Russians. The Republican attack carried no plan of action and was geared to domestic consumption. Nevertheless, the criticism gradually mounted during 1946 and was echoed throughout the country not only by politicians seeking advantage in the mid-term elections that November, but also by academics, publicists, and a large section of the American public. Because the Truman administration was making a strategic reassessment in the eighteen months following the war, it appeared to the American electorate, who were ignorant of this shift, that Truman and the Democrats were drifting in their foreign policy and therefore ineffectual in dealing with the profound foreign challenges of the day. By the election in November this new mood had broken the Democrats' hold over both houses of Congress. When the new Congress met the following January the Republicans, who had been counselling strength against the Red tide, proceeded to seriously undermine the president's ability to do just that by slashing his budget from $41 billion to $31.5 billion. They did this to allow for a twenty percent income tax reduction to stimulate the economy. But much more was eroding here than the president's political base. While Truman feared a Russian attempt to alter the balance of power, and while he talked of meeting it with an iron fist, he at the same time was forced to preside over one of the most complete and rapid demobilizations in military history. When the war ended in 1945 the United States had an experienced army of three and one half million men in Europe. By March

1946, only ten months later, it had only 400,000 troops left, mainly new recruits. A cost-cutting Congress became one of Truman's worst enemies. If the Republicans got their way, warned the secretary of war, the United States might have to withdraw its army from Germany and Japan. At the same time, the secretary of the navy announced that the proposed cut by Congress would reduce the U.S. Navy to impotence. Truman's loss of control of Congress could not fail to give the impression abroad (and at home) of weakness and irresolution. The demobilization almost certainly encouraged Russian belligerence and intransigence in the world and especially in the Middle East.

The mounting criticism at home also affected Truman's handling of a key postwar problem: the international control of atomic energy. In January 1946 Secretary of State Byrnes had appointed a committee headed by Undersecretary of State Acheson to draw up a policy on atomic energy. His committee in turn appointed a board of consultants under the direction of David E. Lilienthal, the administrator of the Tennessee Valley Authority, and made up primarily of nuclear physicists.

The Acheson-Lilienthal Plan that appeared in March 1946—at the height of the Iranian crisis—was based on a revolutionary premise. It suggested that the possession of this unique source of military and industrial power transcended national boundaries. For this reason the plan provided for an international body to control the raw materials and the production facilities used for atomic energy. This was meant to control the military uses of atomic energy and would oversee the mining, refining, and utilization of the world's raw materials. It also called for a freeze on the production of atomic weapons (although the United States reserved for itself the decision as to whether it cease manufacturing bombs of its own) and the inspection of atomic facilities in all affected countries. The report assumed a lengthy American lead in the field and so it basically ignored the question about what might occur if the Soviet Union violated the agreement and began to build bombs of its own.

Sensitive to the criticism that they were making too many concessions to the Soviets and anxious to get the plan through a sceptical Congress, Truman and Byrnes asked Bernard Baruch to present the plan at the U.N. In choosing Baruch the administration made a serious error. A millionaire since the age of thirty and a man of vast political connections, Baruch was nevertheless totally ignorant about atomic-energy policy. He decided to change the Acheson-Lilienthal Plan and chose as his advisors not scientists but Wall Street bankers, who knew as much as he did about the subject.

Baruch's plan inserted a voting procedure that gave the United States control over every step of the process—even the establishment of atomic power for peaceful purposes within the Soviet Union. The plan called for the participating powers to halt atomic research and submit to inspection and to an audit of their fissionable materials. The United States itself would relinquish its own atomic weapons to an international authority when all other stages of the agreement had been completed. It would thus be able to maintain an atomic monopoly through continued American control of fissionable material. Not surprisingly, the Soviets rejected the plan when it was presented to the U.N. in June 1946. In the U.N. Andrei Gromyko suggested instead that all atomic weapons be destroyed immediately and the Great Powers agree not to manufacture anymore. He also called for the sharing of atomic information and materials. The United States rejected this proposal since it failed to provide safeguards. The possibility that an historic chance to cooperate over atomic energy had been missed was felt by a significant section of public opinion and both Baruch and the Truman administration came in for a wave of criticism. Under siege at home and abroad, Truman admitted privately that appointing Baruch was "the worst blunder I ever made . . .!" Before the year was out Baruch had resigned and Congress passed the Atomic Energy Act, which basically forbade any exchange of atomic-energy information. A nuclear arms race was now unavoidable.

If the Truman administration gave the impression of uncertainty and drift it was because, lacking a sophisticated and determined foreign policy vis-à-vis the Soviet Union, it wavered between the set views of the anti-Soviet Right and the Democratic Left. These views were clarified in the public debates of 1946 by Winston Churchill and Secretary of Commerce Henry Wallace.

From the moment he assumed office Truman seemed to be running well-ahead of the majority of the American people on the foreign issues and external dangers confronting the country. It was true that there was a growing unease among the political and academic elites about the apparent hesitancy of the administration to come to grips with things, but polls conducted in early 1946 indicated that the Soviet Union still enjoyed a certain measure of sympathy with the American public. Still very much hungry for great-power cooperation the American people placed great hopes in the U.N. Before Truman could chart a more strenuous foreign policy that defined the problem with exactitude and enabled him to resist the encroachments of the Soviet Union, he had to first sound the alarm about Soviet intentions. This role naturally devolved to the president, and while Truman was in many ways an extremely capable and courageous president he was also a poor public speaker who had had little time to build a public image. His main difficulty, therefore, was in trying to steer his country through one of the most difficult and dangerous periods in its history when he lacked the moral authority to inspire confidence in his people. Truman was enormously unpopular in 1946. His public-approval rating had sunk from a high of 87 percent in mid-1945 following Roosevelt's death to an historic low of 32 percent in 1946. He saw clearly that his prescriptions to meet the crisis might call for great economic and military sacrifices; but who would sacrifice for him? What Truman lacked was the moral authority and stature of Franklin Roosevelt. At precisely that moment Winston Churchill arrived on his doorstep for an American vacation.

Churchill had spent the greater part of his career campaigning against what he perceived to be the Soviet threat. He had for a generation been one of the most passionate and consistent anti-Bolsheviks in Europe. He had tried his best during the war to convince first Roosevelt and then Truman to do their historic duty and assume the burden of containing that Russian challenge. After some encouragement from Truman, Churchill accepted an invitation to speak at Westminster College in Fulton, Missouri. This opportunity gave him the chance to take his case directly to the American people.

It is not stretching things to say that Churchill enjoyed a popularity in the United States in 1946 unrivalled by any foreign political figure in the twentieth century. Churchill possessed what Truman lacked—tremendous stature and an unparalleled record of success in helping to lead the West to victory in World War II.

It is now clear that despite Truman's brief denial of complicity with Churchill in the presentation of the Iron Curtain Speech, he did know what Churchill was going to say to the American people on March 5, 1946, and that he approved of it. He agreed with Churchill that this was a particularly auspicious moment in history that called for a closer collaboration between the two countries outside the purview of the U.N.

Certainly from Churchill's standpoint he viewed the events of the mid-1940s as an alarming repetition of what had transpired only a decade before; once again a bellicose totalitarian expansionism was on the march and had become, like its Nazi predecessor, a threat to the peace of the world; once again his own government was weak and ineffectual and reluctant to do its historic duty; and once again he sensed in the United States the disinclination to become involved in international affairs, the short attention span of the people for matters of public policy, and the requisite need to put their faith in the U.N.

President Truman introduced Churchill somewhat ominously: "We are either headed for complete destruction or we are facing the greatest age in history."[10] He had already privately sounded a similar note over the Iranian crisis. He had told Averell Harriman that a dangerous situation was developing in Iran that might lead to war. Truman had proceeded to Fulton, Missouri, with Churchill on the assumption that Russian aggression in the Middle East was imminent. Believing this, Truman felt that Churchill's speech did not really overstate the consequences of the foreign policy he was trying to implement and convert the American people to.

Churchill began the speech with a dramatic paean to the virtues of American power. With that "primacy of power" went "an awe-inspiring accountability to the future." Central to American predominance was its monopoly of the secrets of the atomic bomb. Churchill asked Americans to recognize that "God has willed" the United States and not "some communist or neo-Fascist state" the monopoly of nuclear weapons. Had totalitarian states enjoyed a similar monopoly they would have unscrupulously sought to impose their political systems upon a vulnerable world. It was important to possess this monopoly and keep it as long as possible because "two gaunt marauders—war and tyranny" had raised their dangerous heads once again in the postwar world:

> From Stettin in the Baltic to Trieste in the Adriatic, an iron curtain has descended across the Continent. Behind that line lie all the capitals of

the ancient states of central and eastern Europe. Warsaw, Berlin, Prague, Vienna, Budapest, Belgrade, Bucharest and Sofia, all these famous cities and the populations around them lie in the Soviet sphere and all are subject in one form or another, not only to Soviet influence but to a very high and increasing measure of control from Moscow. . . . The Communist parties, which were very small in all these eastern states of Europe, have been raised to preeminence and power far beyond their numbers and are seeking everywhere to obtain totalitarian control. Police governments are prevailing in nearly every case, and so far, except in Czechoslovakia, there is no true democracy.[11]

At the heart of the speech was Churchill's call for a "fraternal association of English-speaking peoples." There was a coming "trial of strength," he predicted, and only a political-military collaboration, the kind that helped win the war, would provide the surest protection of Western civilization from the perils of totalitarian incursions and future wars. He therefore appealed to the joint inheritance of the Anglo-Saxon world: the Magna Carta, the Bill of Rights, trial by jury, and the Declaration of Independence. All people should have what the Anglo-American world boasted: free elections by secret ballot and freedom of speech, the "title deeds of freedom." Two peoples such as ours, he said, should pool military advisors and standardize weapons and manuals of instruction. Eventually, he said, there may come the principle of common citizenship.

While Churchill was, in a prophetic sense, calling the non-communist world to arms he at the same time made it clear that he did not believe the Soviets wanted war. "What they desire," he maintained, "is the fruits of war and the indefinite expansion of their power and doctrines. . . . From what I have seen of our Russian friends and allies during the war, I am convinced that there is nothing they admire so much as strength, and there is nothing for which they have less respect than for weakness, especially military weakness." He understood that while the Soviets were obsessed with their state's security, and while they had striven to avoid war they were also driven politically and ideologically to extend their power by shaping the international environment. Preserving the traditional international system was not in the interest of the men of the Kremlin who viewed that system through the lens of the class struggle and were devoted to starting a chain of revolutionary events in that world.

Churchill was trying to do several things in the Iron Curtain speech. First, he was trying to dispel the notion so prevalent in U.S. administrations since 1941 that accommodation and appeasement would produce a lasting agreement with the Soviet Union. Churchill, one of the century's most devoted students of power politics, believed that all conflicts were not susceptible to settlement with the application of persistency and Wilsonian goodwill. The conflict with Nazi Germany could not be resolved that way, and neither would the challenge of the Soviet Union. Obliquely, Churchill was saying that Wilsonianism, regardless of its theoretical merits, was strikingly out of place in the postwar world; that the world was moved by power and not by ideals; that the U.N. was not and probably would not be a good shield for the free world; and that only an Anglo-American "special relationship" underpinning that organization could do the job of maintaining the peace.

Second, under Truman's sponsorship Churchill had come to Fulton prepared to rally mass support against the Soviet threat. He was able to do this as no one else could in the Western world. He had spent most of his career a deadly foe of Soviet communism as he had earlier been an implacable enemy of German power. He had almost single-handedly rung the tocsin against the German threat in the 1930s in a singularly heroic role that most Americans appreciated. Here he was again sounding a similar apocalyptic note against the Red menace.

> The Dark Ages may return, the Stone Age may return on the gleaming wings of science, and what might now shower immeasurable material blessings upon mankind, may even bring about its total destruction. Beware, I say; time may be short. . . .

The Iron Curtain Speech proved quite prophetic in terms of what happened later in the Cold War. Indeed, it almost served as a ticket for the journey. Churchill, as Fraser Harbutt points out, anticipated the Anglo-American "special relationship" as the basis for the Western security system; he correctly foresaw the course the arms race would take; and he brilliantly sketched the theoretical outlines of "containment" and "confrontation-liberation." In doing so he managed to popularize some of the phraseology of the Cold War—terms like "Iron Curtain," "nuclear deterrent," and, of course, the Anglo-American "special relationship." Finally, his call to arms against the Soviet menace for the first time publicly raised the whole question of the price the West would have to pay—in money and in lives—to promote the values it espoused and thought worth defending. In this sense, Churchill played a significant role in influencing the postwar world.

While the contents of this speech shortly became accepted Cold War wisdom, it nevertheless shocked the American public in 1946. The speech created a storm of criticism, much of it at first negative. There was a certain degree of Anglo-phobia in this reaction. It was cynically argued by many hardcore isolationists whose spokesman was the *Chicago Tribune*, that Churchill was trying to hitch a declining British Empire to a rising American star so as to insure his country an important collaborative role in the postwar world. The American Left worried about the negative impact of a policy like this on the U.N. Still others found his apocalyptic vision quite frightening and saw in it a certain element of war mongering. The main spokesman for this latter group was Secretary of Commerce Henry Wallace.

Like Harry Hopkins and Joseph E. Davies, Henry Wallace belonged to that coterie of ardent New Dealers who thought that "British balance-of-power manipulations"—meaning Churchill's leadership—was a policy perverted to its core and one that, if not unheeded, would drag the country closer to the war it sought to avoid. Wallace had been especially exercised by the Iron Curtain Speech. The former vice-president who had been dropped from the Democratic ticket in

1944 expressed his outrage at the direction the administration was moving in a Madison Square Garden rally in September 1946.

Wallace acknowledged in his speech that the Russians were a bit hostile and suspicious in their behavior, but that was a natural reaction of a great people to the aggressive attitudes and policies emanating from Washington and London. Wallace went so far as to assign the lion's share of the blame for the emerging Cold War and the arms race to the West rather than to the Soviet Union. A realistic view of the world, he argued, would recognize the legitimate existence of spheres of influence. The United States had no right to intervene in Russia's sphere in Eastern Europe and Russia had no right to intervene in the American sphere in Latin America, because both regions were vital to the national security of both powerful states. Getting tough with the Russians was precisely the wrong policy to pursue since "the tougher we get, the tougher the Russians will get. . . ."[12]

Wallace enjoyed a good deal of popular support on the left-wing of the Democratic Party and Truman was politically wary of him. Privately he attacked Wallace as one of "the Reds, phonies and the 'parlor pinks' [who] . . . are becoming a national danger." Actually the popular tide had been running against the Wallace view for some time. A growing majority of Americans had remembered Churchill standing up to tyranny in the 1930s and they were predisposed to trusting him again. They endorsed the essential validity of Churchill's case against the Soviet Union, and while hesitant at first about an Anglo-American alliance, they came rather quickly to welcome the remedy he proposed. This was borne out by polls taken just after the speech was delivered. In the first poll taken, only eighteen percent of the American people favored what Churchill said. One month later a similar poll showed that 85 percent approved of his ideas.[13] Because of it, Truman felt confident enough to force Wallace out of the cabinet. Wallace subsequently challenged Truman (unsuccessfully) for the presidency in 1948.

Behind the praise heard for Churchill's ideas in 1946 was the gradual formation of a powerful anti-Soviet front. It included media giants like the *New York Times* and *Time* Magazine; influential political columnists like Walter Lippmann, W. H. Chamberlain, Arthur Krock, David Lawrence, and Drew Pearson; and a large majority of the Congress where there was already heard calls for internal and external vigilance, the removal of pro-Soviet sympathizers from public life and beefing up of the U.S. military to meet the challenge.

The growing hostility to Russia and to communism was accompanied by a corresponding decline in anti-fascist sentiment. This was reflected in the softening attitudes to Franco's Spain, and a growing sympathy for the awful plight of the German people.[14]

Stalin reacted angrily to Churchill's speech. All the talk of an Anglo-American alliance against the Soviet Union, and the continued monopoly of the atomic bomb served to alarm him. It was, said Stalin, nothing less than "a call to war on the USSR." Churchill's "English racial theory" was equally as dangerous, since it bore "a striking resemblance to Hitler and his friends." As far as Churchill's charge of

Soviet expansionism went, it was perfectly normal for the Soviet Union, which made enormous sacrifices in the war, to ensure that the governments of Eastern European states, once so hostile to the Soviet Union, remain friendly to Moscow in the future. These are not expansionist "tendencies," Stalin insisted, but rather "peaceful aspirations." Furthermore, the governments of those states are perfect examples of democracy, whether Churchill thinks so or not. Stalin ended this interview with a warning: if this enemy of Soviet communism succeeds in his appeal to force, as he "and his friends" did during the Allied intervention in the Russian Civil War, "it may confidently be said that they will be thrashed, just as they were thrashed once before, twenty-six years ago."[15]

Kennan's long cable and Churchill's speech, which was in many ways the public expression of the cable, served the Truman administration well. The timing in both cases, separated as they were by days, was perfect. The cable helped to convince the decision makers in Washington that the Soviet Union was responsible for the growing Cold War and explained to them why this was so; it helped convince them of the need for an historical struggle against an imposing adversary, and it assured them that, though the road be long and arduous, the American victory could be won. Churchill's speech had to be more provocative since it was aimed at the widest possible audience. It carried the same message and helped swing the American people around to the same point of view. But in terms of its effect on the administration the Long Telegram had a much more lasting influence on the shaping of American foreign policy for years to come. This was apparent when soon after the Iranian crisis Truman asked Clark M. Clifford, the special counsel in the White House, to prepare the first comprehensive study of United States-Soviet relations, which the president could use as the basis for future policy decisions.

Along with his assistant George Elsey, Clifford consulted with the top officials throughout the government in the summer of 1946 and submitted his report entitled, "American Relations with the Soviet Union,"[16] on September 24. Truman received the report four days after he fired Henry Wallace from the cabinet.

The Clifford Report drew heavily on Kennan's analysis in the Long Telegram, although it somewhat exaggerated the influence of ideology on Russian diplomacy. "The key to an understanding of current Soviet foreign policy," it said "is the realization that Soviet leaders adhere to the Marxian theory of ultimate destruction of capitalist states by communist states." To the leadership in the Kremlin war was inevitable, and "they are increasing their military power and the sphere of Soviet influence in preparation for the 'inevitable' conflict. . . ." The report ruled out concessions and compromises, since they had the effect "of raising Soviet hopes and increasing Soviet demands."

Like the Long Telegram, the Clifford Report exuded a confident and expansive tone that was striking, but it went beyond Kennan's effort in terms of its global reach and its strategies for attaining victory.

Studies conducted by the Joint Chiefs of Staff since 1943 indicated that any power or coalition of powers that succeeded in gaining a dominant foothold on the

Eurasian continent would inherit, as Sir Halford Mackinder predicted so long before, the natural resources, the industrial potential, and the huge manpower reserves to dominate the world. Woodrow Wilson's Fourteen Points, the Atlantic Charter, and the Bretton Woods Agreement were clear indications that U.S. administrations felt that world security and stability and American prosperity depended on an open world—freedom of the seas, open markets, free trade, unhindered access to the raw materials of the world, and the conversion of much of Eurasia to a liberal capitalist economy. The authors of the Clifford Report absorbed these principles, as they did the views of leading defense officials and military analysts who had come to believe since 1945 that the United States could not allow any potential enemy to control the Eurasian land mass. The report echoed this belief—that any power which sought this dominance was to be regarded as a major enemy trying to upset the world status quo and therefore one that could inflict the greatest harm on the United States. It was no accident that the Soviet military presence in Iran was seen in Washington as an attempt to assimilate a key area of the world and deprive the West of a key source of Middle East oil.

It was not the case that the American defense establishment feared a Soviet military invasion of Eurasia; they actually felt reasonably secure in the American military dominance for the moment (despite the demobilization), since the Soviet Union lacked the atomic bomb along with a great navy or air force. But what they feared was the economic and social distress throughout Eurasia and the attempts of Communist parties to agitate and exploit that chaos so as to fan the resentment of millions of desperate people into an ecumenical blaze. There were fears like this during the "Red Scare" following the First World War, and they reemerged in 1945 for even more tangible reasons.

For all of these reasons, U.S. military planners since 1943-1944 had begun to prepare for an elaborate system of overseas bases in Europe, Asia and Africa to counter any overt threat to American interests, and to allow the United States to project its power quickly and effectively against any potential adversary. President Roosevelt endorsed these plans in 1944.

One of the Clifford Report's basic assumptions was that military power could serve as the main deterrent to Soviet aggression in areas deemed vital to American security. Like Kennan, Clifford believed that military power was "the only language which the disciples of power politics understand." Clifford put great stock in American nuclear and biological weaponry, and he felt that the United States should be prepared to use them in the event of war. Nevertheless, it was never Clifford's intention to summon the country to a war footing, but rather to enlighten the president and other members of the administration about the potential dangers facing the nation in the future and the ways in which these threats could be counteracted. In this sense the Report foreshadowed the Truman Doctrine and the Marshall Plan by calling on the United States to "support and assist all democratic countries which are in any way menaced or endangered by the USSR." If there was chaos in Eurasia, the United States must have a decisive response to it.

Like Kennan, Clifford believed that one of the objectives of American policy must be to convince the Soviet leadership that war between the two ideological systems and states need not be inevitable: "It is our hope that they will change their minds and work out with us a fair and equitable settlement when they realize that we are too strong to be beaten and too determined to be frightened."

The Clifford Report represented a major step toward the formulation of an American foreign policy. President Truman found in the Long Telegram and the Clifford Report confirmation of his belief that the danger facing the West came from the Soviet Union, and that the essential policy of the United States must be to resist that danger with all the means at its disposal. Truman began to resist that challenge in Iran and Turkey.

The Iranian crisis was particularly complicated because Soviet forces were arrayed inside Iran. Under the advice of Dean Acheson, Truman was careful not to threaten military action, but at the same time announced that the United States was transferring its Mediterranean fleet to the Persian Gulf. Truman also demanded an accounting from the Russians about the purposes of their troop movements of March and in an attempt to mobilize world opinion he called for a full discussion of the matter in the U.N. In this way (Acheson gave similar advice to President Kennedy during the Cuban Missile Crisis) the Soviet Union would be left "a graceful way out" if she wished to avoid a showdown.

On April 4, 1946, General Walter Bedell Smith, the newly appointed ambassador to the Soviet Union, had a long interview with Stalin. He had been asked by Truman to put the question directly to Stalin: "What does the Soviet Union want, and how far is Russia going to go?" Americans, he said, could relate to Russia's security needs, but Russian "methods" were very disturbing to them. Smith told him that Truman still felt that Stalin was a man who honored his commitments, but he also made it clear that this was not to be interpreted as an indication of weakness. Once again, Smith asked Stalin, "How far is Russia going to go?" Stalin replied that the Soviet Union would not go much farther. He claimed to be bitter about the oil his country was being barred from getting, and about the American opposition in the U.N. He also expressed his resentment over the Iron Curtain Speech. The crisis subsided when Moscow and Teheran agreed on April 4 that a Soviet troop withdrawal would be coupled with an agreement to jointly exploit the northern Iranian oilfields. The Soviet army soon withdrew from Iran, the Iranian army subsequently crushed the separatist movement in the North and, to Moscow's dismay, Iran went back on its agreement with the Soviet Union.

But the crisis of 1946 was not over. When in August 1946 the Kremlin tried to force a treaty on Turkey recognizing joint control of the straits, Truman remarked to a cabinet meeting, "We might as well find out whether the Russians [are] bent on world conquest now or in five or ten years." He then ordered the U.S. Navy's largest aircraft carrier, along with four cruisers and a destroyer flotilla to Istanbul. Turkey, obviously strengthened, rejected the Russian proposal, and the Russians dropped the whole matter.

The Turkish and Iranian crisis constituted the first real skirmish of the Cold War. What Stalin's whole attempt to pursue opportunities in Turkey and Iran had done was clearly imperil American strategic and economic interests and helped forge an Anglo-American coalition armed with atomic weapons. Moreover, having begun the crisis Stalin halted at the very brink of armed conflict and backed down, even though the Russians enjoyed all the logistical and geographical advantages.

The resolution of this crisis not only vindicated the conclusions of the Long Telegram and the Clifford Report, but it also anticipated the strategy of containment and the general pattern of the Cold War.

Kennan and Clifford based their reports on a sense of U.S. invulnerability to Soviet attack. Their argument was that because of its great economy, its monopoly of the atomic bomb, and the security of the American homeland from attack, in a confrontation the Soviet Union could be made to back down. Kennan especially had felt certain about this in his recommendations, and the Soviets had indeed behaved as he predicted they would. This crisis also established a clear precedent for what lay ahead. Whether it was Turkey and Iran or most (but not all) of the crises to come, the Soviet Union assumed certain burdens of risk by their international behavior and the United States in each case resolved to take timely and decisive action—and succeeded in containing the problem.

In the early Cold War crises of the 1940s, when the rivalry had not yet become so intense and bitter, there was no thought given by either side to rationally parcel out territory and economic stakes as victorious states did in previous centuries. This was so because the rivalry was not only based on national factors, but also on ideological ones. By the time Kennan and Clifford came to issue their reports, the United States had come to view the relationship as the Soviet Union did—as a clash of systems. And in that clash neither system *could* allow the other system a share of the spoils since they both regarded each other as illegitimate and therefore not deserving of a share of anything.[17] One year before the Truman Doctrine the leadership of both countries had already come to feel that over the long term they could not really coexist and that one side would inevitably disappear.

Notes

1. R.V. Daniels, *A Documentary History of Communism* (New York: Vintage Books, 1960), 2, 142-47.

2. Robert J. Donovan, *Conflict and Crisis. The Presidency of Harry S. Truman 1945-1948* (New York: W.W. Norton and Company, 1977), 160.

3. Thomas H. Etzold and John Lewis Gaddis, *Containment: Documents on American Policy and Strategy, 1945-1950* (New York: Columbia University Press, 1978), 50-63.

4. Etzold and Gaddis, *Containment*, 84-90.

5. George F. Kennan, *Memoirs. 1925-1950* (Boston: Little, Brown and Co., 1967), 359.

6. Bruce R. Kuniholm, *The Origins of the Cold War in the Near East. Great Power Conflict and Diplomacy in Iran, Turkey, and Greece* (Princeton, N. J.: Princeton University Press, 1980).

7. Raymond Cohen, *Threat Perception in International Crisis* (Madison: University of Wisconsin Press, 1979), 68-70.

8. Dean Acheson, *Present at the Creation: My Years in the State Department* (New York: Viking Press, 1969), 264.

9. Harry S. Truman, *Year of Decisions* (Garden City, N.Y.: Doubleday and Company, 1955), 550-52.

10. Fraser J. Harbutt, *The Iron Curtain: Churchill, America, and the Origins of the Cold War* (New York: Oxford University Press, 1986), 188.

11. Quoted in Robert Rhodes James, ed., *Winston Churchill: His Complete Speeches, 1897-1963* (New York/London: Chelsea House in association with R.R. Bowker, 1974), 3, 7285 ff.

12. Walter Lafeber, *The Origins of the Cold War, 1941-1947: A Historical Problem with Interpretations and Documents* (New York: John Wiley and Sons, 1971), 144-48.

13. *Public Opinion Quarterly* 10 (1946-1947), 24, 265.

14. Harbutt, *The Iron Curtain*, 207.

15. Lafeber, *The Origins of the Cold War*, 139-43.

16. Etzold and Gaddis, *Containment*, 64-71.

17. Seweryn Bialer and Michael Mandelbaum, *The Global Rivals* (New York: Vintage Books, 1989), 38.

8

The Truman Doctrine
and the Marshall Plan

The Second World War, which came to a military end in 1945, was never formally terminated. Treaties dealing with boundaries, reparations, and the limitation of armed forces were concluded with minor Axis enemies like Italy, Hungary, Romania, and Bulgaria, but no assembly of the great powers met to discuss the reconstruction of Europe. Instead, the postwar settlement emerged piecemeal between 1945 and 1949 and in different ways for the two halves of the continent. In Western Europe under allied supervision and protection there was a swift return to the pre-1939 pattern of life. In Eastern Europe the Soviet occupation helped produce a major social revolution. The problem of recovery in both cases was highlighted by the social and economic chaos that accompanied the greatest of all wars.

By war's end at least thirty-two million Europeans had perished, over twenty million on the battlefield. Sixty million had been uprooted from their homes with almost half of that number driven from their countries by force or by force of circumstance. These included a million and a half Poles deported from Polish areas annexed by Germany, one hundred thousand Alsace-Lorrainers expelled into unoccupied France, almost five million foreign workers deported by the Nazis to toil for the Reich, and roughly twelve million Germans who either fled or were expelled from Eastern Europe, of whom it was estimated two million died on the long trek back to Germany.

The devastation produced by the Second World War was far greater and spread over a far wider area than the First World War. By 1945 most of Europe's capitals outside the neutral countries had been subjected to a massive bombardment and some of them, like Warsaw and Berlin, were reduced to rubble. Only Paris and Rome had been spared attack. Because so much industrial plant and equipment were destroyed in these air raids, production was down dramatically across the continent with no country having the financial resources to afford their replacement. Transport was completely disorganized because railway lines, bridges, and ports had been targeted by Allied air forces and systematically bombed. Millions of farms were destroyed as well and huge tracts of arable land, over which armies had fought, were laid waste. The coal and food shortage was particularly acute in the cities and starvation was commonplace. The shortages had the added effect of opposing the towns to the countryside, which helped to multiply political divisions in each country. To make matters worse the winter of 1946-47 was a particularly bitter one. It saw roughly two hundred people freeze to death in Berlin alone. Furthermore, the whole problem of low production in industry and agriculture was aggravated by the high inflation and black marketeering that was rampant, especially in western and central Europe. In money terms, writes one historian, the Second World War cost more than the combined total of all European wars since the Middle Ages.[1] Savings as consequence had been wiped out by the war and foreign exchange reserves were nearly exhausted. These problems were particularly acute in Britain, France, Italy, and Germany.

The United States had responded initially to the looming economic catastrophe with a variety of stopgap solutions. American credits were extended to Britain and interim aid to France and Italy. Behind it was the hope that somehow everything would return to normal and Europe would restore its prewar economic position. But by early 1947 Britain and France, two of the great powers of the modern age, were prostrate and showed no signs of restoring their prewar glory.

France's postwar crisis was both economic and political. It's first major economic problem was reviving the transportation system that had been destroyed both by Allied bombing and the sabotage campaign waged by the resistance. This problem threatened to choke the entire economy. It's second major problem was the shortage of coal. In 1946 France was the world's largest importer of coal. With production down everywhere in Europe and Britain using every bit she mined, scarce francs had to be spent for the purchase of high-cost American coal.

Inflation had been a serious problem since the occupation and only increased, from 1945 on, because of the widening gulf between dwindling supplies and rising demand. Wholesale prices had risen 80 percent during 1946. Attempts in Western Europe to halt its rise were blocked when drought struck in 1947 wiping out between three and four million acres of wheat and sending agricultural prices soaring again. Workers then demanded higher wages and the inflationary spiral began again with prices rising another 50 percent. Dependent as France was on imports she had to suspend them due to the lack of money to pay for them.[2]

The most glaring problem that France faced and the one which produced the greatest discontent arose over the question of food supplies. It has been estimated that the average Parisian lost forty-two pounds of weight during the German occupation. More than any other problem, hunger fuelled the tension and unrest throughout the country.

In the first postwar general election of October 1945, three political parties came to dominate the field: the Communist and the Socialist, parties which had been around for decades, and the new creation of Christian Democracy. In this brief interlude of what was called "Tripartism," the three emerged nearly equal in electoral support.

The Communist Party, which had furnished the wartime resistance to German occupation with much of its punch, emerged from the war extremely large and popular, having polled 26.6 percent of the popular vote, doubling its strength since the last election of 1936, and becoming France's number one party.

The new power and prestige of the Soviet Union also lent glamor to the French communists as did its power to inspire devotion and sacrifice among its adherents. By 1947 the party controlled the largest trade union in the country boasting a membership of 80 percent of France's workers. It also held five cabinet posts in the newly formed Fourth Republic, including the Vice-Premiership and the Ministry of Defense. In other words, communism emerged for the first time as a major force in Western European politics.

Next to the large and popular Communist Party, the Socialist Party (which polled 24 percent of the votes cast) seemed dull and devoid of ideas and led by a cadre of aging men whose best years were behind them.

The third party, which embodied Christian Democracy, was the Popular Republican Movement (MRP). Founded in 1944 by Georges Bidault, one of General De Gaulle's resistance leaders, the MRP based itself on Catholic principles, representative democracy, anti-communism, and commitment to the capitalist system. Like communism, it was closely associated with the resistance tradition. And because it was the only major conservative party, it was able to attract the support of millions of conservatives whose own parties had disappeared and who voted for them because they were the lesser of the three evils. In 1945 they polled 25 percent of the votes cast.

After De Gaulle's resignation in January 1946, a tripartite government came to power made up of Communists, Socialists, and Christian Democrats. This coalition made agreement in policy matters next to impossible to attain. The Communist Party had taken the line since 1944 that it was not going to attempt to seize power by insurrection, but that it would cooperate in the establishment of a coalition government. Their extended goal was to use to coalition to give more power to parliament (the major reason for De Gaulle's resignation) so as to make and break ministries and to control all aspects of government with the hope of one day establishing a version of people's democracy in France. Lacking a coherent economic and social policy, and with large doses of American aid only promised but not yet delivered, the tripartite government simply drifted.

The situation was just as bad in Italy. Like France, Italy experienced mass unemployment and the inflation rate reached 50 percent in the first half of 1947. In the latter half of 1946 the social unrest reached alarming proportions. A revolt of hundreds of former partisans broke out in the hills of northern Italy, while in the industrial cities a wave of spontaneous action against the unemployment and inflation followed with the trade union leadership having lost control of the movement. This was matched in the countryside of the south by an agrarian movement in which, by 1949, 1,187 cooperatives, with a total membership of nearly a quarter of a million, took over more than 165,000 hectares of land. Compounding the problem was the widespread diffusion of arms throughout the country.[3] Like France, three political parties came to dominate the field: the

Christian Democrats, the Communists, and the Socialists.

Founded in 1942 the Christian Democratic Party originally consisted of members of the old Catholic Political Party (the Popolare) and a number of Catholic anti-fascists. Under its leader, Alcide De Gasperi, it sought to encourage Christian values and a sense of fraternity among its people, as well as promote representative democracy, anti-communism, and commitment to the capitalist system.

In the general elections of 1946 the Christian Democrats polled 35.2 percent of the popular vote and became the largest party in Italy. It continued to actively recruit and expand by exploiting its links with the Catholic Church.

The party that placed second, just nosing out the Communist Party with 20.7 percent of the vote (the communists won 19 percent), was the Socialist Party. Under the weak leadership of Pietro Nenni it was pro-Soviet, and therefore subservient to the Communist Party, the more official representative of the socialist bloc. Following the Communist lead as it did, it was never able to establish its own political autonomy.

Like the French Communist Party, the Italian Communist Party emerged from the war tremendously popular with its membership steadily expanding. Under its leader, Palmiro Togliatti, the party joined the Tripartite government and viewed reform under the leadership of the Christian Democrats as attainable. In an important sense they were forced to hold this view because they believed that revolution in postwar Italy was an impossibility. Togliatti felt that an armed insurrection to establish a communist government in Italy would immediately invite an Anglo-American intervention. Togliatti believed instead that the socialist revolution was something that was brought from outside by the Soviet Union. In this sense the Communist Party of Italy was not a genuine revolutionary party. Along with most Socialists the Communists slavishly maintained that the Soviet Union represented the realization of socialism. And it was this which eventually alienated large blocs of Italian voters on the left. More specifically, the party bore the burden of the Trieste issue, which outraged millions of Italians who might have otherwise supported them.

With a mixed Slavic and Italian population, Trieste and its hinterland had for long been claimed by both Italy and Yugoslavia. In 1945 the Yugoslavs had taken over a large part of Venezia Giulia and subjected the Italian population to a harsh occupation. The Yugoslavs were communist comrades and Stalin at first backed their claims. The Italian Communist Party actually went so far as to welcome the Yugoslav "army of liberation." After six weeks the Yugoslavs were forced by the Allies to withdraw, but not until the Italian Communist Party had been made to look like so many pawns of Moscow.[4]

The political crisis in Italy was brought on by the peace treaty in February 1947. The treaty stripped Italy of all her colonies, exacted reparations to the tune of $360 million dollars and, worst of all, gave most of the Istrian Peninsula to Yugoslavia and made Trieste a free territory under international supervision. Signing the treaty proved a grave blow to De Gasperi's prestige. As a consequence, the Christian Democrats lost heavily in the regional Sicilian elections of April. The economic distress peaked at exactly this moment. There was massive unemployment, runaway inflation, and the widespread diffusion of arms. The conditions of daily life were becoming desperate.

Britain's postwar crisis was basically an economic one. Being an island-nation, she was more dependent for her existence upon international trade. With less than 5 percent of her population engaged in agriculture, she had to import much of her food. She also had to import most of the raw materials (coal was the major exception) needed for her industries. What aggravated the problem was the loss of one-fourth of her merchant marine, the liquidation of one-half of her overseas investments, and the depletion one-fourth of her financial reserves. By December 1946, despite an American loan of $5 billion and the continuation of the wartime austerity program, Britain had only reached her prewar level of production. At that point, Britain experienced one of the worst winters in its history. Because of the blizzards and sub-zero weather, the transportation system ground to a halt as did industries that could no longer be supplied with the requisite fuel. When factories closed millions of workers were left jobless, cold, and hungry. By early 1947 Britain's whole export drive had, for the most part, collapsed. Only eighteen months before, when the war ended, all of Britain had been aglow with pride and a sense of comradeship at having come through the war victoriously. One of the victors in that war, Britain's future now appeared bleak.

It was now imperative that the British government face up to the sea change in the country's economic fortunes and trim their sails. The first area of traditional British dominance that came up for harsh review was the eastern Mediterranean. Since the war Britain had been propping up conservative regimes in Greece and Turkey, which would have toppled without such support. In 1946 the British organized elections in Greece that returned a majority for the supporters of the Greek monarch, George II. As a consequence, the Greek communists who had been suppressed by the British at the end of 1944 took up arms once again in September 1946 and made another bid for power. This time they received a great deal of cross-border support from communist regimes in Albania, Bulgaria, and especially Yugoslavia. Once again, the British army was called upon to back up the Greek government. In early 1947, faced with the necessity of reducing its military budget, and despite its eagerness to resist a possible communist takeover, the British decided that they could no longer afford to prop up the Greek government.

On February 21, 1947, the first secretary of the British embassy in Washington delivered two notes to the U.S. State Department that informed Washington that Britain could no longer subsidize the Greek and Turkish regimes. It also informed the administration of its intention to remove the British army from Greece by March 31. These historic notes also expressed Britain's hope that the United States would rise to the challenge and assume the burden that Britain was about to relinquish. History does not afford many examples of a great empire announcing the beginning of its demise and requesting that a rising ally assume the same imperial role.

The British notes came as no surprise to Washington, but the suddenness did. The administration had gradually been preparing for such an eventuality since late 1946. In September 1946 it had prepared programs of military aid for Greece and Turkey, and an attempt had been made in January 1947 to estimate the Greek regime's economic needs. All of this had been hesitant and inconsistent. The British notes now forced Washington to erect a new interventionist foreign policy for the European continent—and to do so on the run.

The American response to the notes was based on the understanding that the Pax Britannica was drawing to a hurried close and that the logic of containment demanded that the American people abandon their aversion to power politics and assume the burdens of world leadership. It was felt by administration officials that it was too late to liberate the peoples of Eastern Europe without precipitating a war; instead, efforts had to be expended on keeping the rest of Europe from sliding into the communist camp. Western Europe, as both George Kennan and Clark Clifford had pointed out, possessed the largest concentration of skilled workers, technicians, and managers outside the United States. It represented the second greatest concentration of industrial power in the world. Should this region pass under Soviet influence it would irrevocably alter the balance of power in the world.

On February 24 a worried Dean Acheson confided to the journalist Louis Fischer that the crisis in Europe had assumed such staggering proportions that the United States had to find some means of preventing a collapse. "The British are pulling out everywhere," he told Fischer, "and if we don't go in, the Russians will." Acheson felt that there were only two powers left; "If the Near East and France go communist," he said, "I fear very much for this country and for the world." It was Acheson's feeling, shared by many in the administration, that the Greek crisis was only one manifestation of a general world crisis brought about by the economic devastation of the war, the decline of Great Britain as one of the world's great powers, and the expansion of a dynamic Soviet Union. Ever since the Turkish straits crisis the year before, Acheson believed that the Soviets would not be content with a limited sphere of influence in Eastern Europe, but had unlimited expansionist goals. His views were especially important because, as much as anyone else in the Truman administration, his outlook and influence helped shape the diplomacy of the United States in the critical postwar years.[5] Acheson was undersecretary of state from 1945 to 1947 and succeeded George Marshall as secretary of state from 1949 to 1953. From 1945 on, the man Henry Kissinger once called, "the greatest secretary of state of the twentieth century," enjoyed President Truman's total support.

Acheson had prided himself on being a student of British history. What he specifically admired was Britain's use of economic and military strength to maintain the balance of power in the long peace following the Congress of Vienna in 1815. It seemed obvious to Acheson that with the impending retreat of Britain, it would naturally fall to the United States to assume the old British role of stabilizing vital parts of the world. In Dean Acheson President Truman found a diplomat-statesman of high calibre with the vision and intelligence to complement his own decisiveness.

Six days after the receipt of the British notes (February 27) Truman, worried about getting vital foreign policy legislation through Congress, summoned the leaders of both houses to the White House for a briefing on his proposed program. Truman, who was curiously passive at this meeting, allowed George Marshall and Acheson to argue for the new policy. Marshall, who was no more articulate than Truman, failed to impress his audience. He led off the discussion with a version of the domino theory but one in which he conveyed the impression that the aid should be extended to Greece on humanitarian grounds and the aid to Turkey to strengthen Britain's faltering position in the Middle East. A that moment the congressional leaders were above all budget conscious, and so their initial reaction was, "How much is this going to cost?" and "Isn't this pulling British chestnuts out of the fire?" At this point Acheson asked Marshall, "Is this a private fight or can anyone get into it?" "This was my crisis," Acheson recalled in his memoirs. "Never," he said, with that consummate confidence that normally irritated congressmen, "have I spoken under such a pressing sense that the issue was up to me alone."

Acheson built his case around the polarization of power in the postwar world, drawing an historical parallel with the situation that existed between Rome and Carthage in the ancient world. Not since that titanic clash had there been such a polarization of power on this earth. But what made the present struggle between the United States and the Soviet Union even worse was that it was being inflamed by ideology. In a preview of the Truman Doctrine speech, Acheson told the legislators:

> The two great powers were divided by an unbridgeable chasm. For us, democracy and individual liberty were basic; for them dictatorship and absolute conformity. And it was clear that the Soviet Union was aggressive and expanding.

Using the domino theory to drive the point home, he said that the "corruption of Greece would infect Iran and all to the east," and "would also carry infection to Africa through Asia Minor and Egypt, and to Europe through Italy and France. . . ." The United States stood at an historical crossroads. "The Soviet Union was playing one of the greatest gambles in history at minimal cost," Acheson told his listeners. "We and we alone were in a position to break up the play."[6]

By the time he finished speaking, Acheson had convinced the congressmen that the basic assumption behind Soviet world politics was that its objectives could be achieved only at the expense of the United States. The crisis they were all facing had, therefore, little to do with "pulling British chestnuts out of the fire," but had everything to do with containing the "infection" of communism and preserving the security of the United States. Acheson had always been strongly sceptical about Wilsonian internationalism and dollar diplomacy, although he was willing to invoke its rhetoric to get his ideas across. In 1947 he wanted the administration to commit itself to stabilizing those areas of the world that threatened to become unglued, and if this meant working with authoritarian regimes like Greece and

Turkey, then so be it; at least they would not threaten the national security of the United States. If Acheson pushed for anything in the crucial discussions of 1947 it was for a truly pragmatic American foreign policy.

Acheson's appraisal of Soviet intentions and the aggressive nature of communism certainly stunned and even shook his congressional audience. His analysis, in fact, thereafter became an accepted American belief. Senator Vandenberg told Truman that if he wanted Congress to vote the requisite monies for his new policy, then he should do what Acheson had just done at the White House: "scare the hell out of the American people."

On March 12, 1947, only nineteen days after the receipt of the British notes, Truman went before a special joint session of Congress and delivered an historic address that set forth what became known as the Truman Doctrine. In a dramatic speech that lasted only eighteen minutes, Truman declared the intention of the United States to supplant Britain as the economic and military guarantor of Greece and Turkey. He asked for $400 million in aid—$250 million for Greece, and $150 million for Turkey. And if this seemed excessive, he reminded his audience that the United States had contributed $341 billion toward winning the Second World War. The request for Greece and Turkey amounted to little more than one-tenth percent of the wartime investment.

But foreign assistance was not to be narrowly confined to the Eastern Mediterranean. "I believe," Truman said, "that it must be the policy of the United States to support free peoples who are resisting subjugation by armed minorities or by outside pressures." Implicit in this was an American pledge to massively employ the country's resources to bolster friendly nations all along the periphery of the Soviet bloc that appeared susceptible to outside pressure from the Soviet Union, or internal pressure from native Marxist parties supported by the Soviet Union.

Truman then came to the heart of what must rank as one of the most important speeches in American history. If America was to survive as a great nation it could only do so in a world where freedom flourished. He then, in a distinction worthy of Woodrow Wilson, graphically divided the world into two opposing ways of life, thus recognizing the Cold War publicly and officially for the first time. One system, he said, was "based on the will of the majority, and is distinguished by free institutions, representative government, free elections, guarantees of individual liberty, freedom of speech and religion, and freedom from political oppression." The other system was "based upon the will of a minority forcibly imposed upon the majority. It relies upon terror and oppression, a controlled press and radio, fixed elections, and the suppression of personal freedoms."[7]

Nowhere in his speech did Truman preach caution and compromise in the face of the crisis. He called for no concessions to expediency. Everything in his speech revolved around his definition of the enemy (who he never named). From the beginning, the speech was couched in the familiar Wilsonian ideological language that Americans understood and had grown used to since 1941. As a matter of fact, George Marshall and Charles Bohlen had objected to Acheson's draft of the speech precisely because they felt it emphasized "a little too much flamboyant anti-communism."[8] But Truman and Acheson, who knew more about political language and its symbols, understood that an ideologically driven speech would have the widest possible appeal in the country. Furthermore, dividing the world into "democratic" and "totalitarian" systems and viewing the current crisis in Greece as part of a much larger global struggle helped to legitimize the new direction of U.S. foreign policy. The Truman Doctrine speech was an historical turning point since it called for a massive intervention into areas of the world the United States never before considered vital to its security. It was at this point that the Cold War was decisively joined, but in only one critical part of the world: Western and Mediterranean Europe. It was not meant to be applied in Asia—at least not yet. This became clear when Dean Acheson had to defend the policy before some hostile critics in Congress.

There was a lot of sharp and valuable criticism directed toward the Truman administration over its new direction in foreign policy. One of the major arguments against the program was that the Greek and Turkish governments were undemocratic, corrupt, and reactionary and to include them in the American definition of the free world was frankly absurd. Acheson's counter argument to this was that countries like Greece and Turkey might, with American aid injected at the right moment, evolve in a more democratic direction. After all, they were not totalitarian states and unlike communist governments they would over the next generation most certainly be cast in a different political mould. When Acheson was then asked by a congressional committee to draw a comparison between U.S. aid to Europe and U.S. aid to China, Acheson faltered. The administration was urging an historical fight with communists in Europe and supplying them with the tools to wage it, but in China it was merely urging its communists to cooperate with the Chiang-Kai-Shek regime. Acheson could only say that the situation was different in Asia, which was so vast. In practical terms what Acheson was saying was that despite the global rhetoric of Truman's speech, the Truman Doctrine was limited to Europe.

The collapse of the Pax Britannica, which underlay the crisis in the Eastern Mediterranean, was now addressed decisively by President Truman in a bold reformulation of American foreign policy. It then became the task of a small group of men—led by Dean Acheson and William Clayton at the State Department to shape the Truman Doctrine into a workable response to Soviet expansionism and, at the same time, to persuade the U.S. Congress and the American people once and for all that the tradition of peacetime isolationism was no longer in the national interest.

The best statement of this case appeared anonymously in the July 1947 issue of the semi-official journal *Foreign Affairs* under the title, "The Sources of Soviet Conduct." George Kennan was the author. In this article Kennan summarized both his ideas in the "Long Telegram" of 1946, as well as official government policy as distilled from the key discussions conducted in Washington since 1945. His target was the political elite of the United States.

Kennan's article added one important thing to his earlier cable: the concept of containment. Kennan's basic argument was that the Russians would prove weak in the face of a determined use of force and would eventually yield to it. In other words, Soviet aggression could be "contained by the adroit and vigilant application of counterforce at a series of constantly shifting geographical and political points." Kennan believed that given the new circumstances of the postwar era, the United States would have to undertake the containment of the Soviet Union alone and unilaterally, but if it could do so without wrecking its economy, the Russian state would undergo a period of immense strain climaxing in "either the breakup or the gradual mellowing of Soviet power."[9]

At its heart, containment was a defensive policy. As its architects envisioned it, it was to be waged by economic assistance, propaganda, military power responding only to military threats, and diplomacy. In other words, it was designed to maintain the status quo by blocking further Soviet expansion and political infiltration. It was not designed to carry the struggle to Eastern Europe and the Soviet Union. Quite the contrary, one of its ironies was that, like the *cordon sanitaire* policy of the 1920s, it told the Soviets that they would be able to consolidate the gains of the Second World War. As the influential political columnist, Walter Lippmann, put it in the public debate that followed Truman's speech and the Kennan article, containment was a policy of "holding the line and hoping for the best." What he felt the policy did in the long run was "concede to the Kremlin the strategical initiative as to when, where and under what local circumstances the issue was to be joined." According to Lippmann, this "would mean for ten or fifteen years Moscow, not Washington, would define the issues, would make the challenges, would select the ground where the conflict was to be waged, and would choose the weapons." And Kennan was hoping for the "mellowing" of Soviet power as that state became more "frustrated."[10] In many ways Lippmann's analysis and criticism were brilliantly drawn, but nevertheless were prophetically wrong. Soviet power *did* bear within itself the seeds of its own decay, as Kennan had said, and would end up one day "as one of the most pitiable of national societies." At the same time, Lippmann seriously underestimated the tenacity of the American people over the long haul. It was true that containment was, as he said, a form of trench warfare, but the American people persisted and did not weary of the struggle. They held the line and adhered to the essential precepts of the containment policy until the Soviet Union *did* weaken internally and its ruling elite lost faith in its reason for being.

It was in Greece that the Truman Doctrine had its first dramatic success. U.S. military aid began to arrive in the summer of 1947 and shortly thereafter, under American supervision, troops loyal to the Athens government began to aggressively clear the communist forces from one region of the country after another. The government was helped by a dramatic change in Soviet bloc politics; in 1948 the split between Marshal Tito and Stalin had become public. In that year, when the rebellion in Greece reached its peak, Stalin had scolded the Yugoslavs for extending too much aid.

What, do you think that Great Britain and the United States—the United States the most powerful state in the world—will permit you to break their line of communication in the Mediterranean? Nonsense. And we have no navy. The uprising in Greece must be stopped, and as quickly as possible.[1]

On the surface of it, this remark suggests that the Truman Doctrine had overdone Soviet expansionism; but on the other hand, it may show that the early strength shown in 1946 in Iran and Turkey was sufficient to make Stalin cautious. At any rate, by 1949 Tito, who was more worried about Soviet attempts to overthrow him, closed the Greek-Yugoslav border, thus effectively cutting off aid to the rebels. By 1950 the civil war was over and for the first time in the Cold War a communist force intent on seizing power was defeated by force of arms. The successful resolution of the Greek crisis helped to convince Washington that the Truman Doctrine and the containment policy were amply justified.

While Americans had been preoccupied with national security since the Japanese attack on Pearl Harbor, it was in 1947 that the term national security itself came into general American use. That it did was in response to what was perceived as the failure of postwar international efforts at maintaining collective security. The concept itself was formalized with the passage of the National Security Act in July 1947. The act provided for separate Departments of the Army, Navy, and Air Force, with a secretary of defense presiding over them. The Joint Chiefs of Staff were to serve as advisors to the secretary of defense and to the president. To coordinate diplomacy and military planning, the act also created a National Security Council (NSC) to consist of the president, certain cabinet members, and other advisors on foreign and military policy. At the same time, two other agencies were created to serve the NSC: a National Security Resources Board and a Central Intelligence Agency. The National Security Act of 1947, along with the Truman Doctrine, reflected a streamlined, single-minded concentration on containing and repelling Soviet expansionism. It all helped make 1947 an historical turning point. It was at that moment that the Cold War was decisively joined.

The Truman Doctrine was directed toward a certain political and ideological and even military problem posed by the Soviet Union in the postwar world. But it soon became obvious that military aid to Europe was not enough to solve the problem. What was needed alongside this bold reformulation of U.S. policy toward the Soviet Union was an equally dramatic approach toward the economic crisis. The continuing economic crisis seemed an open invitation for everything the United States feared the most—namely, the extension of Soviet power working in collusion with native Communist parties and communist-controlled labor organizations. Washington began to address this problem in the summer of 1947.

The Truman Doctrine logically led to a program of economic reconstruction to bolster the stability of Europe and help eradicate the misery out of which the Communist parties in Western Europe were gaining recruits. Returning in April 1947 from the Conference of Foreign Ministers in Moscow, Secretary of State George C. Marshall was convinced that the Russians were interested only in profiting from the economic plight of Europe, not in ameliorating it. He and President Truman were agreed that the only solution lay in aiding European nations that were willing to cooperate with each other in rebuilding their economies.

Marshall announced his proposal for a European recovery program in an address at Harvard University on July 5, 1947. The Marshall Plan, as it came to be known, was preeminently the result of staff work in the Department of State. Kennan had important input here, but its principal author was William L. Clayton who reported in detail to Marshall about Europe's economic problems and about the need for an enormous U.S. relief effort. It was Charles Bohlen who then proceeded to draft Marshall's speech.[12]

The administration understood that their country's economic well-being depended on European economic prosperity. The lessons of the Great Depression of the 1930s indicated that a different global approach was required if the mistakes of the past were to be avoided. According to Michael Hogan, the ideas expounded in the Marshall Plan found their origin in the various experiments of the Hoover and Roosevelt administrations: namely, in a capitalism that combined freer trade and open market forces. This approach, which he calls "corporatism," involved an active collaboration among industrial leaders, labor, and a creatively interventionist state. The plan was plainly intended to be more than a passive reaction to communist pressure and subversion. Its architects were anxious to avoid dividing Europe. Quite the contrary, they sought an integrated European market and to which they held up as a model the U.S. internal market.[13] Central to that European trade area was the restoration of German power, but in a more benign form.

There were two key parts to Marshall's speech. First, that the European governments were to help themselves by drafting a mutual economic aid plan, to which the United States would make a substantial contribution. American aid would be based on need, which meant that all participants must furnish particulars about their economic plight. This would not be a repetition of lend-lease. Marshall urged the governments of Europe to decide among themselves the best allocation of resources. He hoped that all or most of the European nations would agree to joint action.

Second, Marshall made it clear that most European nations could participate in the program, including the Soviet Union and its satellites in Eastern Europe. Nevertheless, Marshall also excluded "any nation attempting to foster adverse economic conditions in order to gain politically from the misery of others." This, of course, was addressed to the Soviet Union. It was recognized that the entrance of the Soviet Union into the program would enormously complicate things (and certainly multiply the costs), and even wreck it. It is difficult to imagine that the U.S. Congress would have supported a reconstruction program that included the Soviet Union. Nevertheless, Russian participation was not rejected out of hand.

At this point the British arranged for a planning meeting in Paris of the European foreign ministers—Britain, France, and Russia. The meeting began on June 27. Britain and France proposed that a joint European proposal be worked out, which presumed a cooperative determination of the needs and priorities of each nation as well as Europe as a whole. Molotov, however, believed that the whole scheme was a cover for United States economic imperialism, and an attempt to rebuild Western European and especially German power at Russian expense. At the same time, it was an attempt to rip Eastern Europe out of the Soviet orbit.

Before Molotov stormed out of Paris he denounced the British and French for being lackeys of the United States and causing the division of Europe. Molotov broke off discussions on July 2 and returned to Moscow. The British and the French then invited all European states except Spain, which was considered fascist, to send representatives to a conference on the Marshall Plan to meet in Paris on July 12. The Poles and Czechs who needed aid desperately accepted the invitation to go to Paris and accede to the plan. But it was clear from Molotov's denunciation that the Soviet Union would not permit any communist participation in the plan.

Why did Stalin reject the Marshall Plan? He certainly understood that his country was as physically devastated as any nation in the world. Not only did vast population centers lay in ruins, but Russia faced a food shortage so acute that it approached famine level. Complicating efforts to economically recover was the fact that vast regions of the western part of the country—particularly Belorussia, Latvia, Estonia, and the Ukraine—were engulfed in partisan warfare, which took the security forces no less than five years to quell. At the same time, Stalin was being publicly attacked by Churchill and Truman while his country was increasingly isolated in the U.N.

According to Dmitri Volkogonov, the anti-communist Truman Doctrine had already confirmed for Stalin that the confrontation with the West had begun. The Marshall Plan, coming so soon after the Truman Doctrine, was a clear indication of the American desire to maintain a serious presence in Europe.[14]

Blinkered as Stalin was by his own propaganda and ideology he also felt that capitalism was nearing a crisis point. The Marshall Plan, seen through the Marxist-Leninist prism, was an instrument to solve the perennial problem of overproduction. Nevertheless, this was where the United States could prove most dangerous. For Russia to accept the Marshall Plan, especially when she was so vulnerable and desperate for aid, would be at the cost of accepting virtual American control over the Soviet economy. Stalin understood that the Soviet hold on Eastern Europe was too recent and too precarious and that a campaign of American economic imperialism would more than likely detach the satellites from Soviet control. Stalin's answer was to reduce all contact with the West and retreat behind the Iron Curtain—and make his satellites do the same.

On July 9, 1947, a delegation from Prague was summoned to Moscow. Stalin told them that the Marshall Plan was directed at the Soviet Union and that if the Czechs attended the discussions at Paris it would be viewed as a hostile act against his country. The Czechs then agreed to revoke their original acceptance of the Marshall Plan. As Jan Masaryk, the Czech foreign minister, said to his friends: "It is a new Munich. I left for Moscow as Minister of Foreign Affairs of a sovereign state. I am returning as Stalin's stooge."[15] And then to the historian, Hubert Ripka, he said: "My dear friend, we are nothing but vassals. The saddest is that there are people of our own blood who are doing the dirty work. The communists have not an ounce of patriotic pride. They are the slaves of Moscow, and they rejoice in their servitude." By July 11 every Eastern European state had rejected the invitation to come to Paris. Western leaders quickly saw the importance of Stalin's intimidation of the satellites to stay out of the program. It would require, they felt, a political clamping down on the entire region, and when this happened, Europe would be permanently split into two camps.

On July 12 the conference convened in Paris and was attended by only the West European states plus Greece and Turkey, and the free state of Trieste. Germany had no government and Spain was not invited. In all, sixteen nations joined a Committee of European Economic Cooperation, which met in September 1947, and presented plans for reconstruction to create a self-sufficient Europe by December 30, 1951, when the plan would end officially.

The participants said they needed $22 billion worth of food, fuel, raw materials, and capital equipment over and above what they could pay for themselves. In December 1947 Truman asked for $17 billion for a four-year program. Opposition to this did form in the U.S. Congress, but in February 1948 it was overwhelmed by a shocked and aroused public opinion when Czech Communists seized power in Prague. By April 1948, less than a year after Marshall's speech and in an election year, the Republican Congress had approved an initial $5 billion. This was more than 2 percent of the U.S. gross national product for that year. It was for this reason that Churchill called the plan "the most unsordid act in history."

Altogether over a three-year period the United States spent $12.4 billion through the plan, with the largest amounts going to Britain, France, and Germany. The plan, in other words, targeted the key industrial nations whose recovery would lift the living standards throughout the region. This it did almost immediately. Its economic consequences surpassed even the most optimistic expectations of its architects. By the time the program was due for termination, European industrial production had risen 35 percent—the most rapid economic growth in Western European history—and agricultural production rose to 10 percent above the prewar level. At the same time, the tremendous growth helped fuel the phenomenal expansion of the U.S. economy during the same period. The commercial links forged between Western Europe and the United States, which complemented their increasingly intimate political ties, forced the United States to develop an important stake in international trade for the first time in its history. This involvement prompted Washington to press the participants in the Marshall Plan to dismantle the trade barriers inherited from the depression years that blocked American access to foreign markets. In the summer of 1947 the United States, along with twenty-two other nations, adhered to the General Agreement on Tariffs and Trade (GATT). In subsequent years GATT served as a forum for periodic negotiations between trading partners aimed at reducing the vast maze of trade restrictions that had accumulated since the 1920s. From the beginning, members of GATT promised to abide by the most-favored-nation trade principle. This principle meant that any bilateral arrangement over trade or tariffs was to be automatically extended to all members. It was this more than anything else that helped to destroy most of the tariff walls and government restraints on trade. By the 1960s, sixty-three nations controlling 80 percent of world trade belonged to GATT. Along with the Bretton Woods Agreement, the Marshall Plan and GATT were momentous acts of statesmanship by which the United States helped to create the postwar world. World trade grew in this vast marketplace at an annual rate of almost 7 percent in real terms between 1948 and 1970 after nearly twenty years of stagnation.

The political consequences of the Marshall Plan were to prove as far-reaching as the economic ones for the future of Europe. The plan, along with the Truman Doctrine, sent a clear signal to Paris, Rome, and Berlin, that the United States would not abandon them. The Soviet repudiation of the plan not only accelerated the political and ideological split throughout the continent, but also increased the polarization within many of the states between those Communist parties which looked to Moscow for their support and those pro-Western parties who looked to Washington for leadership and economic salvation.

The Russian answer to the Truman Doctrine and Marshall Plan was to abandon the whole idea of people's democracy, and with it all the rhetoric about popular fronts and national coalitions, and quickly nail down those areas of Europe Moscow considered within the Soviet sphere. Also abandoned was the idea of seeking "national roads to socialism" (never popular with the Russians anyway). What Moscow intended to do was to create a formal organization of Communist parties through which to direct, coordinate, and control communist policy in Europe. What it wanted to do was retain the unquestioning loyalty of those Communist parties who had now come to power or were very close to attaining it. It would do this by replacing local communists who had spent the war years in resistance movements at home and who might prove too independent, with men who in many cases had for years demonstrated a clear subservience to Stalin and who owed him everything, including in some cases their lives; and it would do this by submitting its whole sphere of influence to the rigors of Marxism-Leninism, as a way of permanently anchoring these men in the Soviet orbit.

Moscow's vehicle for doing this was the Cominform (Communist Information Bureau), which was created in July 1947. From its initial meeting in September 1947 it was used to discipline the Communist parties of Eastern European states, to force their loyalty toward Moscow, and to urge Communist parties to foster strikes and disorder in the West (especially Italy and France). Its membership included the Communist parties of the Soviet Union, Poland, Yugoslavia, Hungary, Romania, Czechoslovakia, and Bulgaria, as well as those of France and Italy. Unlike the Comintern it was to have its seat outside the Soviet Union in Belgrade.

Russia also began to link these countries with the Soviet Union economically. By 1949 this had developed into Comecon (Council for Economic Cooperation), a centralized agency that allowed Moscow to stimulate and control Eastern Europe's economic development.

As it turned out, these were momentous decisions in two ways: politically it meant that Communist parties who were weak and illegitimate to begin with and who willingly (in most cases) submitted to the dictates of Moscow would never be able to free themselves from the stain of being creatures of a foreign power. By ruthlessly imposing the Stalinist model on the region Moscow assumed an imperial burden of maintaining order and stability over an area full of millions of restless people who hated their regimes and whose aspirations to freedom and independence were unquenchable. What the political decisions of 1947 meant in the long run was that submission to communist rule could only be maintained by the threat of Soviet military intervention.

Economically, the decision to create Comecon was just as important because it helped condemn the Soviet Union and its satellites to economic backwardness relative to the West and in the long run helped to contribute to the economic failure of the whole Communist system.

At the Cominform's opening conference in September 1947, Andrei Zhdanov, the Kremlin's leading ideologue and heir apparent to Stalin, delivered the keynote address. This speech would serve as the most significant statement of communist internationalism until Stalin's death six years later.

Going much further than Stalin's speech of February 6, 1946, Zhdanov made it abundantly clear that the wartime collaboration of the Grand Alliance was now irrevocably over. In fact, he insisted that the members of the Grand Alliance had entered the war for different reasons; the Soviet Union for the best of reasons, to destroy Nazism, and the West for the worst of capitalist motives, to destroy commercial rivals and establish their dominant economic position. In a classic statement of the two-camp thesis he divided the world between imperialists who wished to politically subjugate large parts of the world and were planning a new war against socialism, and the peace loving socialist world that was combatting imperialism and fascism. The American challenge, he felt, must be countered immediately, and the main battleground for this Manichaean struggle would be France and Italy. The French and Italian Communist parties were therefore accorded a special responsibility. "They must take up the standard in defense of the national independence and sovereignty of their countries." Moscow now ordered those parties to foment massive demonstrations and strikes to destroy the Marshall Plan.[16]

The economic crises in France peaked in 1947 as did French anxieties about the internal and external Soviet challenge to its security. Earlier that year, Georges Bidault, the minister of foreign affairs, told the American ambassador to France that his government more than anything else feared that Germany might fall completely into the Soviet orbit, thus endangering the security of France and its neighbors. Hemmed in by the pressures of coalition politics, the French government was at first unwilling to take sides with the West against the Soviet Union. The Truman Doctrine speech changed all of this once and for all. It told the French that Washington was willing to forge a security link between the states of Western Europe and take a firm stand against the common enemy.

At the Moscow Foreign Ministers Conference of March-April 1947 Bidault asked George Marshall for economic aid. It was here that Marshall gave the French a preview of his plan. Both men agreed that Germany should be included in it. Paris now declared itself ready to align itself with London and Washington in a new postwar security system.[17]

In the spring of 1947 the French Communist Party attacked the Truman Doctrine and in the summer it began to attack the Marshall Plan. Echoing Moscow's line parrot-like, it condemned the U.S. relief effort as thinly disguised imperialism. Under Moscow's thumb, the party leadership seriously underestimated the emotional dynamism of nationalism. It actually stressed openly the importance of France achieving an agreement with the Soviet Union even at the expense of French national interests. The communist trade unions even went so far as to adopt a resolution rejecting desperately needed Marshall Plan aid. It was this attitude, coming as it did at the height of the 1947-1948 crisis that, more than anything else, helped to erode the party's substantial support throughout the country.

On May Day 1947, the Communist Party fomented large demonstrations throughout France and later that month bread riots broke out in the country. This was followed by strikes that quickly spread from the public sector to the Renault factories to the department stores and the transport system. The premier, Paul Ramadier, did not hesitate to ascribe it to "the conductor of a secret orchestra." On May 4 the Communist Party refused to vote confidence in the government's economic and social policy. Bolstered by promises of American aid, Ramadier on May 5 expelled the Communist ministers from the government. This rupture of the Tripartite system was then made definitive by the formation of the Cominform in September. What the Cominform served to do was give official form to the policy of hostile blocs. This was followed by yet another and greater wave of strikes in November and December 1947, involving more than two million workers. The strikes were to be the party's clearest answer to the Marshall Plan. All the essential services were struck—food supplies to the large cities were cut off and badly needed coal was not mined. In the National Assembly where the communists were a major force they helped to paralyze the government. In parts of France the imminence of the Communist takeover was expected on a daily basis.[18] The Great Fear of 1947-1948, as it came to be known, was fed not only by the strikes but also by several acts of sabotage, including the derailing of a train that killed sixteen people. The fears of the moment were also aggravated when it was learned that communists had extensively infiltrated the Ministry of Ex-Servicemen. The country was also rife with rumors. For example, it was reported that an international brigade of communists was being formed on France's borders and that there were secret arms caches at key points in the country that were to be used in a coup d'etat. And all the time the economic crisis worsened. By the fall of 1947 the government had to reduce the bread ration to 200 grams—75 grams less than at the worst point of the war. The crisis was so bad that Vincent Auriol, the President of the Fourth Republic, was moved to observe that "the unrest is close to panic. . . . The government appears to lack the means to get its authority respected."

On November 22 Robert Schuman of the MRP succeeded Ramadier. A week later Schuman recalled eighty thousand men to military service in order to maintain order and keep the essential services running. Propped up by the promise of Marshall Plan aid, the government remained firm and had the strength to ride out the storm. Steeling it from the beginning was its knowledge that the public was on its side. The public was, of course, exasperated, and did not doubt for a moment that the Russians were responsible for the chaos.

Earlier in 1947 General De Gaulle had founded a new party, the Rassemblement du Peuple Français (RPF). It had a pronounced anti-Soviet and anti-communist posture. Along with the strike movement it helped to polarize the political issue around the struggle for or against communism. Backed up by American aid, which began arriving in France by 1948, anti-communism had once again become legitimate. That it did was in no small way accelerated by the communist coup in Czechoslovakia in February 1948.

As much as any other single contemporary event, the destruction of Czech democracy stiffened the resolve of the French government and its people. As a consequence, the strike movement weakened, the strikers lost confidence in their leadership, and their movement splintered into communist and socialist unions. The result was the general collapse of communist power in France.

Did the Communist Party ever really have a chance? From Truman's speech in March 1947 the party realized that it was waging a losing battle. Its leadership often drew envious comparisons between themselves and the people's democracies of Eastern Europe. The party in France had none of the advantages of, for example, the Communist Party in Czechoslovakia. It was represented in the cabinet, but it didn't have enough time to infiltrate the army, police, and bureaucracy; it polled a large vote, but never more than 27 percent of the electorate; it was not in close proximity of the Red Army but isolated in Western Europe in the shadow of the Anglo-American armies.[19]

There was in the resistance of the French Communists to the Marshall Plan a certain desperation, a sense that in the political struggle being waged, and with the Anglo-American shield so close, they were to be the victims. Nevertheless, they convinced themselves that they were saving France from the hated system. Above all, they correctly judged the power of the Truman Doctrine and the Marshall Plan. They understood that if the American program could be fulfilled, it would keep France in the Western column and keep the Communist Party out of power.

The Communist Party did not fare much better in Italy. Ever since De Gasperi's visit to the United States in early 1947, the Truman administration had made its position clear. If there was to be a large U.S. relief effort for Europe in the future, it would most certainly include Italy as an integral partner in the program. But there was to be no blank check. If the United States was to distribute enormous sums of money to its allies in Europe, then it could be done only for those governments that were relatively free of communists and could make clear economic choices to participate in the plan. Certainly by May, the Truman administration was strongly urging De Gasperi to govern without the communists.

Encouraged by the promise of American support, and prompted by the successful French action in April to exclude the left from the Paris government, De Gasperi now decided to move directly to end the coalition with the left. On May 31, 1947, he succeeded in forcing the Communist and Socialist parties from the coalition government. Less than a week later the Marshall Plan was announced and immediately received Rome's unconditional support.

Unlike the French Communist Party, the Italian Communists more reluctantly took Zhdanov's speech like a call to arms. Nevertheless, the strike wave that now broke over Italy and that was reminiscent of 1919, was designed to prevent an economic revival by heading off Marshall Plan aid and bring the Italian government down.

The Communist Party in Italy labored under the same restrictions as the party in France. Its leadership lacked charisma and could not mount a strong appeal to those people outside the party. Added to this burden was the onus of appearing to take its orders from a foreign country. All this allowed De Gasperi to move with confidence and fully exploit the anti-communist mood of the country.

The anti-communist campaign began in the summer and autumn of 1947 and reached its peak in the weeks preceding the general election of April 1948. The struggle was not merely between the Christian Democrats and the Communists, but as Truman defined it in March, it was between two opposing ways of life. And what reinforced this Manichaean struggle—as it did in France—was the formation of the Cominform and the coup in Czechoslovakia.

Coming as it did during the election campaign, the Czech coup provided Italians with a dramatic example of what happens when a Communist Party, though a minority, seizes power in a democratic society through a coup d'etat. It made a profound impression on Italian voters in 1948. Be that as it may, the greatest influence on the way Italians voted in their most important postwar election came from the United States.

The United States responded to the election of 1948 by injecting large doses of "interim aid" into Italy in the first three months of 1948. Each instalment was made with a great public display by the American ambassador. And lest anyone miss the point, the aid was often transported across Italy on a special "friendship train" and then distributed with the customary ceremonial at each station along the line. At the same time, the United States gave Italy twenty-nine merchant ships and returned large amounts of gold that the Nazis had looted from Italy during the war. And as if this was not enough, the United States, Britain, and France promised that the city of Trieste would be returned to Italian rule. Finally, George Marshall made it absolutely clear that U.S. aid would abruptly stop in any country that voted the communists into power. In the event that this campaign failed and the Communist Party won the election, the United States had a military option it was prepared to exercise. Washington had plans to encourage an anti-communist insurrection on the mainland, while it directly occupied Sicily and Sardinia. To give thrust to this, the United States and Britain strengthened their Mediterranean fleets off the Italian coasts.[20]

The election of April 18, 1948, represented a resounding victory for the Christian Democrats. They received twelve million votes, raising their 1946 vote by five million, or 48.5 percent of the total, and an absolute majority in the Chamber of Deputies. The Communist Party polled eight million votes, or 31 percent of the total. The election reflected the effort of voters to concentrate their votes on a major party that they felt would constitute the most powerful bulwark against communism.[21]

Never in American history had the foreign policy of the United States been developed so quickly or so creatively. In the formative postwar years that policy had to be constructed on the run in response to the swiftly developing challenges of war and devastation and the geopolitical threat of Soviet power. Never had relations before or since between the United States and its European allies been so close or so cordial. All through the period 1945 to 1950 the United States, despite its lack of international political experience, pursued a coherent policy of supporting and strengthening European governments of the democratic center. What the Truman administration had hoped from 1946 on was to stimulate the growth of a "Third Force" in Europe—a moderate, responsible conservatism that would prove equally resistant to the pressures of communism on the left and to the blandishments of ultra-conservatives on the right, who advocated a return to the authoritarianism of the 1930s. It was this policy that helped bring the Christian Democrats to power in France, Italy, and Germany. In all these cases the new regimes were propped up from within by Marshall Plan aid, and protected from external threats and the fate of the Eastern European satellites by the Truman Doctrine and the American military shield. While it is certainly true that American policy bore a certain responsibility in helping to divide the world into rival political and economic blocs, it at the same time deserved most of the credit for preserving the freedom and independence of millions of people in a critical part of the world.

Notes

1. Richard Mayne, *The Recovery of Europe 1945-1973* (New York: Anchor Books, 1973), 39.

2. Jean-Pierre Rioux, *The Fourth Republic, 1944-1958* (Cambridge: Cambridge University Press, 1989), 17-28.

3. Paul Ginsborg, *A History of Contemporary Italy. Society and Politics, 1943-1948* (New York: Penguin Books, 1990), 106.

4. Ginsborg, *A History of Contemporary Italy*, 103-4.

5. David S. McLellan, *Dean Acheson. The State Department Years* (New York: Doff, Mead and Company, 1976).

6. Dean Acheson, *Present at the Creation. My Years in the State Department* (New York: Signet Books, 1970), 293.

7. Joseph Marion Jones, *The Fifteen Weeks (February 21 - June 5, 1947)* (New York: Harcourt Brace Jovanovich, 1955), 269-74.

8. Charles E. Bohlen, *Witness to History, 1929-1969* (New York: W.W. Norton and Co., 1973), 261.

9. Thomas H. Etzold and John Lewis Gaddis, *Containment: Documents on American Policy and Strategy, 1945-1950* (New York: Columbia University Press, 1978), 84-90.

10. Walter Lippmann, *The Cold War. A Study in United States Foreign Policy* (New York: Harper and Row, 1972), 6, 7, 22.

11. Milovan Djilas, *Conversations with Stalin* (New York: Harcourt, Brace and World, 1962), 182.

12. The speech can be found in Jones, *The Fifteen Weeks*, 281-84.

13. Michael J. Hogan, *The Marshall Plan: America, Britain, and the Reconstruction of Western Europe, 1947-1952* (Cambridge: Cambridge University Press, 1987).

14. Dmitri Volkogonov, *Stalin. Triumph and Tragedy* (Rocklin, Calif.: Prima Publishing, 1992), 530-31.

15. Quoted in Jacques Rupnik, *The Other Europe* (London: Weidenfeld and Nicolson, 1989), 96.

16. Gale Stokes, ed., *From Stalinism to Pluralism. A Documentary History of Eastern Europe since 1945* (New York: Oxford University Press, 1991), 38-42.

17. David Reynolds, ed., *The Origins of the Cold War in Europe. International Perspectives* (New Haven, Conn.: Yale University Press, 1994), 105.

18. Rioux, *The Fourth Republic*, 126-32.

19. Irwin M. Wall, *The United States and the Making of Postwar France 1945-1954* (Cambridge: Cambridge University Press, 1991), 63-77.

20. Ginsborg, *A History of Contemporary Italy*, 115-18.

21. Giuseppe Mammarella, *Italy after Fascism. A Political History 1943-1965* (Notre Dame, Ind.: University of Notre Dame Press, 1966), 191-92.

9

Constructing the Soviet Bloc, 1945-1953

The smashing Russian victory over Nazi Germany in the Second World War foreshadowed the establishment of Soviet control over the states of Eastern and Southeastern Europe. The West was forced to watch impotently as the Soviet Union at first satellized the states of the region and then eventually communized them. Never in their foreign policy had the West ever really guaranteed the security of this area. As we have seen in chapter five, it was in vain that the West hoped that the Russians treat the region with a measure of generosity.

Communism had never been an important force in this large area of Europe before the Second World War. Only in Czechoslovakia, the most highly industrialized state in the region, was there anything like a large Communist following. In fact, the Communist parties of Western Europe were a good deal larger and more active and popular than those of Eastern Europe. The Communist parties in each Eastern European state faced a people and a native intelligentsia that were profoundly anti-communist. The only democratic regimes that existed in the pre-1939 period could be found in Czechoslovakia and briefly in Germany. Nevertheless, while the other states could be classified as quasi-authoritarian, they did possess functioning parliaments, which at their best boasted very lively debates. These regimes also allowed their citizenry a large measure of freedom of the press, as well as private enterprise and freedom of religion. This vast and highly complicated area of the world had nothing in common with the Soviet Union.

The countries that were now included in the Soviet sphere of influence (Albania, Bulgaria, Czechoslovakia, Hungary, Poland, Romania, and the Soviet zone of Germany) covered an area of 400,000 square miles and had a population of over one hundred million. By the end of the Second World War it was in a state of anarchy. Its political and economic institutions had collapsed and many of the beliefs and values and political ideas around which the social structures of many of these states had been organized had either waned or disappeared. For example, fascism had been thoroughly discredited and small pockets of its faithful rendered impotent. This was also true, to a certain extent, of conservatism and capitalism. The liberal parties were all but broken by 1945, their best days now only to be found in the past. Democratic socialism was still numerically important but, like liberalism, it lacked the punch it once had before the 1930s. Everywhere in the region the Communist Party capitalized on the conditions of disorder and confusion and on the general craving for change.

From 1944 to 1947 Eastern Europe was increasingly satellized; that is, the states of the area were gradually bound politically to the Soviet Union with their decision-making power increasingly shifted to Moscow. From 1947 on, under the pressure of the Truman Doctrine and especially the Marshall Plan, the region was swiftly Sovietized.

Generally speaking, the process of satellization conformed to three basic stages. The first stage began with the formation of broad anti-fascist coalitions, which included communists, socialists, agrarians and liberals. Power at first was not wielded exclusively by the Communist Party. Stalin was reluctant to maintain communist control by direct force, and he realized that he needed the help of all non-communist groups in rebuilding the region's war-torn economies. The non-communist elements who were weary of the postwar chaos, tamely cooperated with the Communist Party because the party seemed to be the only group which possessed a program for change and was capable of real action. At the same time, the communists made sure they took over the key ministries of the interior and defense.

The second phase began when the Communist Party felt sufficiently confident to go on the offensive. Through its control of the police, the party waged a gradual and one-sided battle for position with the other parties, often outlawing them and arresting their leaders on the pretext that they had aided and abetted fascism. Through its monopoly of communications it also deprived its enemies from using the press, radio, and meeting places to fight back. In the process the Communist Party succeeded in removing their rivals piecemeal from one vital center of government after another and replacing them with loyal communists. The Hungarian communist leader, Matyas Rakosi, called this "salami tactics," a slicing off of political enemies in which the party achieved exclusive control. In the Soviet-controlled countries and Yugoslavia, this phase occupied most of 1946 and part of 1947.

The third phase was characterized by the structural reorganization of the state and the consolidation of communist political monopoly. In this phase all organized opposition was liquidated as was the removal of all fundamental liberties of expression, conscience, association, movement, and teaching. At the same time, most of the economy was nationalized and forced-labor camps either opened, or in some cases, expanded. This final phase was reached in Albania, Bulgaria, Romania, and Yugoslavia by the end of 1947. It was reached in Poland, Czechoslovakia, and Hungary in 1948, and East Germany in 1949.[1]

The only resistance, small as it actually was, came from the Catholic Church. This was especially true in Poland, Czechoslovakia, and Hungary, where Catholics enjoyed a majority. Here too, the battle was hopelessly one-sided. The Communist Party simply arrested, brought to trial, and imprisoned a certain number of cardinals, archbishops and bishops (like Cardinal Mindszenty in Hungary and Cardinal Wyszynski in Poland), which intimidated the rest of the clergy. At the same time, the communist regimes stripped the church everywhere of its wealth rendering its clergy politically impotent and somewhat superfluous.

To a certain extent the Sovietization of Eastern Europe, which was accelerated after 1947, became imperative from Stalin's point of view. Building "socialism in one zone" fulfilled certain objectives for him. First, it provided the Soviet Union with a defense in depth against a possible future attack from the West. Second, it ensured that within that buffer zone the new political ruling class was loyal and oriented economically and diplomatically toward Moscow, rather than toward Paris, Berlin, or Washington. Third, it was felt by the Soviet leadership that they could not rebuild their country alone, and that therefore Eastern Europe, whose resources were indispensable, had to be forcibly made to help. This region certainly held Stalin's attention more than any other. According to Nikita Khrushchev,

> Stalin took an active personal interest in the affairs of [Poland and Hungary] as well as Czechoslovakia, Bulgaria and Romania. The rest of us in the leadership were careful not to poke our noses into eastern Europe unless Stalin himself pushed our noses in that direction.[2]

Until 1946 the Russians seemed to work from a rather flexible strategy. After 1947 the pace of change was accelerated and the blueprint for communizing Eastern Europe was tenaciously pushed. Viewing Europe's future through the lens of the class struggle, the program of Sovietization lent substance to Stalin's earlier pledge to extend the social system of the Soviet Union to other countries.

It was the Cominform, formed in 1947, that spearheaded the movement to Sovietize Eastern Europe. Through the Cominform Stalin sought to regulate the domestic and foreign policies of the "people's democracies" in accordance with the radicalization of Soviet international behavior. At the same time, it was designed to suppress local ambitions and initiatives wherever they arose. It was Stalin's intention to convert these states into small replicas of the Soviet Union, and their regimes into reproductions of Stalinist rule. It helped that the native Communist parties were at first so small, since Stalin could then work from scratch to create subservient regimes once the non-Communist ruling groups were eliminated. If Stalin enjoyed a cult of personality at home, he allowed each subordinate leader of a communist state to clone for himself a similar cult of unswerving loyalty to the ruler. According to the Polish leader, Wladislaw Gomulka, the cult of local Stalinism "could be called only a reflected brilliance, a borrowed light. It shone as the moon does."[3]

In practical terms, what did Sovietization mean? Soviet domination of the Eastern European satellites could be ensured by altering all economic, political, cultural, and institutional life in accordance with the Soviet model. That model, Stalin felt, had universal applicability.

Sovietization in the economic realm was two-pronged; in industry, which was soon nationalized, it called for the introduction of the command economy model, complete with state planning commissions that were to draw up the economic goals for each state-owned economy. It also meant increased investments in heavy industry everywhere in the Soviet bloc, and often beyond realistic levels. In agricultural countries like Romania and Bulgaria the industrialization was unnatural and only helped to destroy a productive source of economic growth. In agriculture it meant the hurried conversion of the previous system of private ownership of land to state-owned collectives. In each case, a reformed satellite was to synchronize its economy with the Soviet Union's in preparation for any international crisis in the future.

Administratively, Sovietization meant the overhaul of all the institutional life that had held the pre-1945 states together. The trade unions were neutralized, the churches intimidated and Marxism-Leninism enthroned in their place, the non-Communist parties hounded out of existence, the legal system overhauled, the security apparatus and military establishment purged and taken over by communists. The overall object in each case was the same. The individual must not feel that there was any shield that could afford him protection from the state. If there was to be an arbiter of his destiny, it was the party—the one new institution that held the whole system together.

Sovietization in the cultural realm, or "Zhdanovshchina," as it was called pejoratively, meant the reorganization of art, literature, music, and film along Soviet lines. This campaign had been started by Zhdanov in the Soviet Union in 1946. At that time he had denounced Western culture as "putrid and baneful in its moral foundations," and had tried to enforce communist orthodoxy and expunge foreign influences from Soviet cultural life. This was now extended to the satellites. Writers and artist unions and all cultural publications throughout the bloc were taken over by the Communist Party and grafted on to the political sphere. Art was made subservient to the needs of the party and creativity was carefully modulated by the party whose sole objective was to eradicate all forms of independent thought. Stalin called writers and artists "the engineers of human soul" and he wanted them to produce works featuring "positive heroes" that he and the party thought people should emulate. The communists knew that one of the marks of a true religion was its ability to unite intellectuals with the masses, and on that score (which was ultimately a resounding failure) "Socialist Realism" in art and literature was meant to be the social cement. In the 1940s the Marxist intellectuals showed a peculiar deference to Stalin's political and cultural wisdom, a deference that assumed many forms—from a slavish loyalty to an unenthusiastic adherence to a cynical determination to make the most of a bad thing and get ahead. Nevertheless, the Stalinist practise of strict economic, political, and cultural controls contained the seeds of its own destruction. This kind of policy replete with calls for vigilance against internal and external enemies could only be offensive to intensely nationalist peoples and would eventually even offend the communist leadership in each satellite. But hard-line communists like Jakub Berman of the Polish Party, felt that regimentation needed time to work its necessary changes. "I understand that for a nation to be able to shift to a new set of values," he said, "a new shape, it has to experience a breakthrough of a kind it was never known throughout its thousand years of history."[4] The long-term ideological object was to produce a new Soviet man, or *Homo Sovieticus*, as Soviet dissident writers called him. In other words, Stalin was calling for a total social and economic transformation of society. What he succeeded in creating was a series of states that were duplicates of the Soviet Union. The Communist Party in each state aimed at total power and got it, creating in the process a new command economy and society with everything emanating from the center and tied closely with Moscow. Under the guise of working for the common socialist good, the ruling group in each state succeeded in strengthening the centralized tyrannical state. Paternalistic and repressive, they institutionalized violence and terror in the secret police and the army. In each state could be found a people traumatized by recent events, habituated to violence and a sullen silence, and regarding its regime as clearly illegitimate. Unlike the Communist Party of the Soviet Union, the Communist parties of Eastern Europe never really achieved a complete break with the past, but they did succeed in creating the postwar era's first set of totalitarian societies. In the next generation Eastern Europeans were schooled in cynicism and the realities of the Cold War, and the widespread conviction that the world was irreparably divided into mutually exclusive spheres.

From Stalin's point of view, he had increased the power of his country territorially, and completely subordinated Eastern Europe to Soviet geopolitical interests. By the 1950s, international communism came to look more like an empire ruled from Moscow. In practical terms, this meant that he had created a vast Soviet rimland behind which he could better protect his borders, and from which he could extract reparations and resources to rebuild the Soviet Union. One expert has placed a value of $14 billion on the amount of reparations in kind extracted from the satellites in the period from the mid-1940s to the early 1950s.[5]

The Soviet leadership was certainly under no illusions about the popularity of communist regimes in Eastern Europe. No amount of propaganda and indoctrination could win the allegiance of the region's peoples. In the long run there were alternative approaches to securing Soviet domination on stronger foundations than just naked repression. One approach that Stalin could have pursued was to allow the satellites to introduce a measure of political pluralism into their systems, and the other was to allow each Communist Party the freedom to pursue its own path to socialism, one in line with its own national needs. Other empires in the past had been quite flexible in this regard. Both options were rejected, first in the Czech coup of 1948, and then in the split with Yugoslavia. In both cases, there were extremely important effects on the monolithic unity of the Soviet bloc, and on the developing Cold War.

In the case of Czechoslovakia (as in Yugoslavia and Poland), the German invasion, which destroyed the old political structures, represented the crucial turning point in its history. Just as important, the Western betrayal at Munich in 1938 haunted the Czech political elite. And they were reminded of it again when the U.S. Army in 1945 reversed its progress and left Czechoslovakia when it could easily have liberated most of the country. The political implications of this were clear: Czechoslovakia was now irreversibly in the Soviet sphere. Czech President Eduard Benes understood the position clearly. His country boasted the region's strongest democratic tradition, but because of a geopolitical accident it had to declare its friendship and cooperation with a country it intensely mistrusted. As the Czech historian, Jacques Rupnik, puts it, Munich was to the Czechs what Katyn was to the Poles, but with one major difference; the Munich debacle forced the Czech political elite to desperately look to the Soviet Union as the future guarantor of Czech statehood, thus reversing Thomas Masaryk's (the republic's founder) historical policy of looking westwards.[6]

In 1943 Benes travelled to Moscow to forestall the creation of a Moscow-sponsored Czech government-in-exile. Transcripts of Benes's discussions with Stalin and Molotov strongly suggest that it was Benes who took the initiative and offered his country as an instrument of Russian expansion in Central Europe.[7] Benes promised Stalin that his government would always speak and act in a manner agreeable to the Soviet government. In fact it was Benes who invited Soviet interference in his country's internal affairs. For example, it was Benes who requested that the Soviets aid his government in punishing the Slovaks and the Sudeten Germans for their wartime collaboration with Nazi Germany. The transcripts show that the Russians were very reluctant to do this. Nevertheless, the record shows that Benes, who had written off these peoples politically, was directly involved in the plan to expel three million Sudeten Germans from Czech soil.

To the surprise of Stalin and Molotov, Benes also called for a sweeping confiscation and nationalization of property and banks, not only those of the Czech Germans, but also of large-scale Czech capitalists. Benes seemed to be calling for a swift transition to socialism—far beyond what Stalin asked for or expected.

Benes was not merely settling old scores with political enemies at home, he was also acquiescing in the reduction of democracy and leading his country into the Soviet orbit. Why would Benes, not a communist himself, do this? According to Edward Taborsky, private secretary to Benes when he went to Moscow in 1943, Benes assumed that Europe was moving into the Russian orbit anyway, and that the Russian version of communism would adapt itself to the Czech national tradition. Czechs like Benes in the last stage of the war thought that their own Communist Party would be only a pale reflection of the Russian party, and more like a bellicose Social Democratic party. Second, Benes assumed, said Taborsky, that the Soviet Union would be exhausted at war's end and desperate for American aid. He believed that all these circumstances argued for his country being a "test case of goodwill" in the postwar era, and something of a "useful bridge" between East and West.[8] For these reasons, Benes thought that the Russians would respect Czech independence.

This view was reinforced in 1945 when Klement Gottwald, leader of the Czech Communist Party, explained to his eager colleagues that "in spite of the favourable situation, the next goal is not soviets and socialism, but rather carrying out a really thorough democratic national revolution." The Communist Party was very cleverly linking itself to the Czech democratic tradition—Gottwald even claimed to be a disciple of Thomas Masaryk—as it was trying to link communism with Czech nationalism by capitalizing on the intense anti-German feelings of the Czech people.

Like the French and Italian communists, the Czech Communist Party had a clean wartime record and identified with the Soviet Union, the liberator of Czechoslovakia. Like Communist parties elsewhere, its primary political task was to become the leading political force in the country without alarming the West as it had between 1917 and 1923. The Communist Party had been a powerful force in Czech politics since the 1920s and had for the years of the German occupation cooperated with non-Communist parties. By 1945 after six years of occupation, the party began to swell—from 40,000 in 1945 to 1,350,000 by 1948. This growth reflected the popular revulsion to Nazi rule, the longing for real change that followed it, and the new political realities of living within the Soviet orbit.

All of this told in the general election of May 1946. The Communist Party emerged as the strongest party with 38 percent of the vote. No Communist Party in Europe has ever done as well in a free election (in Hungary in 1947 it could only get 22 percent).

President Benes therefore invited Klement Gottwald to be premier. Gottwald then formed a government containing nine communists and seventeen non-communists. Benes still hoped for a restraint in the emerging American and Soviet power blocs that would allow Czechoslovakia to survive. He also hoped that the communists "having already come so far on the way to real power [would] understand that they must impose some restraint on themselves, that while they need not retreat anywhere they must have the patience to choose the correct moment for continuing in a reasonable way along the evolutionary road."[9]

Actually the Communist Party that initially took over the police and the army, came to dominate the other key ministries as well. The minister of information and education was a communist who led the drive to capture the mass media and, through that, the Czech mind. Opposition newspapers were gradually suppressed and the recent history of the country was rewritten in a communist direction. Because the party controlled the ministries of social welfare and agriculture it fast became the source of employment for thousands of people. At the same time, the civil service was inflated in size and stuffed with communists.

Nevertheless, by the summer of 1947 the party had only succeeded in alienating whole blocs of potential voters, partly because in a democratic society the activities of the Ministry of the Interior and the police were acutely offensive to otherwise respectable people; and partly because farmers had begun to balk at the idea of collectivization; and workers were angry because communists were demanding that they increase their labor but not their salaries. National elections were slated to be held in May 1948, and everyone expected the Communists to be soundly defeated.

The deterioration in the climate of East-West relations in the spring and summer of 1947 and the related changes in Soviet policy toward its sphere of influence precipitated the crisis that would snuff out Czech independence for the next forty years.

When the Czech government unanimously accepted the invitation of the

United States to participate in the Marshall Plan, Stalin, who feared the entry of democratic forces into Eastern Europe, stopped it cold. The Soviet Union, Stalin told a shaken Gottwald, would never allow the Czechs to be used as an instrument against the Soviet Union. At Stalin's insistence the Czechs obediently complied and withdrew their acceptance.

At the first Cominform meeting in September 1947, Zhdanov pointedly said that the Soviet victory over Nazi Germany had helped to bring about "the complete victory of the working class over the bourgeoisie in every East European land except Czechoslovakia, where the power contest still remains undecided." The implication was clear. It was now time for the Czech communists to accelerate their drive for nailing down total power in their country. The Czech Communist Party archives which were opened during the Prague Spring of 1968 showed that Stalin gave up the whole idea of a parliamentary path for the Czechs when the Communist parties of France and Italy faltered in 1947 and 1948.

The Czech representative at the Cominform meeting, Rudolph Slansky, returned to Prague with a plan to proceed to the final acquisition of power. According to the plan, the security forces were to crush the party's enemies and purge all dissident teachers, students, priests, and civil servants. "As in the international field," said Slansky, "we have gone on the offensive on the domestic front as well."

In early February 1948, the communist minister of the interior, Vaclav Nosek, attempted to purge what remained non-communist in the National Police Force. On February 12, the non-communists in the cabinet demanded that this subversion cease but Nosek, backed by Gottwald, refused. On February 21, twelve of these ministers resigned in protest. They assumed all along that President Benes would refuse to accept their resignations, thereby embarrassing the communists enough to make them back down. But in an atmosphere of mounting tension, and with massive communist-led demonstrations occurring throughout the country, Benes felt that he must remain neutral over the issue, lest the communists foment an insurrection and provide the Red Army with an excuse to invade his country and restore order.

While the non-communist ministers seemed to behave as if this was just an old-fashioned pre-1939 governmental crisis, the communists were mobilizing from below. To help them do this the Soviet Ambassador, Valerian Zorin, arrived in Prague to arrange a coup. Communist "Action Committees" and trade union militias were quickly organized, armed, and sent into the streets. In a speech before 100,000 of these people, Klement Gottwald threatened a general strike unless Benes agreed to form a new communist-dominated government. Zorin at one point offered the services of the Red Army which was camped on the country's borders, but Gottwald wisely declined the offer. He understood that the threat of violence combined with lots of political pressure was sufficient to force Benes's hand. As he said when it was all over, Benes "knows what strength is, and this led him to evaluate this [situation] realistically."

On February 25, 1948, Benes capitulated and appointed a communist-controlled government under Gottwald's leadership. The only important post in the new cabinet that went to a non-communist (Jan Masaryk) was the Ministry of Foreign Affairs. Two weeks later, however, Masaryk was found dead, probably assassinated by the communists. Consumed by these events, Benes soon resigned the presidency thereby allowing Gottwald to take his place. In September 1948, Benes died, bestowing a sense of finality on the whole sequence of events. He was buried before an enormous and silent throng who were there to mourn not only the passing of a popular leader, but also the democracy he had come to represent.

For millions of people in the West, the Czech coup of 1948 became synonymous with the Cold War. The loss of Eastern Europe's only democracy came as a profound shock to millions of people. For the second time in a decade Czech independence and democracy had been extinguished by a totalitarian dictatorship bent on dominating a small and decent country. To people everywhere, it seemed that history was repeating itself. Because the Soviet Union now seemed to have completed the formation of a monolithic Soviet bloc in Eastern Europe and concluded the partition of Europe, it seemed to vindicate the pessimistic appraisals of Soviet power in the West on the part of people who felt certain that cooperation with the Soviet Union was clearly unrealistic. And because it was as horrifying to Western Europeans as it was to Americans, it helped to unify the Western world against the communist countries. It also made the governments of France and Italy appear very prescient in having driven the communists out of their administrations.

The impact of the Czech coup in the United States was immediate. A shocked and aroused public opinion succeeded in overwhelming the opposition that had developed in the U.S. Congress toward the Marshall Plan. Congress promptly approved over five billion dollars for the first year of the European Recovery Program.

Until the Czech coup Washington placed its emphasis in the Cold War on the economic containment of communism, the main instruments of which were the Truman Doctrine and the Marshall Plan and a heavy reliance on atomic power as a shield to support it. Truman understood that in 1946 and 1947 the American people were not prepared for either a massive conventional arms buildup or a confrontation with the Soviet Union so soon after the Second World War. This was why he had not acted immediately on the Clifford Report, despite his general agreement with its conclusions. For similar reasons he was reluctant to increase the military budget dramatically and opted instead for a gradual and balanced buildup. With the large economic outlays expected to come through the Marshall Plan, Truman sought to keep the annual defense budget below $15 billion.

But the Czech coup served to expose the limitations of U.S. conventional military forces, and Washington's overreliance on atomic power. During the crisis in Prague roughly ten ill-equipped and poorly trained U.S. and West European divisions lamely faced more than thirty Soviet divisions in Eastern and Central Europe. Moreover, the Department of Defense complained that the U.S. atomic arsenal and the airpower to use it were woefully inadequate. Lagging behind the policy of economic containment, Washington lacked a credible military deterrent in Europe.

The Czech coup changed the whole tenor of the debate on the U.S. military budget. It helped spark a renewed effort in lobbying on the part of the Pentagon for a substantial rise in the military budget, while at the same time the NSC called for "a worldwide counter-offensive" against the Soviet bloc, including U.S. military aid to the West European Union.[10]

Truman responded to the crisis with a renewed call for selective service, which had been allowed to lapse the year before. He also sought congressional authorization for a program of Universal Military Training (UMT). It was Truman's aim to send a signal of determination to the Soviet Union that its military posture was a strong one and that the United States with this expansion of military preparedness was also prepared in the future to rearm massively if necessary. Congress did not approve UMT, but it did vote to resume selective service, and it did vote the money for a seventy group air force, 25 percent larger than the official request. The remobilization of the U.S. armed forces had begun.

At the very moment the Czech coup seemed to establish Stalin's monolithic rule over Eastern Europe, the Yugoslav communists were falling out of step with Moscow and creating serious difficulties for the Soviet dictator.

To many communists across Eastern Europe the founding of the Cominform and the ideological and economic tightening up in the bloc was greeted warmly. the Yugoslav communists were, from the beginning, a highly visible exception. Communists in most of the bloc countries were an insecure minority; the Yugoslavs were not. The Soviet authorities already had misgivings about Tito and his fellow communists and this was probably the reason why the headquarters of the Cominform was placed in Belgrade and not elsewhere in the bloc, so as to keep an eye on a potential rebel.

From the German invasion of the Balkans in 1941 Tito had asked to be treated differently. Unlike many bloc leaders, Tito was not a "Muscovite" who spent the war years in Russia dogmatically supporting Stalinism and waiting for the first chance to return to his capital behind a wave of Russian tanks. Instead, Tito was a so-called "national communist," a man who spent the duration of the struggle in Yugoslavia building a national resistance movement of partisans, who at their peak numbered 800,000. Moreover, when he began to construct that movement the Soviet Union was not yet in the war and still allied with Nazi Germany. He was the only communist leader in Europe who succeeded in doing this during the war. Tito from the beginning was acutely conscious that he and his movement were on their own. "I felt myself to be an independent leader from the very beginning in 1941," he later recalled. "I felt completely independent, especially when we saw that nobody would help us and we were on our own."[11]

Tito received a big boost in his wartime effort, not from the Russians who were rather stingy with their aid, but from the British who in 1943 decisively switched their support from the royalist General Mihailovich to the partisans as the only real anti-German force in the region.

Tito displayed a shrewd grasp of war and politics in the Balkan setting.

Possessing the stature to forge a strong national authority, he did not appeal to the Yugoslav people on a strictly ideological basis (any more than Stalin did), but on a popular front basis. The man who would later coin the term "people's democracy" played down Marxism-Leninism and instead emphasized traditional patriotism and nationalism. Eschewing communist propaganda at the beginning of the war, he resorted to it rather heavily wherever his army liberated territory from the Germans and began to govern it as a small state. Only then did the communists impose their ideas on the population and try to put into practice their political theories.

Composed mostly of peasants, the Yugoslav Communist Party was not cast in the Leninist mould. Like the Chinese Communist Party whose effort during the war resembled their own, the partisans came to communism during and as a result of an intense national experience, when the interest of their country, rather than the interest of world communism and the Soviet Union was paramount for them. Like Mao-Tse-Tung, Tito created a revolutionary army and not just a resistance movement.

Tito and Stalin quarrelled continually during the war and almost always over aid. Tito was particularly bitter about the small amount of aid he was being given, especially in view of the fact that he was fighting both a war against the Germans and a civil war against Mihailovich and the Cetniks. Stalin was not forthcoming with much aid because he considered the partisan war in the Balkans to be a mere sideshow. And so he consistently devalued Tito's reports and pleas for aid with a monumental ignorance.

Because of the accidents of war, Yugoslavia was fortunate not to be subjected to a Russian occupation. In the last stage of the war the Red Army immediately withdrew to fight on other fronts and so Tito could remain strong and independent in his own right and his country never had to suffer satellization like other bloc countries. Because of the accident of geography, Yugoslavia lay on the western border of the Soviet sphere of influence and thus enjoyed the possibility of direct relations with the West. Yugoslavia was unique in one more critical way; Tito and his partisans had succeeded in creating their own state machine without the benefit of Russian input, and just as important, he got Stalin to agree that Soviet forces should have no administrative powers in Yugoslavia. Consequently, Tito had his own power base from which he could act independently in the world. It was this independence of Tito and the partisans, and their successful attempt to shape their own national liberation, which was basically incompatible with total acceptance of Russian authority.

There was also a curious personal element in the clash of the two regimes. During and after the war, while Tito displayed an unquestioned loyalty to Stalin as one of the giants of twentieth-century communism, he never showed him the unctuous respect the other communists throughout the bloc did. An old Comintern agent who had struggled in the communist movement since 1917, Tito took a rather romantic view of the revolution and the struggle of the working class. Like Stalin he had come to view himself as a man of destiny who was entitled to assume ever greater responsibilities. Like Milovan Djilas, Tito felt ill at ease in the company of the Russians and offended by their personal behavior. Once after a Kremlin state dinner, Tito remarked, "I don't know what the devil is wrong with these Russians that they drink so much—plain decadence."[12] It is clear that while Tito admired the communist system and regarded the Soviet Union as his doctrinal homeland, he did not think the Russian version was the best example of a communist polity.

The animus between Stalin and Tito grew worse after 1945. There were two sources for this friction that led eventually to the final break. The first sprang from the domestic arrangements the Yugoslavs made to rejuvenate their economy. The Yugoslav industrialization and collectivization followed the Soviet model closely, but without Soviet interference. Of all the bloc countries, it was only in Yugoslavia that there was resistance to Moscow's attempt to form satellite economies on behalf of the Soviet Union. At the same time, the Yugoslavs resented Soviet attempts to penetrate their party, army, police, and economic agencies. After all, what distinguished national communists like Tito was their belief that a communist's first loyalty after coming to power was to his own country. They felt responsible to their own people and were bitter about Russian attempts to exploit them. Tito's argument against Marshall Plan aid—that it would subvert his regime and make Yugoslavia a puppet of the United States—was also used by him against the Russian attempt to draw his country ever closer economically to the Soviet Union. Meanwhile, in a growing war of words that touched Yugoslavian pride, Moscow claimed that the partisan role in the war was nothing but a myth, and that it was the Red Army that had really liberated Yugoslavia.

The other source of friction sprang from Tito's view of himself as the foremost of the communist leaders in Eastern Europe. The war had transformed Tito from an armed revolutionary and guerrilla leader into a regional leader, and Tito revelled in his new role. From well back in the war Stalin had been deeply suspicious of a Yugoslav leadership that was ultra-radical and intensely nationalist. Stalin from 1945 watched with alarm as Tito made every attempt to project his image and his strategic influence to other areas of the Balkans.

Tito displayed a belligerent nationalism in 1945 when he had his army "liberate" Trieste. He had made it clear during the war that Trieste and its hinterland, as well as Zara, Fiume, and Istria, were ethnically and historically Yugoslav lands. The angry deadlock between Tito and the West over who actually controlled Trieste, which lasted for some weeks, was broken when Stalin withdrew his support and the Yugoslavs withdrew from Trieste. The Russians, of course, were worried about the reaction of the Italian communists if they backed Tito, and they were not ready for a confrontation with their Western allies. Tito felt that the Russians had let him down and cheated him out of something that was rightfully Yugoslav. Thinking the "percentages agreement" of 1944 was responsible for it all, Tito rebuked the Russians in a speech following the crisis. "We do not wish to be used as small change in international bargaining," he said.[13] Tito's behavior during this episode won him the support of millions of his countrymen, but strong disapproval from Moscow.

Tito and Stalin were also at loggerheads over the Greek rebellion. On his own initiative Tito had extended considerable help to the Greek rebels. Stalin, who in 1944 acknowledged that Greece lay within the British sphere of influence, and who was reluctant to confront the West over an area it deemed vital to its security, angrily ordered the aid to the rebels to stop.

Ever since the war ended Tito had taken the lead in establishing close relations with the other "people's democracies." He made a point of visiting most of these countries and in each case he had been given a hero's welcome. It was this growing influence in Eastern Europe that led him to propose a Balkan federation.

The idea of uniting Yugoslavia, Albania, and Bulgaria into a Yugoslav federal union was an old idea in the communist world and one that Tito thought Stalin might approve of. Rather than endorse it, however, Stalin squelched the idea and scolded the Yugoslavs and Bulgarians for having taken any initiative in the direction of foreign policy. In a Kremlin meeting with George Dimitrov of Bulgaria and Edvard Kardelj of Yugoslavia, Stalin treated his guests to an angry monologue in which he ominously proposed a federation in Eastern Europe linked to the Soviet Union. Stalin may not have been altogether serious about this, but the Yugoslavs believed that in the back of Stalin's mind was the idea that all of Eastern Europe should be included in some fashion in the Soviet Union. Moreover, there was a growing awareness in Belgrade that to create a truly monolithic Soviet bloc, Stalin was compelled to subjugate Yugoslavia. In this seemingly one-sided struggle, it was felt that Stalin anticipated an easy victory.[14]

In February 1948, Tito was summoned to an urgent meeting in Moscow. Tito pleaded ill health and refused to go. Enraged, Stalin told Khrushchev, "I will shake my little finger and there will be no more Tito." Like the measures used to destroy Czech independence, the pressures now applied to Yugoslavia revealed more than anything else the nature of communism in power.

The Russians began their campaign of intimidation by questioning Tito's loyalty to the communist bloc. In March Stalin refused to conclude a promised commercial treaty with Yugoslavia, and later that month he withdrew all Soviet military and civilian advisors from the country. In the meantime, Stalin was completing the takeover of Czechoslovakia, which from the standpoint of Belgrade appeared to be a warning to the Yugoslav communists to go carefully.

At this point, an exchange of letters between Stalin and Tito followed which served to widen the split. The correspondence revealed anger and grievances on both sides that had been building since the war. In Stalin's letters he accused the Yugoslavs of violations of Marxist-Leninist dogma, and drew exaggerated comparisons between Yugoslavian leaders and Leon Trotsky (the ultimate heretic). He accused the Yugoslavs of falsely criticizing the Soviet Union for "great power chauvinism," and he condemned the claim that Yugoslavia was the only true exponent of revolutionary socialism. He attacked the Yugoslav Communist Party for its lack of democracy, and for its alienation from its own masses. In response, Tito's letters advanced what became Tito's political credo—"No matter how much each of us loves the land of socialism, the USSR, he can in no case, love his country less, which is also developing socialism."[15]

In June 1948, Stalin called a Cominform meeting in Bucharest to discuss his differences with the Yugoslavs. Tito, claiming that he could not accept the meeting's agenda, and probably fearing arrest or even assassination, refused to attend. On June 28, Stalin ordered Yugoslavia expelled from the Cominform, and "loyal" Yugoslavs were encouraged to remove "the Tito clique" from power. Stalin almost immediately threw up an economic blockade against Yugoslavia with all the communist countries in the Cominform participating. And to give a menacing thrust to all of this, Stalin massed Soviet troops all along Yugoslavia's borders, ready to act at the first sign of popular protest.

Steel-nerved, distant, and extremely ignorant about developments in other countries, Stalin tried to create division and collapse in Yugoslavia. All his efforts failed. Instead, his attacks only served to cement the Yugoslav people behind their leader. Communists and non-communists alike had every reason to prefer Tito's rule to the more extreme form of Soviet communism. Knowing this, Tito was able to fully exploit the anti-Soviet mood of his country and for the first time render Stalin helpless against a communist opponent. As Milovan Djilas pointed out, Stalin was caught in a trap of his own making. He created his own personality cult of the leader and therefore was in no position to resist the cult of Tito, which "would serve to strengthen Yugoslavia's capacity for independent resistance."[16]

Despite Tito's political and personal triumph, the expulsion from the Cominform and the trade embargo had serious consequences for his country. By 1949, a year after the economic blockade began, Yugoslavia's imports from the Soviet bloc declined drastically. Tito and his party were intensely Marxist and since the war had adopted an extremely belligerent attitude toward the capitalist West. But with their country so politically and economically ostracized, the moment called for a very pragmatic change in the way Belgrade conducted its affairs. This shift moved in both an ideological and economic direction.

The Yugoslavs at first framed their defense (and attack) in an ideological way. Tito and his advisors formulated a communist ideology quite different from the one they were reared on. Reacting to a Stalinism based on the total centralization of power from above, the Yugoslavs attacked the Soviet bureaucracy as a serious obstacle between the government and the people. In an analysis that resembled Trotsky's in *The Revolution Betrayed* (1937), the Yugoslavs labelled Stalinism a bureaucratic perversion and accused it of deviating from Marxism-Leninism and of causing the revolution to degenerate. In its place the Yugoslavs emphasized the concepts of decentralization and power from below.

Second, the Yugoslavs practiced what they preached. Despite the fact that most decision making was still retained in Belgrade, the party was no longer the sole authority at the local level of society. Decision making was increasingly assumed by local communes and worker's councils in industry, with workers given a greater voice in the management of their factories. Tito gradually introduced the market forces of supply and demand and profit in the running of the country's factories. In other words, Tito had, under the intense pressure from Moscow, opened another road to socialism, and one that eventually provided a model for many developing countries as well as an inspiration for other countries in the Soviet bloc.

Yugoslavia was also forced to turn to the West for its capital resources and much of its trade. American aid and trade, comprising 34 percent of Yugoslavia's total imports, helped the country through the extremely difficult years of the economic blockade (1949-1952). In return Tito no longer advocated world revolution, but peaceful coexistence with the West. In the long run it was Yugoslav nationalism and American aid that enabled the country to withstand the Soviet economic assault and maintain its independence.

Why didn't Stalin invade? He certainly considered it, especially after Yugoslavia established ties with the United States. But Yugoslavia was not Czechoslovakia. Under democratic leaders the Czechs had a long record of accommodation with totalitarian dictators. The Yugoslavs, on the other hand, had a well-defined tradition of violent resistance to foreign intruders. Moreover, they were under a charismatic and ruthless leader who had succeeded in creating a great national resistance movement and was quite prepared to create another one. Later, Tito would explain how he was able to challenge Stalin and get away with it.

> Stalin envisaged us as being his satellites after the war. We did not even think of it as a possibility. Still in 1948 he was clever enough not to attack us when he saw what the consequences would be and he saw that we were ready to fight. He did everything possible to provoke a fight and he had his forces massed on our frontiers in case the opportunity should arise. But he recognized what the situation was in our country and he came to the right conclusion.[17]

The defeat Stalin suffered at Tito's hand did irreparable damage to Stalin's authority and prestige. Tito's successful quest for a separate road to socialism now served as an example to communists everywhere in the Soviet bloc who also chafed under the Russian yoke and who longed to establish their own autonomy. It was clear to communists throughout the bloc that there were now serious limits to Stalin's power in Eastern Europe. Tito's success shattered the Soviet claim that there was a monolithic unity and stability in the region.

This was the moment for Stalin to take stock and reassess Soviet methods for interfering in the bloc. After 1949 his interest in the Cominform certainly waned. Following the debacle with Belgrade the Cominform met only a few times and then was allowed to quietly slide into obscurity. As a command vehicle for Soviet goals, the Cominform had clearly failed. But instead of altering Soviet command methods along liberal lines to accommodate the new nationalist realities of holding the bloc together so as to avoid a repetition of Titoism, Stalin was determined to clamp down even harder in the region and cauterize the wound before the infection spread. Smarting after his worst defeat, Stalin was determined to reassert his leadership over the international communist movement.

Stalin began by declaring it treason for communists to show sympathy with Titoism, or in any way to maintain contact with Belgrade. At the same time, he cracked down ruthlessly on all the Eastern European satellite regimes. In the next three years the Stalinist terror of the 1930s was extended to all the Communist parties of Eastern Europe. Leading members of Communist parties in every bloc country were often arrested, with virtually every communist member everywhere at one time under suspicion. It has been estimated that, on the average, one out of four party members was purged throughout the bloc. Altogether some 550,000 party members were purged in Czechoslovakia, 300,000 in Poland and East Germany, and only slightly fewer in the other satellites. A key feature of this massive purge were the show trials for treason resembling in form those that sent the old Bolsheviks to their deaths in Russia in the 1930s. Vladislaw Gomulka in Poland, Laszlo Rajk in Hungary, Traicho Kostov in Bulgaria, and Rudolph Slansky in Czechoslovakia, and countless others were accused of collusion with Titoism, branded as wreckers and spies, tortured and made to publicly confess to crimes they never committed. In most cases they were then executed. It was indeed rare that a leader like Gomulka was allowed to simply draw a prison term.

Stalin also turned inward and extended the purge to Soviet society itself. The regime directed its attack against writers, scholars and artists, who it felt were guilty of "homeless cosmopolitanism," and "national nihilism." At the same time, it extended the purge to those members of his own party who Stalin thought politically suspicious. In this assault Andrei Zhdanov died mysteriously in 1948 and his chief supporters were arrested and shot. The details of this so-called Leningrad Affair are still obscure.

In the purge that took place between the events in Czechoslovakia and Yugoslavia in 1948 and the death of Stalin in 1953, Moscow aimed at complete conformity within the Soviet bloc. It sought to create a true Soviet-dominated monolith in which the national interests and differences of the individual states were suppressed, and the absolute priority of Soviet interests were made permanent. In what must be considered as stage four in the Sovietization of Eastern Europe, the system was reinforced by the presence of tens of thousands of Soviet personnel—troops, military commissars, economic experts, diplomats, and secret policemen. In the meantime, the satellites were sealed in from the West by a rigid "Iron Curtain."

In the Czech crisis Stalin feared the seepage of democratic values into the Soviet bloc. With the Yugoslav crisis he feared that Belgrade's autonomy posed a direct threat to Soviet hegemony in the region. Developments in Czechoslovakia and Yugoslavia exposed what in normal times could easily be hidden—the inherent instability and fragility of the Soviet communist system.

Notes

1. Hugh Seton-Watson, *The Pattern of Communist Revolution* (London: Methuen, 1953), 248-56.

2. Strobe Talbott, ed., *Khrushchev Remembers* (Boston: Little, Brown and Company, 1970), 361.

3. Zbigniew K. Brzezinski, *The Soviet Bloc. Unity and Conflict* (Cambridge, Mass.: Harvard University Press, 1960), 65.

4. Teresa Toranska, *"Them." Stalin's Polish Puppets*, trans. A. Kolakowska (New York: Harper and Row, 1987), 353.

5. Cited in Charles Gati, *The Bloc That Failed. Soviet-East European Relations in Transition* (Bloomington: Indiana University Press, 1990), 24.

6. Jacques Rupnik, *The Other Europe* (London: Weidenfeld and Nicolson, 1988), 87.

7. Vojtech Mastny, *Benes-Stalin-Molotov Conversations in December 1943: New Documents* (New York: Columbia University Press, 1983).

8. Michael Charlton, "On the Origins of the Cold War. The Eagle and the Small Birds," *Encounter* (1983), 49.

9. Eduard Benes, *Memoirs* (Boston: Houghton Mifflin, 1954), 285.

10. Michael J. Lacey, ed., *The Truman Presidency* (Cambridge: Cambridge University Press, 1989), 221.

11. Phyllis Auty, *Tito. A Biography* (London: Penguin Books, 1980), 213.

12. Milovan Djilas, *Conversations with Stalin* (New York: Harcourt, Brace and World, 1961), 115.

13. Auty, *Tito*, 287.

14. Vladimir Dedijer, *The Battle Stalin Lost. Memoirs of Yugoslavia 1948-1953* (New York: Viking Press, 1971), 33-34.

15. Gale Stokes, ed., *From Stalinism to Pluralism. A Documentary History of Eastern Europe since 1945* (New York: Oxford University Press, 1991), 58-65.

16. Milovan Djilas, *Tito: The Story from the Inside* (New York: Harcourt, Brace, Jovanovich, 1980), 30.

17. Quoted in Auty, *Tito*, 297.

10

The Berlin Blockade
and the Formation of NATO

It is a truism in international relations that dire circumstances often give birth to extremely desirable and beneficial developments. In terms of postwar Europe this meant that the social chaos and the Cold War tensions that arose in the late 1940s gave an impetus to the political integration of Europe and eventually led to tremendous economic growth and continental stability. Even though the Soviet leadership was trained to think dialectically and was expected to understand something of this process, it nevertheless drew the wrong conclusions. This was so because men like Stalin traditionally viewed politics, society, economics, and even war itself, through the lenses of the class struggle and the correlation of forces, and not in terms of the historical clash between competing states and the balance of power between them. Thinking dialectically, they assumed that the dire circumstances in which Europe found itself would produce the socialist continent that Marx and Lenin had dreamed of. And had it not been for the intervention of the United States in the problems of the postwar world, they might have been right. What Moscow failed to appreciate was that in testing the American will in those states that were normally viewed as bastions of Western civilization, the United States would come to define its security in the broadest terms, that its resolve would therefore stiffen, and that the dialectical forces of history would ultimately turn against the Soviet Union.

The lessons of this were learned by Stalin and then relearned by his successors through trial and error. Khrushchev, for example, despite his belief in the class struggle, showed some understanding when he said in the 1960s, "If a man sticks out a bayonet and strikes mush, he keeps on pushing. But when he hits cold steel, he pulls back." The Berlin Blockade was a classic example of what Khrushchev meant.

The Marshall Plan was intended to provide Western Europe with enough economic steel to resist the pressure of domestic communism. Economic containment in this case was meant to be an alternative to a military solution. But it should have been clear to the Russians that there was a short and logical step from an economic strategy to a military alliance. And the initiative for such an alliance came not from the United States but originally from Washington's Western European allies.

European coalitions in the past were usually grouped around one power that had the will, the experience, and the economic resources to maintain continental resistance against the threatening state. In the threats to the balance of power following the Thirty Years' War of the seventeenth century, Britain led the coalitions that eventually checked French and German expansionism. It could play this role because it was realistic enough to assess the foreign situation as it was, and as it might be. In November 1944 when Winston Churchill proposed an Anglo-French military alliance to Charles De Gaulle, there was no longer any one country in Europe that could play that role.

Churchill was more than aware that British and French confidence in the international arena had flagged as their power had obviously waned. There was in Churchill's suggestion for an alliance a recognition of this weakness as there was a fear of the revival of German power. Churchill was asking De Gaulle to recognize that there was a new power constellation in the world and that their two countries recognize that a community of aims existed between them. At the time De Gaulle rebuffed the offer, wanting to instead wait until the future of Germany was settled.

By late 1946 Léon Blum was briefly premier of France and much more amenable to such an alliance. Blum understood that the economies of France and Britain were in a shambles and he was looking for a political success to counterbalance economic weakness. At this point the two governments agreed to enter into negotiations to conclude a treaty of alliance. In March 1947 (the month the Truman Doctrine was issued) Ernest Bevin and Georges Bidault arrived at Dunkirk (the scene of the lowest point of Anglo-French fortunes in the war) to sign a mutual defense treaty. The two governments pledged that their nations would remain allies "for all time." The vagueness of the language recalled the Anglo-French Entente of 1904. Like that earlier understanding the agreement of 1947 was less than specific in its terms and less binding in its obligations. Nevertheless, both signees, and those states that joined thereafter, came to feel that they had no future without it. What made the alliance grow and become stronger were the economic and political crises—the recurring crises of the 1940s and 1950s that gave the Western alliance a renewed lease on life. Like the diplomatic combinations that led to the Triple Entente of 1907, this was a traditional response to a threatening state—Germany in 1907 and the Soviet Union in 1947. In other words, this rather emotional signing on the beach at Dunkirk and what would naturally follow from it, represented the seminal moment in the subsequent formation of NATO two years later.

Originally a bilateral pact between two neighbors trying to cope with internal disorder and worried about the Soviet peril, it soon became, under the force of circumstances, the first multilateral military pact of the postwar era. And the catalyst for this diplomatic arrangement was the Czech coup of February 22, 1948.

Despite the fact that the Czech coup did not itself mean that the Soviet Union was going to hurl its army into Western Europe, the governments of the region and the Truman administration were sufficiently alarmed to believe that it might. Under the shadow of the events in Prague, Paris and London pressed the United States for a military alliance.

All through 1947 Ernest Bevin had worked diligently toward extending the Dunkirk Pact to something much broader and substantial. He had been alarmed by the Eastern European states not entering into the Marshall Plan as he was of the purge of the old Social Democratic parties that was taking place throughout the Soviet bloc. He was also alarmed at the Greek civil war being stepped up at that moment and he was worried about the crisis in France and Italy. Bevin now began to talk of the creation of an Atlantic security system that would stretch from Greenland and Newfoundland to the Azores and Casablanca. Less than two weeks after the Prague coup he was warning that "The cardinal error is ever to let them (the communists) in a Government in the vain hope that they will play the game according to Westminster rules." He also made it clear to the Americans and anyone else who would listen that inadequate defense spending would demoralize friends and allies and lead them to think that communism was the wave of the future.

Statesmen like Bevin were preoccupied not only with European economic recovery, but even more so with European security. In a memorandum he wrote on March 3 entitled "The Threat to World Civilization" he drew the dramatic picture of how the Russians aimed to secure "physical control . . . of the whole World Island."[1] When Bevin broached the subject of a military alliance in late 1947 he meant a Western democratic system which included the Americans, the French, the Italians, and the British dominions. He was not thinking of a formal alliance, but an understanding backed by American power and money and the political will of all its members. It resembled the traditional coalitions of the past but with the biggest punch coming from outside Europe. He made it clear that an entente like this would send the clearest signal to Moscow that Soviet advancement was at an end.

The United States had already signed in September 1947 a permanent defensive alliance with what would eventually include twenty-one Latin American republics. The Rio Treaty was designed to repel aggression originating both inside and outside the hemisphere. In the spring of 1948 the signees endowed this alliance with a formal political structure by transforming the Pan American Union into the Organization of American States (OAS). While the Latin American members viewed the OAS from the beginning as a multilateral mechanism for the maintenance of regional security, the United States came to view it, especially after the outbreak of the Korean War, as a regional security system defending the free world against Soviet expansionism. At the same time, Truman's speech of March made it abundantly clear that, while Latin America was important to the United States, it was in Europe that the real battles of the Cold War promised to be won or lost. As the U.S. ambassador to Brazil declared, Europe suffered from "a case of smallpox," while Latin America only had "a common cold."

By the time of the Czech coup in early 1948 the European continent had been split into two political and economic blocs. Until this point, Western and Soviet representatives had communicated in regular convocations at the foreign minister level. By removing the last link between East and West the Czech coup constituted the final rupture in relations between the two superpowers.

Western Europe now signalled its determination to commit itself to collective self-defense. The concept of European unity now flourished as it had not done for generations. In March 1948, five European nations—Britain, France, the Netherlands, Belgium, and Luxembourg (the latter three collectively designated as Benelux) signed the Brussels Pact to extend their mutual defense. Much stronger than the Rio Treaty, it provided for an "automatic" military response to an act of aggression against any of the signatories. The pact was to last for fifty years. The Brussels Pact nations would, of course, have been too weak to resist Russia alone and so they assumed that the support and protection of the United States would, in an emergency, be forthcoming. The signatories of the pact, popularly known as the Western Union, also pledged themselves to economic, social, and cultural collaboration—and not just to collective self defense. When Ernest Bevin first raised the idea for such a coalition with George Marshall, the secretary of state encouraged the effort but made it clear that any such combination would of necessity be European and that the United States, while willing to extend material assistance to it, would nevertheless remain outside the alliance. Like Marshall, President Truman was also anxious about adhering to such an alliance lest it complicate congressional approval of the European recovery program by interjecting the security problem. The Marshall Plan had been designed to draw Western Europe closer to the United States economically, but Washington in early 1948 was reluctant to add a military dimension to the relationship. Congress also disapproved of a military alliance especially when Marshall Plan legislation was still pending. At the same time, the Joint Chiefs of Staff were concerned about the virtual exhaustion of the Second World War stocks of equipment. In early 1948 the Americans were simply not enthusiastic about an open-ended security commitment to Western Europe. This was why, when Washington opened exploratory talks with Britain and Canada in March 1948 on the establishment of an Atlantic Pact, the talks were really designed on the American side to improve European morale and combat Communist subversion in Western European countries. Truman had to go carefully because 1948 was an election year and he was well down in the opinion polls. The feeling in the White House was that big military spending, coming on top of Marshall Plan spending, would sink him in the election.

But support for a new international role for the United States had been growing in Congress. Arthur Vandenberg, a staunch advocate of bipartisanship in the U.S. Senate, took the initiative and drafted a Senate resolution on June 11, 1948, that opened the way for U.S. participation in an Atlantic Pact. He and other senators believed that the time had come for the United States to abandon its traditional policy of remaining aloof from European coalitions. The Vandenberg Resolution permitted the president to develop regional arrangements for collective defense, and it stressed the need to work within the U.N. Even though the resolution did not authorize a blank check for European rearmament, Truman was now able to carry the American public and Congress in the policy of underwriting the creation of a Western European defense community.

This trend toward military preparedness and trans-Atlantic cooperation in security matters was now given its greatest boost by the head-on collision between the Soviet Union and the West in what was always one of the most important battlegrounds of the Cold War: Germany.

As we have seen in chapter eight, the division of Germany was not deliberate but followed from the existence of military sectors originally set up to administrate the country. When allied unanimity and the Potsdam plan for eventual German unification broke down, the lines of occupation became lines of partition.

In 1945 Stalin set all Berlin clocks to Moscow time and began clamping down on his zone in Germany as he did everywhere else in the Soviet bloc. From the Potsdam Conference on the Soviets had sought to profit from their military control of the eastern part of Germany by forcibly extracting the reparations allocated to them by mutual agreement of their wartime allies. They also reneged on their pledge to supply agricultural products from their zone to the western zones in exchange for industrial plant.

This made the situation even more desperate than it was. Throughout Germany, while millions of people lived amid the rubble of war, the cigarette had replaced the Reichsmark as the prevailing unit of monetary exchange. Food rations in the western zones were originally set at 1,500 calories daily, but soon fell to 900, well below the normal requirement. In the bitter winter of 1946-1947 there were hunger marches in many urban areas, as there were large strikes and increasingly violent demonstrations. By 1946 the U.S. Army of occupation was spending one billion a year in relief funds to feed the hungry population.

In late 1946 ex-President Herbert Hoover was asked by the White House to investigate the food needs of twenty-two countries. He found the situation in Germany the most desperate of all. A good deal of the policy that President Truman subsequently pursued in Germany was based on Hoover's report, which was submitted on February 27, 1947.

The Hoover Report called the housing situation in Germany "the worst that modern civilization has ever seen," and the death toll among the elderly "appalling."[2] West Germany, it claimed, faced famine in food and coal and it pointed out that 30 percent of German babies were dying before they reached their first birthday. The report helped convince Washington that the German economy was vital to the economic recovery of Europe as a whole and that the German people had to be allowed to earn their own way. The report therefore called for the German retention of the Ruhr, the Saar, and the Rhineland, much to the annoyance of the French and the Russians who were thinking of ways to keep the Germans weak. It also recommended that the removal of war plants for reparations be stopped immediately and that German capital equipment be used for productive purposes since it was vital for European revival.

The Western allies (dragging the French with them) were determined to bring the collapsed German economy to its feet again. In an attempt to get western Germany organized economically the Western allies agreed to fuse their three zones and to integrate the new entity into a Western European community linked to the United States. In the spring of 1948 a conference of the Brussels Pact nations and the United States held in London invited the Germans to elect delegates to a constitutional convention that would create a new government for West Germany. Pursuant to this decision, the Western allies introduced a major currency reform in June 1948 to stabilize the Reichsmark. The reform repudiated 90 percent of the currency then circulating and substituted for it a new and more sound Deutschmark, backed by American financial power under the Marshall Plan. The economic effects of this reform were almost immediate—the German "economic miracle" had begun.

The political and economic reforms and the growing revival of west German fortunes had begun in the industrialized part of Germany, which contained three-fourths of the country's population. This had made Stalin very uneasy. He told General Walter Bedell Smith that he feared that the recent events in the western zones were a prelude to their political integration in the form of a west German state dependent on and loyal to the United States.[3] Such a prospect could not fail to alarm the Russians. A new, revived, and possibly irredentist west German state integrated in the West would menace Russian influence in eastern Germany and perhaps elsewhere in Eastern Europe. Had the Russians been more clever they could have exploited divisions in the West. Many Germans were critical of the formation of a separate west German state because they saw that it would lead to the permanent partition of their country. There was also some anxiety in France about an economic resurgence in a country that Frenchmen had come to fear. Instead of diplomatically exploiting the divisions, Moscow decided to bring the whole German problem to crisis by blockading Berlin.

Restrictions on the flow of western traffic to Berlin actually began in small ways as early as January 1948 and were then gradually stepped up in the next few months. As early as April General Clay warned the Pentagon that "extension of the blockade to cut food off from the German population might succeed in forcing us out. . . ." In his warning he used a domino argument to make his point:

> When Berlin falls, Western Germany will be next. If we mean . . . to hold Europe against communism, we must not budge. . . . If we withdraw, our position in Europe is threatened. If America does not understand this now, does not know the issue is cast, then it never will and communism will run rampant. I believe the future of democracy requires us to stay.[4]

On June 24, 1948, the Russians threw up a full blockade around Berlin cutting off access to the city, as well as electric current and all deliveries of food and coal. The blockade trapped two and a half million west Berliners with enough food for thirty-six days and enough coal for forty-five days. Russia had challenged the West at its most vulnerable point.

Until 1948 Berlin had never been terribly important to the West. In the closing days of the war, General Eisenhower had advised against the Western Allies taking Berlin ahead of the Russians. As he informed Washington, "May I point out that Berlin is no longer a particularly important objective." The Joint Chiefs of Staff agreed, and so did President Truman, and Berlin was instead conquered by the Russians. With Berlin thereafter in the Soviet zone of occupation, the Allies were allowed to occupy specified sectors within the city with access to those sectors only through Russian-held territory. The western position within this isolated outpost was always militarily untenable. "The city has no military value," said General Bernard Montgomery in 1948. "It is in fact a first-class military liability." And because it was, it was lightly defended. Available for immediate action were only 6,500 Allied combat troops facing 18,000 Russians in the city itself and an estimated 300,000 nearby. Stalin understood this predicament and so thought the risk worth taking, since it was unlikely that the Western Allies with such inferior military forces would take the initiative and force their way into the beleaguered city. In fact, with only two-and-a-half divisions in reserve, George Marshall felt that the United States needed another eighteen months to prepare for a war over Berlin.[5] This was reflected in the standing orders given to Western commanders in Germany in the event of a Russian attack—to withdraw to the Rhine and wage a defensive battle, giving up Berlin in the process.

But political considerations were just as important as military ones. It was clear that what the Soviet Union meant to do in the blockade was to put pressure on the West to drop plans for a west German government and bring them to the bargaining table with Moscow holding all the cards. If this was allowed to happen, the prestige of the West would take a devastating blow throughout the world and millions of people both inside and outside of Europe might conclude that the wave of the future lay in the East and not the West. Certainly millions of Europeans must have recalled the West's record of compromise in the 1930s and were fearful of concessions to yet another totalitarian dictator. According to opinion polls taken during the crisis, the hard-pressed Berliners themselves had little confidence in the Western Allies. The stakes, after all, in the Berlin crisis were very high. If the West did not choose to negotiate but withdrew from the city leaving millions of people to their fate, the Soviet Union would have eliminated a very embarrassing Western enclave behind the Iron Curtain and vastly consolidated the Soviet bloc, restoring the prestige within the bloc that was shaken so badly by the rift with Tito's Yugoslavia.

Considerations of prestige were certainly important in determining the course of the crisis. Once the blockade began, both Truman and Stalin became prisoners of recent history. Truman, for example, sought a rational way out of the crisis but he feared (once again in an election year) being stained with the brush of appeasement. The "Munich analogue" was used both within the political community and the media throughout the crisis. People in and out of government were more than aware that military necessity might now—like 1938—force all sorts of compromises with ideological principles. When Truman tried to break the deadlock by sending Chief Justice of the Supreme Court Fred Vinson to Moscow to talk to Stalin, it was leaked to the press and there was a public outcry. Vinson was never sent. And if Stalin had any thought of compromising, his hands were tied by Tito's challenge to his authority. Stalin too had to avoid the appearance of looking weak, lest he send the wrong message to millions of people throughout the Soviet bloc.

From the very beginning of the crisis the members of the Truman administration were very clear in their own minds as to the nature of Soviet intentions. In his memoirs, President Truman writes:

> General Lucius Clay later blamed himself for not having insisted on a confirmation of the agreement [on access] in writing. It is my opinion that it would have made very little difference to the Russians whether or not there was an agreement in writing. What was at stake in Berlin was not a contest over legal rights, although our position was entirely sound under international law, but a struggle over Germany, and in a larger sense, over Europe. In the face of our launching of the Marshall Plan, the Kremlin tried to mislead the people of Europe into believing that our interest and support would not extend beyond economic matters and that we would back away from any military risks. What the Russians were trying to do was to get us out of Berlin.[6]

At the first White House meeting to discuss the blockade the question of whether to stay in Berlin came up. Truman made it clear that there was to be no discussion of the point. "The United States is going to stay," he said. "Period."

The Truman administration interpreted the blockade as a test of American resolve and four days later it began a massive airlift of food, fuel, and other supplies into west Berlin. In Stalin's initial calculations he had made no allowance for the use of Allied air power. Soviet officials were quite sure that Berlin could not be supplied by air and that a total economic collapse would result from the blockade. At the same time, the Soviet military was convinced that the United States was not serious about staying in Berlin, in spite of the firm public statements of U.S. generals in Germany.

There were three air corridors into Berlin and if the Russians chose to close them they could only have done so by using force. At the very beginning of the airlift the Soviet air force harassed the cargo planes, but when a British plane crashed on its approach to the city, the harassment stopped. Stalin wanted to force the West's hand, but not precipitate a war in the process. At the same time, the Soviets never withdrew their people from the Berlin Safety Center and the center continued to operate all through the blockade. In other words, Stalin did not press his advantage and acted with a great deal of caution. He had at least some evidence that if he went further he would be faced with war.

From the beginning of the crisis Truman thought of the airlift as a means of stretching existing rations in Berlin and gaining more time for diplomatic negotiations. Few in the West believed it could supply the city for very long.

George Marshall told the National Security Council in September that time was on the side of the Soviets.[7] The airlift was a brilliant improvisation but when it failed to break the deadlock more serious measures were contemplated.

Both the British and the Americans felt that a squadron of B-29 bombers must now be stationed in Britain and several in Germany. Two squadrons of B-29's were promptly dispatched to British airfields in July and a third in August. The hint was given out that they were all atomic-capable. The arrival of the planes in Britain and the knowledge that they might be carrying atomic bombs became front-page news in the British press and the British public welcomed their deployment.

The Russians might have held an advantage in conventional arms on the ground in Germany, but the United States now had acquired the capacity to deliver nuclear weapons behind the Iron Curtain. George Marshall observed that the Russians would at last have to face up to the likelihood that "the United States would really use the atomic bomb against them in the event of war." The Russians, of course, lacked superiority in the air and they had no atomic capability of their own.

Almost from the beginning of the crisis American generals in Germany were sufficiently alarmed by the blockade and its implications to seek White House approval for the use of force. It was General Clay's idea to form an armed Anglo-American convoy of 200 trucks escorted by three infantry divisions to force the blockade. Clay's argument throughout the crisis was that the Russians thought an airlift too weak a response to a Soviet provocation, and so they kept up the pressure of the blockade. Clay was of the opinion that the Russians did not really want war and so forcing the blockade did not run great risks.[8] The Joint Chiefs of Staff issued a memorandum in July recommending that the armed convoy scheme be seriously considered. Truman, and eventually the Pentagon, firmly vetoed the idea of an armed convoy on the grounds that it was not justifiable to run the risk of armed conflict. While the Truman administration proceeded to seek a solution through diplomatic channels, General Curtis LeMay, commander of the U.S. Air Force in Europe, on his own initiative established strategic bases behind the American forces and behind the Rhine (he had received two squadrons of B-29's that summer) where he began stockpiling supplies. He was ready, he said, to provide air support by ordering an attack upon East German airfields. Many generals were clearly unhappy with their standing orders to fight, in the event of war, a defensive action on the Rhine, and they felt driven to take initiatives because of what they felt was the uncertainty prevailing in the White House.

The pressure on President Truman was enormous in what was one of the most dangerous crises of the Cold War. His own secretary of defense, James Forrestal, wanted Truman to authorize use of the atomic bomb. He even made the request during the summer of 1948 to hand over control of the atomic bomb to his department. Truman refused and kept control of the bomb firmly in his own hands. Support for a nuclear solution, in the event of armed conflict, came from the NSC, which warned Truman that the refusal to use the bomb would only encourage Soviet aggression and demoralize America's European allies who were counting on American strength and the will to use it. When Secretary of the Army Kenneth Royall went so far as to urge a preemptive nuclear strike against the Soviet Union during the height of the crisis, Truman made it clear where he stood and how much he had changed since 1945. He said "You have got to understand that this isn't a military weapon. It is used to wipe out women and children and unarmed people, and not for military uses. You have got to understand that I have got to think about the effect of such a thing on international relations. This is no time to be juggling an atom bomb around."[9]

As the crisis grew the martial spirit grew among the American people. The Russians, after all, had miscalculated and made a serious propaganda blunder. Their use of starvation as a tool of foreign policy was never popular in the Western world, much less in the United States. When the American public was polled in 1948 on whether the United States should use force to break the blockade, 86 percent responded yes, and only 8 percent said no. "I have a terrible feeling," Truman recorded in his diary, "that we are very close to war."

Truman's advantage all along had been his country's nuclear monopoly and, no less important, the indomitable spirit of the people of Berlin. The Berliners were always of two minds about the blockade. On one hand, they felt that the West was not being forceful enough in removing the blockade; and on the other, they showed themselves quite willing to suffer the privations of the blockade—notably the lack of heating, light, and work—so as to avoid falling under communist rule. Tens of thousands of Berliners attended rallies to show their resolve to stick it out, their spirits kept up by the relief flights that arrived in the city at sixty second intervals. Allied bombers by October 1948 were supplying Berlin with an average daily airlift of food and fuel approaching 5,000 tons.

The Berlin Blockade and the Allied effort to relieve it represented one of the great confrontation crises of the Cold War. From the beginning Truman viewed it in two ways. First, he understood that Stalin was not seeking a military contest but rather certain political objectives. And these goals could be attained by bending the American will and making Washington capitulate over the running of Berlin and West Germany. This was why Stalin did not interfere with the airlift and eventually lifted the blockade on May 12, 1949. He did this when he realized that the West would not back down and that East Germany suffered even more from the economic effects of the crisis than did West Germany.[10] And he backed down when he understood that it was the West that had scored the political victory. Second, Truman saw the blockade in terms of the larger problem—the defense of the West. His dispatch of B-29's to Europe in the summer of 1948 and the massive use of U.S. Air Force personnel to operate the airlift represented a major step in assuring America's European allies that the United States was assuming a major role in the defense of the continent, and that it was prepared to use its nuclear advantage to offset the threat of Soviet military strength. In either case, Truman understood that a withdrawal from Berlin in the face of Soviet pressure would, like the Munich crisis of 1938, constitute a political defeat of the greatest magnitude. Reining in his less cautious generals, Truman kept his head and provided sensible, decisive, and courageous leadership throughout the crisis.

The Berlin Blockade had far-reaching consequences. It succeeded in accelerating the West's plan for a separate west German state comprising the three western zones, and it provided a powerful stimulus for the integration of western Europe into a military alliance led by the United States.

During the final week of the blockade in May 1949, the Allies permitted the establishment of the Federal Republic of Germany with its capital in Bonn. It conducted its first postwar elections in August 1949, which resulted in a victory for Konrad Adenauer and his pro-Western Christian Democratic Party. At the same time, the West German Communist Party was reduced to a small splinter group. The policy pursued by Adenauer for the next fourteen years was extremely anti-communist and intensely pro-American. Indeed, the entire political leadership of West Germany was now aligned solidly with the West. Representatives of all the major political parties were absolutely clear and consistent in following Adenauer's lead in building the West German state, in maintaining West Berlin as a free outpost in communist-held territory, and in his commitment to the economic recovery of the rest of non-communist Europe. Adenauer received a big boost in governing the new West Germany because almost from the day the blockade began the German nation ceased to be treated as a former enemy. Instead, the new Federal Republic was regarded as an essential bulwark against the Soviet menace and as a vital spur to the economy of Western Europe. The blockade therefore succeeded in furthering the very developments it was intended to prevent.

The Berlin Blockade was the first postwar crisis in which the powers of Europe and the United States found themselves completely involved over a single issue. For the first time since the mid-1930s one crisis melted into another—the Czech coup, the Tito-Stalin split, the blockade, the formation of NATO, and the Korean War. From 1948 on we find Europe and the world perpetually in crisis and living in an atmosphere of universal tension.

Because the crisis took on the semblance of warfare, it confirmed the growing opinion in the United States and throughout the West that the Soviet Union was irredeemably hostile. The crisis therefore brought the United States and Western Europe as close as they had been in the Second World War, and underlined the need for aid to Europe. By the time the crisis had ended Berlin had become a symbol of firmness in the face of the most dire Soviet threats and attempts at expansion, and succeeded in forging a Western consensus about the nature of that challenge. The idea of collective security, allowed to lapse at war's end, now staged a return to allied diplomacy. This became clear early in the blockade crisis when Britain invited the United States to join her allies in military talks. General Lyman Lemnitzer arrived in Britain in a matter of days to discuss ways of improving the military capabilities of the allied armies, to give consideration to a unified headquarters in Europe, and to appoint a supreme commander. Included within this emerging security shield was the new West German state.

President Truman had for months understood that on top of feeding hungry western Europeans, the United States had to protect them as well. In Dean

Acheson's phrase, he was "the captain with the mighty heart." Nevertheless, until the blockade, the Truman administration had been extremely reluctant to participate in a European alliance. It was the Europeans, led by the British and the French, who all along pressed the United States to make such a commitment. Memories of the diplomatic disasters of the 1930s, when appeasement in Europe and isolationism and neutrality in the United States had contributed so much to Hitler's successful aggressions, added force to the impulse to build a collective bulwark against the new aggressor. It was the Europeans who pleaded for the Americans to move in and lead the alliance.

In November 1948, Truman won an astonishing election victory and his party recaptured both houses of Congress. From the events of 1946 and 1947, which led to the Truman Doctrine and Marshall Plan and from the Czech coup and the Berlin Blockade, the Truman administration had allowed public opinion to form around events, rather than appeals. In 1946 there was absolutely no thought in Washington to erect an American-led defensive alliance. By 1949 it was a reality. With the election of 1948 over, it was clear that an alliance with Europe was acceptable to the American people and that, along with the bipartisan nature of congressional support over foreign policy, Truman had a solid base to work from. With the election behind him Truman was determined that the key foreign policy goal of his second term as President was a collective-defense alliance with Europe.

Negotiations between the United States and its Western allies began in July 1948. The negotiations on the European side were undertaken by virtually the same British, French, and Benelux diplomats who had drafted the Brussels Treaty. The participation of the United States, Britain, and Canada involved all three in unprecedented peacetime defense commitments. The North American allies had never assumed advance obligations of military action in Europe, and Britain had never kept armed forces on the European continent in time of peace. The demands of the moment for all three called for a fundamental repudiation of isolationist traditions. On April 4, 1949, and one month before the Russians lifted the blockade ten European countries (Britain, France, Belgium, the Netherlands, Luxembourg, Denmark, Ireland, Norway, Italy, Portugal) joined with the United States and Canada to form the North Atlantic Treaty Organization (NATO). Greece and Turkey acceded to it in 1951, the German Federal Republic in 1955, and Spain in 1982. Appropriately the treaty was signed in Washington.

The treaty provided "that an armed attack against one or more of them in Europe or North America shall be considered an attack against them all; and consequently they agree that if such an armed attack occurs, each of them . . . will assist the Party or Parties so attacked by taking forthwith, individually and in concert with other parties, such action as it deems necessary, including the use of armed force, to restore and maintain international peace and security."[11]

The treaty also provided for the creation of an executive body, a North Atlantic Council of foreign, defense, and finance ministers. Beneath an overall commander, there were to be three separate commands controlling military units contributed by the member states: an Atlantic Command, a Channel Command, and a Central

Command supervising the European forces, including Turkey, under the direction of a Supreme Allied Commander for Europe. The treaty did not provide for the establishment of an integrated NATO force, but merely for the strategic coordination of the military actions of members of the alliance. Only under the impact of the Korean War was a standing army created under NATO command. Four days after the ratification vote in the U.S. Senate on July 21, 1949, President Truman asked for a military-aid program for NATO totalling $1.4 billion dollars to prime the pump of European rearmament.

The original assumption behind the formation of NATO was the American belief that the nuclear umbrella could prevent Moscow from trying to subvert the economic recovery and political stabilization of countries that were participants in the Marshall Plan. The original strategy that underpinned the alliance was that the NATO members would form the "shield" against an invasion from the east, while the U.S. nuclear arsenal would provide NATO with its nuclear "sword" that in a war would strike decisively against the Soviet Union. In 1949 the administration and the Congress saw the American role as limited to aid to the Europeans to enable them to defend themselves, backed up by the American nuclear monopoly. The strategy underlined the essentially defensive character of NATO whose forces were hopelessly inadequate for an attack on the Soviet Union. The American monopoly of the atomic bomb tended to freeze the territorial and military status quo during the blockade in the sense that it set a limit to how far the Russians were willing to go in ejecting the West from Berlin. But in July 1949 the Soviet Union exploded its first nuclear bomb, thus ending the U.S. nuclear monopoly that had been expected to last for years. As Senator Vandenberg wrote in his diary, "This is now a different world."

Coming as it did between the Berlin Blockade and the Korean War, the explosion of the first Russian atomic bomb helped turn NATO into something stronger than a mere defensive alliance. Thereafter the Allies, led by the United States, set out in earnest to construct a strong military force in Western Europe. At the same time, President Truman authorized work to begin on building a thermonuclear hydrogen bomb as the only way to retain the American nuclear lead over the Soviet Union.

These strategies and weapons of mass destruction were as new in the history of international conflict as was the helplessness of the traditional European powers, Britain, France, and Germany. But the way that both sides in the Cold War after 1948 came to define power in military and political terms suggests to us something of the international struggles of the past. Whether it was the French challenge to the balance of power in the Napoleonic Wars, the German challenge in the two world wars, or the face off over Berlin in 1948-1949, in each case we can see the same kind of powerful protagonists drawing the sword, the same challenge to the territorial status quo, the same kind of defensive coalition against the aggressor, followed by the same kind of dangerous arms race.

After the Czech coup no other country in Europe fell under communist rule. The communists had lost the Greek civil war, as they did the Italian, French, and

Finnish elections. By the end of the Berlin Blockade anti-communism was popular in virtually all of Western Europe. Seen from the American perspective, containment was working because the Soviet advance in Europe had been stopped in its tracks. But the Chinese communist victory of 1949 and the Korean War that followed in 1950 signalled a shift in the focal point of the Cold War from Europe to Asia. It also led to a globalization of the East-West confrontation and an intensified campaign to prepare for a third World War.

Notes

1. Quoted in C. J. Bartlett, *The Global Conflict. The International Rivalry of the Great Powers, 1880-1970* (London: Longman, 1992), 275.

2. Ann and John Tusa, *The Berlin Blockade* (London: Hodder and Stoughton, 1989), 107-8.

3. Tusa, *The Berlin Blockade*, 265.

4. Quoted in Jean Edward Smith, *The Defense of Berlin* (Baltimore, Md: Johns Hopkins University Press, 1963), 105.

5. Robert Murphy, *Diplomat among the Warriors* (Garden City, N.Y.: Doubleday and Co., 1964), 316.

6. Harry S. Truman, *Years of Trial and Hope* (Garden City, N.Y.: Doubleday and Co., 1956), 122-23.

7. W. Phillips Davison, *The Berlin Blockade. A Study in Cold War Politics* (Princeton, N.J.: Princeton University Press, 1958), 190.

8. Davison, *The Berlin Blockade*, 126.

9. Quoted in Gregg Herken, *The Winning Weapon. The Atomic Bomb in the Cold War 1945-1950* (New York: Alfred A. Knopf, 1980), 260.

10. Davison, *The Berlin Blockade*, 275.

11. Quoted in Don Cook, *Forging the Alliance. NATO, 1945-1950* (New York: William Morrow, 1989), 214.

11

The Perils of Containment:
The Korean War

In the five-year period following the end of the Second World War the United States witnessed nothing less than the unsettling of the geopolitical and socioeconomic bases of world order. This unravelling began with the collapse of German military power in 1945 and the creation of large power vacuums in Europe, which the Soviet Union tried to fill. At the same time, the erosion of British imperial power was in no small way the cause of the crisis of 1946. In early 1947 Britain announced her intention to give Burma self-government, to quit India, the jewel of her empire, by June 1948, and to send the whole Palestine problem to the U.N. This latter move served to encourage Zionist claims to statehood in the region, and in turn aroused an implacable Arab resentment toward the West in a critical area of the world.

Likewise, the Japanese role in eroding the foundations of international affairs in Asia was just as indispensable as the German role in Europe from 1939 to 1945. In 1942, for example, the Japanese victories over the French and Dutch in Southeast Asia dealt a fatal blow to those empires, and led to the proliferation of national liberation movements seeking to exploit the resulting chaos. This was the situation in Malaya, Indochina, Indonesia, Burma, and the Philippines. This transformation from empire to independence naturally put the West at a disadvantage. Marxism in an important sense attracted the future leaders of Asia precisely because its message was so anti-Western. The rapid changes and internal conflicts taking place in many societies in Asia, and the message of violence and radicalism preached against the West, seemed to fit the mood of non-Western peoples just when they were ripe for revolting against imperial dominance. Nowhere was this more evident than in China.

The Japanese role in bringing about upheaval in China was critical. Especially in the first phase of the war, the Japanese succeeded in demoralizing the Chinese bureaucracy and army, greatly weakening the upper classes, and driving the Nationalist regime from its home base. With the government absent from large stretches of China, Mao Tse-Tung found it relatively easy to substitute his own regime.

It is now a commonplace to say that time was on the side of Mao and the communists. Like Stalin in 1941, Mao succeeded in bringing about a fusion of Chinese nationalism and communism. Unlike Mao, the government under Chiang Kai-Shek never made any real military effort to recover lost territory. The longer the war lasted, the deeper and more intense the communist control of occupied areas became. By 1945 the communist army had become identified in the minds of the people with the Chinese resistance.

By the last stage of the war the United States had begun to appreciate the inherent danger in the nationalist-communist rivalry. Washington feared that it might lead to a civil war that would considerably damage the war effort against the Japanese and, at the same time, allow the Soviet Union to back the communists. The United States then strove to encourage a political settlement between the two sides while at the same time it tried to get the national government to reform itself. As it turned out, reform was hopeless and the United States placed its remaining hopes on a political settlement to which both sides at first gave their verbal assent.

With the collapse of Japanese power in 1945 the rich provinces of Manchuria and the populous and urban northeast were occupied for a time by the Russian army and opened suddenly to communist Chinese penetration. This proved to be an enormous boon to the Chinese communist army, which fought against the Nationalist army for possession of the occupied areas. The Russians collaborated with Mao's armies, turning over large stocks of captured Japanese arms and ammunition to them, even as they looted most of Manchuria's industrial plants and equipment. They also frustrated Nationalist attempts to reestablish authority over Manchuria. Strategically placed as the Russians were, they succeeded in delaying the arrival of Chiang's troops by many critical weeks. Nevertheless, the Soviet attitude toward the Chinese civil war was an ambivalent one. There is some evidence that while the Russians cut rail lines linking Manchuria to the main body of Chiang's army, and while it allowed the communists to recruit freely in Manchuria, Stalin also tried to discourage the Chinese communists from making an attempt to capture the whole country. Like the Americans, he even urged Mao to join a coalition. Only gradually did Moscow realize how powerful the Chinese communists were, and how weak and indecisive their enemies were. When it did, it moved steadily to a policy of open and firm support for the communists.

Much of Moscow's misunderstandings and underestimation of Chinese communist power was shared by the United States. Washington was almost totally ignorant of the inner nature of the communist movement in China. It did not seem to occur to anyone in the State Department that the communist movement of China, modelled as it was on Lenin's, was inherently totalitarian, and that its leadership aspired to total power as a means to effect rapid and profound changes in the social order. As late as the civil war in that country there were still officials in Washington who judged the Chinese Reds as being something other than dedicated communists. James F. Byrnes once referred to them as "so-called communists," and even Dean Acheson insisted that they were "agrarian reformers." Acheson and Byrnes were not in the minority. Washington appeared to be fooled by the growing popular support for the communists in China, and took the leadership's invocation of democratic symbols at face value. Washington seemed to act on the assumption that America's interests in Europe were a lot more essential than its stake in China; that when the smoke cleared in Asia the new communist regime would not be able to menace the United States because it would take years for China to recover and become a strong state. Forgotten was the lesson of a backward Russia between the wars rehabilitating herself and industrializing at a breathtaking pace and becoming a superpower by 1945. A closer look at the movement would have told them that Mao subscribed to the two-camps doctrine, adhered to the Comintern in the 1920s and 1930s, viewed the states of the League of Nations as capitalist enemies, and enthusiastically endorsed every move the Soviet Union had made in its foreign policy, including the Nazi-Soviet Pact. The United States was paying for the provincialism and isolationism of the interwar period.

This appalling ignorance of Chinese politics lay behind American efforts to end the civil war by forging a coalition government between Mao and Chiang, something along the lines of the tripartite governments that existed in Western Europe. For this purpose General George C. Marshall was sent to China in December 1945 to broker a similar arrangement. At first he obtained a cease-fire and encouraging signs of accommodation, but the differences between the "two Chinas" were irreconcilable. The Marshall mission was a clear indication that the United States had decided against armed intervention. This reluctance to use ground forces in China reflected the almost universal feeling of the American people. Even the most outspoken critics of the administration's policy never proposed massive intervention by the United States in China, nor could they, given the reduction of the United States military since 1945. By the summer of 1946 when the civil war had spread from Manchuria to China proper, the U.S. Army had fallen to less than two million—a decrease of over six million in nine months since the Japanese surrender. At any rate, Washington was acutely aware of the limits of American power and the internal weaknesses of Nationalist China. The Nationalist tactics were outmoded, Chiang's troops demoralized and defecting to the enemy, their society corrupt and riddled with inflation. The communists continued to recruit massively in the countryside, their army grew in numbers as a consequence, and they waged war against Chiang's army more aggressively. By October 1948 Mao's armies forced a surrender of the Manchurian garrisons. It was in Manchuria that one of the truly large wars of modern times was decided.

Franklin Roosevelt had wanted to make China one of the world's great powers for the purpose of building a postwar political order in the Far East. It was for this reason that he included China as one of the "Four Policemen." Roosevelt's objective was to make China a counterweight to Soviet power in Asia and a model for former colonial peoples seeking self-government. It was felt, at the time, that political and economic reforms would accomplish much in this direction as would a coalition government in Beijing that would be linked ideologically and economically to the United States.[1] By the time of the Truman administration Soviet expansionary behavior in Eastern Europe was linked to its role in the

Chinese civil war. The Soviet Union seemed to be exploiting revolutionary nationalism in both places. Washington's objective became "the prevention of revolutionary change linked to global Soviet expansion."[2]

President Truman did not request large-scale Marshall Plan aid and massive intervention in China in part because of the sheer size of the country and the logistical problems associated with it, and in part because he detested the leaders of the Kuomintang, the political elite of the country, who he thought represented a lost cause. "They are all thieves," he once claimed, "every last one of them." American resources were, of course, finite, and massive aid to China would have interfered with the U.S. program of containment in Europe. Maintaining stability in Europe was of primary importance and the Germans, French, and British were solid vehicles for achieving it.

The collapse of Chiang's army in 1949 was rapid and by the end of the year it had fled with its leader to the island of Formosa (Taiwan). All of mainland China was now under a new regime that rejected Western democracy and regarded Washington as the world center of imperialism and reaction.

Even before the end of the civil war, the United States had begun to distance itself from the debacle. The China White Paper, which was issued by the Truman administration in the summer of 1949, attacked the Chinese communists as tools of the Soviet Union but disclaimed any responsibility for the defeat—which it attributed to the failures of the Kuomintang. Anxious as they were to distance themselves from a losing cause, Truman and Acheson made it clear in January 1950 that U.S. forces would not be used to defend Taiwan "at this time." On the other hand, the United States refused to recognize the new government of China, even though some Western European nations did so, and instead blocked its entry into the U.N. for decades to come. At the same time, with Red China proclaiming its propaganda to all of East Asia (national liberation movements were in full course in Malaya, Indochina, Indonesia, and Burma), and with the Russians having exploded their first atomic bomb, Truman decided that the Yalta system was dead. The moment had come to make a reexamination of U.S. objectives in peace and war and the effect of those objectives on U.S. strategic plans. The result was a new approach to the rehabilitation of Japanese-American relations, the go-ahead on the development of the hydrogen bomb, and a new blueprint for U.S. postwar foreign and defense policy, known as NSC-#68.

Ever since the war the National Security Council (NSC) and the Joint Chiefs of Staff had acknowledged that Japan was of central strategic importance to U.S. security interests in the Far East. Not only was the country a potential industrial powerhouse, but it occupied an important geographical location astride the key trade routes of the North Pacific. Japan could then provide the United States "with staging areas from which to project our military power to the Asiatic mainland and USSR islands adjacent thereto."[3] It was believed that if Japan was added to the Soviet bloc the balance of power in the world would clearly shift to the disadvantage of the United States. Washington was equally aware that a weak and disarmed Japan, living as it did in the shadow of a militant communist China, gave encouragement to a native communist movement that, while still small, was nevertheless well led and aggressive. The spreading chaos on the Asian mainland heightened the importance of Japan to Washington.

Beginning in 1946, as China tumbled into civil war and revolution, the United States government introduced new reform policies in Japan to strengthen that nation in a manner similar to the rebuilding of West Germany. The reform measures helped democratize the Japanese government, expanded its educational system, and instituted sweeping land reforms. The United States throughout enjoyed the full support of Emperor Hirohito and succeeded very quickly in rebuilding Japanese self-esteem. In the process, the United States became Japan's most important export market while Japan became a model for economic modernity. What the United States succeeded in doing was creating a dynamic alternative to communism as an economic model, which in the long run served to undermine the Soviet Union's client states in Asia.

The news that Russia exploded her first atomic bomb was just as shocking in the United States as the communist conquest in China and the treaty of alliance between Mao and Stalin that followed it. Truman and Acheson had expected Mao's triumph but they thought that the Russians would not test an atomic bomb for years to come. It now was patently obvious to all Americans that they were just as vulnerable to mass destruction as the Russian people were. Equally alarming was the realization that the Russian bomb weakened the deterrent effect of United States power against a Soviet attack on Western Europe. As Gregg Herken points out, "The Russian atomic test signalled not only the end of the American nuclear hegemony but the start of the Soviet-American arms race."[4]

In January 1950 Truman asked his secretary of defense, Louis Johnson, to begin a reexamination of the Soviet Union's thermonuclear capabilities and, at the same time, he authorized research on the hydrogen bomb in an attempt to restore the United States's technological advantage.

It was clear to the White House that with the Russian bomb and the fall of China the Cold War had entered a new stage. A new approach had to be found to wage that war more effectively, one that could mobilize the American people to more vigorously support the struggle. Acheson was determined to recapture the initiative and counter the impression fostered by recent events that communism was the wave of the future. The National Security Council was now ordered to undertake a comprehensive reevaluation of American policy toward the communist world. Paul Nitze, a veteran hard-liner, was chosen to oversee this broad review of the nation's objectives in peace and war and its foreign and defense policies. The product of this investigation was a top secret document known as NSC-#68, which was submitted to the president in April 1950.[5]

From the outset, NSC-#68 asserted apocalyptically that the American people "in the ascendance of their strength stand in their deepest peril." It was clear where the danger lay. While it was true that the Soviet Union worked from no master plan, it did, however, aspire ultimately to world hegemony. It moved relentlessly toward this goal by preserving its own autocratic power base, gradually extending its control over its satellites, and trying at the same time to weaken all opposing power centers. Despite the internal weaknesses of the system—the poor agricultural output, the ugly relationship with its own people, and the stresses within its empire—the United States could expect rapid economic growth in the Soviet Union, the maintenance of a large military establishment (even as the United States demobilized), and a growth in its nuclear capability that would close the gap with the United States within a five-year period. The report made the dire prediction that the Soviet Union would have the capacity to launch an atomic attack against the United States by 1954. Furthermore, Soviet expansion was progressing "because the Kremlin was inescapably militant," fired as it was by a messianic faith that was antithetical to the American way of life. Any further extension of its area of domination "would raise the possibility that no coalition adequate to confront the Soviet Union with greater strength could be assembled." It had already subjected Eastern Europe and China and substantially eroded the U.S. power position. The authors of the report assumed a Russo-Chinese monolith that, unless stopped, would appropriate the rest of the Eurasian land mass. The original containment policy of 1947 did not go far enough and had obviously failed to stem communism's advance in the world. Next to communism's gains since the war, the United States appeared irresolute and desperate. A new global strategy which would restore the initiative to the United States and enable it to roll back the communist tide was therefore needed. Unless this was done, America's allies might drift into a dangerous neutrality or worse, the United States itself might retreat to a policy of isolation.

NSC-#68 recognized for the first time that the Soviet breaking of the U.S. nuclear monopoly had increased the possibility of piecemeal aggression. Deliberately playing down diplomacy as a means of dealing with Moscow, the authors recommended nothing less than a sweeping militarization of the Cold War in peacetime.

NSC-#68 represented a significant departure from the assumptions of the early Cold War years (1945-1949). First, it had been thought unlikely that Moscow would deliberately resort to armed aggression to secure its goals. The original containment policy was primarily political and economic and targeted at critical areas on the Soviet periphery, particularly military-industrial centers. The policy was not based on conventional forces but rather on the nuclear shield, which was supposed to reassure the American people and their allies. But the Russian bomb and the loss of China brought a radical rethinking of U.S. policy. From NSC-#68 on, the Russian threat was defined almost exclusively in military terms and containment was broadened to include everything on the Soviet perimeter.

In a very American attempt to reconcile the nation's moral convictions and its strategic responsibilities, Paul Nitze and the other authors of NSC-#68 believed that "a defeat of free institutions anywhere is a defeat everywhere," and that a vigilant and well-armed United States should be prepared to resist communist aggression wherever it occurred. They now recommended not only the prompt development of the H-bomb, but a vast increase in conventional Western rearmament which would enable the United States to wage a struggle of global dimensions. This included the erection of a vast alliance system along with a global network of military bases. Without superior strength, they argued, the policy of containment was little more than "a policy of bluff." Second, to sustain this military growth NSC-#68 called for a dramatic mobilization of the country's economic resources. Believing that a strong foreign policy dictated great military strength, the report called for a vast increase in military spending. Despite the large disparity between the industrial capacity of the United States and the Soviet Union, the report maintained that the United States spent only one-half of what Moscow did on defense as a proportion of gross national product. The United States could easily afford to spend as much as 20 percent of its gross national product on armaments without jeopardizing its economy or lowering its standard of living. It could, the report argued, raise taxes significantly (from roughly thirteen billion to fifty billion) without incurring inflation. In other words, in waging a global struggle the United States could afford both guns and butter.

Finally, the battle would have to be waged as long as it took for the Soviet Union to accommodate itself to coexistence, gradually withdraw from the field, and radically change its policies.

The buildup and projection of U.S. military power called for in the final draft of NSC-#68 represented an extremely dramatic change in the way the United States conducted itself in peace time. The report arrived on Truman's desk with an intense debate swirling around it. Ranged against Acheson and Nitze were Kennan and Bohlen who felt that the report exaggerated Moscow's intentions and power, and Louis Johnson who questioned whether the country could really afford to spend such money on a sustained basis. The critics of NSC-#68 felt that an acceptance of the report would destroy any diplomatic relations between the superpowers for decades to come, drain the nation economically, and lock the two camps into a permanent struggle lasting indefinitely. Using the Second World War as an example, Acheson and Nitze argued that the country could afford to escalate spending and they insisted that the increased defense outlays would give a lagging United States economy a much needed boost.

There is indeed evidence that the report deliberately exaggerated the Soviet threat. It should have been apparent to anyone who knew something about the Soviet Union and China that there was no Russo-Chinese monolith, and it should have been equally clear that predictions of a Soviet nuclear Pearl Harbor in the early 1950s were alarmist. But the authors of NSC-#68 understood that Truman was dead set against a quantum leap in defense spending and that he believed that only a national emergency could justify such a program. As Acheson made clear in his memoirs, "The purpose of NSC-#68 was to so bludgeon the mass mind of 'top government' that not only could the President make a decision but that the decision could be carried out."[6]

Truman, who did not need to be convinced of the geopolitical danger presented by the Soviet Union, was nevertheless cool toward the conclusions of NSC-#68. The mid-term elections were due in November and Truman was very worried about large deficits and crippling inflation. Truman had initiated this strategic assessment, but he did not endorse its findings. Instead of accepting the report he instructed the Bureau of the Budget, the Treasury Department, and the Council of Economic Advisers to review it, thus effectively placing it on hold. In fact, NSC-#68 might have been relegated to the footnotes of diplomatic history "had not the Russians been stupid enough," as Acheson once put it, "to have instigated the attack against South Korea and opened the 'hate America' campaign."

If there was a watershed in postwar U.S. defense policy, it came with the Korean War. Until the North Korean attack on June 25, 1950, the policy of containment was based on the belief that communist penetration of vulnerable societies would be economic and political rather than military. The invasion of South Korea for the first time clearly demonstrated the military nature of the Soviet threat, thus confirming the most dire predictions NSC-#68 had made about Soviet intentions. The North Korean attack provided the international crisis that made national security the prime determinant of the defense budget. Under its impact the United States began its great postwar rearmament program. What had been politically unfeasible prior to June 1950 was now highly popular. When Truman raised the military budget from thirteen to twenty-two billion dollars in fiscal year 1951 there was little opposition from Congress or the American public. The Korean War was a crisis that committed the United States to draw the line against aggressive communism and which allowed the administration to adopt the objectives of NSC-#68 that September. As Samuel F. Wells, Jr., points out, "The real significance of NSC-#68 was its timing—the Tocsin sounded just before the fire."[7]

Caught between the Asian giants, China and Japan, Korea occupied a strategic position and a tragic history of victimization not unlike Poland's. In the last one hundred years three significant wars were fought for control of that country. At the Cairo Conference of 1943 Franklin Roosevelt had tried to enlist the Soviet Union in a new international system in Asia. Believing that the Koreans were not ready to govern themselves, the Allies envisaged a period of joint trusteeship for the country lasting for a lengthy period, followed by unity, freedom, and independence. Roosevelt was trying to enlist the Russians, an old contender for influence in Korea, in a mutually beneficial relationship for the good of all Koreans.

With the sudden collapse of Japanese power in 1945, and the Red Army poised to enter the country, Washington hastily proposed that the United States accept the surrender of the Japanese army in the southern half of Korea, up to the 38th parallel (the farthest limit likely to be acceptable to the Russians), and that the Russians do the same in the northern half. The partition was meant to be temporary but, like Germany, the Korean problem was swallowed by the Cold War and the occupied zones quickly became the frontiers of separate and hostile states. North of the 38th parallel the communists under Kim Il Sung developed a hostile "people's government" with a strong aggressive army. In the south elections were held in early 1948, which brought an authoritarian government to power under the intensely nationalistic anti-communist, Dr. Syngman Rhee. The border between the two Koreas thereafter became the one place outside of Europe where the United States and the Soviet Union directly confronted each other. One historian has described the decision to divide Korea at the 38th parallel as "the first postwar act of containment."[8]

From 1947 to June 1950 the Truman administration and its military advisers were fairly consistent in defining the U.S. line of defense in the Pacific just short of the Asian mainland. The administration was guided in its strategic thinking by the belief that the United States ought not to overextend itself and that it could not protect its friends everywhere in the world. It therefore did not interpret the Chinese civil war in the same strategic terms as the Greek civil war or the Berlin Blockade. This thinking was reflected in Truman's speech of January 5, 1950, in which he publicly declared that the United States would not intervene in the Chinese civil war and that Taiwan was Chinese. At this point in his administration the president believed that the Chinese communists had national interests not identical to those of Russia and that a clever foreign policy could exploit this natural antagonism by turning China's hostility toward the Soviet Union. This rather sophisticated policy was quickly submerged during the Korean War and did not reappear until the Nixon administration.

In the period between the end of the Chinese civil war and the summer of 1950 the United States defined its commitment in Asia in a peripheral way. As early as September 1947 the Joint Chiefs of Staff recommended that, because of the shortage of resources, the United States "has little strategic interest" in keeping bases and troops in Korea. In the event of war the line could be held in Korea by air power based in Japan.[9] Military thinking never wavered from this line. Whenever politicians or generals applied the language of containment to Asia and communism and spoke of the U.S. defense perimeter in the Pacific, they judged Korea strategically unimportant and outside the pale. In March 1949, for example, General Douglas MacArthur, commander of America's forces in the Pacific, stated in an interview with a British journalist that Korea and Taiwan lay outside the U.S. defense perimeter. "Our line of defense," he said, "runs through the chain of islands fringing the coast of Asia." Those islands were the Philippines, the Ryukyus, Japan, and the Aleutians.[10] Dean Acheson said virtually the same thing in a speech before the National Press Club on January 12, 1950. Like MacArthur, he defined the U.S. defense perimeter in Asia in a way that excluded Korea and Taiwan. Going even a bit further, he declared that states in this area had to look to their own devices for their defense and rely upon the diplomatic efforts of the U.N. to help protect them.[11] Six months before, all U.S. forces, with the exception of a small advisory mission, left South Korea. That country was now left considerably weaker than its more heavily armed neighbor to the north. Syngman Rhee, in fact, accused the United States of abandoning his country and he was left begging for assurances that he would be protected in the event of a North Korean invasion. Acheson's speech was anything but reassuring.

Did Acheson "invite" the North Korean attack as his Republican critics alleged? General Matthew B. Ridgeway, soon to be commander in chief of U.S. forces in Korea, thought this a "gross and misleading simplification." Nevertheless, the Acheson statement coming when it did "did nothing to give the enemy even momentary pause."[12] According to a senior North Korean official interviewed in recent years, the policy statements of Truman and Acheson convinced Kim Il Sung that "the United States would not enter the Korean War," or "even if they did enter the war, they would not hold sway over the destiny of the war."[13] At the very least, it seems that Kim used Acheson's speech to strengthen his case with Stalin to support the idea of an invasion.

Stalin was of two minds about Kim's plans to unify Korea with a stroke of the sword. On one hand, being a genuine Marxist-Leninist, he believed firmly in the inevitability of a third world war with the West and the ultimate victory of the Soviet Union. Toward the end of his life, Molotov quoted Stalin as saying: "The First World War tore one country away from capitalist slavery. The Second World War created the socialist system, and the Third World War will finish imperialism forever."[14] Stalin apparently believed that this war would break out within twenty years. Speaking to Tito in 1945, he declared "the war shall soon be over. We shall recover in fifteen or twenty years, and then we'll have another go at it."[15]

Preparing his country for this eventuality lay at the heart of Stalin's domestic and foreign policy until his death. However, just as in the 1930s, he had to buy time, since he did not want to get involved in a great war before his country was ready. This is what caused Stalin to doubt the wisdom of Kim's plans to invade South Korea. Just as Stalin had once been extremely cautious over aiding the communist guerrillas during the Greek civil war, so he was equally worried over the potential dangers of a Korean conflict. In both cases he was concerned that his country might be drawn into a wider struggle before it was ready to wage it. It was also clear that Stalin at first feared U.S. intervention. "The Americans," he told Kim, "will never agree to be thrown out of [Korea and] lose their reputation as a great power."[16]

Despite the fact that North Korea was a Soviet satellite, its leader seems to have held all the initiative in convincing Stalin to back his plans for the invasion. The argument that changed Stalin's mind was complex. First, it was clear that North Korea enjoyed an overwhelming superiority in armor and air power, and that by comparison the South Korean army was extremely weak. This was an important argument for Stalin, a man who understood the mathematics of power. Second, a North Korean invasion would, Kim assured Stalin, ignite a rising in the south of 200,000 communists who were prepared to support the invasion. The Russians were convinced that Kim's estimate of these forces was correct and that a genuine revolutionary situation existed in South Korea. Between the overwhelming military advantage and the enormous fifth column within South Korea, Kim predicted a blitzkrieg that would carry North Korea to victory in three or four weeks. Furthermore, with only four undermanned and underequipped divisions in Japan to race to the aid of South Korea, the Americans would not have the manpower or the time to intervene. Third, Kim argued, there was the recent example of the

Chinese civil war. According to senior Soviet diplomat, M. S. Kapitsa "The Koreans were inspired by the Chinese victory and by the fact that the Americans had fled from mainland China completely; they were sure that the same could be accomplished in Korea quite quickly."[17] Why, Kim argued, would the Americans fight for little Korea, if they relinquished giant China without a scrap? If they had not fought for Chiang Kai Shek, why would they fight for Syngman Rhee? And did not Acheson exclude Korea from the U.S. defense perimeter? Kim used all of these arguments in a secret visit he made to the Soviet capital from March 30 to April 25. According to Nikita Khrushchev, Kim Il Sung "was absolutely assured of success" and transmitted this confidence to Stalin, a classic example argue the authors of *Silent Partners* "of the weak manipulating the strong." According to Molotov: "It seemed that [The Korean War] was not needed by us. The Koreans themselves had forced it on us. Stalin was saying that we cannot avoid the national question concerning a unified Korea."[18] Lee Sang Jo, the North Korean ambassador to Moscow at the time, relates that all the initiative came from Kim, "who persuaded the Soviet leader of the success of the plan for a 'national liberation war' personally devised by himself. Although Stalin worried about the possibility of Washington's interference, he at last gave his approval."[19]

Stalin's backing of a North Korean adventure could be rationalized as promising great advantages to the Soviet Union with minimal risks. If the United States intervened, a war in Asia would drain away critical American resources and serve to reduce the U.S. commitment in Europe. It might even lead to a clash between the United States and China that would only increase China's dependence on the Soviet Union. And if the United States stood down and did nothing, it would damage its reputation irrevocably and probably loosen its hold on Japan, which, after the passive American response to recent events in China, might force the Japanese to conclude that communism was the wave of the future.

Before their meeting ended in April, Stalin urged Kim to consult with Mao and warned him: "If you should get kicked in the teeth, I shall not lift a finger. You have to ask Mao for all the help."[20]

On his way back from Moscow Kim paid a secret visit to Beijing. Mao at first seems to have disagreed with Kim's idea to invade South Korea and wanted him to reconsider the whole adventure. But Mao's reluctance did not last long. After all, the Chinese had fought their own civil war and were pursuing the unification of their own country. How could Mao deny his fellow communists in North Korea the chance to do the same? At the same time, Mao was preoccupied with Taiwan and had already secured a Soviet promise for an invasion of that island. "How could Mao express his fears of American intervention in Korea," ask recent historians of the subject, "without admitting to Stalin the likelihood of the same U.S. involvement in Taiwan, thereby jeopardizing that support. Mao had to be positive."[21] Like Stalin, Mao expressed his fears of U.S. intervention and asked Kim if he wanted China to send troops to Korea in case of such a contingency. Kim declined the offer, believing that the war would be over and done with quickly, and that Soviet aid was all that he really needed. And that aid began to arrive in substantial amounts as soon as Kim returned home, where it was immediately distributed along the 38th parallel.

On June 25, 1950, Kim Il Sung hurled tens of thousands of Russian-trained troops across the 38th parallel into South Korea. The South Korean army, which had only been lightly armed by the United States, was unable to defend itself.

The intelligence failure over the possibility of an invasion in 1950 was appalling. The CIA was only a fledgling organization and not held in high regard in Washington. The CIA station in Tokyo consisted of three men working out of a hotel room whose reports were completely ignored by General MacArthur. As Joseph Goulden points out, between March 1 and June 25 Korea was not even mentioned in the CIA's daily summaries.[22] What was all but ignored was the rapid buildup of North Korean armor close to the parallel, the evacuation of thousands of families near the border, the closing of rail lines to the border to anything but military traffic, the recruitment of women to nursing positions and, most tellingly, the mass conscription of young men. U.S. Army Intelligence read the signs but did not draw the proper conclusions. Neither did the army's leaders who seriously underestimated the North Koreans. As General Omar Bradley later recalled, "I don't think any of us knew . . . what would be involved. No one believed that the North Koreans would be as strong as they turned out to be."[23] Much of this mixture of ignorance and complacency was reflected in the Truman administration. When questioned before the House Committee on Foreign Affairs on June 20, 1950, Assistant Secretary of State for Far Eastern Affairs Dean Rusk claimed that an invasion of South Korea was out of the question. Even if they attacked, he went on, the South Korean army "could meet credibly the kind of force which the North Koreans have established."[24]

Compounding these errors in intelligence-gathering and sound judgment was the lack of U.S. military preparedness in Asia. Preoccupied as they were by the containment of communism in Europe where the great battles of the Cold War promised to be won, the White House and the Joint Chiefs made the wrong assumptions about the prospects of future wars. The term "limited war" was not then in current use. When the concept of war was discussed in the White House or in the Pentagon it was total war that was meant—war that was to be waged against the Soviet Union, not conventionally, but by long-range air power and nuclear weapons. This being the case, it seemed wrong-headed to defend small pieces of the Asian mainland, especially when they had, like Korea, been cast outside the U.S. defense perimeter. For all these reasons the United States was unprepared militarily and psychologically for the Korean War.

From the early hours of the invasion Washington viewed the struggle not as a civil war or as an isolated incident, but as a clash having global implications. The Truman administration strongly believed that the invasion was part of a larger Sino-Soviet strategy. To Truman, the attack seemed to represent an ominous change in Soviet tactics—from political pressure to the overt use of military force.

> The attack upon Korea makes it plain beyond all doubt that Communism has passed beyond the use of subversion to conquer

independent nations and will now use armed invasion and war. It has
defied the orders of the Security Council of the United Nations issued
to preserve international peace and security.[25]

Truman's response to the events in Korea was also framed in historical terms.
Having lived through the 1930s he understood that the Western failure to stand up
to Hitler only encouraged Nazi aggression and ultimately led to the Second World
War. He felt that if the American will was tested and found wanting in Asia, it
might set in motion a similar chain of events that would not only undermine the
American position in Asia but also endanger the whole edifice of containment and
lead to another world war. Like the Berlin problem of 1948, the low strategic value
of Korea stood in stark contrast to its political importance as a democratic bastion
on a communist mainland. Truman and Acheson now immediately reversed their
original policy of withdrawing from the Asiatic mainland. They understood that
failure to respond to the invasion would be regarded as a sign of weakness
undermining American prestige. For the first time, a feeling for a moral
commitment to the freedom of the South Korean people became an important
factor in U.S. policy. The containment theory, once confined to Europe, was now
almost automatically extended to Asia as well. After his initial briefing on the
invasion Truman remarked, "By God, I'm going to let them have it."[26]

On June 25 Truman brought the question of the invasion before the U.N.
Security Council. The council could act more quickly than the General Assembly
and at the moment the Russians, because Red China was not allowed to replace
Taiwan on the council, refused to attend its meetings. Throwing away its veto
power was an enormous tactical blunder. With it Russia could have prevented any
concerted U.N. action over developments in Korea. Instead, on the 25th, with
Russia absent, the council called upon North Korea to halt the invasion and to pull
back her forces to the 38th parallel. Two days later it called upon member nations
to "furnish such assistance to the Republic of Korea as may be necessary to repel
the armed attack."

On June 27 Truman sent U.S. air and naval forces into Korea and, at the same
time, he dispatched the Seventh Fleet into the Formosa Strait to serve as a barrier
between the Chinese mainland and Taiwan. This latter move was, to a certain
extent, made in response to mounting Republican criticism in Congress, which had
been particularly intense since the fall of Chiang in China. What it served to do was
neutralize Taiwan and commit the United States to the losing side in the Chinese
civil war. The historic implications of earning the enmity of the new China were
not considered. The two countries would for years remain frozen in mutual
hostility. Mao certainly considered the U.S. intervention toward Taiwan a virtual
declaration of war and he concluded that the real United States aim was to
eventually invade China itself. This belief only grew as the U.N. forces fought their
way up the Korean Peninsula.[27] For Beijing, the permanent presence of a hostile
force on one of its borders was an intolerable situation.

On July 7, 1950, the Security Council placed its troops under a unified
command headed by the United States. President Truman appointed General

MacArthur commander-in-chief of the U.N. armies. The United States supplied roughly 48 percent of the military force to the Korean War; South Korea provided 43 percent and the fifteen nations fighting under the U.N. flag mustered the remaining 9 percent.

The Korean War seemed to confirm the most dire conclusions made only months before in NSC-#68. First, it validated the idea that all interests in the world, no matter how peripheral, were of equal weight and that any shift in the world balance of power, no matter how small, might conceivably upset the whole system of international relations built up since 1945. Second, it confirmed the report's prediction that the Soviet Union might resort to piecemeal aggression employing proxies to do its dirty work. Third, it reinforced the report's argument that the American military establishment needed a dramatic overhaul and expansion. The Soviet Union now seemed bent on using military force to achieve political objectives. It was now clear to the administration that to draw the line against communism and to mobilize the U.S. economy and people behind rearmament, the Cold War had to be militarized and NSC-#68 implemented immediately. At the beginning of 1951 Truman submitted a defense budget of $50 billion, roughly quadrupling the previous budget of six months before. He also increased the size of the standing army by 50 percent to three and a half million men. At the same time, the United States created an integrated military force in Europe under a unified command, while it moved to increase the size of the U.S. military contingent on the continent. In December an integrated defense system was created under the supreme command of General Eisenhower. Because of the Korean War the United States was able to pressure its allies in Europe, especially France, to accept the idea of West German rearmament. Washington also made its first significant commitment to Vietnam and Taiwan, and Japan agreed to allow long-term U.S. military bases on its territory. In other words, the Korean crisis forced the United States to assume its global responsibilities and bring its military assets in line with those commitments. The original emphasis on containing Russia's expansion toward Western Europe was now superseded by the commitment to project U.S. power to the heart of that continent and beyond that, to Asia. With the implementation of NSC-#68 the United States had clearly decided to subordinate its economic interests (at least in the short run) to its geopolitical needs.

In the first phase of the war, with the North Korean army threatening to capture the entire peninsula, the use of the atomic bomb was seriously contemplated in Washington. A nuclear strike was seriously discussed at the Pentagon, not only to stave off a military disaster but also to counter a possible Russian intervention. U.S. planes frequently bombed targets only a few kilometers from the Soviet border and at one point mistakenly bombed a Soviet airfield just south of Vladivostok.[28] Indeed, at one point Secretary of the Navy Francis Matthews was actually fired by President Truman for advocating a preventive attack on the Soviet Union. Nevertheless, on the day of the invasion the commander of the U.S. Air Force, General Hoyt Vandenberg, was authorized to draw up contingency plans for atomic strikes against Soviet bases in Siberia. The situation on the ground in Korea was at first so serious that by mid-July General MacArthur and the army chief of staff were already discussing the bomb's use. Before the war was over, a frustrated MacArthur would demand the use of "thirty to fifty" atomic bombs against Manchuria and the establishment of a "radioactive cobalt barrier" along the Yalu River.[29] Truman himself saw the bomb as "a weapon of last resort," as Gregg Herken puts it. No less frustrated than MacArthur, especially when peace talks were stalled, Truman told his aides that if the North Koreans and Chinese refused to agree to or violated an armistice, he would consider using the bomb.

Despite all the private saber rattling, Truman resisted military attempts to wrest the bomb from civilian control as he did during the Berlin Blockade. He insisted that the war be fought with conventional weapons and he deliberately ruled out the use of nuclear bombs. MacArthur may have advocated extending the war to mainland China and using the bomb, but other generals, like Omar Bradley, never recommended its use. Bradley and others simply felt that the bomb was not suitable for that kind of war.[30] Furthermore, Truman could not have dropped the bomb on North Korea or China and, at the same time, held the U.N. coalition together.

In one other sense Korea was an example of a limited war; Truman insisted that the war be localized geographically and not extended, even to a China, which intervened and came into the war on the side of the North Koreans.

Laboring under these limitations, MacArthur's first task was to stop the complete rout of the South Korean army. With only a few U.S. divisions at his disposal, MacArthur nevertheless succeeded in stabilizing a short front at the Pusan perimeter. In mid-September, with the North Korean army poised to drive the U.S. divisions into the sea, MacArthur conducted an amphibious landing on the Korean coast at Inchon that succeeded in cutting the North Korean army's supply lines. The North Korean army was thrown into total disarray and a headlong retreat, as the U.N. forces moved to the offensive. It was the Korean War's first turning point.

After the North Koreans were turned back by the Inchon landing, the next critical decision in Washington was whether to take the war north of the 38th parallel.

From the beginning of hostilities in June, a feeling began to grow in Washington that whatever the outcome there should not be a return to the original Korean status quo. Despite opposition from within the State Department by George Kennan and others, the administration was intoxicated by the brilliant possibilities then opening up before it: namely, the destruction of the North Korean army and the unification of the country. This was why the United States at first refused to negotiate a peace. Even before Inchon, on September 1, the Security Council voted down a Soviet motion for a ceasefire. Mao apparently viewed this vote as a lost opportunity. He had misjudged the American resolve to stay the course and the unwillingness to negotiate from weakness. What did Truman want, Mao asked: to negotiate an end to the war, or an extension of it?[31] The answer from Washington was to extend it, and the political and military goals had to be reshaped to fit the new battlefield realities.

The United States came into the war with one set of political and military goals. Applying the containment doctrine, the original goal was to repel the invasion, and to do this meant sending U.S. planes to bomb across the 38th parallel. By September and the Inchon landing the goal was to destroy the North Korean army, and to accomplish this required the United States to send ground troops across the parallel. Nothing illustrates the perils of containment more. With the mounting success of the U.S. Army in Korea, what had begun as a war to defend South Korea was quickly transformed into an offensive war to unite all of Korea by destroying the communist regime in the north.

There was also a domestic reason for the escalation in goals. More than one historian had pointed to the administration's anxiety about the Republican opposition in Congress, which, it felt, would make political capital out of any White House attempt to end the war short of total victory. After the loss of China to the communists, Truman's critics at home were claiming that the administration did not have the necessary determination to vigorously deal with communism in the world. If Truman stopped the American march at the 38th parallel, the Republicans would no doubt have used it to make political gains in the elections in November 1950.[32]

On September 27 MacArthur was given new instructions. He was now ordered to cross the 38th parallel and destroy the North Korean army—provided that Soviet or Chinese troops did not intervene and enter the war or threaten to do so. General Marshall even cabled MacArthur: "We want you to feel unhampered tactically and strategically to proceed north of the 38th parallel."[33]

On October 1, 1950, South Korean troops surged across the parallel and MacArthur demanded the unconditional surrender of North Korea. At this point, the Allies heard from China for the first time.

Little was heard from China during the first month of the war. This was understandable as the North Korean army swept southward past Seoul in what appeared to be a triumphant march to conquer all. At the same time, units of the Chinese army stationed opposite Taiwan began to be deployed. When the U.S. Army went on the offensive and South Korean troops approached the parallel, China began to be heard. On October 3, 1950, Chou En-Lai, the Chinese foreign minister, conveyed a clear warning to the United States through the Indian ambassador in Beijing: "The U.S. troops are going to cross the 38th parallel in an attempt to extend the war. If the U.S. troops really do so, we cannot sit idly by and remain indifferent. We will intervene. Please report this to the prime minister of your country."[34] The message was relayed to Washington where it was dismissed by Acheson. The Indian ambassador, K.M. Pannikar, was dismissed as a pro-communist and anti-American alarmist. Aside from a concerned president with nagging doubts, the only people truly alarmed about the prospects of a Chinese intervention could be found in Eighth Army Headquarters in Korea. They believed that the Chinese would soon enter the war and they even accurately predicted the Chinese order of battle along the Yalu frontier when they did. At this point, to get a more accurate picture of developments in Korea (and to relieve his anxieties) Truman elected to meet with MacArthur at Wake Island in the Pacific for a personal briefing.

From the beginning MacArthur, who felt himself to be a special student of the Oriental mind, did not believe that the Chinese would risk war against an advanced country like the United States, which boasted a victorious army. MacArthur clearly undervalued his own military intelligence as he did the fighting capacities of the Chinese communists. He also overestimated his own air power. If the Chinese did enter the war, he told Truman, U.S. air power would inflict on their armies the "greatest slaughter." MacArthur's optimistic forecasting was confirmed by the CIA, which felt that a Chinese intervention was highly unlikely.

The underestimation of Chinese intentions and the lack of political knowledge about that country was appalling. The Chinese people and their regime and the revolution they had made were much more complicated than Washington liked to believe. From the beginning, the Chinese viewed the struggle in Korea as a defensive war against imperialism, and Mao had made it abundantly clear to his colleagues that a Sino-American conflict was inevitable. The United States, after all, had not only blocked the conquest of Taiwan but, according to Mao, it was intent on subverting the communist revolution and ultimately invading China itself. There was a genuine fear in Beijing that a triumphant United States could ignite another revolution among the millions of Chinese on the mainland who were anti-communist and who in thousands of cases were in open revolt. From the beginning of the war rumors spread on the mainland about an impending invasion of China and the landing of Chiang Kai-Shek to reclaim his former position. There was indeed genuine turmoil in the country and the ruling Communist Party had to overcome the perception of weakness. As Mao put it, "If we do not send troops [to Korea], the reactionaries at home and abroad would be swollen with arrogance when the enemy troops press to the Yalu River border."[35]

Mao was also under pressure from Stalin to intervene in the Korean War. "The Americans," Stalin said, "cannot make a war on two fronts. The two fronts are the wars in Korea and China. Because of that, there will be no war with China. Therefore, right now it is possible for you to help." Stalin also lectured the Chinese on what a continued American presence on the Yalu might mean for the future: "The economic recovery of the Northeast probably will be out of the question. Thereafter, [the Americans] at will could harass [you] from the air, land, and sea."[36] At the same time, Stalin made it clear that the Soviet Union would not enter the struggle because it would mean a world war with the United States and Russia had still not recovered from the last one. Mao clearly understood Stalin's position. Stalin believed that after Inchon the U.S. armies had to be stopped but that a direct clash between the Soviet Union and the United States was to be avoided. It therefore fell to communist China to prevent a U.S. victory. There would, of course, be Soviet arms extended to the Chinese but not nearly in the numbers that Mao wanted or asked for. This lack of genuine Soviet support, coming on top of the meager support extended to Mao during the war of 1937-1945, helped plant the seeds for the later Sino-Soviet conflict.

On October 20, 1950, Pyongyang, the North Korean capital, was captured by the advancing Eighth Army. On October 24 MacArthur ordered all his forces to proceed rapidly toward the Yalu. At a moment when MacArthur was talking about bringing the boys home for Christmas, 300,000 Chinese troops were being infiltrated into the mountains north of Pyongyang. On October 26 a Chinese soldier was captured, and four days later fourteen more were taken. By November 4, eight Chinese divisions had been spotted by U.S. intelligence and Russian-made fighter planes had engaged the U.S. Air Force. MacArthur ignored it all and kept pressing ahead. On November 9, a massive Chinese attack broke out all along the Yalu, hurling back the U.N. armies with heavy losses. Through December the U.S. Army waged a fighting retreat from North Korea. At this point, the U.N. tried to open negotiations with the Chinese, but Beijing, as its armies swept below the 38th parallel and recaptured Seoul, set impossibly stiff terms. In March 1951 the United States Eighth Army counterattacked and for a second and final time captured Seoul and recrossed the 38th parallel. After mid-1951 the war settled down into a protracted and bloody war of attrition near the parallel. Cease fire talks finally began on July 10, 1951, and dragged on until an armistice was concluded at Panmunjom on July 27, 1953.

The Korean War has to be viewed as a major war in the twentieth century because of the carnage that resulted from it. Over four million people were killed in the war, mostly Koreans, along with one million Chinese. By 1953 the whole country was laid waste. The revival of South Korea and its future transformation into one of the "Asian Tigers" began at once. The North, on the other hand, remained broken economically and in the iron grip of Kim Il Sung.

The war was also important in terms of its geopolitical impact. It taught the United States that containment was, at least in Asia, a very costly thing. While it was true that the communist invasion was contained, the front stabilized and the Korean status quo rendered unalterable, it was also clear that the Cold War assumed for the first time a military dimension and a global extension that both sides did not want. For the first time in its history the United States created and maintained a vast military apparatus in peacetime. As Raymond Aron writes, while the European problem first made the United States think of the world, it was in Asia that it first assumed an imperial burden.[37]

Second, the Korean War must be viewed as one of Stalin's greatest foreign policy blunders. While it was true that in the war the Chinese and North Koreans assumed all the burdens of fighting and risk at no cost to the Russians, Stalin had inadvertently raised to new stature a resurgent China whose power in Asia would eventually surpass Russia's. China's performance against the United States in the war helped generate the nationalist pride on the mainland that helped the communists to more speedily consolidate their rule. Between this and the meager Soviet aid extended to the Chinese during the war, one is justified in saying that the seeds of the Sino-Soviet conflict were planted here.

While it was also true that Stalin's main enemy, the United States, was drawn into a costly conflict with proxies, he had also made the serious error of failing to keep his enemies disarmed. The United States that Russia faced after 1953 was infinitely stronger economically and militarily than it was going into the summer of 1950.

In the long run, the interests of the Soviet state were badly served. All of Stalin's efforts since 1945 to achieve a breakthrough and alter the balance of power only succeeded in stiffening American resolve, creating a determined alliance against his country, provoking an unprecedented nuclear buildup in the United States, and hastening the decline of Soviet security. By 1953, when Stalin died, the lines were drawn in the Cold War, which endured for forty more years.

Notes

1. Warren I. Cohen, *America's Response to China* (New York: John Wiley and Sons, Inc., 1980), 172-75.

2. Michael Schaller, *The United States and China in the Twentieth Century* (New York: Oxford University Press, 1979), 113.

3. NSC-#49, "Strategic Evaluation of United States Security Needs in Japan," in *Containment: Documents on American Policy and Strategy, 1945-1950*, eds. Thomas H. Etzold and John Lewis Gaddis (New York: Columbia University Press, 1978), 231.

4. Gregg Herken, *The Winning Weapon. The Atomic Bomb in the Cold War, 1945-1950* (New York: Alfred A. Knopf, 1980), 304.

5. Ernest R. May, ed., *American Cold War Strategy: Interpreting NSC 68* (New York: St. Martin's Press, 1993), 21-82.

6. Dean Acheson, *Present at the Creation. My Years at the State Department* (New York: New American Library, 1967), 488.

7. Samuel F. Wells, Jr., "Sounding the Tocsin: NSC 68 and the Soviet Threat," *International Security*, 4 (1979): 139.

8. Bruce Cumings, *The Origins of the Korean War. Liberation and the Emergence of Separate Regimes 1945-1947* (Princeton, N.J.: Princeton University Press, 1989), 131.

9. Joseph C. Goulden, *Korea. The Untold Story of the War* (New York: Times Books, 1982), 25.

10. Goulden, *Korea*, 31.

11. Acheson, *Present at the Creation*, 466.

12. Goulden, *Korea*, 31.

13. Sergei N. Goncharov, John W. Lewis, and Xue Litai, *Uncertain Partners. Stalin, Mao, and the Korean War* (Stanford, Calif.: Stanford University Press, 1993), 142.

14. Goncharov, Lewis, and Litai, *Uncertain Partners*, 55.

15. Milovan Djilas, *Conversations with Stalin* (New York: Harcourt, Brace and World, Inc., 1962), 114-15.

16. Goncharov, Lewis, and Litai, *Uncertain Partners*, 142.

17. Goncharov, Lewis, and Litai, *Uncertain Partners*, 138.

18. Quoted in Goncharov, Lewis, and Litai, *Uncertain Partners*, 139.

19. Quoted in Goncharov, Lewis, and Litai, *Uncertain Partners*, 139.

20. Quoted in Goncharov, Lewis, and Litai, *Uncertain Partners*, 145.

21. Quoted in Goncharov, Lewis, and Litai, *Uncertain Partners*, 146.

22. Goulden, *Korea*, 39.

23. Callum A. MacDonald, *Korea. The War before Vietnam* (New York: Free Press, 1986), 36.

24. Goulden, *Korea*, 41.

25. Harry S. Truman, *Years of Trial and Hope 1946-1952*, 2, (Garden City, N.Y.: Doubleday and Co., 1956), 339.

26. MacDonald, *Korea. The War before Vietnam*, 30.

27. Goncharov, Lewis, and Litai, *Uncertain Partners* 158-59, 181, 184.

28. R. Craig Nation, *Black Earth, Red Star. A History of Soviet Security Policy, 1917-1991* (Ithaca, N.Y.: Cornell University Press, 1992), 192.

29. Nation, *Black Earth*, 193.

30. Herken, *The Winning Weapon*, 332.

31. Goncharov, Lewis, and Litai, *Uncertain Partners*, 173.

32. MacDonald, *Korea. The War before Vietnam*, 50.

33. MacDonald, *Korea. The War before Vietnam*, 50.

34. Goncharov, Lewis, and Litai, *Uncertain Partners*, 179.

35. Goncharov, Lewis, and Litai, *Uncertain Partners*, 181.

36. Goncharov, Lewis, and Litai, *Uncertain Partners*, 189.

37. Raymond Aron, *The Imperial Republic. The United States and the World 1945-1973* (Englewood Cliffs, N.J.: Prentice-Hall, 1974).

12

Eisenhower and Dulles:
From Massive Retaliation to Covert Action

On January 20, 1953, General Dwight D. Eisenhower was sworn in as the thirty-fourth president of the United States. Harry Truman, who had occupied the office since April 1945, had decided not to run for another term in 1952 because he felt that he was too unpopular to win reelection. Eisenhower, on the other hand, was persuaded to run, not only to end twenty years of Democratic Party rule, but because he was determined to keep the Republican nomination out of the hands of the isolationist wing of his party.

With the Korean War still dragging on in 1952 and the American electorate so troubled by it, it was not surprising that they turned to a successful and popular general who was nevertheless closely linked to the military and foreign policies of the two previous administrations. They gave him a landslide victory.

Raised in humble beginnings in Abilene, Kansas, Eisenhower spent his whole adult life in the military, his career reaching its peak as Supreme Allied Commander of the D-Day invasion forces in 1944. After three years as U.S. Army chief of staff from 1945 to 1948, and a brief and unhappy spell as president of Columbia University, he was appointed in 1951 to the overall command of NATO's military forces. Eisenhower therefore came to the American presidency imbued with the habit of command. This was reflected in his whole style of governance. From the White House down he established a chain of command; through the cabinet and through numerous committees, administrators arrived at important policy decisions, which they then referred to the president. In this sense, Eisenhower was not a "hands-on" president such as Truman was.

Less than two months after Eisenhower took office, Stalin died. His death together with the fact that the new Soviet premier, Georgi Malenkov, appeared conciliatory, opened the possibility of an end to the Korean War and perhaps some moderation of the Cold War.

On July 27, 1953, a final armistice agreement was signed in Korea that provided for a cease-fire and withdrawal of both armies two kilometers back of the existing battle line. A political conference to seek the peaceful unification of Korea was to be held, but it never took place. Instead, the cease-fire was followed by an uneasy and protracted armed truce.

On October 10, 1953, the United States signed a security pact with South Korea that provided that country with a guarantee of joint defense if the war was renewed by North Korea. South Korea would henceforth be protected, but the dream of unification would remain unfulfilled.

Eisenhower's choice of secretary of state, John Foster Dulles, exerted a commanding influence over American foreign policy until his death in 1959. Dulles was from an old, established American family. Two of his relatives, including Robert Lansing, had been secretaries of state before him. A corporate lawyer with experience in international affairs, Dulles came to office anxious to seize the initiative from the communists, or at least to throw them off balance with a steel-like display of American resolve. In many ways his personality was suited for this role. He was dogmatic and unbending, often lecturing Western statesmen (and Eisenhower) arrogantly on the complexities of international relations. Anthony Eden once described him as "a preacher in world politics," and, more unkindly, Dean Acheson placed him among that breed of "single-minded concentrators" who lacked a broad, geopolitical perspective. Although he would have bristled at the comparison, his view of international relations resembled that of Woodrow Wilson's, at least in one fundamental sense; both men perceived America's relation to the world in moral terms. Both felt that American foreign policy must ultimately be based on morality and principle. This being the case, Cold War negotiations with the Soviet Union should be avoided at all costs—at least until the dreadful Soviet system altered its shape drastically.

Eisenhower and Dulles were extremely critical of the Truman-Acheson foreign policies as they evolved until 1952. They believed that those policies placed too great a strain on American resources and were less than effective abroad. Dulles, in particular, felt that the policy of containment was no more than a passive reaction to evil.

> We shall again make liberty into a beacon light of hope that will penetrate the dark places. It will mark the end of the negative, futile and immoral policy of 'containment' which abandons countless human beings to a despotism and godless terrorism, which in turn enables the rulers to force the captives into a weapon of our destruction. . . . The policies we espouse will revive the contagious, liberating influences which are inherent in freedom. They will inevitably set up strains and stresses within the captive world which will make the rulers impotent to continue in their monstrous ways and mark the beginning of the end.[1]

Critical as he was of the containment policy, this statement of purpose, which originally appeared as a plank in the Republican Party Platform of 1952, closely resembled George Kennan's critically moral view of the communist system and the confident hope for internal Soviet change.

Despite the new administration's anxieties about all the sacrifices that went into the Cold War, it was adamant that the Soviet Union disgorge what it had swallowed in Eastern Europe, that the communist tide be rolled back, and that under no circumstances should an accommodation be made with the enemy. Communism, they felt, was a coherent and radical ideology that helped to fuel and coordinate a series of global assaults wherever the Kremlin thought the West weak.

It was the administration's intention to replace the objective of containment with the more positive goal of liberation. The new foreign policy was directed at liberating the captive nations of Eastern Europe. The policy proved politically irresistible—however impractical—to a political party that had been kept from the White House since 1932. The appeal to voters of Eastern European background was too tempting to ignore. At the same time, Eisenhower sought a change in defense policy. Believing that the price of the NSC-#68 was too draining on the economy, and the prospect of a whole series of inconclusive limited wars too onerous for the country to bear, Eisenhower sought a cut in the expensive military budget to something—he was never sure how much—a good deal less than the high figure of 1952. He was clearly bothered by the almost unrestrained spending ushered in by the Korean War. Under the new policy, the Pentagon would shift its emphasis to thermonuclear weaponry and its delivery by the air force. This was popularly called at the time, getting "more bang for the buck," and closely resembled the defense strategy of Truman on the eve of the Korean War. On one hand he wanted to resist communism everywhere. "As there is no weapon too small," Eisenhower said in 1953, "no arena too remote, to be ignored, there is no free nation too humble to be forgotten."[2] On the other hand, if spending to fuel the military establishment persisted it would eventually alter the very nature of American society. After all, how do you deal with the warweariness of the American people and their fear of nuclear retaliation *and* the enormous expense of the Cold War, and at the same time assure them that their government was waging an aggressive battle on their behalf against world communism? The new White House policy of "massive retaliation" seemed to resolve this problem. According to Dulles, the United States would no longer worry about Soviet sponsored brush fires around the globe (despite what he was saying about resisting communism everywhere) but would rely instead on "the deterrent of massive retaliatory power . . . a great capacity to retaliate instantly, by means and at times of our own choosing."

Dulles also had a tactic to go with massive retaliation: brinkmanship. It was a dangerous foe the American people were facing, he claimed in a *Life* magazine interview of 1956, and sometimes you have to take risks to maintain the peace. What really counted was deterrent power and the nerve to use it. Dulles called it, "the ability to get to the verge without getting into the war is the necessary art. If you cannot master it, you inevitably get into a war. If you try to run away from it, if you are scared to go the brink, you are lost."[3]

If Dulles was to be taken literally, then Washington was prepared to turn every local conflict, both in the third world and behind the Iron Curtain, into a nuclear showdown. Dulles always claimed, for example, that he brought the Korean War to an end by directly threatening a recalcitrant China with the bomb if the Chinese did not agree to end hostilities. In fact, there is no record of Dulles having done any such thing. Brinkmanship rang as hollow as "massive retaliation." In all the critical moments of the Cold War in the 1950s, the Eisenhower-Dulles policy became indistinguishable from the Truman-Acheson policy of containment. After all, the Russians tested their first H-bomb in 1953, which only made "massive retaliation" a double-edged sword. There were now enough bombs on the other side to transform the strategical landscape. What would winning a war mean now? With the monopoly of nuclear weapons a thing of the past, Eisenhower certainly saw that the purpose of diplomacy was to avert war. The American people did not see this at first. Comfortable with a foreign policy imbued with moral purpose, they were drawn to a set of slogans that promised swift action at low cost.

The new Eisenhower-Dulles foreign policy was first applied successfully on a small scale just off the Asian mainland. In December 1953, a U.S.-Nationalist Chinese alliance was concluded and in the summer of 1954 the Red Chinese began shelling the islands of Quemoy and Matsu. The islands were situated between Red China and Taiwan and garrisoned by Chiang Kai-Shek's troops. Laying just five miles off the mainland, they commanded the approaches to important harbors in the Fukien province of China and therefore they had some strategic value. With the sudden Chinese shelling went threats of invasion. The administration felt that if the Red Chinese were allowed to seize the islands, they might feel encouraged to extend their attacks to Taiwan and beyond that to Japan and the Philippines. The situation caused such anxiety in Washington that Eisenhower actually got a joint resolution through Congress which declared that U.S. forces would be deployed in the event of a communist attack, to protect the islands from invasion. The crisis eventually subsided, and for Dulles the successful defense of Quemoy and Matsu represented the triumph of brinkmanship.

When Eisenhower took office in 1953 he had promised to "wage peace" as he had waged the Second World War, using every means at his disposal. This included covert operations by the CIA, which it had been authorized to do since 1948. From 1948 the CIA had begun to grow in size—its foreign stations alone rose from seven to forty-seven by 1952, and its budget from $4.7 million in 1949 to $82 million in 1952, as its personnel grew by thousands of people.[4]

A clear sign that the CIA was given an expanded role was the appointment of Allen Dulles, the brother of John Foster, to head the agency. On intelligence matters, the two brothers communicated almost daily with the secretary of state becoming a natural "conduit" for intelligence to the White House. The Department of State and the intelligence community never worked more closely.

Massive retaliation may have been a myth, and the costs of the containment policy somewhat prohibitive, but covert operations promised large returns on a modest investment. This became clear almost at once in the subversion and overthrow of hostile regimes in the Middle East and Latin America.

The situation in postwar Iran found the young Shah, Mohammed Reza Pahlevi, sitting uneasily upon the Peacock Throne. In 1951 the Iranian legislature appointed Dr. Mohammad Mosaddegh, the head of the National Front Party, prime minister of the country. One of his first acts in office was to undercut the power of the Shah and call for the nationalization of the British-owned Anglo-Iranian Oil Company. Mosaddegh's action spoke for a popular grievance; royalties paid to the Iranian government by the oil company amounted to half the country's revenues, while at the same time, the company earned nearly five times that amount from the oil it extracted from its fields. In fact, the British government received more taxes from the company than Teheran received from its own natural resource. This is what Mosaddegh meant when he said, "The source of all the misfortunes of this tortured nation is only the oil company."[5] The nationalization was popular with the Iranian people.

Anglo-Iranian retaliated by withdrawing all of its personnel from Iran and threatening legal action against any foreign buyers of Iran's oil. Oil provided 30 percent of the country's total income and 60 percent of its foreign exchange.

In response, Mosaddegh requested aid from the United States as Iran had in 1946. Eisenhower refused, on the grounds that Mosaddegh was a tool of the communists. Mosaddegh was not a communist, but increasingly came to rely on them as allies. With the American door firmly shut Mosaddegh demanded that he be given extraordinary powers to deal with the crisis. The Shah refused and instead asked for Mosaddegh's resignation. Aided openly by the Iranian Communist Party (the Tudeh), Mosaddegh's party began massive rioting in protest. According to Daniel Yergin, Mosaddegh became the first Middle Eastern leader to use the radio to arouse his followers.[6] The rioting forced the Shah's hand and he reappointed Mosaddegh prime minister. The Shah felt powerless in the face of popular demonstrations as he would twenty-five years later. "What can I do?" he pleaded to the American ambassador. "I am helpless."

Once back in office, the prime minister broke off relations with Britain and made diplomatic overtures to Moscow. From Washington it looked as if Mosaddegh was moving his country into the Soviet orbit. Rumors of a Soviet loan swept the country and more ominously, the new Soviet ambassador chosen for Teheran was the same man who presided as ambassador to Prague in 1948.

In February 1953 the crisis worsened when the Shah announced that he would abdicate. This set off another round of rioting, this time between Mosaddegh's followers—once again supported by the Tudeh Party—and thousands of the Shah's supporters. Encouraged by the demonstrations on his behalf, the Shah decided to remain on his throne.

For the British, the situation was unstable and they threatened military action. Anxious that this might provoke a Soviet move into Iran, worried about an East-West confrontation like the crisis of 1946, and inclined to view third world nationalism with suspicion, Washington authorized a CIA-led covert action (code named AJAX) to topple Mosaddegh and anchor the Shah firmly on his throne.

In mid-July, the Shah met secretly with the CIA officer, Kermit Roosevelt, who assured him of Washington's firm support. The Shah in turn agreed to participate in the CIA operation. Acting in concert with the Iranian army and security forces, where the Shah had many loyal supporters, and the British Secret

Intelligence Service (the idea for a coup was originally theirs), which had many contacts in the officer corps, Roosevelt and a handful of operatives orchestrated the coup that ousted Mosaddegh.[7]

On August 9, the Shah signed a decree removing Mosaddegh from his position and appointed a loyal general to replace him. At this point, the Shah removed himself to Italy to await the outcome of events.

On August 19, the new prime minister, General Fazollah Zahedi, led a huge mob—in many ways financed and mobilized by the CIA—backed by a column of tanks, to the Mosaddegh residence in Teheran. After a brief battle, Mosaddegh fled over the back wall of his garden, and the capital now belonged to the Shah's supporters. "I knew that they loved me," said the Shah when he heard the good news. He soon returned to Iran and resumed his throne. At a celebration that followed, the Shah offered a toast to the top CIA agent: "I owe my throne to God, my people, my army, and to you."[8] Mosaddegh was soon arrested, tried for treason, and permanently exiled to his home village.

When the smoke cleared, a new oil consortium was established giving the British 40 percent of Iranian oil production, five American firms another 40 percent, and Dutch Shell and French Petroleum 20 percent. Profits were to be split evenly between the consortium and Iran. Oil once again flowed into western markets, the British oil monopoly was broken, and the United States now possessed a large economic and political stake in the stability of the Shah's regime. Not only had the United States gained a staunch ally in Iran for the next twenty-five years, but it had also taken yet another major step in assuming Great Britain's power role in the Middle East.

Another example of a successful covert action in a third world country was the American intervention in Guatemala. This attempt to change the politics of a Latin American country, like the later attempts in Cuba and the Dominican Republic, involved obsessive American security concerns about international communism, and Washington's belief that it could unilaterally invoke the Monroe Doctrine to protect its vital interests. The United States, of course, had a greater concern for events in neighboring Latin America since, if a country fell to communism there, it could spread to other nations in the region and even, through Mexico, reach the borders of the United States. Through the Rio Pact of 1947 and the Organization of American States (OAS) established a year later, and through its enormous investments in the region and economic assistance and by its support for many of the dictators of the continent, the United States was able to maintain a dominating influence over its neighbors to the south. Millions of Latin Americans chafed under this relationship and their nationalism grew strident.

In 1951 Jacobo Arbenz Guzmán came to power in Guatemala after a free election that gave him 60 percent of the nation's electorate. Determined to aid the nation's poor, Arbenz's program emphasized social and economic reform. Central to this was land reform—in 1951 2 percent of the population owned 60 percent of the land—and the reduction of the power of foreign interests in the country. In 1952 Arbenz signed into law a bill that expropriated much of the 225,000 acres of unused land owned by the United Fruit Company. For over a century the company had exercised a strangle hold over the Guatemalan economy. In all that time, it had been the country's biggest employer, monopolizing shipping, communications, and railroads. Known popularly as "the Octopus," it had for decades shaped the nation's politics.[9] The attack on it by a government embarking on a program of economic nationalism was enormously popular with most Guatemalans. More of a reformer than a communist, Arbenz offered to compensate the company for the land, but United Fruit demanded much more.

Pursuing a policy of economic nationalism was in Washington's eyes dangerous enough, but in his struggle with United Fruit Arbenz welcomed the support of the Guatemalan Labor Party, as the communists in the country called themselves. While only four communists sat in the Guatemalan parliament, the party did grow in popularity especially in rural areas of the country and among union workers. They were also represented within the Ministry of Education and the National Agrarian Department, the latter being the agency directly involved in the expropriation of United Fruit's leadership.

As for the Soviet Union, it showed little interest in Latin America in the 1950s. Moscow did not take non-communist reformers like Arbenz very seriously, especially in what it perceived as the American sphere of influence, and it gave little support to the Guatemalan Communist Party. Nevertheless, native communists were vocal in support of Arbenz's program and that was enough to convince many officials in Washington that Arbenz was establishing a communist beachhead in Latin America. As the newly appointed American ambassador to Guatemala, John E. Peurifoy, declared, Arbenz "talked like a Communist, he thought like a Communist, he acted like a Communist, and if he is not one . . ., he will do until one comes along."[10] Eisenhower was certainly convinced that Arbenz was a communist; he later said that if nothing was done, in six months Guatemala would "fall completely under communist rule."[11]

Afraid that communism was indeed gaining a foothold in Latin America under the guise of economic nationalism, Dulles attended an inter-American conference in Caracas, Venezuela, in March of 1954 and demanded the condemnation of "international communism." He received this from the meeting, but the resolution they passed only focused on communist influence outside the hemisphere and not inside as Dulles had wanted. In May at a meeting of the OAS Dulles got the organization to declare that the domination of any American state by international communism would constitute a threat to the hemisphere. Nevertheless, he was unable to get the OAS to take collective action against Guatemala since he admitted to them that it was "impossible to produce evidence clearly tying the Guatemalan government to Moscow."[12]

The success in Iran the year before already inclined the American policy-makers to place a great reliance on the CIA as an instrument of foreign policy. At this point, Eisenhower called in the CIA to organize the overthrow of Arbenz. He approved a CIA plan (code named Operation Success) to train Guatemalan exiles in camps in Florida, Nicaragua, and Honduras and prepare them for an invasion of their country.

Feeling isolated within the OAS, and no doubt sensing that the United States was plotting his overthrow, Arbenz played into Eisenhower's hands when he requested and received two thousand tons of light arms and artillery from communist Czechoslovakia. It was this action that triggered the CIA invasion.

On June 18, 1954, Colonel Carlos Castillo Armas led a small force of three hundred men across the border of Honduras toward Guatemala City. This modest incursion was supported by the CIA bombing of the capital and a large propaganda campaign designed to convince Arbenz and his supporters that they faced an overwhelming force of three thousand. By June 27 Arbenz stepped down and fled into exile in Mexico City.

The American-trained Colonel Castillo quickly reversed Arbenz's reforms and slaughtered thousands of his supporters. American aid then began to pour back into the country and the United Fruit Company was restored to its former position. And when it was over, Dulles, in a television address of June 30, 1954, remarked that "the situation is being cured by the Guatemalans themselves."[13]

The crises in Iran and Guatemala illustrated the problems Washington had in dealing with third world nationalists throughout the Cold War. In postwar Western Europe there was no shortage of politicians of the conservative but democratic center whom the United States could help shape into a third force that stood midway between communism and right-wing dictatorship. In the more politically unstable third world, however, Washington usually ended up trying to topple determined nationalists who wished to seize full control of their national resources, and replace them with more pliant authoritarian figures with no popular roots in their countries, but willing to cooperate with the United States in exchange for continued financial support. Washington seemed unable or unwilling to make proper distinctions between Marxist-Leninists like Ho Chi Minh and Fidel Castro, and nationalists like Mosaddegh and Arbenz. In most cases the United States underestimated the power of determined and well-organized nationalists over the long haul, and overestimated the power of international communism to capture and hold them. Covert action policies to remove troublemakers, real and imagined, went just so far. They could only be successful in the short run. The coup in Iran, for example, brought twenty-five years of stability in a key state; but placing a generally unpopular Shah back on his throne only "identified Iran and the Shah more closely with the United States then it was good for either one of them," writes Gregory Treverton. "It also set in motion a kind of psychological dependence by the Shah on the United States that Americans no doubt liked initially but came to lament in 1977 and 1978."[14] Finally, covert action and palace coups such as those in Iran and Guatemala would never suffice in provoking popular risings against entrenched regimes like that of Nasser in Egypt or Castro in Cuba.

Notes

1. Robert H. Ferrell, *American Diplomacy. A History* (New York: W.W. Norton and Co., 1969, 883.

2. Quoted in John Lewis Gaddis, *Strategies of Containment. A Critical Appraisal of Postwar American National Security Policy* (New York: Oxford University Press, 1982), 130.

3. James Shepley, "How Dulles Averted War," *Life XL* (January 16, 1956), 78.

4. Gaddis, *Strategies of Containment*, 157.

5. Quoted in Daniel Yergin, *The Prize. The Epic Quest for Oil, Money and Power* (New York: Simon and Schuster, 1992), 455.

6. Quoted in Yergin, *The Prize*, 466.

7. Kermit Roosevelt, *Countercoup. The Struggle for the Control of Iran* (New York: McGraw-Hill, 1979).

8. Quoted in Walter Lafeber, *The American Age. United States Foreign Policy at Home and Abroad*. 2nd edition (New York: W.W. Norton and Co., 1994), 545.

9. Hubert Herring, *A History of Latin America* (New York: Alfred Knopf, 1961), 456.

10. Quoted in Richard H. Immerman, *The CIA in Guatemala* (Austin: University of Texas Press, 1982), 181.

11. Dwight D. Eisenhower, *The White House Years: Mandate for Change, 1953-1956* (London: Heinemann, 1963), 422.

12. Blanche Wiesen Cook, *The Declassified Eisenhower* (Garden City, N.Y.: Doubleday, 1981), 276.

13. Quoted in Robert H. Ferrell, ed., *America in a Divided World* (New York: Harper and Row, 1975), 223.

14. Gregory F. Treverton, *Covert Action: The Limits of Intervention in the Postwar World* (New York: Basic Books, 1987), 176.

13

The Suez Crisis

American interests in the Middle East were not just concerned with Iran and oil. The region had also entangled the United States originally in the question of Palestine. Since the nineteenth century, Zionists had sought a Jewish homeland in Palestine, and at the end of the Second World World War they pressed Great Britain—still the principal foreign power in the area—to open British-mandated Palestine to Jewish refugees from Europe. The British, who had troops stationed in Jordan, Iraq, and Egypt, and who supplied arms to a number of Arab states, retained major assets in the region in oil and the Suez Canal. Determined to maintain friendship with the Arabs, the British resisted the Zionist pressure. But the same appeals made to Washington received a more sympathetic audience.

President Truman felt that at least part of the Zionist program could be accommodated. He moved to this position because he genuinely wanted to resettle thousands of displaced Holocaust survivors in the land of their forefathers and because he was also an American politician. "I have to answer to hundreds of thousands who are anxious for the success of Zionism," he said just after the war. "I do not have hundreds of thousands of Arabs among my constituents."[1]

The beleaguered British who were forced to keep 100,000 troops in Palestine to maintain order despaired of ever finding a solution to the problem to which Arabs and Jews could agree. Remaining in Palestine became less and less of an option, and London finally decided to abandon the whole Palestine problem to the U.N. by mid-1947. A special U.N. commission had already recommended partitioning the country into Jewish and Arab states, but it also urged that the economic unity of Palestine should be maintained.

On November 29, 1947, the General Assembly voted for partition. The Jews were willing to accept partition, but the Arabs were adamantly opposed to it. Both Britain and the United States felt that partition would have to be enforced by military means, but both were unwilling to do it. The infant Jewish state was therefore left to fight for its own survival.

Fighting between Arabs and Jews broke out openly in December 1947 and soon grew into an all out war. Outnumbered and outgunned, the Jews astonished everyone by going on the offensive in July 1948 and defeating the Egyptian army in January 1949. By the spring, the Arabs sued for an armistice and Israel had won the first Arab-Israeli War.

From the beginning of the Palestine problem Washington was caught between two clashing nationalisms: an irredentist Jewish Zionism seeking to redeem the Holy Land and establish its own state upon it and an Arab nationalism seeking to rid the region of foreign interests and traditional pro-Western regimes, and a Palestinian branch seeking to redeem the same bit of contested soil. At first Truman resolved the problem by opting for partition and then, ignoring the advice of his State Department that a pro-Israeli policy would alienate the Arab world, he tilted toward Israel even more by extending it diplomatic recognition only moments after it became a state, on May 14, 1948.

The Russians also at first pursued a pro-Israeli policy, voting for partition and then extending the new state recognition. While they took a dim view of Zionism as a nationalist ideology, which could potentially alienate Soviet-Jewish citizens, the Russians also calculated that a pro-Israeli policy was yet another way to expel Britain as the hegemonic power in the Middle East and fill the vacuum it left. However, this was not a well-thought out policy and certainly it was a short-lived one. Once Israel won its war of independence, it made a formal request in 1950 to purchase arms from the United States. Even though Washington was cool to the idea, the Russians understood that Israel would probably pass into the American orbit. More important, it became geopolitically obvious to Moscow that the side to back in the Middle East were the Arabs. They constituted the vast majority of people in the region, they possessed most of its oil, and Arab nationalists increasingly targeted Western interests for special hatred. It was therefore inevitable that the Cold War moved into a fierce competition for Arab loyalty, as the superpowers strove to recruit surrogates to assist them in their respective security systems.

The victory of Israel in 1949 constituted a watershed in the history of the Middle East. Arab nationalism, which for years had been gathering like so many clouds, now broke like a storm over the region. The humiliation of losing a war to tiny Israel, and the creation of what Arabs regarded as a Western-sponsored Zionist enclave on Arab soil, provided the catalyst for many political changes in the Middle East. The first and seminal of these changes occurred in Egypt.

In 1952 Gamal Abdul Nasser led a group of Egyptian army officers in a bloodless coup against King Farouk, the pro-Western ruler of the country. Nasser became prime minister in 1954 and president a year later. Soon after taking office he initiated a program of land reform, which included the breaking up of large landed estates and the opening up of new areas for cultivation. He also initiated a program to industrialize the Egyptian economy. Central to Nasser's economic reforms was the building of a dam on the Nile River at Aswan, which would provide irrigation for the new land he sought to reclaim and hydroelectric power for industrial development.

Raising the standard of Egyptian nationalism, he also pledged to eliminate British control of the Suez Canal. The proceeds from canal operations, he felt, could help pay for a good deal of his program. In 1954 he signed an agreement with Britain that provided for a phased withdrawal of 80,000 British troops from the Suez Canal Zone by mid-1956.

Washington reacted to these events in two ways: first, to keep Nasser's Egypt in the Western column it offered to finance the Aswan Dam. This alone succeeded in drawing the United States directly into the problems of the Middle East. Second, it wanted to, as Dulles put it, "create a solid bond of resistance against the Soviet Union." It did this by drawing some of the states that rimmed the Soviet Union into a regional defensive alliance. Signed in 1955, the Baghdad Pact was a military alliance that included the United States, Britain, Turkey, Iran, Iraq, and Pakistan. It was the first time an Arab country (Iraq) was added to the Northern Tier defensive shield of Greece, Turkey, and Iran.

Immediate reaction to the pact in the Middle East was intensely negative. Both Israel and Egypt found the pact offensive. Israel hated it because she feared that Jordan might adhere to it and be armed by the West, thus increasing Israel's isolation and feelings of insecurity. Nasser hated it as well, as did most Arabs who were excluded from the coalition, because it seemed to be yet another neo-imperialist combination between Britain and the United States and the traditional and reactionary regimes of the region. But just as important, arch-rival Iraq was to be armed by the West and could therefore now bid for the leadership of the Arab world, a role coveted by Nasser and Egypt. For Nasser and other Arab leaders, communism was not the powerful emotive weapon in the political struggles of the Middle East that the West wanted it to be—however, Israel, Western imperialism, and inter-Arab rivalries were.

In 1955 Nasser's preeminence in the Middle East seemed assured. With the gradual withdrawal of the British army from the Canal Zone, he stood before his people as the century's first truly independent ruler of modern Egypt. He also presented himself as an implacable enemy of Israel.

By 1955 guerrilla raids from Egypt against Israel became more frequent and bloody. Israel, which had come to view Egypt as its most dangerous enemy, saw these raids (as well as those on her other borders) as posing a long-term threat to the country's survival. On February 28, 1955, Israel mounted a huge retaliatory raid, led by General Ariel Sharon, against Egyptian positions in the Gaza Strip. Thirty-six Egyptian soldiers and two civilians were killed, exposing Egyptian military weakness. The Baghdad Pact and the Gaza raid challenged Nasser in two ways: on one hand, the pact seemed to blunt Nasser's bid for revolutionary pan-Arab leadership and instead aggravated an injured Arab nationalism; on the other hand, the raid produced a military humiliation at the hands of a hated enemy. In response, Nasser decided to conclude an arms deal with Czechoslovakia—acting for the Soviet Union. The Baghdad Pact, as one historian writes, "aimed at excluding Soviet influence from the Middle East, had resulted in bringing it in."[2]

Under the agreement with the Czechs, Egypt was to sell cotton to the Soviet bloc in return for 300 medium and heavy tanks of the latest Soviet type, and 200 MIG-15 jet fighters. As the Israeli General Moshe Dayan, concluded: "In quantity alone, they tipped the arms balance dramatically against Israel; in quality, the tilt was even more drastic."[3] Almost immediately, Israel began to plan for a preemptive strike against Egypt. It was the introduction of new Soviet weapons into the sensitive Middle East balance of power which created the crisis of 1956.

New elections in France in January 1956 brought the socialist Guy Mollet to power. For ideological reasons he was inclined to help a fledgling Israeli democracy. More important, he was bothered by Nasser's extension of aid to the Algerian revolution against French control. Even before the nationalization of the Suez Canal, Israel and France had therefore forged a close relationship. In the spring of 1956 the French began to redress the balance of power between Egypt and Israel by selling arms to Israel, including thirty-six of their latest fighters. For the first time since Israel's founding she had broken out of her isolation. Even more important, the United States, it was learned, had approved of the sale. In May 1956, Nasser responded to this by withdrawing diplomatic recognition from Chiang Kai-Shek's regime in Taiwan and shifting it to communist China. This, of course, only served to deepen Washington's disillusionment with Nasser.

In April 1955, Anthony Eden succeeded Winston Churchill as prime minister of Great Britain. Like Dulles, he believed at first that Nasser could be held in the Western camp by helping him finance the Aswan Dam. The finance needed was to be provided by the World Bank, on condition that the United States and Britain contributed as well. If the West did not do this, Eden argued, the Soviet Union probably would, and thus gain entrée into the Middle East. Nevertheless, the breach between Britain and Egypt widened in the year following Eden's assumption of office. Part of the reason for this was the strident pan-Arab and anti-British propaganda campaign waged by Nasser all over the Middle East. It was particularly strong in King Hussein's Jordan, where it was Nasser's objective to prevent that country from joining the Baghdad Pact. Nasser's anti-imperialist message with the Jordanian people was so powerful that the King bowed to pressure and replaced the British Commander of the Arab Legion, a symbol of British paternalistic hegemony in the Middle East. Along with the Soviet arms sale to Egypt, these developments served to convince Eden that Nasser's was a dangerous regime seeking to undermine the British position in the Middle East, and that it could now be written off as a possible ally.

On June 13, 1956, the last of the British troops left their bases in Suez. On July 19 under pressure from Britain and France, as well as the U.S. Congress, the Eisenhower administration withdrew American financial support for the Aswan Dam. Adding insult to injury, it even publicly insulted the Egyptians when it claimed that their credit was no good. "May you choke to death on your fury," Nasser cursed.[4] Using the American withdrawal from the Aswan project as an excuse, Nasser announced the nationalization of the Suez Canal on July 26.

In the Middle East Nasser's move produced jubilation, as he became a hero to millions of Arabs. In the West it produced panic, since two-thirds of Western Europe's oil passed through the Suez Canal. It was certainly clear even then, that Eden overreacted to Nasser's move. His first reaction was to say, "The Egyptian has his thumb on our wind-pipe." Exaggerating the economic threat to the West, feeling personally humiliated by developments in Cairo, and being a new prime minister pressed hard by his party's right wing, Eden was prepared to personalize his quarrel with Nasser and embark on a very ill-considered military adventure.

The pressures on Eden to take a firm stand were very strong. They not only came from his own party and a section of the British press, but from his own experiences as a diplomat during the 1930s. Those experiences with appeasement, argues Hugh Thomas, scarred Eden for life, so that he came to view the nationalization of the Suez Canal through the prism of the Rhineland crisis of 1936.[5] But Nasser, troublemaker as he was, was no Hitler. In misjudging him, Eden made the mistake of overestimating Egyptian power, even as he underestimated Arab nationalism.

Only one day after the nationalization of the canal, the British Cabinet decided to prepare a military option. There was general agreement that in the final analysis Egypt would be attacked, the Canal Zone seized, and Cairo forced to accept an internationalization of the canal ensuring free passage through it permanently.

In Paris Guy Mollet was just as determined to remove the Nasser regime as was Eden. Like Eden, he took an exaggerated view of Nasser as the new Hitler, and equated the nationalization of the Suez Canal with Hitler's remilitarization of the Rhineland. Mollet and the French people took Nasser's move as a personal affront, since it was France that built the canal in 1869, and since it was French shareholders who held a majority of stock in the Suez Canal Company in 1956. But more important, Mollet's real concern was in putting down the rebellion against French rule in Algeria, which Nasser was aiding. The French, therefore, worked very hard to forge a military alliance with Britain.

What determined the events of late 1956 that led up to the intervention in Egypt was the conflict between the geopolitical interests of Britain and France and the Arab nationalism of Nasser's Egypt. And it was precisely this fact that placed Washington on the horns of a dilemma. Britain and France were old and loyal allies who assumed all along that the United States would accept their fait accompli in the Middle East and provide them with oil supplies when they needed them. But the United States was not just a powerful state that helped the allies restore their economies after the war; it was also a superpower that was bidding for the friendship of the Arab peoples by insisting that it was free of a colonial past. To support the allies in an unjustified colonial war to crush Arab nationalism would have placed the United States in an untenable position in the Middle East and turned the whole Arab world against the West. Dulles at one point told the National Security Council in a now famous comment, that for many years the United States had been "walking a tightrope" between backing Europe's empires and trying to win the friendship of countries escaping from colonialism. The Americans always insisted that their major European allies give priority to the Cold War over their empires. Dulles even suspected that London was trying to maneuver Washington into reasserting British colonial supremacy.

Eisenhower decided very early that Egypt's nationalization of the Suez Canal was not a cause for war, and Anthony Eden was repeatedly told by him during the crisis that the Americans were unalterably opposed to force in removing Nasser from power. Eisenhower therefore instructed Dulles that his task was to help the British find a peaceful solution to the problem. By July 31 Dulles was on his way to London to do just that.

On August 16 a conference of twenty-four maritime powers convened in London to deal with the Suez problem. Dulles, who had played a role in creating the conference, returned to Washington and boasted that he alone had prevented Britain and France from going to war.[6] Dulles was clearly out of touch with the situation. Actually, the British and the French were just stalling for time while they secretly moved into a coalition with Israel and prepared to intervene militarily in the Middle East. Fooled by this, Washington would later feel betrayed by London.

At the conference eighteen of the twenty-two nations supported a scheme for a group of user nations to jointly run the Suez Canal with Egypt. Robert Menzies, the prime minister of Australia, was dispatched to Cairo to present the plan. But the Russians, who had been one of the four dissenters at the conference, had already made it clear that the plan was neo-colonial in content and should be withdrawn. It was clear at this point that Nasser and Egypt had found a powerful patron in the Soviet Union and therefore had every incentive to reject the plan. In the meantime, the British and French waged a psychological war aimed at pressuring Egypt to come to terms. For example, elements of the British and French fleets began to arrive in the east Mediterranean as troops poured into Cyprus and Malta. At the same time, the British and French gave orders to begin the evacuation of their nationals from Egypt, Jordan, Syria, and Lebanon.

When Robert Menzies presented the eighteen-nation plan in Cairo, he also tried to make Nasser understand that the British and French were bent on military action. But at that moment, Eisenhower was telling a Washington press conference that the United States would go to any length to secure a peaceful resolution to the crisis. This, of course, was what Nasser wanted to hear, and along with Russian support he found it easy to reject Menzies's proposals as infringing on Egypt's sovereign rights. On his way home to Australia, Menzies stopped off in Washington and chided Eisenhower for "pulling the rug out from under his feet." Eisenhower lamely replied: "What can I do, this is a democratic country!" Menzies then told him that it was the task of a president to be a leader.[7]

A second conference was convened on September 21 and its proposals were also rejected by Nasser. Britain and France then took their dispute to the Security Council of the U.N. This was clearly a diversion, since Eden at this point was determined to have his intervention.

In one sense, the alliance that brought together Britain, France, and Israel was a natural one. All three felt that they had a clear interest in attacking Egypt and politically destroying Nasser. But in another sense, it was an extremely contrived coalition. France, after all, was extending real support to Israel while Britain was allied with some of the Arab states. Until late in the planning of Operation Musketeer, as the invasion of Egypt was called, Eden wanted the Israelis excluded from the conflict lest Britain's Arab friends be antagonized more than necessary.

The British attitude toward Israel became clear in September 1956 when Jordan became the victim of two Israeli reprisal raids. Britain condemned them in very strong terms and reaffirmed her loyalty to Jordan. According to Eden, the moment was so tense that he was on the verge of sending British planes to aid Jordan.[8] Nevertheless, because of Washington's coolness toward an intervention, and the lack of popular support at home for his policy—an opinion poll conducted in September suggested that slightly less than half the British people were behind him—Eden rather late in the day came to accept an Israeli role in the assault on Egypt.

From October 22 to 24, the British, French, and Israelis held secret discussions at Sèvres, a suburb of Paris. It was the French plan to have the Israeli army attack Egyptian positions in the Sinai Desert and sweep down to the canal. In the second phase of the operation, the British and French would pretend that they were not in collusion with the Israelis and they would issue an "ultimatum" to both sides to cease hostilities and withdraw their forces ten miles from the canal. The Egyptians would then have to accept a temporary occupation of the Canal Zone pending a final settlement. The belligerents were to be given twelve hours to comply. The Sèvres Agreement assumed that Nasser would reject the ultimatum. In the final phase of Operation Musketeer an Anglo-French armada would invade Egypt and occupy the Suez Canal Zone on the pretext of separating the combatants and safeguarding the traffic through the waterway.[9]

David Ben-Gurion, the prime minister of Israel, had some serious reservations about the plan. He disliked a scheme that called upon his country "to mount the rostrum of shame so that Britain and France could lave their hands in the waters of purity." General Moshe Dayan, however, the man who would lead the attack into Sinai, showed Ben-Gurion that unless Israel played that designated role it would not secure anything like the goals it needed. After all, he argued, Britain and France could easily defeat Egypt without Israel's help. "The sole quality we possessed, relevant to this contest, and they lacked, was the ability to supply the necessary pretext. This alone could provide us with a ticket to the Suez Campaign Club."[10]

Ben-Gurion was also bothered by the timing of the invasion. He wanted his allies to put off the assault until after the U.S. presidential elections the following month. But the British and French felt that it was perfectly timed since it would make Eisenhower think twice about the Jewish vote in the United States and the concomitant pressure of the Jewish lobby in Congress. But Ben-Gurion had little faith in the lobby and he knew that the majority of Jewish-American voters traditionally cast their ballots for the Democratic Party. For Eisenhower and Dulles, the Jewish vote would not be an important factor.[11]

On October 29, 1956, after French fighter planes blanketed Israeli cities with a defense umbrella, and the French navy took up positions off the Israeli coast, the Israeli army began its invasion of Sinai. On October 30, Britain and France sent their ultimatum to both sides to withdraw from the canal and gave Egypt twelve hours to comply. Nasser, however, managed to keep his head and began to rally his people for a defense of their country. When the ultimatum expired on October 31, the R.A.F. began bombing Egyptian airfields. At the same time, the Israeli army swept all before it and succeeded in expelling the Egyptians from the entire peninsula. By November 5 it had captured Sharm Al-Sheik where Egyptian artillery had for so long closed the Gulf of Aqaba to Israeli shipping. On the same day, British and French paratroopers were put ashore in the Canal Zone, and the next day the main amphibious landing took place at Port Said. By the 9th the allies were in complete control of the Canal Zone. Militarily, all seemed to be going according to plan. Politically, however, everything went wrong from the start.

Washington reacted very angrily to the news of the invasion. "Nothing justifies double-crossing us," a furious Eisenhower told his aides. "We're going to apply sanctions, we're going to the United Nations, we're going to do everything we can to stop this thing."[12] On October 30, the United States introduced a resolution in the Security Council calling on all countries to stop fighting in the Middle East and withdraw all military forces. Eisenhower rested his case on the status and role of the U.N., a clever move, since he could distance himself from an irresponsible adventure without taking sides with Egypt. Britain and France vetoed the resolution. Eisenhower then publicly attacked the British and French for playing into Russia's hands by distracting the world from the brutal repression of the Hungarian Revolution (see chapter fourteen).

All three allies had badly miscalculated about American reaction. Eisenhower made it perfectly clear that he would not back any of them. And he had the economic leverage to force his allies to withdraw from Suez. The Suez Canal was severely damaged in the fighting and would remain closed to navigation for an indefinite period. The United States was therefore in a strong position to dominate the world oil market. Eisenhower felt that those who began the crisis to secure oil supplies, should be left to "boil in their own oil." Indeed, he threatened to cut off oil supplies to Britain and ruin the British currency unless the war was stopped. Gold reserves in Britain had fallen by 100 million pounds during the first week of the invasion, and the U.S. Treasury opposed Britain's request to withdraw capital from the IMF. When Washington finally did agree to an IMF loan of 300 million pounds to hold the British currency intact, it was linked to a British declaration of a cease-fire. As one historian puts it, the United States "seemed to hold Britain to ransom."[13]

The Suez crisis deeply divided the British people and their government. The opinion polls certainly showed a very confused public on November 1 and 2. Thirty-seven percent of those answering the question: "Do you think we were right or wrong to take military action in Egypt?" thought Eden had acted correctly, and 44 percent thought him wrong. But on November 10-11 the approval rating rose to 53 percent. Nevertheless, almost half the British people disapproved of what their government was doing. Eden also received heated criticism from within his own government. A number of people in the Foreign Office circulated a letter condemning the government's action, and several junior members of the Foreign Service resigned in protest. The Labour Party was united in vehement opposition to the government. Lacking a consensus at home and strongly pressured by the

United States, Eden's government began to lose its resolve.

The pressure on all the Suez partners was considerable, since there now appeared a danger of bringing a Soviet intervention against them. The Russians, who had been preoccupied with events in Hungary, waited nearly a week before they were satisfied that the United States was not behind the invasion. Their response to the crisis was then two-pronged; on one hand, Khrushchev, who saw a chance to pose as the protector of the Arabs, proposed that the Soviet Union and the United States take joint action to force the aggressors out of Egypt. Khrushchev knew that Eisenhower would reject this "but by putting him in the position of having to refuse," he told Molotov, "we'll expose the hypocrisy of his public statement condemning the attack against Egypt. We'll make him put his money where his mouth is. If he were really against the aggression, then he'd accept the Soviet Union's proposal for us jointly to safeguard Egypt's independence."[14] On the other hand, Nikolai Bulganin, the premier of the Soviet Union, sent notes to all three Suez partners, which blustered in the most intemperate language that the Soviet Union was ready to crush all three, by use of "every kind of modern destructive weapon." Foreign Minister Dimitri Shepilov warned the West that its resort to force might provoke "a serious conflict which would encompass the whole of the Near and Middle East and perhaps go even further." On November 5 Bulganin sent Israel a very ominous note that said that Israel's action "places in question the very existence of Israel as a State." On November 7, the CIA "leaked" a report—attributed to U.S. ambassador Bohlen in Moscow—that the Russians intended to "flatten" Israel on the following day.[15] Eisenhower also increased the pressure on Israel when he sent Ben-Gurion a message (through Rabbi Abba Hillel Silver) asking him to withdraw his forces and "return immediately to your own borders. . . . The President emphasizes that, despite the temporary convergence of Israel's interests with those of France and Britain, you shall not forget that Israel's strength is primarily dependent on the United States."[16]

For the moment Ben-Gurion chose to ignore these warnings and on November 7 he delivered a vigorous victory speech in which he said that "the Armistice lines have no more validity." He also waved aside any prospective U.N. force to maintain any future peace. He affirmed: "on no account will Israel agree to the stationing of a foreign force, no matter how called, on her territory or in any of the territories occupied by her."

Eisenhower was very bothered by Ben-Gurion's speech. His undersecretary of state, Herbert C. Hoover, Jr., made the president's anger clear to Israel the next day: "Israel's attitude will inevitably lead to most serious measures, such as the termination of all [U.S.] governmental and private aid, United Nations sanctions, and eventual expulsion from the U.N." Hoover also warned that if Israeli intransigence continued, and the Soviet Union entered the Middle East, "Israel would be the first to be swallowed up."[17] This was the sort of threat designed to snap a small country back to reality. So was the General Assembly resolution to get Israel to withdraw immediately from Egyptian soil; it passed by a vote of 65 to 1.

The British and French also chose to ignore the Russian warnings, believing as they did that the Russian missile threat was false. If they were worried about anything, it was Soviet intervention in the form of volunteers. There were, in fact, serious rumors circulating throughout the Middle East of Russian jets flying to Syria over Turkey. Eden and Mollet remained cool about the Soviet missiles because they assumed that the United States would fulfill her NATO obligations, although no one could say whether those obligations extended to allied forces outside Europe. A partial answer to this question was supplied by General Gruenther, the Nato commander, on November 13. At a press conference he warned that if Khrushchev followed through with his threats, "Moscow would be destroyed as night follows day."[18]

As early as November 4, the General Assembly called on the Secretary General to arrange a cease fire. Between the pressure from Washington and the attainment of most of its objectives, the Israelis stopped fighting. Guy Mollet wanted to thumb his nose at the U.N. for a bit longer, but Eden (who was physically ailing during the crisis) saw no alternative to accepting the cease fire on November 6. The Anglo-French troops then handed over the Canal Zone to a U.N. peacekeeping force and the British and French finally left Egyptian soil on December 23. Only after the United States threatened sanctions did the Israelis disengage from Sinai in March of 1957.

The biggest political casualty of the Suez crisis was Anthony Eden, who resigned in disgrace and was replaced by Harold MacMillan. Ironically, MacMillan had been the strongest proponent of the Suez invasion in the British cabinet. Eisenhower subsequently received both prime ministers of Britain and France and the Western alliance was patched up. On April 24, 1957, the Egyptian Canal Authority opened the Suez Canal to traffic once again and the crisis was over.

The clearest winners in the Suez crisis were Egypt and Israel. Even though its military reputation took a severe blow at the hands of little Israel, Egypt did establish control over the Suez Canal. Moreover, it eventually got the Aswan Dam built with Soviet aid, and it gained the region's first clear victory over "imperialism." From 1956 the Arab world for really the first time realized the importance of oil as a weapon of diplomacy. Nasser's personal prestige remained enormous throughout the Middle East until his death in 1970.

Israel was able to free the Gulf of Aqaba from Egyptian control and destroy the terrorist bases in Gaza. In the process she won a clear victory and proved for the first time that she was a regional force to be reckoned with. The resolution of the Suez crisis bought ten years of peace for Israel, time in which to absorb its waves of immigrants—thousands of whom came from Egypt and North Africa—build up its economy and military even further, and strengthen her very important relations with the United States.

The crisis accelerated British decline. Among the losers, Britain saw her influence wane both in the Middle East and in Washington. It would now be a very difficult thing for Britain to act in the world independently of the United States.

The French who had placed a great deal of trust in its Anglo-Saxon allies would never do so again to the same extent. The Suez setback helped to bring back

Charles de Gaulle to power eighteen months later. Under his leadership, France would veto Britain's entry into the Common Market, eventually withdraw from the military structure of NATO, concentrate on an independent deterrent, and be very cool to U.S. policy in Vietnam.

For the Soviet Union the Suez crisis was indeed an historic turning point. It gained a great deal of credibility in the Middle East and in the third world by siding with Egypt and by helping to construct the Aswan Dam. Every Soviet move during the crisis was calculated to win Arab support. Nevertheless, the Russians also demonstrated their inability to decisively effect the outcome of events. It was now clear to Arab leaders that American nuclear supremacy would not soon be challenged by the Soviet Union.[19]

Moscow's relationship with radical Arab regimes like Nasser's were merely partnerships of convenience. Egypt, for example, proved to be a less than solid ally. In December 1958 when a coup in Iraq toppled a pro-Western monarch and brought to power rulers who professed friendship to the Soviet Union, Nasser reacted by arresting hundreds of Egyptian communists. While the Soviet Union would maintain a major influence in the Middle East, the Arab regimes were as unwilling to accept Soviet domination as they were Western.

The crisis definitely ended European claims to hegemony in the Middle East, and left the Western bloc in disarray. The United States by 1957 was left as the uncontested representative of Western interests in the Middle East. It now saw Soviet-backed Arab radical regimes exploiting the vacuum (a notion deeply resented by Arab nationalists) left by Britain and France. Eisenhower and Dulles now felt that the moment had come for a new application of containment to the region. It was vital to do this because, as Eisenhower put it: "The Bear is still the central enemy."[20] On January 5, 1957, Eisenhower requested authorization from Congress to use the U.S. armed forces in the Middle East to help nations there resist "overt armed aggression from any nation controlled by International Communism," and authorization to extend military and economic assistance to the region.[21] The Eisenhower Doctrine, as it came to be called, was soon tested. In April 1957 King Hussein of Jordan was nearly toppled by pro-Nasser Jordanians. Eisenhower ordered the Sixth Fleet to patrol off the coast of Lebanon and he threatened to send in the marines. The immediate object of the Eisenhower Doctrine in this case was Nasserite Arabs who might eventually be backed by the Soviet Union. Another test came in Lebanon in May of 1958 when civil war erupted between Christians and pro-Nasser Muslims. When a few months later the pro-Western regime in Baghdad fell, Washington, fearing the spread of Arab radicalism, landed troops in Lebanon to prop up the pro-American regime. Communism was only distantly in the picture, and the United States through its invocation of the Eisenhower Doctrine was prepared to use force where it served American interests. Lebanon and Iran endorsed the Eisenhower Doctrine, while Syria, Egypt, and Jordan soundly rejected it.

What the Suez crisis did in the final analysis was to help the United States and the Soviet Union translate their Middle Eastern policies into the global terms of the Cold War.

Notes

1. Quoted in George Lenzcowski, *American Presidents and the Middle East* (Durham, N.C.: Duke University Press, 1990), 30.

2. Conor Cruise O'Brien, *The Siege. The Saga of Israel and Zionism* (New York: Simon and Schuster, 1986), 385.

3. Moshe Dayan, *Story of My Life* (London: Weidenfeld and Nicolson, 1966), 146.

4. Quoted in Gail E. Meyer, *Egypt and the United States* (Rutherford, N.J.: Fairleigh Dickinson University Press, 1980), 146.

5. Hugh Thomas, *Suez* (New York: Harper and Row, 1967), 37-38.

6. Sherman Adams, *First Hand Report. The Story of the Eisenhower Administration* (New York: Harper, 1961), 200.

7. Thomas, *Suez*, 72.

8. Anthony Eden, *Full Circle. The Memoirs of Anthony Eden* (London: Cassell, 1960), 512.

9. Thomas, *Suez*, 63-122.

10. Dayan, *Story of My Life*, 175.

11. O'Brien, *The Siege*, 289.

12. Quoted in Peter L. Hahn, *The United States, Great Britain, and Egypt, 1945-1956* (Chapel Hill: University of North Carolina Press, 1991), 230.

13. Thomas, *Suez*, 147.

14. Nikita Khrushchev, *Khrushchev Remembers*, trans. Strobe Talbott (Boston: Little, Brown and Company, 1970), 434.

15. Michael Brecher, *Decisions in Israel's Foreign Policy* (London: Oxford University Press, 1974), 285.

16. Brecher, *Decisions*, 277.

17. Brecher, *Decisions*, 286.

18. Quoted in Thomas, *Suez*, 147.

19. Oles Smolansky, *The Soviet Union and the Arab East Under Khrushchev* (Lewisburg, Pa.: Bucknell University Press, 1974).

20. David Schoenbaum, *The United States and the State of Israel* (New York: Oxford University Press, 1993), 117.

21. Quoted in Stephen F. Ambrose, *Eisenhower, The President* (New York: Simon and Schuster, 1984), 382.

14

The Death of Stalin
and the Revolutions of 1956

By 1953 Stalin's rule in the Soviet Union was as firmly established as it had ever been. He was still admired as one of his country's greatest historical figures, second only to Lenin, and "the standard bearer of his genius and his cause."

To the very end of his life Stalin was anxious to safeguard his power. By 1953 it was clear that he was laying the ground work for a third great purge of the Communist Party. All of the old guard communists began to fear for their lives when each in turn was eased out of their important positions. Even Lavrenti Beria lost sole command of the secret police, and one of his key protégés was arrested. Like the "Kirov Plot" which helped to trigger the Great Terror of the 1930s, this purge was to be preceded by a "conspiracy" as well.

In January 1953 the Soviet government announced that nine doctors, all but two Jewish, had been arrested and charged with murdering Andre Zhdanov and other members of the party elite. They were accused of having acted on orders from Israel and the American and British security services. It was also alleged that they planned to liquidate the rest of the country's leadership. The government's use of the "Doctor's Plot," as it was called, was designed to arouse the country against internal and external enemies and, at the same time, rekindle a latent anti-Semitism within Soviet society. The unfortunate doctors were arrested, tortured, and made to confess to crimes they did not commit. Jews in prominent positions were now particularly vulnerable and thousands of arrests followed.[1] At this point, with the axe poised to fall on the party itself, and with mass terror about to break over the country, Stalin died on March 5, 1953.

Stalin's death touched off a political struggle in the Soviet Union among its leading power centers—the party, the organs of security, and the army. At the same time, it touched off a personal struggle among the old guard Stalinists who, now with Stalin's death, returned to their former positions—Beria as head of the secret police, Malenkov as premier and briefly party chief, Molotov as foreign minister, Bulganin as minister of defense, and Nikita Khrushchev, who quickly won the party post.

The collective leadership that replaced Stalin had to adjust to an atmosphere of insecurity and suspicion. Stalin's death was unsettling enough, but Khrushchev feared that the worst was still to come. Like the rest of the leadership he feared the power of the secret police. "I already sensed that Beria would start bossing everyone around and that this could be the beginning of the end. . . . I considered him a treacherous opportunist who would stop at nothing to get what he wanted. . . . He was a butcher and an assassin."[2] The fear that Beria might establish a personal dictatorship drew the other members of the leadership together in a conspiracy against him. Led by Khrushchev and with help from the army leadership, Beria was trapped in a Kremlin conference room and arrested. The key factor here was the use of the Russian army to settle a personal struggle for power. The important result was that for the first time since the 1920s, the party recaptured its former preeminence, and the secret police was once again subordinated to party control.

The last years of Stalin's rule witnessed great industrial expansion as the Soviet Union sought to recover from the war and meet the new geopolitical challenges of the Cold War. But the costs of production were extremely high and living standards actually declined. Tremendous shortages throughout the economy—always an endemic problem in Soviet history—imperilled future economic growth. By Stalin's death economic hardship was almost as acute as it was in the 1930s. The command economy was notoriously inefficient and corrupt, the bureaucracy stifling and run by apparatchiks who blindly obeyed the orders of their superiors. Both Malenkov and Khrushchev understood, as Gorbachev would thirty years later, that the Soviet Union was ripe for a major economic reform.

The new leadership began to institute changes in the economy immediately. Malenkov began by lowering prices and devoting more resources to consumer goods. At the same time, Khrushchev took charge of agricultural production and, in an attempt to raise living standards, he launched a vast program to grow grain on land previously not cultivated in Kazakhstan and western Siberia. In the short run this "virgin lands" program produced dramatic results.

Malenkov and Khrushchev also understood that Stalin's foreign policy since the war had been counterproductive. Through all of Stalin's efforts to take advantage of postwar chaos, he had failed to achieve a revolutionary breakthrough. All he had accomplished by trying to pressure the West in Iran, Berlin, and Korea, was the formation of the Western alliance and the rearmament of the United States and West Germany. The failure of Stalin's major policies in Europe and Asia had left the Soviet Union as isolated as it ever was. The new leadership therefore moved quickly to restore the contacts lost during the previous eight years and reduce tension with the West. Diplomatic ties were then restored with Israel and Greece, and Moscow began to heal the rift with Yugoslavia. At the same time, it repudiated all previous claims to Turkish territory and together with the Chinese sought to revive the armistice talks in Korea. Less than two weeks after the armistice was signed in Korea, Malenkov made a major speech to the Supreme Soviet in which he seemed to cast off the adversarial "two camps" doctrine, and he became more conciliatory toward the West. It was clear that Moscow was striking out on a new path when Malenkov declared: "We firmly stand by the belief that there are no disputed or outstanding issues today that cannot be settled peacefully by mutual agreement between the parties concerned."[3]

At the Conference of Foreign Ministers held in Berlin from January 25 to February 18, 1954, the Soviet Union and the Western powers made an attempt—their first since 1949—to reach an agreement on European security. Molotov proposed that all foreign troops disengage from Germany and allow that state to become neutral. This would lead, he said, to reunification and then to a general European security treaty open to all those states on the continent that promised to settle their disputes peacefully. Cleverly employing the language of the North Atlantic Treaty, Molotov said that in the event of war, an attack against one state would be considered an attack against all, and "each one of the parties, in the exercise of the right of the individual or collective self-defense, shall assist the state or states which had been so attacked by all the means at its disposal."

The Soviet initiative at Berlin was all very well, but from Washington's standpoint the neutralization of Germany seemed designed to destroy NATO; and the proposal to withdraw troops from Europe seemed like a transparent attempt to get the U.S. military back across the ocean while the Red Army, camped on its own border, was still within striking distance of all the continent's major centers.

The proposals were rejected. The Russians spoke the language of accommodation, but in November 1954 they began to construct their own military counterweight to NATO. This would in 1955 become the Warsaw Pact and would give Moscow a perfect excuse to maintain a military presence in Eastern Europe. This was why Dulles initially opposed direct contact with the new Soviet leadership. Even though Winston Churchill, as early as April 1953, urged direct contact with the new ruling group in Moscow, Dulles refused to believe that the Soviet Union had changed under new communist leadership. After all, Malenkov, Molotov, and Khrushchev made a clear distinction in their speeches between softening their posture toward the West and maintaining a rigid control over what they had won in the Second World War. Moreover, Malenkov and Khrushchev may have attacked the rigidities and excesses of the Stalin regime, but they clearly, at every opportunity, affirmed the essential validity of the communist ideology. They let it be known that Marxism-Leninism would remain the basis of communist party rule. Nor was this fidelity to the ideology simply career opportunism. For them the ideology remained eternally true and stood the test of time.

In charting a new domestic and foreign course for his country, Khrushchev was prepared to go much further than his rivals in the Politburo. A peasant of little schooling, Khrushchev was a man of tremendous energy who was highly flexible and pragmatic in his whole style of governing. He was also a dedicated communist. For example, in discussing Stalin's encouragement of Kim Il Sung's attack on South Korea, Khrushchev made it clear in his memoirs that he approved on ideological grounds. "In my opinion, no real communist would have tried to dissuade Kim Il Sung from his compelling desire to liberate South Korea from Syngman Rhee and from reactionary American influence. To have done so would have contradicted the Communist view of the world."[4] Like Stalin, his whole career had revolved around the concept of force. He had shrewdly and single-mindedly engineered his own rise to power in a time of Byzantine treachery and unbelievable mass violence. In 1953 alone, he had clearly demonstrated that he was an accomplished student of the Stalinist system when he furthered his position by manipulating the power blocs of the party, the bureaucracy, and the army. He proved then that he could be alternately accommodating and ruthless and he did so when one false move could have cost him his life. Finally, he knew when to forge personal alliances with competitors and discard them when they were no longer useful.

The weak and indecisive Malenkov proved no match for the tough and unscrupulous Khrushchev. Shunting Malenkov aside in early 1955, Khrushchev then turned his attention to the hardline Stalinists on the Politburo led by Molotov. Khrushchev's main argument in the struggle with Malenkov was that his rival was wrong to support consumer industries at the expense of heavy industry needed for defense. This was a clear Stalinist line and briefly won Molotov to his side. Khrushchev then showed himself a student of Stalin's attack on the left opposition in the late 1920s when he isolated Molotov by attacking his rigid stance on foreign relations. His vehicle for doing so and the key to his radical break with Stalinism was his attempt to reestablish diplomatic relations with Yugoslavia. The unimaginative Molotov openly criticized the new policy, objecting to any attempt to patch up things with a country that since 1948 had proved itself to be anti-Soviet.

At the end of May 1955, and accompanied by defense minister Nikolai Bulganin, Khrushchev visited Belgrade. Molotov was deliberately left behind. Under the Belgrade Agreement, Khrushchev formally acknowledged the principle of "separate paths to communism." Khrushchev made a point of repudiating the Stalinist attempt to impose ideological purity on the regimes of Eastern Europe. This was reinforced a year later when Khrushchev dissolved the Cominform. In acknowledging that there was no longer a Soviet monolith in Eastern Europe, Khrushchev was, in effect, giving the go-ahead to the future growth of nationalistic Communist parties throughout Europe.

Khrushchev made other dramatic moves that augured well for the reduction of Cold War tensions. He normalized relations with West Germany in 1955 and in the same year the Russians withdrew from Austria and signed a treaty with the West which guaranteed Austrian neutrality. This was the first instance of a Soviet military and political withdrawal from an area in Central Europe under their control.

Khrushchev also forged closer relations with the non-aligned countries of Asia. Thus Moscow supported a Chinese proclamation in April 1955 on peaceful coexistence at the Bandung Conference of non-aligned nations in Indonesia. Along with Bulganin, Khrushchev then visited India, Burma, and Afghanistan and once again professed his devotion to the doctrine of peaceful coexistence and the respect for the sovereignty of nations. In each case, Khrushchev also promised economic assistance and scientific and technical cooperation. Khrushchev was not just establishing his credentials as a world statesman to enhance his prestige at home, he was gaining some real influence among the underdeveloped nations of the world, as he would again when he helped Egypt build the Aswan Dam. What Khrushchev was also doing in the 1950s was buying time and avoiding direct confrontation with the West after the failed policies pursued by Stalin in the Berlin Blockade and the Korean War. In many ways, this was the traditional Russian response to foreign policy disasters on one hand, and economic backwardness on the other. Khrushchev's eagerness for peaceful coexistence and the quest for allies was used as a means to achieve a breathing spell in order to catch up with the rest of the world's more powerful rivals. This accounts, argues Jack Snyder, for the reduction of ideological militancy, the "appeasing while catching up" and the remaining open to the importation of technologies from more advanced societies. Snyder argues that peaceful coexistence should be understood against the historical precedents of Stolypin's detente with Germany following the Russo-Japanese War, Stalin's popular front strategy and pact with Hitler, and Gorbachev's use of a peace campaign to head off the American Strategic Defense Initiative in the 1980s. All these examples, he concludes, "conform to a general pattern of a backward state hoping to postpone a sharpening of international competition until it can catch up."[5] And while it was catching up, Moscow found it useful to promote national liberation struggles in the third world in conjunction with the attainment of nuclear immunity. Its long-range goal was the defeat of containment through encirclement.

It nevertheless appeared to many in the West that a new era in East-West relations had been achieved when in July 1955 the Geneva Summit convened. Attended by the United States, Britain, France and the Soviet Union, this was the first summit conference since Potsdam in 1945. Coming on top of all the initiatives taken by Moscow since Stalin's death, the conference presented an opportunity to open a new dialogue between the two blocs.

The atmosphere at Geneva was congenial throughout. Eisenhower wisely chose to ignore Dulles's advice to keep an "austere countenance" when dealing personally with the Russians. At their first official dinner, Eisenhower, impatient with formalities, told Khrushchev that it was vital to "find some way of controlling the threat of the thermonuclear bomb. You know, we both have enough weapons to wipe out the entire northern hemisphere from fallout alone." Khrushchev agreed: "We get your dust, you get our dust, the winds blow and nobody's safe."[6] A bit later Eisenhower proposed his "open skies" plan, whereby the two countries would have the right to photograph each other's territory and exchange blueprints of military installations. Khrushchev angrily called it "espionage." "Who are you trying to fool?" he asked. "This kind of plan would be fine for you because it would give your strategic forces the chance to gather target information and zero in on us." The Russians, after all, already had access to information on American installations through their intelligence efforts, and from U.S. periodicals. The arrangement therefore would be too lop-sided. Eisenhower replied that nevertheless the plan was an important step that would "dispel fear and suspicion and thus lighten international tension by reassuring people against the dangers of surprise attack."[7] Eisenhower later remarked: "We knew the Soviets wouldn't accept it. We were sure of that, but we took a look and thought it was a good move."[8] The U.N. General Assembly eventually endorsed the plan, but the Russians rejected it outright as an American espionage scheme that would infringe on Soviet territorial sovereignty.

Eisenhower did not make a good impression on Khrushchev at the conference. Khrushchev thought the president a good man, but a weak president who was too dependent on his advisors, especially Dulles, who Khrushchev once referred to as the "chained cur of capitalism." Khrushchev made a better impression on Eisenhower. The president found Khrushchev "round and amiable, but with a will of iron only slightly concealed."[9]

The summit also concerned itself, albeit briefly, with the issues that had produced the Cold War; namely, the German question, and the Soviet hold over Eastern Europe. Eisenhower did call for free elections in Germany, while Dulles added his voice by advocating the liberation of Eastern Europe. And it was these questions that especially angered Khrushchev. The West wanted "the reunification of Germany," he recalled, which really meant the formation of a single capitalist Germany as part of NATO. Khrushchev made it clear that Russia would not permit free elections in East Germany until West Germany had disarmed. Nevertheless it was here that Moscow formally recognized West Germany. Khrushchev also felt that the Western leaders at Geneva were out "to restore capitalism in the countries liberated by the Soviet army after World War II, and they particularly wanted to tear Poland away from the Socialist bloc." Khrushchev made it clear that the bloc would remain under Soviet control. This was actually signalled to the West two months before, on May 14, 1955, when Moscow created the Warsaw Pact. The pact was a defensive alliance of European communist nations, which represented the Soviet response to the American integration of West German troops into NATO. Ten years after the war the West could do little but grudgingly acquiesce to Soviet domination of Eastern Europe.

The summit accomplished little of consequence on the problems of disarmament and European security. Nevertheless, it was generally free of rancor, as both sides were eager to make good impressions. Many people were fooled by the new style of the Russians and misinterpreted it—as did the Western media—as a basic change in Soviet attitudes. When Eisenhower returned home, he applauded "a new spirit of conciliation and cooperation" he thought now existed in the Kremlin. The "Spirit of Geneva" even infected Dulles. "The Soviet policy," he said, "is now based on tolerance which includes good relations with everyone."[10] Khrushchev declared that the conference was actually useful, since "it gave the leaders of the four great powers an opportunity to see each other at close quarters and to exchange views informally among themselves." And yet, he went on: "If anybody thinks that for this reason we shall forget about Marx, Engels, and Lenin, he is mistaken. This will happen when shrimps learn to whistle."[11]

During the great thaw of 1955 it was also apparent that there were serious rifts in the Kremlin leadership between "Stalinists" led by Molotov and "reformers" led by Khrushchev.

In February 1956 Khrushchev used the meeting of the Twentieth Congress of the Communist Party to deliver a scathing denunciation of Stalin and the "cult of the individual" and, at the same time, to bid for the leadership of the country. Until this point, Stalin was still regarded as a rather god-like figure in party circles and throughout the communist world. Khrushchev's speech, which lasted over four hours, was remarkable for the honesty and vehemence of its attack. In his speech, Khrushchev revealed Stalin's ruthless destruction of loyal party and government workers and thousands of professional army officers. He told about the persecution of the nation's important people—scientists, artists, writers, composers, and millions of ordinary people trapped in the absurdities of a system that had become perverted. Throughout the speech there were thinly veiled attacks on those who had been the hard-core Stalinists in the 1930s and who had done the dictator's bidding, namely, Molotov, Malenkov, and Kaganovich, Khrushchev's rivals in the Politburo. His audience already knew at least part of the truth, but Khrushchev for the first time exposed the true extent of the problem. In his indictment of the system, Khrushchev tried to depict Stalin's despotism as an aberration of Leninism rather than its logical extension. At the same time, he demythologized Stalin's image as the all-wise war-time leader when he revealed how Stalin had miscalculated during the German attack in June 1941, and how, for a time, he had even lost control and come close to a breakdown. He also attacked Stalin for fabricating the Leningrad Affair and the Doctor's Plot, and held him responsible for the break with Tito.[12]

It was obvious that the Stalinist regime had lost its moral compass and the problem of rehabilitating millions of victims had to be faced squarely. According to Roy and Zhores Medvedev, by 1957 between seven and eight million people who were still alive in the Gulag prison camp system were released and allowed to return to their homes. Another five to six million were posthumously rehabilitated. This kind of pardon had important consequences for the surviving families, since they had lived under the stain of treason ever since their relative's arrest. They could now apply to live in Moscow, receive a pension, and if they still wished, be reintegrated into the Communist Party. Before the rehabilitation, Khrushchev had limited the powers of the secret police and reduced it substantially in size.[13]

Khrushchev was trying to remove the dead hand of the past and alter a system that ruled through naked force alone. He believed that a more relaxed political atmosphere would promote new levels of prosperity. In denouncing the crimes of the Stalin era, it was his basic intention to condemn Stalin's vicious treatment and demotion of the Communist Party. He made a point in the speech of not questioning the country's one-party system, nor did he question the collectivization of the Russian countryside in the 1930s. He therefore only indirectly addressed himself to the sufferings of the Soviet people since, after all, he himself had been involved in the crushing of the peasantry on Stalin's behalf. Khrushchev, no less than the other Stalinists in the Politburo, had a vested interest in one kind of society. Nevertheless, Khrushchev's reform of the more criminal aspects of the system was so extremely radical that it encouraged the post-Stalin crisis to grow.

As an empire, the Soviet Union and its satellites closely resembled the Habsburg and Ottoman empires. Like them, it boasted a contiguous accumulation of territory held together by military and administrative power, and dominated by a powerful core. Unlike the other empires, however, it was ruled by a political party which tried to refashion it all into a communist regime. It was different in one more way; the western borderlands of the empire were in some cases more advanced culturally and economically than the imperial core. And for this as well as the obvious reasons, states like Poland, Hungary, and Czechoslovakia seethed under the Russian yoke.

Khrushchev understood that attempts to de-Stalinize the Soviet Union would probably be followed by similar attempts to reform the miniature Stalinisms throughout the Soviet bloc. To a certain extent, Khrushchev encouraged it. But what he may not have appreciated was that a sweeping reform of the imperial core of the empire, accompanied at the same time by a power struggle, might even lead to revolt in the borderlands, as it did in Poland in 1863 and again throughout the Russian empire in 1917. People all over the bloc were encouraged by the political thaw following Stalin's death and the execution of Lavrenti Beria. Crises arose in the Soviet bloc since 1953, argues Charles Gati, when Eastern Europeans sensed drift and uncertainty and division in Moscow. "Kremlin turbulence does not create crises in Eastern Europe; it turns inherent instability into explicit regime demands or popular explosions."[14] The reduction of the power of the Soviet secret police and Khrushchev's attack on Stalinism served to undermine the legitimacy of the ruling clique and greatly increased anti-Soviet feelings among millions of ordinary people throughout the bloc, as well as among younger members of Communist parties.

The first sign that there might be an irreversible dynamic in de-Stalinizing came in Czechoslovakia right after Stalin's death. It began with a demonstration in Prague in which workers voiced both economic and political demands. They called for free elections, and carried aloft pictures of Thomas Masaryk and Edouard Benes, the first two presidents of a free Czechoslovakia. The Kremlin handled this bloodless outburst carefully, and allowed the Czech militia to quell it.

Two weeks later, On June 17, 1953, a workers' revolt broke out in East Germany. Stalin's death coincided here with a mounting economic and political crisis. The East German government under Walter Ulbricht had instituted an austerity program that called for a raising of quotas in industrial plants and a reduction in worker's income—the regime subjected the recalcitrant to a number of show trials in which workers were made to confess to the crimes of slacking and sabotage. The crisis was also agricultural. Collectivization proceeded so quickly that by the end of 1952 nearly 15,000 farmers and their families had fled to West Germany, leaving roughly 13 percent of East Germany's arable land untended. This of course produced a food shortage, which led to more unrest in the cities and more arrests and show trials. By June 1953, at least 2 percent of the population had fled to the West, making the economy a shambles.[15]

The explosion in East Berlin began among some construction workers who quit their jobs in protest over an increase in work requirements. As they marched down the Stalin Allee they called upon other workers to join them. It quickly turned into a riot as hundreds of workers went on a rampage tearing down propaganda posters and billboards. It soon included the entire populace of East Berlin. Encountering little resistance at first, it quickly became the first attempt at a revolt within the Soviet bloc as workers set fire to Communist Party buildings and released prisoners from jail. The revolt spread to other cities in East Germany; there were mass meetings throughout the country in which workers demanded that the Ulbricht government step down and that free elections be held. Terrified at first, the besieged government pleaded with the rioters to go back to work and, when that failed, called for Russian help. The revolt did not subside until Soviet troops broke up the demonstrations with tanks and until it became obvious that no help from the West would be forthcoming. Hundreds were killed and wounded in the suppression and when it was over the Ulbricht government took vengeance and executed eighteen workers and sentenced 1,300 to long prison terms.

It had all been a genuine proletarian uprising that had embarrassed the communist world. It had served to discredit a communist regime in a key satellite that had been in power for eight years. It also showed clearly that Moscow's domination over Eastern Europe was maintained by force and that no matter how it advanced reform and preached peaceful coexistence, it was determined to preserve Soviet rule.

Khrushchev's "secret speech" sent a shock wave through Eastern Europe, but particularly through Poland and Hungary. Poland was certainly Russia's most important satellite. She was among the largest of the bloc states, and the original bone of contention between East and West during the last stage of the war. Moreover, Moscow's communications with East Germany crossed Polish territory and therefore she was strategically vital to the Soviet security system. Determined to turn Poland into a Soviet-controlled state, Stalin had purged national-communists like Wladyslaw Gomulka as potential Titoists, and erected a loyal regime in Warsaw under an old Comintern agent, Boleslaw Bierut. To prop him up he installed a Soviet general, Marshal Konstanty Rokossowski, as deputy premier and minister of defense. To Sovietize the economy, heavy industry was emphasized at the expense of agriculture, the trade unions were crushed, and the economy directed by a central plan. In an attempt to stifle the traditional Christian Culture of the country, the privileges and possessions of the Catholic Church were curtailed and many bishops and priests were arrested and imprisoned. To reorganize Polish cultural life along Soviet lines, writers and artists unions and all cultural publications were taken over by the Communist Party.[16]

In December 1953, Colonel Josef Swiatlo, an important member of the Polish secret police, defected to the West. He had been the man in charge of arresting Gomulka and other party members in 1948-1949. In speeches on Radio Free Europe he admitted that he was ordered to falsify evidence against Gomulka so that the state could arrest him. He also revealed that Communist Party members often spied on each other. These revelations served to shake up the party and undermine the legitimacy of the ruling clique. The reduction of the powers of the secret police in Russia was therefore quickly imitated in Poland, as Gomulka was released from prison in 1954.

Khrushchev's attack on Stalinism had been preceded in Poland by a period of intellectual ferment. The first discussion clubs of intellectuals were formed in Warsaw in the spring of 1955 and took aim at the sorry state of communist culture. Khrushchev's speech of 1956, which had been read out at Communist Party meetings throughout Poland, intensified these discussions as intellectuals began to question the monopoly of the Communist Party over Polish cultural life. The old Stalinist leaders also found themselves on the defensive against younger and more liberal and nationalistic party members who increasingly sought "a Polish road to socialism." A few weeks after Khrushchev's speech, Bierut suddenly died and the political and ideological underpinnings of the regime began to unravel. At this point Khrushchev engineered the selection of Eduard Ochab as Bierut's successor. As it turned out, Ochab proved to be a flexible communist and soon threw in with the reformers.

A number of reformers now called for Gomulka's elevation to the Polish Politburo. Still a popular figure in the party, Gomulka had been a resistance fighter during the war and a victim of Stalinism. While ruthless in his determination to eliminate "class enemies," and contemptuous of "bourgeois democracy," he nevertheless sought to establish a socialist system independent of the Soviet model. Overnight he became a popular symbol of resistance and reform.

In June 1956, 15,000 steelworkers in Poznan escalated a pay dispute into a massive riot, the first manifestation of its kind in Poland since 1939. The workers demanded "Bread and Freedom" and carried signs that read, "Down with Communism" and "Throw the Russkies out." They assaulted some party officials along the way and the first troops sent to the scene fraternized with the rioters. When the Polish army finally restored order—by firing into the crowd—fifty-three workers lay dead and more than 300 were wounded.

At this point, the Communist Party leadership split into a reformist and Stalinist wing full of enemies of Gomulka. The reformists soon gained the upper hand as Gomulka emerged as its leader on the central committee. Gomulka then promptly turned up the heat when he vowed that he would enter the party's Politburo only if the Stalinists were purged from it.

In October the workers movement exploded again right across the country with demonstrators demanding the withdrawal of the Soviet army from Poland. "We had every right to move troops in Poland," recalled Khrushchev. "It looked to us as if Polish events were rushing forward on the crest of a giant anti-Soviet wave. . . . We were afraid Poland might break away from us at any moment."[17]

On October 19, 1956, the Polish central committee met to select a new Politburo. A powerful Soviet delegation including Khrushchev, Mikoyan, Molotov, Kaganovich, and a dozen Russian army generals in full dress uniform arrived that same day in Warsaw uninvited. The Soviet delegation proceeded immediately to the meeting of the Central Committee. At the time, Soviet tank forces began to advance on the capital. Khrushchev's worry, he later said, was that Gomulka's elevation to power (he was elected first secretary of the Communist Party at the meeting) was engineered by the "political machinations of certain anti-Soviet forces." A military intervention seemed, at least for the moment, the best way to set things right.

The reformers, however, presented a united front as Gomulka prepared to go on the radio to endorse the Titoist idea of separate paths to socialism. Khrushchev, of course, was afraid that Gomulka could explain the situation in a very anti-Russian way that could ignite things into a full-blown revolution. At the same time, Marshal Rokossowski informed Khrushchev that the Polish military would not put down the movement on behalf of the Soviet Union. Indeed, Gomulka had ordered the Polish army into defensive positions around Warsaw, and along with thousands of workers were prepared to defend the capital.

Khrushchev was afraid that if he did nothing the movement might spread to other bloc countries. On the other hand, if he called for a military repression and a blood bath resulted, it would spell the end of his reformist policies and erode his own position in Moscow. Ochab agreed with Khrushchev that if things were not soon controlled than chaos would ensue and the revolutionary movement might succeed in destroying communism in Poland. It would be best, he argued, to keep Gomulka in power since a majority of the party and the people placed their trust in him. The Polish people needed to be led by someone who is "free from Stalinist stigma."[18] Khrushchev realized that Gomulka and his supporters were reformers, but they were still communists who, while they would like to build a socialist society different from that of the Soviet Union, would still remain allies of Moscow and remain in the Warsaw Pact. Gomulka made this clear when he told Khrushchev: "Poland needs the friendship of the Soviet Union more than the Soviet Union needs the friendship of Poland." After several tense days, Khrushchev decided to compromise with Polish nationalism and pulled his troops back to their bases, and sent his congratulations to Gomulka.

From the Poznan riot to the moment when Soviet troops returned to their bases, Gomulka understood the limits of Russian tolerance. It was clear to him that he had to steer a moderate course in which the Communist Party continued to play a dominant role in the country's political life. He could do this because he had a firm base in the party and in the factories of Poland. He could therefore maintain control of the popular movement and avoid a military showdown with the Soviet Union. Instead of yet another Russian repression of Polish freedoms, Gomulka was able to bring off a genuine Polish-Soviet compromise in which he achieved some substantial modifications in communist rule. For example, Poland obtained full domestic autonomy—a curtailment of Russian military authority within Poland, an almost complete lifting of the Iron Curtain to the West, less censorship than could be found in other bloc countries, a reintroduction of religious instruction into the school system, and the dismantling of collective farms and their return to the peasants. Poland could now run her internal affairs her own way, and in return she had only to bend her knee to Moscow and remain in the Warsaw Pact and consistently proclaim her loyalty to Soviet foreign policy.

In November 1956 Gomulka was warmly received in Moscow where he spoke like a loyal ally and reassured Khrushchev. To cement the new relationship Moscow cancelled Poland's debts to the Soviet Union and extended Poland a Russian loan of 700 million rubles and one and a half million tons of wheat to help her through the winter. Gomulka had proven himself one of the most gifted politicians in Polish history.

The events in Poland in 1956 indicated once again that a communist bloc country could take a separate path to socialism, one in line with its own national traditions.

The competing forces in Poland in 1956 could also be found in Hungary: A hated Stalinist ruling clique, a liberal opposition group within the Party and energized by Khrushchev's speech, a group of rehabilitated former leaders, thousands of restless and angry workers, and the support of the country's intellectuals. Unhappily, the result in Hungary was tragic.

Like the Polish movement, the Hungarian Revolution was preceded by a strong period of intellectual ferment. In Hungary, as in Poland, the Communist Party leaders faced a native intellectual class, the majority of whom were bitterly opposed communism.

Like Poland, many intellectuals organized themselves into discussion groups, which challenged the Communist Party's monopoly of truth. They consistently maintained that the press must be unshackled and allowed to publish the truth, show trials and torture to extract false confessions must be condemned and the perpetrators punished, and the rule of law restored to the Hungarian nation. Above all, the arts must no longer be subservient to the Communist Party. There were echoes of 1789 and 1848 in the message and activism of what writers and artists, academics and students were saying and doing in 1956. All across the bloc, but particularly in Poland and Hungary, men and women were calling for a return to the ideals of those eventful years: liberty, equality, and fraternity, and the nationalism of 1848. The events of 1956 and again in 1989 are dramatic examples of the great democratic revolution of the eighteenth century working its way through once again.

But Hungary was different from Poland in one important sense. It had been an Axis power during World War II and contributed troops to the German invasion of the Soviet Union. Moscow treated the Hungarians like former enemies after 1945 and the scale of oppression was therefore greater here than it was in Poland. The unpopularity of the communist regime in Hungary was correspondingly greater as was the intellectual ferment.

Under the iron hand of Matyas Rakosi, as hard-line a communist chieftain as could be found in the bloc, Hungary was converted into a communist state in 1949. With Stalin's death in 1953 Rakosi did his best to resist the winds of change blowing in from Moscow. Instead of responding positively to the demands for economic and political reforms, he clamped down even more severely than before.

In June 1953, after being summoned to Moscow, Rakosi was forced to resign as prime minister (although he remained on as party first secretary) and was replaced by Imre Nagy, a reform-minded communist. Two years later Nagy was dismissed and Rakosi returned as prime minister. Rakosi soon proved that he had learned nothing in the interim. Instead of responding positively to the demands for reforms advocated by intellectuals and progressive communists around Nagy, he clamped down even more severely than before. The intellectuals were intimidated and Nagy was expelled from the party. Once again, Rakosi was replaced, this time by a close associate, Erno Gero. Hardly less hated as a Stalinist than Rakosi, Gero failed to provide any firm national direction to the intellectuals, students and workers who were clamouring for change. Nagy was the only potential Gomulka the nation could have rallied around, but lacking Gomulka's mettle, he refused to organize an opposition. The opposition movement then grew spontaneously, encouraged by the divided leadership within the Communist Party and inspired by the events in Poland.

On October 23, the day after Gomulka's formal return to power in Poland, students spearheaded a massive demonstration in Budapest on behalf of the Polish uprising. Like the crowds of 1848 the crowd here was a mixture of students, workers, and soldiers. They carried Hungarian and Polish flags and sang the Marseillaise, Louis Kossuth's anthem of 1848. The students demanded freedom of speech, a trial for the Stalinist leadership, Imre Nagy's return to office, and the removal of the Russian army from Hungarian soil. The crowd soon swelled to 200,000 and called for Imre Nagy. When he addressed them in Parliament Square, he began by calling them "comrades." The crowd yelled back, "We are not comrades." Still very much a reformed communist, he promised to introduce democratic procedures into the communist system, and asked for the people's confidence.

During the evening of the 23rd the Hungarian security forces opened fire on the demonstrators. What had until this point been a peaceful demonstration, now turned violent as the rising began to spread throughout the country. By the following day Hungary flamed with rebellion.

It soon became obvious that the people wanted not just reform but an end to the whole regime. Gero at this point asked the Soviet troops in the country to restore order. At first they moved in hesitantly, reluctant to intervene. In several places Russian troops actually fraternized with the demonstrators who climbed on their tanks waving flags. The Hungarian politburo was too uncertain of their own army's loyalty and on the 24th it lost its nerve; in an effort to contain the situation, it appointed Imre Nagy prime minister. But the rising quickly turned into national rebellion anyway. Government buildings were seized and communist emblems torn down. At one point, the Red Star was turned off atop the parliament building.

On the day Nagy was appointed prime minister, two emissaries from the Kremlin, Anastas Mikoyan, a skilled negotiator, and Mikhail Suslov, the party's ideologist, arrived in Budapest to assess the situation. By the 28th they came to agree that the Soviet intervention had been a mistake and they concluded that a Polish solution might be the answer. They then consented to the dismissal of Gero and his replacement by Janos Kadar, a man who had spent five years in prison on the charge of Titoism. The Soviet tanks were then withdrawn from the capital.

On his first day in office Nagy had declared martial law. In his radio address to the nation he announced a "greater democratization of public life" and stated that those who laid down their arms would not be subject to martial law. He also announced that negotiations for the withdrawal of Soviet troops from Hungary had commenced. But Nagy was not the master of events and he allowed himself to be swept along by the popular tide.

Revolutionary committees sprang up spontaneously in the cities calling themselves "councils," and reminding some people of the Soviets of 1917. While the call for a general strike went out, these councils broadcast over the radio and demanded the departure of the Russians from the country. More important they also controlled the movement in the provinces and threatened to march on the capital.

At the end of Nagy's first day in office he announced the end of one-party rule and formed a coalition government modelled on the one existing in 1945 before Communist Party rule was imposed on Hungary. Quickly the old political parties reopened their offices and began to publish newspapers. At the same time, Cardinal Mindszenty, the primate of Hungary and the symbol of opposition to communism who had been jailed in 1949, was freed and began to address huge crowds in Budapest. The revolution also took a grim turn when rebels seized the Communist Party office in Budapest and massacred its inhabitants.

Moscow then sent a clear signal to Nagy that it would not allow "reactionary forces" to undermine the foundations of socialism. The Russian message here was clear; tragically for the rebels, the American signals were mixed. On October 27, John Foster Dulles delivered a speech in Dallas, Texas, in which he said that any East European state that broke with Moscow could expect American aid. This could only fuel the hopes of the rebels in Hungary. But on the 29th he made it clear that the United States did not consider either Poland or Hungary as potential allies. But what the revolutionaries paid more attention to were the inflammatory broadcasts emanating from Radio Free Europe, which urged them to reject compromise solutions and step up the pace of change. Despite the fact that Washington funded Radio Free Europe, its independent board received no official instructions from the United States. Misled by these broadcasts, the Hungarian rebels begged for Western aid. But Eisenhower denied permission to air-drop arms and supplies, and troops were out of the question. Hungary was, he said privately, "as inaccessible to us as Tibet."[19]

Nagy seemed oblivious to most of this anyway. What he tried to do was steer a moderate course that would appease the revolutionaries and not alarm Moscow so much that it would intervene and crush the whole reform movement.[20] In the end he made the worst possible mistake—he announced Hungary's neutrality and its withdrawal from the Warsaw Pact, and he asked that the U.N. recognize that neutrality.

All along the rebels had rejoiced in the sympathy of the rhetorical support that filtered through from the West, but remained ignorant of the fact that the West's real attention was riveted on what was happening in the Suez Crisis. The events in Egypt provided the Russians with an exceptional diversion. In the Kremlin the prospect of Hungary breaking free of the communist grip set off alarm bells. If Nagy was allowed to get away with it, his example could have encouraged similar movements across the bloc. In this sense, it is important to note that some of Khrushchev's biggest support for a repression came from Gomulka and Tito, as it also did from the communist leadership in Bulgaria, Romania, and Czechoslovakia.

On November 4, 1956, Soviet forces consisting of fifteen army divisions and 200,000 troops began the suppression of the Hungarian Revolution. By the time the rebellion was crushed, roughly 3,000 Hungarians were killed and another 13,000 were wounded, and tens of thousands of people fled into hiding or exile. Imre Nagy was arrested by the Russians after being given a guarantee of safe-conduct by them. He was later executed. At the same time, the Russians installed Janos Kadar as the new prime minister of Hungary. Originally a cautious reformer and a victim of the Stalinist regime, Kadar worked to restore some semblance of order in his shattered country. Kadar understood that Moscow was willing to allow some degree of autonomy and independence in Hungary in return for an assurance that Hungary would not permit any return of multiparty democracy or Hungarian neutrality. Kadar quietly charted the course of Hungarian autonomy laid out by Imre Nagy, relaxing the restrictions of the centralized state and allowing some scope for an eventual return of private enterprise. All of it made Hungary a generation later the most prosperous state in the communist bloc. As Francois Fejto points out, in Hungary "it became evident that Stalinist methods of repression had been used, not to restore Stalinism, but to institute a Khrushchevist regime similar to Gomulka's."[21]

The bloc leaders quickly learned that de-Stalinization would not be tolerated if it eroded the power of the Communist Party, and that a leader who was not master of the public mood would soon be abandoned by the Kremlin.

When the revolution was over, Dulles tried to put the best face on America's lack of response to the crisis. Despite all of the administration's rhetoric about massive retaliation and the liberation of captive peoples, the United States seemed impotent to do anything in the face of the most dramatic events in the communist bloc since Tito's break with Stalin. At no point in the crisis did Washington spell out the limitations of American support to Budapest. It omitted to tell them that the United States was not prepared to go to war because its security interests were not involved. Nor did Washington remind the Kremlin of the political and economic costs of the repression. The United States talked a lot tougher to its allies over the Suez intervention than it did to the Soviets over the Hungarian Revolution. On December 18, six weeks after the revolution was crushed, Dulles explained the flaccid American response to the uprising:

> we have no desire to surround the Soviet Union with a band of hostile
> states and to revive what used to be called the *Cordon Sanitaire*, which
> was developed largely by the French after the First World War with a

view to circling the Soviet Union with hostile forces. We have made clear our policy in that respect in the hope of facilitating in that way an evaluation—a peaceful evolution—of the satellite states toward genuine independence.[22]

Dulles seemed to scrap the whole concept of containment and tacitly recognize that there were spheres of influence in the world and that the Soviet Union could now feel secure in its own sphere. And what of the Hungarians? "There was no basis for our giving military aid to Hungary," Dulles said. "We had no commitment to do so, and we did not think that to do so would either assist the people of Hungary or the people of Europe or the rest of the world."[23] The captive peoples would have to look elsewhere for support.

While the events in Poland and Hungary once again demonstrated the force of nationalism and even foreshadowed the eventual disintegration of the Soviet empire, the West had looked weak during the crisis and the Russians improved their relative position. Emboldened by the developments in Europe and Egypt and the weak response from Washington, Khrushchev now became more adventuristic in his foreign policy as his domestic position became more secure. He now decided to challenge the West over Berlin.

Notes

1. Arkady Vaksberg, *Stalin against the Jews*, trans. A.W. Bouls (New York: Alfred A. Knopf, 1994).

2. Nikita Khrushchev, *Khrushchev Remembers*, trans. Strobe Talbott (Boston: Little, Brown and Company, 1970), 323-24.

3. The whole speech is in Myron Rush, ed., *The International Situation and Soviet Foreign Policy: Reports of the Soviet Leaders* (Columbus, Ohio: Ohio State University Press, 1970), 155-65.

4. Khrushchev, *Khrushchev Remembers*, 368.

5. Jack Snyder, *Myths of Empire. Domestic Politics and International Ambition* (Ithaca, N.Y.: Cornell University Press, 1991), 216-17.

6. Quoted in Michael R. Beschloss, *Mayday. Eisenhower, Khrushchev and the U-2 Affair* (New York: Harper and Row, 1986), 101-2.

7. Beschloss, *Mayday*, 103.

8. Quoted in Herbert S. Parmet, *Eisenhower and the American Crusades* (New York: MacMillan, 1972), 406.

9. Beschloss, *Mayday*, 103-4.

10. Quoted in Henry Kissinger, *Diplomacy* (New York: Simon and Schuster, 1994), 517.

11. Quoted in Denis Healey, "When Shrimps Learn to Whistle," *International Affairs* XXXII (January 1956), 2.

12. The entire speech is in Khrushchev, *Khrushchev Remembers*, 559-618.

13. Roy A. Medvedev and Zhores A. Medvedev, *Khrushchev: The Years in Power* (New York: W.W. Norton and Company, 1978), 13-23.

14. Charles Gati, *Hungary and the Soviet Bloc* (Durham, N.C.: Duke University Press, 1986), 214.

15. Henry Ashby Turner, Jr., *The Two Germanies since 1945* (New Haven, Conn.: Yale University Press, 1987), 116-24.

16. Richard Hiscocks, *Poland. Bridge for the Abyss? An Interpretation of Developments in Postwar Poland* (London: Oxford University Press, 1963), 163-65.

17. Nikita Khrushchev, *Khrushchev Remembers. The Last Testament*, trans. Strobe Talbott (Boston: Little, Brown and Company, 1974), 196-99.

18. Konrad Syrop, *Spring in October: The Polish Revolution of 1956* (London: Shenval Press, 1957), 96.

19. Beschloss, *Mayday*, 138.

20. Bela K. Kiraly and Paul Jonas, eds., *The Hungarian Revolution of 1956 in Retrospect* (New York: East European Quarterly, 1977), 42.

21. Francois Fejto, *A History of the People's Democracies: Eastern Europe since Stalin* (London: Harmondsworth, 1974), 122-23.

22. Quoted in Kissinger, *Diplomacy*, 565.

23. Quoted in Kissinger, *Diplomacy*, 565.

15

Khrushchev and the Berlin Problem, 1958-1963

Khrushchev emerged from the revolutions of 1956 weakened politically. At home he faced major opposition from Stalinists in what he called the "anti-party" group. The crisis came to a head in June 1957 over the issue of how best to reform the economy. The Politburo by a vote of seven to four voted Khrushchev out as general secretary. Not the kind of man to go quietly, Khrushchev then appealed the vote to the Central Committee where half the members had been elected thanks to him. With the support of the army under Marshal Zhukov, military aircraft flew the supporters of Khrushchev in from the outlying provinces and even from foreign countries for the key vote. Khrushchev won the vote and then turned on his enemies. Instead of liquidating them as Stalin would have, he expelled them from the Central Committee and the Politburo, and from the capital as well. Molotov was assigned to the obscure post of ambassador to Mongolia, and Malenkov was sent to manage a power station in Kazakhstan. He also turned on his erstwhile ally, Marshal Zhukov and removed him from the Politburo on the charge of building a personality cult in the army. In March 1958 he took Bulganin's place as prime minister, thereby making himself the official head of the government as well as the party. At this point, the period of collective leadership was over as the power struggle to succeed Stalin was settled. Nevertheless, Khrushchev's opponents were not dead, merely in exile, and his power would never be completely secure. He felt under constant pressure to succeed, not only in the realm of the economy but especially in foreign affairs.

Khrushchev's winning of the power struggle coincided with an upturn in the Soviet economy and the successful launching of Sputnik, the world's first man-made satellite, on October 4, 1957. The Russians had also made progress in armaments. By 1958, they had developed long-range bombers capable of striking the Untied States and they had fired an experimental intercontinental ballistic missile (ICBM) a distance of 4,500 miles. Khrushchev took these developments as proof that the Soviet Union was about to pass the United States not only scientifically and militarily, but even economically, and become the most productive society in the world. It also seemed to lend substance to Khrushchev's contention that the planned society was inherently superior to the free market economy of the West.

The testing of Sputnik certainly came as a shock to the American public who, since the Manhattan Project, had grown accustomed to its country's lead in science and technology. The administration had known for years that the Russians were laboring hard in the area of ballistic missile development. In fact, the administration was grudgingly coming to accept the prospect of Soviet parity in nuclear strike capability. Eisenhower had been urged to explain to the American people the full implications of the nuclear arms race for American power and security.[1] "Operation Candor," as it was called, was rejected on the grounds that it would only serve to alarm the American people. As a result, Sputnik came as a shock to American complacency and Moscow scored a great propaganda victory.

The testing of Sputnik also coincided with the submission of the Gaither Report, a secret report commissioned by the president in 1957. Co-written by Paul Nitze, the report was filled with the most dire warnings concerning the supposed vulnerability of the U.S. strategic arsenal to a surprise first strike, and the glaring inadequacies in U.S. civil defense policies and programs. The report concluded that the United States needed to improve virtually all aspects of its military posture. Like NSC-#68, it warned the president that the balance of power might be shifting to the Russians unless defense spending was raised significantly. Despite the fact that Sputnik was a prototype and Moscow had only test-fired six ICBMs, the Gaither Report succeeded in feeding popular fears that the Russians had gained an insurmountable lead over the United States. Khrushchev only made it worse when he bragged that Russia could turn out rockets "like sausages."[2]

Eisenhower seemed to be the only one in Washington to keep a cool head throughout the Sputnik alarm, despite a sudden drop in his public opinion rating of 22 percent, and a strong attack on the "missile gap" by the Democratic Party. More than anyone else, the president understood that Sputnik had not compromised U.S. security. Since 1956 the U-2 spy plane had been overflying Russian airspace and probing Soviet military weaknesses. Through that secret reconnaissance Eisenhower learned that the Russians were far from achieving an operational capability in ICBMs, and that their whole program was floundering. Eisenhower therefore rejected most of Gaither's recommendations. When he was urged by Gaither and others to spend $30 billion over a five-year period in the building of fallout shelters against atomic radiation, he replied that no real defense existed against such a war. Eisenhower was more worried about the impact of increased defense spending on inflation and the economy. Nevertheless, however grudgingly, he agreed to upgrade U.S. nuclear forces into the solid-fueled Minuteman ICBM that, along with the missiles carried by nuclear-powered Polaris submarines and the B-52 strategic bomber fleet, would make up the U.S. strategic "Triad" that far outmatched any Soviet equivalent. What Sputnik had therefore in the long run done was make Americans think there was a missile gap, provide a much-needed spur to U.S. scientific research, and accelerate the arms race.

Nevertheless, believing that a major shift in the world correlation of forces had taken place, Khrushchev felt ideologically obliged as a Marxist-Leninist to translate this into a dynamic foreign policy. He now looked around for a suitable place to press his "advantage."

Khrushchev had once described West Berlin as a bone stuck in the Soviet throat. Situated 110 miles inside communist East Germany it formed the escape route since 1949 for over three million East German refugees from communism. That manpower drain threatened the very existence of the East German state. Almost ten years after the Blockade crisis, the prosperity of West Berlin stood in stark contrast to the drab and economically inert East Germany. This was alarming enough to Khrushchev, but what also bothered him was the West's refusal to recognize East Germany, the continued rearmament of West Germany, and its integration into NATO. For this reason, Moscow had strongly endorsed the Rapacki Plan in October 1957 (named after Poland's foreign minister), which called for a nuclear-free zone in Central Europe, principally in the two Germanies, Poland and, Czechoslovakia. On March 31, 1958, the Soviet Union unilaterally suspended nuclear testing, beginning a process that was supposed to lead to a conference on the problem in November. There was in these moves an attempt at blocking the nuclear arming of NATO, especially at a moment, despite Khrushchev's bluster about technological breakthroughs, when the Soviet strategic arsenal was vastly inferior to the American. The United States rejected the Rapacki Plan because it perpetuated the division of Germany and never really dealt with the arms problem in a balanced and equitable way.

Eisenhower's problem with the suspension of nuclear testing was that nuclear weaponry was the only way for the United States to counter Russia's and China's advantage in land armies. He was willing to halt the atomic testing if Russia would agree to adequate inspection. He decided to suspend tests for one year beginning October 31, 1958, and if a proper program of inspection and safeguards were developed the moratorium could be renewed. Khrushchev denounced this as a "trick," as he had criticized the "open skies" plan, and announced that Russia would resume testing. He also decided to take matters a dramatic step further and test the resolve of the United States and its European partners at their most vulnerable point.

On November 10, 1958, Khrushchev told a group of visiting Polish party officials that the time had come to end Berlin's four-power status, and he warned that Moscow intended to turn control of its access routes to the city over to East Germany. This would then create what he called a "normal situation" in the East German capital. On November 27, he issued the Cold War's first ultimatum when he demanded the total evacuation of all four occupation forces from Berlin within six months (i.e., by May 27, 1959), failing which the Soviet Union would hand over control of its routes to the city to the East German government. Since the Western Allies never signed an access agreement with the East German government, nor extended it diplomatic recognition, they labored under an enormous disadvantage; they knew that a deal with East Germany over Berlin would automatically confirm the existence of two Germanies. The western enclave in Berlin seemed about to disappear into the Soviet bloc.

There were both domestic and foreign reasons for Khrushchev's ultimatum and the beginning of what became the second Berlin crisis. Never exercising as complete an autocratic control over the Soviet Union as Stalin had, Khrushchev was influenced by domestic pressure, particularly from his generals. His attempts to reach accommodation with the West after 1953 and his pronounced cutbacks in the size of the Russian armed forces alienated many generals who felt that Khrushchev's program was eroding the security of the nation. Khrushchev aimed to pacify this key power bloc and shore up his domestic position.

The ultimatum was also designed to achieve important objectives in foreign affairs. In a very narrow sense, it was meant to remove the irritating West Berlin impediment in a Soviet satellite. But more important, the policy of squeezing the Allies out of Berlin was meant to rupture the intimate connection between the United States and West Germany. If Russia got away with this and the Allies negotiated with East Germany thus extending it a de facto recognition, it would radically change West German politics. The Adenauer regime had come to regard Berlin as the critical test of America's determination to protect West Germany. "If Berlin were to be lost," Konrad Adenauer warned, "my political position would at once become untenable. The socialists [who were at the time neutralist] would take over power in Bonn—they would proceed to make a direct arrangement with Moscow, and that would be the end of Europe."[3] If Washington withdrew from Berlin, the U.S.-German relationship would receive an irreparable blow. Adenauer therefore strongly objected to conceding anything to Khrushchev's ultimatum.

Khrushchev's other objective was the weakening of NATO. If he could successfully incorporate West Berlin into the communist world, the Allies might lose heart and abandon the alliance. As the tension mounted, Moscow made it clear that if the crisis led to a nuclear exchange between the superpowers, the West European nations would be destroyed as well. The threat was intended to keep the NATO members from establishing missile bases on their soil. Khrushchev had made similar threats during the Suez Crisis and all the belligerents at that time chose to remain impervious to them. This was true in the Berlin Crisis as well, but with one exception—Great Britain. Harold Macmillan took the threat seriously judging from his behavior during the crisis. He was extremely reluctant to go to war for the sake of two million Berliners. Eight nuclear bombs, he told Eisenhower emotionally, would kill thirty million Britons.[4] Macmillan therefore broke ranks with his allies and elected to try personal diplomacy. Flying to Moscow on February 21, 1959, he only managed to dangle the prospect of a full summit before Khrushchev, who treated him discourteously.

French President Charles De Gaulle, who had just returned to office after twelve years, felt that Khrushchev was bluffing. If Moscow really wanted war it was not by making concessions over Berlin that it would be avoided, and if they were seeking to avoid it then it was useless to make concessions to them. De Gaulle was positioning himself, writes Henry Kissinger, in "the role of defender of the European identity and used the Berlin crisis to demonstrate France's understanding of European realities and its sensitivity to German national concerns."[5] De Gaulle's fear was that if the West backed down in the face of an ultimatum the Germans would then pursue their national goals in collusion with the Russians.

From the beginning of the crisis Eisenhower had tried to defuse its dramatic content. He was worried not only over an ultimatum but also over the American public's growing alarm about the crisis and the growing martial spirit in Congress. Members of Congress, with a mixture of anger and panic, demanded a mobilization of the U.S. armed forces and a steep rise in the defense budget. In press conferences in February and March 1959 he both assured the American people about the prospects of war and, at the same time, sent a warning signal to the Kremlin. "We are not going to fight a ground war in Europe," he said, and it was unlikely that the United States would "shoot our way into Berlin."[6] The implication was clear — the Kremlin would have seen it, the American people not at all; if war came, Eisenhower was saying it would be nuclear. Eisenhower could remain calm and take this position because he knew the Soviet Union was militarily inferior and that Khrushchev was probably bluffing. The West, he felt, had to first remain resolute until Khrushchev backed down. The Allies then unanimously followed the American lead, rejected the Soviet ultimatum, refused to recognize the transfer of Russia's authority to the East German regime, and the United States slightly beefed up its troops in Western Europe. It was necessary to send a military signal of U.S. intentions because in January 1959 the Russians immobilized an American convoy on the Berlin highway for several hours. This was a very dangerous moment. Army Chief of Staff General Maxwell Taylor urged the president to test Soviet intentions by sending a small military force through the corridors of West Berlin. Like Truman in 1948, Eisenhower resisted any idea of forcing the pace of events and making the crisis even more dangerous than it was.

Khrushchev had repeated Stalin's mistake of 1948; he had misjudged the West, which once again presented the Russians with a united front. The Kremlin now backed down and in March 1959 it revoked the deadline for the transfer of sovereignty to East Germany and acknowledged the rights of the Allies to maintain a military presence in the city. At this point, Khrushchev accepted an American invitation to visit the United States. "I'll admit I was curious to have a look at America," recalled Khrushchev. "America occupied a special position in our thinking and view of the world."

Richard Nixon had suggested to Eisenhower that when Khrushchev arrived he should be given an escorted trip through the country, which would give him "a subtle feeling of the power and the will of America." Khrushchev's tour through America lasted from September 15 to September 27, 1959. He was the first Soviet leader to visit the United States. He visited factories and farms, shopping centers and housing projects; he met with business tycoons in New York City, labor leaders in Pittsburgh, and show business people in Hollywood. The only low note in an otherwise warmly human tour came with his appearance before the National Press Club in the nation's capital. When asked probing questions about his role in the suppression of the Hungarian Revolution, Khrushchev lost his temper and refused to answer that "provocation." Instead, he shook his fist at the reporters and stormed that "communism is a science" and predicted that "we will surpass you." But in his calmer moments he assured the American people that remarks like this should not be taken in a military sense. "I say it again — I've almost worn my tongue thin repeating it — you may live under capitalism and we will live under socialism and build communism. The one whose system proves better will win."[7] A month later Khrushchev made his definition of peaceful coexistence even clearer:

> Coexistence means the continuation of the struggle between two social systems, but of a struggle by peaceful means, without war, without the interference of a state in the domestic affairs of another state. One should not be afraid. We must struggle resolutely and consistently for our ideals, for our way of life, for our socialist system. The partisans of capitalism, too, will not, of course, abandon their way of life, their ideology; they will fight. We hold that the struggle must be economic, political, and ideological, but not military.[8]

He also reminded Americans of their often mixed relationship with the Soviet Union—how Americans had intervened in the Russian Civil War and how in recent years they had been close allies in the war against fascism. "The plain people of America like me," he said, "It's just those bastards around Eisenhower that don't."[9]

Dulles had died of cancer in April, and so it was Eisenhower who handled the diplomacy of Khrushchev's visit. Dulles's death seemed to signify the end of the U.S.-Soviet hostility. The two leaders then settled down to a series of private discussions at Camp David, the presidential retreat in the Maryland mountains.

Eisenhower told Khrushchev that the United States had no intention of staying in Berlin forever. "Clearly," he said, "we did not contemplate 50 years in occupation there."[10] Eisenhower even recognized that the Berlin situation was "abnormal," but Khrushchev failed to press him on this. Discussions between the two men were even more amiable then they were at Geneva four years before. The media of both countries waxed lyrical about the "spirit of Camp David" as they had formerly celebrated the "spirit of Geneva." Khrushchev had indeed made a strong and favorable impression on the American people, and he regarded the trip as a personal triumph. He also viewed the trip as a milestone in the growing relationship between the two countries: "We were proud we had finally forced the United States to recognize the need for closer contact with us."

Actually, nothing of substance resulted from the Camp David talks save a general understanding that the Berlin problem was to be deferred to a conference to meet the following year. In a speech to the U.N. General Assembly a bit later, Khrushchev called for general and complete disarmament within four years. A few months after his return home, he announced a cut in the Soviet army by one million men. A summit conference was scheduled in Paris for May 1960, after which Eisenhower planned a trip to the Soviet Union. Two weeks before the Paris summit, on May 12, a U-2 spy plane on a CIA mission was shot down over the

Soviet Union.

The U-2 reconnaissance flights had violated Soviet airspace for four years, military planners feeling secure that at extremely high altitudes the planes were immune from missile attack. Almost from the beginning, the flights were something of an open secret. Articles on the black plane of unique design appeared in American popular journals and in at least one Soviet publication. The Soviet government had filed three protests against the flights in 1956 and 1958 and in each case Washington had denied the charge. At Camp David, Khrushchev had not raised the matter at all. As he would later recall, the Americans "knew they were causing us terrible headaches whenever one of these planes took off on a mission." This kind of espionage, he said, "was war — war waged by other means."[11] As Michael Beschloss puts it, "The U-2 was capable of arousing virtually every major Soviet anxiety." Further, he states:

> it took off from Turkey, Japan and other Western bases (encirclement) to violate Soviet frontiers (invasion) for espionage (espionage) in the course of which it photographed and eavesdropped on the Soviet military (lack of secrecy) and confirmed Soviet weakness (military inferiority). The black plane had the potential to undermine the authority of the regime: what might the Soviet people say if they learned that their government was unable to perform the most fundamental task of protecting them from foreign invaders?[12]

Allen Dulles, the head of the CIA, had given the president every assurance that if something went wrong on a mission over the Soviet Union, the aircraft would automatically self-destruct and the pilot would be killed in the process. While the full story of the U-2 flight has not yet been told, it would seem that the plane, either through engine trouble or pilot error, had lost altitude and become vulnerable to attack. After the crash, the Russians recovered the aerial photography equipment intact and captured the pilot who had parachuted to safety. Years later, Eisenhower's son, John, insisted that "Allen Dulles had lied to Dad."[13] The president had from the beginning kept a tight rein on the U-2 program approving the missions on a flight-by-flight basis. But it is not clear even today why he approved a flight so close to the summit in Paris.

At first Eisenhower lied about the flight because he believed that the equipment and pilot could not have survived the mission. When Khrushchev first revealed the episode to the world he went out of his way not to accuse Eisenhower personally. Instead, he made a point of accusing Allen Dulles and the military establishment, thus giving Eisenhower the chance to blame his subordinates. But Eisenhower candidly admitted he knew about the flights and assumed full personal responsibility. And when he promised that there would be no more U-2 flights, it fell on deaf ears. The "spirit of Camp David" had evaporated and Khrushchev reacted very angrily. Eisenhower, he said, "had, so to speak, offered us his rear end, and we obliged him by kicking it as hard as we could."[14] When Eisenhower refused to apologize for the U-2 flights, Khrushchev withdrew his invitation to visit the

Soviet Union. Then in a press conference Khrushchev promised that if there were anymore U-2 flights, not only would the planes be shot down but the bases they took off from would be attacked as well.

Once the summit conference was cancelled, the captured pilot, Gary Francis Powers, was placed on trial in the Soviet Union in August 1960. The televised trial became the greatest show trial in Cold War history. Powers received a sentence of ten years imprisonment, but in 1967 he was exchanged for Colonel Rudolf Abel, a leading Soviet spy captured in the United States. Any chance for an entente between the superpowers became impossible for the rest of the Eisenhower presidency.

Why did Khrushchev choose this moment to wreck the summit, especially when he looked forward to making some progress toward a limited test ban treaty, and toward a solution to the perennial problem of Germany? He could have handled the whole matter through private channels as he had transmitted his earlier concerns over the same flights. But if he did this he would encourage his enemies to attack him for being "soft" on matters of Soviet security. But Khrushchev was worried about more than domestic "hawks"; he was worried about his largest ally, Communist China. While the Americans and the Russians were squabbling over access routes to Berlin and intelligence planes over the Soviet Union, Mao Tse-Tung had begun to challenge Khrushchev for the leadership of the world communist movement.

The left wing of the Chinese Communist Party gained an ascendancy in 1957 and advocated a very accelerated pace of economic development to break out of the backward torpor the country found itself in. Like their Russian cousins on the left in the 1920s and 1930s, they had a mystical faith in the power of the masses, and the use of propaganda to ideologically mobilize them into action. In 1958 China launched its Great Leap Forward. The slogan of the day was "permanent revolution on both the domestic and foreign fronts."

The Great Leap Forward called for the merger of China's collective farms and their transformation into communes. At the same time, tens of thousands of tiny industrial plants were set up throughout the country to compensate for the lack of heavy industry. It was all an aggressively ambitious plan for a basically rural society to leap over the socialist stage of history and reach the final stage of communism. The Communist Party of China believed that this could be done by industrializing at a breathtaking pace, defying all the laws of economics. The whole campaign carried a tone of aggressive utopianism. By 1959 the party claimed that what had been accomplished in China should serve as the model for building communism in all underdeveloped countries. The Chinese insisted that in the commune they had discovered the basic unit of the future communist society.

The Sino-Soviet dispute, which was about to break out openly, was centered on two things: the special path the Chinese had chosen to "leap into the future," and the question of Mao Tse Tung's global strategy.

Moscow took the Great Leap Forward as a challenge to her leadership of the revolution in Asia, Africa, and Latin America. It was also seen as a rejection of

Soviet economic planning, which was considered too slow by Beijing standards. The two countries were, of course, in different phases of their revolutions, and their Communist parties were mobilizing different social elements: workers in Russia and peasants in China. The Russians always talked about raising production levels, while the Chinese were talking about maintaining ideological fervor and maintaining momentum. The Chinese certainly considered themselves ideologically purer than the Russians and, because they were, would outrace them to the goal of achieving a communist society. The Chinese program appealed to far left groups throughout the communist world (and beyond) and gave them a weapon in bloc debate. Mao was thus able to present himself not only as the commander who held off the Untied States in Korea, but as an original theoretician who already stood as one of the giants of twentieth-century communism. Next to that image, Khrushchev appeared to be a cynical politician who had failed to stand up to the Americans over Berlin.

Khrushchev thought the communes were a lot of utopian rubbish. He had witnessed the early failures of the Soviet experiment in this direction and he had become a communist-pragmatist as a result. Russia was headed toward the final stage of communism, but in its own good time. The commune idea, he once told Senator Hubert Humphrey, had failed in Russia in the 1920s because "you can't get production without incentive." When Humphrey replied that that sounded capitalistic, Khrushchev said: "Call it what you will, it works."[15]

The other point of contention fuelling the Sino-Soviet dispute centered on global strategy. Mao had been as excited by the Sputnik breakthrough as Khrushchev had. He urged Khrushchev to use his advantage in rockets to launch all sorts of small wars of liberation, since the United States would now be too frightened to wage nuclear war. The United States was just a "paper tiger" he told Khrushchev in 1957, and the communist world should meet the West head on and not flinch from a war the forces of communism could only win. "If the imperialists unleash war on us, we may lose more than three hundred million people. So what? War is war. The years will pass and we'll get to work producing more babies than ever before."[16] Mao's speech disturbed Khrushchev as it also did Gomulka and the other European communists who spoke for small populations. In reply to this, Khrushchev made it clear to Mao that nations could no longer calculate "the alignment of forces on the basis of who has the most men." Bullets and bayonets may have been adequate for wars in previous eras, but "when the machine gun appeared, the side with more troops no longer necessarily had the advantage. And now with the atomic bomb, the number of troops on each side makes practically no difference to the alignment of real power and the outcome of a war. The more troops on a side, the more bomb fodder."[17] Khrushchev concluded that Mao was a "lunatic on a throne," and a "megalomaniac warmonger." Mao, on the other hand, was genuinely distressed at the discrepancy between Russia's military assets and its lack of resolve to use them. He was bothered by Russia's mere bluster during the Suez Crisis, and its almost total silence during the Taiwan Straits crisis of 1958. Worst of all, Russia refused to back China during its border conflict with India in

1962.

Mao had an extremely low opinion of Khrushchev. He thought Khrushchev to be anything but a Leninist. He was sharply critical of Khrushchev's reconciliation with Tito's Yugoslavia and he reacted very negatively to Khrushchev's attack on Stalinism in 1956. When Khrushchev first met Mao in 1957 he was struck "by how much he sounded like Stalin." He felt that Mao had "the same diseased outlook on other people."[18]

While Stalin lived, Mao deferred to him as the senior leader in the communist world. After his death, Mao claimed that honor for himself. In 1957 on the eve of the Great Leap Forward, unity was still maintained in the communist bloc. At Communist Party meetings in Moscow that year Mao had declared: "The Communist Party of the Soviet Union should be the one and only center of the international Communist movement, and the rest of us should be united around that center."[19]

By mid-1959, as Khrushchev sought an accommodation with the United States, he tried to induce Beijing to moderate its aggressive ideological and political strategy for the communist bloc. Mao would have none of it. To do as Khrushchev asked, Mao felt, was to renounce the messianic goals of world communism. When Khrushchev visited Beijing in 1959, he realized that a break in relations was imminent. Soviet advisors and specialists were being deliberately humiliated and their homes ransacked by Red Guards. In Russia itself, according to Khrushchev, Chinese students circulated anti-Soviet leaflets and organized anti-Soviet demonstrations.

In 1960 the long-simmering quarrel erupted publicly. At a world communist meeting in Bucharest the Chinese condemned Khrushchev's whole policy of peaceful coexistence with the capitalist West, especially the United States. The Chinese accused the Soviet Union of violating the revolutionary principles of Marxist-Leninism, of which the Chinese branch of the world communist movement had become the most orthodox adherent. When Mao published an article attacking Moscow on similar grounds, Khrushchev lashed out at the Chinese leadership by calling them "children," "nationalists," "adventurers," and "madmen." They were, he claimed, seeking to engulf the world in a nuclear holocaust. He then abruptly recalled all his advisors in China and expelled the Chinese students from the Soviet Union. Economic aid stopped as well. A year later Khrushchev would do the same to Albania, China's ideological ally. A large number of Chinese industrial projects suddenly ground to a halt. The industrialization of China may have been set back by as much as five years.

The Sino-Soviet conflict had a major impact on Khrushchev's behavior during the U-2 affair. Mao certainly exploited the episode to undermine Khrushchev's position in the Kremlin and throughout the socialist camp. It became important for Khrushchev to show his detractors at home and abroad that he was a legitimate heir to Lenin and Stalin, that he was a resourceful leader who could stand up to the West and who could seize the initiative throughout the third world. To Khrushchev's dying day he believed that the U-2 incident eventually proved his political undoing. In fact, he traced his political decline to that day in May 1960 when the crisis began. From then on he was never again master in his own house but had to share power with hard-liners who defined any accommodation with the United States as so much weakness.[20] He may have been trying in this explanation, as Michael Beschloss suggests, to shift the onus for the breach between the superpowers to Washington and explain the inadequacies of his personal rule, but the whole crisis did set back East-West dialogue for years and it did play into the hands of Khrushchev's more "hawkish" rivals. If Khrushchev did not labor under the same domestic restraints of a democratic system like Eisenhower, he nevertheless had to always remain cognizant of his rivals to the right and left of him, and the power struggle swirling around him. Too often in the Cold War the Kremlin remained insensitive to the checks and balances of democracy in Washington, while Washington too often ignored the precarious position of the Kremlin leadership, which could only go just so far in forging a detente with the West. How much of a detente could have been achieved in 1960 without the U-2 episode is therefore problematic. For Marxist-Leninists, since 1917 there was no real distinction between war and peace—each was but a phase in the larger historical process of the class struggle. Marxist-Leninists before Khrushchev were captives of this because they had not as yet been exposed to the perils of the nuclear age. Khrushchev was the first communist to both understand those dangers and seek some sort of peaceful coexistence with the West. In the process he had to keep one eye on communism's long-range ideological goals, and the other on the intricate problems of foreign relations. The problem for Khrushchev (and Brezhnev) was to avoid war and at the same time extend Soviet power by making the international system serve the Soviet state. This did not preclude the occasional probing and even bullying of the West where it was deemed vulnerable and when it was weakly led.

Still desperately needing a triumph in foreign policy to shore up his precarious position at home, Khrushchev resolved once and for all to settle the Berlin issue on Russia's terms. A change in the U.S. administration in 1960 offered him the chance to do this. Khrushchev took the occasion of a summit conference at Vienna to present the new American president, John F. Kennedy, with another ultimatum demanding the end of the Allied presence in West Berlin and the transformation of the area into a free city. Khrushchev threatened to sign a separate accord with East Germany if no general agreement over Germany had been concluded by December 1961. In the meantime, he placed thousands of troops into position along Berlin's border sealing off West Berlin from East Berlin. Kennedy then sent General Lucius Clay, the hero of the Berlin Blockade of 1948-1949, to West Berlin, and reinforced the U.S. garrison in the city. On August 21, the Kremlin announced its resumption of nuclear testing after a nearly three-year hiatus. Russia then proceeded to test no less than fifty nuclear bombs over the next two months.

Like the other two Berlin crises, all the initiatives were Russian and it was the Kremlin that decided just how far the crisis would grow. At the same time, Washington signalled its determination to remain in Berlin, as it had in the earlier challenges. Kennedy did this despite his reluctance to run great risks over the city. He made this clear to his advisors after his Vienna meeting:

> it seems particularly stupid to risk killing a million Americans over an argument about access rights on an Autobahn . . . or because the Germans want Germany reunified. If I'm going to threaten Russia with a nuclear war, it will have to be for much bigger and more important reasons than that.[21]

Be that as it may, Kennedy, like Eisenhower, remained cool and stubborn during the crisis, even though Khrushchev at one point told the British ambassador that it would take only six atomic bombs to destroy Great Britain and nine to wipe out France.

On August 13, 1961, East Germany with Moscow's approval suddenly constructed the Berlin Wall sealing off West Berlin from East Germany. At one point, Soviet and American tank units confronted each other in a potentially dangerous situation until cooler heads prevailed.

The Berlin Wall revealed the bankruptcy of the East German regime, which could find no other human formula to keep its citizens contented and at home. And it certainly became a symbol for all the tyrannical rigidities of the Cold War. But from the standpoint of Khrushchev and Walter Ulbricht, it was the perfect solution to not only stem the tide of emigration from East Germany, but put an end to the recurring Berlin crises. Kennedy saw this immediately when he told his aides, "Why would Khrushchev put up a wall if he really intended to seize West Berlin? There wouldn't be any need of a wall if he occupied the whole city. This is his way out of his predicament. It's not a very nice solution, but a wall is a hell of a lot better than a war."[22] The West German people were highly critical of Kennedy's reluctance to destroy the wall. But the president, despite his famous speech at the wall where he proclaimed, "I am a Berliner," actually had little sympathy for the Berliner's plight. They had fifteen years, he said privately, "to get out of their jail."[23] Once again the status quo was maintained in Berlin, and the Berlin Wall helped to make it permanent. In January 1963 and just after the Cuban Missile Crisis, Khrushchev acknowledged that the Berlin Wall made a separate peace treaty with Berlin unnecessary. The status of Berlin would no longer be a problem in the Cold War.

In the three Berlin crises Stalin and Khrushchev had initiated direct challenges to the United States, and each time the United States had contained the Soviet threat. Those challenges were posed in an area of Central Europe where the Soviet Union enjoyed a measure of regional military superiority. The final direct challenge to the United States came in 1962, in Cuba, where the United States enjoyed a preponderance of power.

Notes

1. W.W. Rostow, *The United States in the World Arena* (New York: Harper and Brothers, 1960), 316-19 ff.

2. Quoted in Gregg Herken, *Counsels of War* (New York: Oxford University Press, 1987), 130.

3. Quoted in Charles de Gaulle, *Memoirs of Hope: Renewal and Endeavor*, trans. Terence Kilmartin (New York: Simon and Schuster, 1971), 223.

4. Michael R. Beschloss, *Mayday. Eisenhower, Khrushchev and the U-2 Affair* (New York: Harper and Row, 1986), 175.

5. Henry Kissinger, *Diplomacy* (New York: Simon and Schuster, 1994), 577.

6. Kissinger, *Diplomacy*, 574.

7. *Khrushchev in America* (New York: Cross Currents, 1960), 120.

8. Quoted in R. Craig Nation, *Black Earth, Red Star. A History of Soviet Security Policy, 1917-1991* (Ithaca, N.Y.: Cornell University Press, 1992), 202.

9. Quoted in Beschloss, *Mayday*, 201.

10. *Diplomacy*, Kissinger, 580.

11. Nikita Khrushchev, *Khrushchev Remembers. The Last Testament*, trans. Strobe Talbott (Boston: Little, Brown and Company, 1974), 444, 446.

12. Beschloss, *Mayday*, 157.

13. Beschloss, *Mayday*, 8, 9, 65.

14. Khrushchev, *Khrushchev Remembers*, 446-49.

15. Donald S. Zagoria, *The Sino-Soviet Conflict 1956-1961* (Princeton, N.J.: Princeton University Press, 1962), 99.

16. Khrushchev, *Khrushchev Remembers*, 255.

17. Khrushchev, *Khrushchev Remembers*, 255

18. Khrushchev, *Khrushchev Remembers*, 252.

19. Khrushchev, *Khrushchev Remembers*, 254.

20. Harrison E. Salisbury, *A Journey for Our Times. A Memoir* (New York: Harper and Row, 1983), 489.

21. Quoted in Michael R. Beschloss, *The Crisis Years. Kennedy and Khrushchev, 1960-1963* (New York: HarperCollins, 1991), 225.

22. Quoted in Beschloss, *The Crisis Years*, 278.

23. Quoted in Beschloss, *The Crisis Years*, 278.

16

The Cuban Missile Crisis

From the end of the Second World War to the late 1950s Washington paid scant attention to Latin America and its growing vulnerability to communist influence. With the exception of the Guatemalan intervention of 1954, all seemed well and correct in the relations between the United States and the states of Latin America. The nations of the region joined the U.N. after the war and entered into various pacts and organizations (like the Rio Treaty and the OAS) with the United States providing for mutual action whether in defense or economic cooperation. All this came in a period when the region's population began to significantly increase and when it was in the process of industrializing. At the same time, the United States and Latin America became increasingly interdependent economically. By the end of the 1950s trade with Latin America accounted for a third of the imports and a quarter of the exports of the United States. The region seemed to be what it always was—a secure American sphere of influence.

Despite the close economic ties, the United States still appeared to be a distant giant to its neighbors, the "Colossus of the North," which did little to advance social, economic, and political progress directly in the region. American presidents periodically paid lip service to the Good Neighbor Policy but, in fact, they poured billions of dollars into Europe and Asia to win the battles, real and potential, of the Cold War, and generally neglected Latin America.

Washington remained relatively indifferent to the festering problems of Latin America until May 1958, when Vice-President Richard Nixon during a trip to the region was mobbed in Lima and Caracas. In the aftermath of these incidents, Washington began to gradually alter its policy toward Latin America. It worked with the nations of the region to raise the price of coffee and some metals and it promoted the creation of a regional common market among the republics. When in 1958 Brazil proposed an Operation Pan-American to speed regional development, Washington agreed to furnish nearly half the capital for a new InterAmerican Bank to make development loans.

Despite the shift in policy, Washington's program in Latin America was denounced as "Yankee imperialism" by the region's communist spokesmen. One of these "spokesmen," hidden from Washington's view for most of the 1950s, was Fidel Castro.

That the first real revolution after the war in Latin America occurred in Cuba came as something of a shock in Washington. Since the Spanish-American War of 1898 the United States had dominated the economic and political life of the island. The United States, for example, owned nearly all the mines and ranches in the country and half of its sugar, and forged very close links with the regime of General Fulgencio Batista.

Nothing in Castro's background predetermined that he become one of Latin America's most famous revolutionaries. He had a middle-class, Roman Catholic upbringing, and later trained as a lawyer. Normally these things in a man's background argue for a figure of rather conservative leanings. But Castro, who originally imbibed his radical politics at the university, was embittered by the appalling conditions in his country. Cuba was notoriously corrupt, its unemployment extremely high, and its prostitution a national scandal. Like so many potential rebels in the region, he held American influence responsible for making it all worse and deliberately perverting the natural development of Cuba. The Batista dictatorship seemed to leave no alternative to resistance except a resort to armed force.

All that Cubans knew about Castro was that in 1953 he had made a pathetic attempt to overthrow the government, and that he was captured and imprisoned. His career at this point bordered on the ridiculous. No one in the country took him seriously, including those in the Cuban Communist Party who believed him incapable of aggressive leadership. But like all successful revolutionaries, Castro learned from his mistakes. He learned that a frontal assault on the state would not succeed unless it had the backing of a large section of the people. Castro used his two years in prison to read Marx and Lenin, organize his fellow inmates, and develop a program of socioeconomic change that he could take to the Cuban people.

Released from prison in 1955 he went to Mexico to gather money and arms for another try at revolution. In 1956 he once again landed in Cuba with a small band of men and succeeded in winning the support of the Cuban peasantry and other anti-Batista forces. By 1958 he was scoring military victories as all classes began to coalesce against the regime. In late 1958 Washington suggested to Batista that he resign in favor of a military junta, which could then offer liberal concessions to defuse the revolutionary movement. Batista refused to cooperate. The Cuban army began to crack, and on New Year's Day 1959, Castro victoriously entered Havana.

By April the United States still had not recognized the new Cuban government. The U.S. State Department recommended that President Eisenhower do so, but the CIA felt that Castro might well be a communist and urged caution. The new government in Havana still represented a broad coalition of forces and at first Castro appeared to be a tough but reforming nationalist. He began by imprisoning or purging the police, bureaucracy, and army of the most ruthless supporters of the previous regime. In February he postponed elections indefinitely. While this did anger Washington, Castro had as yet not seized foreign-owned enterprises or attacked the property owners as a class.

In April Castro accepted an invitation to speak in Washington before the American Society of Newspaper Editors. Eisenhower refused to meet him, but Richard Nixon invited him to his office for a long conversation.

In a meeting that lasted three hours Nixon tried to get Castro to agree to hold free elections, to moderate the executions of his enemies and, at the same time, to determine how far left Castro's politics really were. To Nixon's request for free elections, Castro responded, "The people did not want elections because the elections in the past had produced bad government." To Nixon's call for an end to the bloody executions (some of which were shown on Havana television), Castro responded that he was carrying out "the will of the people." As to Castro's politics, Nixon was uncertain. "He is either incredibly naive about Communism or under Communist discipline—my guess is the former, and as I have already implied his ideas as to how to run a government or an economy are less developed than those of almost any world figure I have met in fifty countries." The only positive thing Nixon managed to say about Castro was that he had "the great gift of Leadership."[1]

Treading carefully in the shadow of the United States, and remembering what happened to Arbenz, Castro only declared himself to be a Marxist-Leninist in December 1961. Yet almost from the beginning he was prepared to initiate profound social and economic reforms designed to reduce America's extensive interests in the country. The first hint of this came in May 1959 when he proclaimed the Agrarian Reform Law. It limited the size of holdings to 1,000 acres for small farms and 3,300 acres for grazing operations. Anything in excess of this was to be expropriated. This did not seem to bother Washington as much as Castro's attempts to purchase arms. At first he approached suppliers in the United States and Western Europe, but when Washington refused to permit sales and its allies followed suit, he threatened to buy arms from Eastern Europe.

At first the Soviet Union took a guarded approach to the Cuban revolution, but with tensions between the United States and Cuba steadily mounting, the Kremlin saw an opportunity to establish a beachhead in Latin America. In February 1960, Anastas Mikoyan, the first deputy premier, visited Havana. The two countries quickly signed agreements committing the Cubans to sell the Soviet Union sugar in return for shipments of oil and industrial goods. Castro then demanded that the U.S. oil firms in Cuba refine the Soviet oil. When the State Department in Washington ordered the companies to refuse, Castro promptly nationalized the oil companies. Eisenhower then cut the sugar quota, and ended it completely by year's end. Russia then promised to increase its purchases of sugar and granted $200 million in low-interest loans to the financially hard-pressed Castro regime. Moscow became the mainstay of the Cuban economy for the next twenty-five years. Amid the most vehement anti-American oratory, Castro repudiated the Rio Pact and called for revolutions throughout Latin America. At the same time, Khrushchev publicly boasted that the Monroe Doctrine was dead. By the summer of 1960 Castro moved to confiscate privately owned firms—mining companies, hotels, banks, etc.—both foreign and domestic. Eisenhower responded to this by imposing a trade embargo on Cuba, exempting only medical supplies and some food staples.

As early as Mikoyan's arrival in Cuba, Eisenhower had embraced the thesis that the Castro regime had moved from neutralism to communism. On January 3, 1961, as he prepared to vacate the White House, Eisenhower broke diplomatic relations with Cuba. Thousands of Soviet technicians, military advisors, and diplomatic personnel were already streaming into Cuba to lend assistance to the new revolutionary regime. To Washington, the island nation of Cuba appeared to be rapidly changing into a Soviet satellite. To stop the Cuban revolution from going too far, Eisenhower had earlier secretly ordered the CIA to organize and train Cuban exiles for an eventual invasion of their homeland. This was the situation when John F. Kennedy assumed the presidency in January 1961.

The new president had made Cuba an issue in the 1960 election campaign and was determined to oust Castro. At the same time, more and more voices were being raised in Congress, the military, and the media, demanding action against this new Soviet satellite. The momentum in Washington as Kennedy took office was clearly on the side of invasion.

Under the supervision of the CIA an exile army composed of refugees from Cuba had for months been armed and trained at clandestine camps in Florida, Guatemala, and Nicaragua in preparation for an invasion of the island. Blinded by the quick and easy success of the Guatemalan invasion of 1954, the CIA (known among the Cuban exiles as the Cuban Invasion Authority) assured the new and inexperienced president that a small group of paramilitary fighters could be safely landed in Cuba and that their mere presence—once they established a small foothold—would ignite an internal uprising by thousands of alienated victims of communist tyranny. According to a CIA estimate there were roughly 3,000 activists in the anti-Castro underground, and they were supported by 20,000 sympathizers. The CIA counted on a disgruntled 25 percent of the Cuban population to actively support the invaders.[2] The plans were approved by the Joint Chiefs of Staff, although they felt that the element of surprise would be critical to the whole operation. Dean Rusk, the new secretary of state, and the presidential assistant, Arthur Schlesinger, Jr., both advised against the invasion on the grounds of feasibility and on their belief that whether it was successful or not, world opinion would be negative and the United States would find itself isolated in the world community. But Kennedy feared that if he cancelled the operation he would be accused of being soft on communism. Striking a hopeless middle course, he approved the operation but on one major condition: that American forces not be involved. This meant that the United States would not provide air cover. The few Second World War B-26 bombers that would be used would be flown by Cuban pilots and they would be kept under tight rein. Kennedy was determined to maintain the fiction that, the invasion was a purely Cuban affair, because he was afraid that, as American involvement grew and became known, Khrushchev might retaliate by invading West Berlin.[3] The Cuban leaders of the invasion were told in general terms that they were on their own, but they apparently believed that the CIA would not allow the venture to fail. Even the CIA did not protest Kennedy's conditions because, as Allen Dulles later put it, "We felt that when the chips were down, any action required for success would have been authorized [by the President] rather than permit the enterprise to fail."[4]

On April 17, 1961, between 1,400 and 1,500 Cuban guerrillas were placed ashore at the Bay of Pigs and the disaster began at once. The Americans, who had pioneered amphibious landings in the Second World War had apparently forgotten the lessons fifteen years later. The beachhead turned out to be indefensible, the military intelligence poor, and the lack of proper air cover doomed the invasion from the beginning. Worst of all, the underground had not even been informed when or where the invasion would begin and the men were put ashore too far from the mountains, which could have provided them with safety. Moreover, the Castro government was not taken by surprise, and so a little under 1,500 men were pitted against a Cuban militia of 250,000, who remained loyal to Castro. Within hours the invasion was wiped out and 114 anti-Castro guerrillas were killed while more than 1,100 were taken prisoner. It had all been a fiasco and President Kennedy was personally humiliated. "All my life I've known better than to depend on the experts," he said. "How could I have been so stupid, to let them go ahead?" Nevertheless, public opinion polls held just after the disaster gave him the highest approval ratings of his presidency (83 percent). "It's just like Eisenhower," Kennedy joked. "The worse I do the more popular I get."[5]

The Bay of Pigs was a setback for the Kennedy administration but the struggle against communism in the Caribbean was relentlessly pursued. While no covert plan existed to restage the invasion, Washington continued to seek ways to dislodge Fidel Castro from power. Following the invasion the United States tightened the trade blockade around Cuba, directed a huge propaganda campaign at the regime, and marshalled enough votes to get Cuba expelled from the OAS. At the same time, the CIA planned to assassinate Castro in cooperation with figures of organized crime. With the backing of the president the CIA also launched Operation Mongoose. Under this program the CIA, using anti-Castro exiles, staged a series of hit-and-run sabotage raids against various strategic targets, including oil refineries, bridges, communications networks, and sugar mills. The object of all this was to not only create chaos and destabilize the regime but also to isolate Cuba economically and politically. Ultimately, it was hoped, a popular rising would follow. The results were disappointing. Castro remained strong, popular, and very much in power.

With the new and untested American president recently installed in Washington, Khrushchev resolved to once and for all settle the outstanding issues between the two countries. He took the occasion to do this at the Soviet summit conference at Vienna in June 1961. It was here, as mentioned in the previous chapter, that Khrushchev delivered his final ultimatum on Berlin, and it was here that Khrushchev took Kennedy's measure by successfully bullying him.

When President Kennedy extended the invitation to meet with Khrushchev he knew next to nothing about Khrushchev the communist politician. As a student at Harvard he had immersed himself in the great-power diplomacy of the 1930s, but he knew little of Russian history and even less about Marxism-Leninism and the role it might play in the shaping of Khrushchev's foreign policy. And Kennedy was warned about how potentially dangerous Khrushchev could be. The CIA report to Kennedy made it clear that Khrushchev was "imbued with the idea that he can utilize Soviet power to move the world toward communism during his lifetime." This was a sound view but it did not make much of an impression on Kennedy. Warned by the columnist Walter Lippmann that Khrushchev was a "committed revolutionary," Kennedy replied, "He's not a *real* revolutionist. He's never going to carry a revolution to the point where he thinks it is going to produce a war with us."[6]

Kennedy was also well-briefed by the CIA on Khrushchev the man. A sound CIA psychological profile was prepared for the president, which warned him about Khrushchev's mood swings and how quick he was to anger and bluff, cajole and threaten. He was warned that in all likelihood Khrushchev would try to knock him off balance at the conference. If Kennedy quickly found himself on the defensive, it was his own fault. He had been adequately briefed.

The man who went to Vienna to show the Soviets that they "must not crowd him too much" was, at the age of forty-three, the youngest president in American history. He was very conscious of his youth as he was of the slim victory he won in 1960, the closest presidential race in seventy-two years. His experience was reflected in a certain ambivalence about the Cold War and what the United States could do about it. On one hand, he understood that "there cannot be an American solution to every world problem," and on the other, he called for a Wilsonian crusade against atheistic world communism.[7] It was this inexperience that served him so badly in the Bay of Pigs. When asked by former President Eisenhower why he had failed to provide air cover during the invasion, Kennedy replied that he had been worried by a Soviet thrust at West Berlin. Eisenhower then angrily explained that "that is exactly the *opposite* of what would really happen. The Soviets follow their own plans, and if they see us show any weakness, that is when they press us the hardest." Eisenhower then predicted that "the failure of the Bay of Pigs will embolden the Soviets to do something that they would otherwise not do."[8] Adding his voice to Eisenhower's Richard Nixon also conveyed the practical lessons of realpolitik in dealing with the Soviets. "Khrushchev will prod and probe in several places at once," he said. "When we show weakness, he'll create crisis to take advantage of us. We should act in Cuba and Laos, including, if necessary, a commitment of U.S. air power."[9]

To Khrushchev, of course, Kennedy's failure to back up the Bay of Pigs invasion and finish off Castro was a sign of weakness. After all, Cuba was in the American sphere of influence. If he was reluctant to fight there, why would he show strength in Berlin, Laos, or anywhere else? Khrushchev knew about Kennedy's private reservations about Berlin and his fear during the Bay of Pigs of a Soviet move against that city. According to Arkady Shevchenko of the Soviet Foreign Ministry, the Bay of Pigs "gave Khrushchev and the other leaders the impression that Kennedy was indecisive."[10] Fyodor Burlatsky, an assistant to Khrushchev, suggests that Khrushchev saw a golden opportunity to exert pressure on a young president who, unlike the "political wolf" Eisenhower, had proved himself indecisive. Khrushchev had gained a great deal of confidence since his Camp David meeting with Eisenhower. "If before his meeting with Eisenhower he had been concerned not to lose face, before meeting Kennedy he was more preoccupied with how to put the young president 'in his place' and secure the concessions he wanted from him."[11] Anatoly Dobrynin, the former Soviet ambassador to the United States, who was present when Khrushchev made his pre-Vienna report to the Politburo, corroborates this. He has recently written that only Anastas Mikoyan dissented from the hard-line approach of exploiting an inexperienced president. He argued instead for the "entering into a reasonable and constructive dialogue which would lead to a positive development of Soviet-American relations." Khrushchev brushed this advice aside and insisted that this was "a favorable situation that must be exploited."[12]

Kennedy was aware, as he admitted to Richard Nixon in April, that the Bay of Pigs might lead Khrushchev to think that he could "keep pushing us all over the world." In fact, the desire to convey a stronger impression about his leadership prompted Kennedy on the eve of the summit to ask Congress to allocate more funds for defense and fall-out shelters, and to give the space program a significant boost as well.

At the Vienna meeting the two leaders talked at cross purposes. Kennedy had just finished reading Barbara Tuchman's *The Guns of August*. He had been very impressed with her thesis that through a series of stupid mistakes and miscalculations the great states of Europe in 1914 stumbled into the First World War. Kennedy was quite taken with the idea of "accidental war" and he tried to convey his concerns about it to Khrushchev in their first meeting at the summit. Kennedy told Khrushchev that he worried about Soviet attempts to encroach on new areas of the world (like Cuba) and the possible conflict that might arise between the two countries. "My ambition is to secure peace," he said. "If we fail in that effort, both our countries will lose. . . . Our two countries possess modern weapons. . . . If our two countries should miscalculate, they would lose for a long time to come."[13] Kennedy was really arguing for the status quo as American Presidents have since the Wilson administration. Khrushchev would have none of it. He was trained as a Marxist-Leninist to disdain the status quo and view the world in dynamic and dialectical terms. For every Russian leader since Lenin, who believed passionately in the dialectical forces of history, the revolution was always in the making because the world was not static but dynamic, and it was the historic duty of the Soviet Union to seek a revolutionary breakthrough in it. When Kennedy finished making his point Khrushchev began to yell, "Miscalculation! All I ever hear from your people and your news correspondents and your friends in Europe and everyplace else is that damned word miscalculation." Did America want the Soviet Union "to sit like a schoolboy with hands on top of the desk? . . . You ought to take that word and bury it in cold storage and never use it again."[14] Khrushchev was not interested in Kennedy's view of accommodation and he made it clear that the Soviet Union would continue to challenge the capitalist system everywhere in the world. Three years later Khrushchev told Senator William Benton that Kennedy had missed the real point. "We in the U.S.S.R. feel that the real revolutionary process should have the right to exist. The question of the right to rebel, and the Soviet right to help combat reactionary governments . . . is the question of questions . . . . This question is at the heart of our relations with you. . . . Kennedy could not understand this."[15]

At their last session in Vienna, Kennedy once again raised the question of miscalculation. Khrushchev brought his fist down on the table and thundered, "I want peace. But if you want war, that is your problem." At this point Khrushchev threatened to sign a separate peace treaty with East Germany and unilaterally alter West Berlin's status. Dobrynin says that Khrushchev was "obviously bluffing," that "he feared a new war and never considered a possibility of one waged over Germany or other international disputes."[16] But Khrushchev's bluff worked. "If that is true," a shaken Kennedy responded, "it's going to be a cold winter."

In contrast to Khrushchev's performance throughout the summit, Kennedy appeared weak and vacillating. He even at one point drew attention to his own weak political position at home. Dean Rusk, Kennedy's secretary of state, later said that Kennedy was very upset by this last encounter with Khrushchev. "He wasn't prepared for the brutality of Khrushchev's presentation. . . . Khrushchev was trying to act like a bully to the young President of the United States." Kennedy's own entourage had been stunned by the president's poor showing at Vienna. Charles Bohlen felt that Kennedy was "a little bit out of his depth," and Averell Harriman thought that he was "shattered by the experience." When James Reston, the Washington bureau chief of the *New York Times*, interviewed Kennedy just ten minutes after his last meeting with Khrushchev, he found the president in shock. When he asked Kennedy how the summit had gone, Kennedy replied, "worst thing in my life. He savaged me. . . . I think I know why he treated me like this. He thinks because of the Bay of Pigs that I'm inexperienced. Probably thinks I'm stupid. Maybe most importantly, he thinks that I had no guts."[17] According to Fyodor Burlatsky, "Khrushchev thought Kennedy too young, intellectual, not prepared for decision making in crisis situations."[18] It was clear that Khrushchev never questioned American power. What he questioned was John Kennedy's readiness to use it. This was what Paul Nitze meant when he said the summit was a "disaster." "Khrushchev was frightening," he told the CIA station chief in London. "I'm scared to death about what will happen next."

As early as the summer of 1960 Khrushchev made the assertion that Soviet rockets might be used in Cuba's defense. After the Vienna summit he halted the reduction in the size of the Red Army and instead increased the military budget by one-third. If Khrushchev had any lingering doubts about Kennedy's mettle, they were dispelled by the president's lack of a strong response to East Germany's erection of the Berlin Wall, and to Russia's resumption of nuclear testing, when Khrushchev broke his promise without warning. Eisenhower, Acheson, Lucius Clay, Charles De Gaulle, and even his own vice-president felt that Kennedy could have responded more strongly to Khrushchev's challenge and prevented the wall from being erected. Vice-President Lyndon Johnson, speaking to reporters off the record, said that the Berlin crisis was the result of the administration's poor record in the previous crises. "He had tasted blood in Cuba and Laos and now Berlin, and he's out for more. He thinks he can push a young President and a new administration and is probing to see how far he can go."[19]

In the months following the Vienna summit Kennedy remained obsessed with Cuba, and with trying to dispel all notions in the Kremlin that he was a pushover. In early October 1962, Kennedy decided to escalate Operation Mongoose to increase the number of raids on the island. At the same time, large-scale military exercises were conducted in the Caribbean at various times during 1962. One such exercise conducted in the spring involved 79 ships, 300 aircraft and more than 40,000 troops. All of this served to convince Castro that the Bay of Pigs was merely a first step in Washington's campaign to destroy his regime. Consequently, he desperately asked Moscow for military protection against what he felt was the imminent U.S. invasion of his country.

Khrushchev, who was constantly attacked by Mao's China for softness against the West, was inclined to extend Castro the firmest support to sustain his regime. He had already retreated from two separate ultimatums about Berlin; to stand by and allow the United States to dismantle the first real Marxist-Leninist revolution in the western hemisphere, was therefore unthinkable. "We were sure," Khrushchev said in his memoirs, "that the Americans would never reconcile themselves to the existence of Castro's Cuba. They feared, as much as we hoped, that a Socialist Cuba might become a magnet that would attract other Latin American countries to socialism. . . . It was clear to me that we might very well lose Cuba if we didn't take some decisive steps in her defense." Khrushchev claimed that on his visit to Bulgaria in May 1962 he had the idea of installing missiles in Cuba "without letting the United States find out they were there until it was too late to do anything about them."[20] Given the risks involved, however, the defense of Cuba was not the only motive for installing missiles there. According to Khrushchev, the other reason was his desire to close the missile gap with the United States and set right the strategic balance in one bold move.

> We had to establish a tangible and effective deterrent to American interference in the Caribbean. But what exactly? The logical answer was missiles. . . . In addition to protecting Cuba, our missiles would have equalized what the West likes to call 'The balance of power.' The Americans had surrounded our country with military bases and threatened us with nuclear weapons, and now they would learn just what it feels like to have enemy missiles pointed at you; we'd be doing nothing more than giving them a little of their own medicine.[21]

On hearing of Khrushchev's plan, some of the civilian members of the Politburo registered their disapproval. Anastas Mikoyan doubted whether missiles could be installed in Cuba without the United States knowing, and he felt that Castro would reject the idea because it might provoke an American invasion.

Andre Gromyko warned Khrushchev that the missiles would "cause a political explosion in the U.S.A." On the other hand, Marshal Malinovsky felt that it could be done quickly and remain undiscovered to the end. According to Mikoyan's son, Sergo, the army approved of the missile deployment "as a deterrent measure."[22] Both Sergo Mikoyan and Fyodor Burlatsky believe "that Khrushchev did not think through the American reaction." Not thinking it through, Khrushchev relied on the impression of weakness he received when he met Kennedy at Vienna, and on Kennedy's lack of strength since the Bay of Pigs. What must have struck Khrushchev more than anything else was the growing strategic superiority of the United States and its reluctance to use it to force major concessions from the Soviet Union.

The traffic of Russian weapons to Cuba was tracked carefully by U.S. intelligence for months. On August 29 the first surface-to-air missiles (S.A.M.s) were sighted, but since they were defensive weapons Washington chose to tolerate them. "Were it otherwise," Kennedy said on September 4, "the gravest issues would arise." The complacency of the CIA analysts and the Kennedy administration was fed by a careful Soviet disinformation campaign. For example, on September 4 Anatoly Dobrynin carried a confidential message from Khrushchev to Robert Kennedy promising that he would create no problems for the administration during the 1962 congressional elections. Khrushchev conveyed similar messages through private channels at various times during September and October.

The first shipment of offensive nuclear missiles arrived in Cuba on September 8. Another shipment arrived a few days later. But on reviewing the evidence the CIA concluded that Moscow would not place offensive nuclear weapons in Cuba. The performance of the intelligence community during the missile crisis left much to be desired, Walter Laqueur argues, because of its tendency toward "mirror imaging," "the assumption that an adversary will behave in a rational manner calculated to secure national security *as we understand those terms*."[23] Heretofore, the CIA argued, the U.S.S.R. had refrained from locating strategic nuclear missiles in other countries, not even in Eastern Europe. Why would Khrushchev now do anything so reckless as to put missiles in Cuba?

There was also a failure of intelligence on the Soviet side. No one there, least of all Khrushchev, was able to predict how even a "weak" President might react if his hand was forced. No one in the Kremlin seemed to give any thought to American considerations of its own prestige, its own domestic politics, or the vulnerability of Strategic Air Command (SAC) bases to Soviet attack, if the missiles were installed in Cuba.

In early October 1962 Moscow began construction of sites for forty-eight medium-range missiles and twenty-four intermediate-range ballistic missiles in Cuba. Soviet military and political officials have asserted ever since that Moscow gave clear orders that none of the missiles in Cuba would be placed on alert or in firing position. That is, the warheads would not be attached to the actual missiles. Nevertheless, they could be mounted and readied for use in a very short space of time, which would have immediately doubled the Soviet Union's first strike capability against the United States. According to Georgi Shaknazarov, an aid to Mikhail Gorbachev in 1988, "It is the ability to deliver a missile that is important for parity, not the quantity, of missiles. We had no missiles near the United States. The United States had bases encircling the Soviet Union." Installing the missiles, he says, "was an attempt by Khrushchev to get parity without spending resources we did not have."[24] Arthur Schlesinger at a conference in 1987 summed up the Soviet Union's move in political terms. The missiles had, he says, "a considerable effect on the world *political* balance. The emplacement of nuclear missiles in Cuba would prove the Soviet ability to act with impunity in the very heart of the American zone of vital interest—a victory of great significance for the Kremlin, which saw the world in terms of spheres of influence and inflexibly guarded its own."[25] What Khrushchev wanted, Donald Kagan argues, was "a credible nuclear force that would paralyze the Americans and prevent them from using their nuclear threat to prevent Soviet advances around the world."[26]

The U.S. Congress was increasingly worried by the general arming of Cuba and many of the leaders of the opposition called for a blockade of the island to end Soviet military assistance. On September 26 the Congress passed a resolution authorizing the president to stop "by whatever means may be necessary, including the use of arms, the creation in Cuba of a foreign military base that endangered United States security." Kennedy signed it on October 3 and on the same day twenty Latin American foreign ministers formally condemned any Soviet attempt to make Cuba an armed camp for the communist subversion of the hemisphere. On October 8 the U.S. Congress passed legislation to withhold aid from any country found trading with Cuba. All these steps were taken before a single offensive missile was discovered in Cuba.

But Khrushchev chose to ignore the changing political climate in the United States and he refused to halt the growing spiral of confrontation. In a meeting with the visiting Austrian vice-chancellor, Khrushchev "proclaimed to all and sundry that the Americans had lost their fighting spirit. . . . In short, he seemed confident at the time that all he had to do was raise his voice a little. Khrushchev's heightened self-assurance of those days was that of a gambler who had made his move."[27]

Khrushchev certainly made his move and U.S. intelligence sources began picking up information about missiles being unloaded at Cuban ports. On October 1 evidence of missile sites was presented to Robert McNamara, the secretary of defense, and the Joint Chiefs of Staff. The Defense Department then began contingency planning for an invasion of Cuba. Publicly the administration continued to deny that there was any evidence of nuclear missiles in Cuba. But on October 14 a U-2 spy plane photographed medium-range missile sites under construction there. Two days later American officials informed the president that the Soviet Union had indeed placed offensive missiles in Cuba.

To help advise him on the unfolding crisis, Kennedy created an Executive Committee of the National Security Council which came to be known as Excom.

Besides the president's brother, Robert, and the vice president, it contained Robert McNamara, Dean Rusk, Treasury Secretary Douglas Dillon, National Security Advisor McGeorge Bundy, General Maxwell Taylor, the chairman of the Joint Chiefs of Staff, Theodore Sorensen, Under Secretary of State George Ball, John McCone, the head of the CIA, and experienced people from the Truman years, like Dean Acheson, Paul Nitze, and Robert Lovett.

Excom met for the first time on October 16, 1962. For both military and political reasons it was agreed that the United States could not accept the presence of Soviet missiles in Cuba trained on the United States. If the United States passively accepted the missiles, it would constitute a terrible blow to its prestige in Latin America. It would expose the hollowness of its treaty commitments to use its great power in defense of not only the states of Latin America but of nations everywhere. The United States would then have looked like a fading giant. Moreover, coming so soon after the Bay of Pigs fiasco, a do-nothing policy would have exacted an enormous political toll on Kennedy's political party in the congressional elections of November 1962. Kennedy told his brother at the end of the crisis that if he had done nothing he would have been impeached. The only real alternative, therefore, was to do something.

The president's initial consideration was to strike hard and remove the missiles. The Joint Chiefs tried to reinforce the president's original plan to strike. The Air Force argued that a "clean surgical operation" to take out the missile sites would not be as effective as a more massive attack involving hundreds of planes flying hundreds of sorties, striking all missile sites, airfields, ports, and gun emplacements. In the early meetings of Excom the view of the Joint Chiefs was supported by Rusk, Dillon, McCone, and Acheson. Acheson was for an air attack followed by an invasion. Some of these men would, before the crisis ended, change their minds. When the president asked Air Force Chief of Staff General Curtis LeMay what the Russian response might be to the attack he proposed, the general assured him that, given the strategic superiority of the United States, the Russians would do nothing. According to Robert Kennedy, the generals assumed that a war was in the American national interest and to the last day of the crisis they wanted to attack Cuba.[28] President Kennedy, who realized that the kind of attack that the military was proposing would produce many casualties among civilians, as well as among Cuban and Soviet military personnel, felt that the Russians would be compelled to respond militarily. "If they don't take action in Cuba," he said, "they certainly would in Berlin." At the same time LeMay could not guarantee that all of the missile sites would be destroyed. What if only one was fired against the United States by a panicky ground crew? At this point in the discussion, Robert Kennedy passed a note to the President: "I now know how Togo felt when he was planning Pearl Harbor."[29] What he meant was that a massive air raid by a superpower on Cuba in a surprise attack would possibly kill thousands of civilians and violate the very canons of decency the United States was built on. A course of action like this would make the United States appear to be a bully and imperil its moral standing at home and around the world. As the president told Arthur Schlesinger after the crisis: "An invasion would have been a mistake—a wrong use of power. But the military are mad. They wanted to do this. It's lucky for us we have McNamara over there."

The other serious alternative to a surprise attack was to blockade or quarantine the island of Cuba. Robert McNamara was its strongest advocate in Excom. The pressure of the blockade, he argued, would be dramatic and forceful, it could be increased incrementally if events warranted it, and it would leave the control of the situation in the hands of the United States. Gradually, the majority of the committee swung around to the idea of the quarantine. By October 20 the president was committed to it. He called it "the only course compatible with American principles. The only dissenting approach was Adlai Stevenson's, the U.S. representative to the U.N. He wanted to tell the Russians that if they withdrew their missiles from Cuba, the United States would withdraw theirs from Turkey and Italy and give up the Guantanamo Naval Base in Cuba. He was shouted down.[30]

The discussions held between October 16 and October 22 remained a closely guarded secret. Whenever either Kennedy met with Anatoly Dobrynin or Andre Gromyko they never tipped their hand, even when the Russians continued to assure them that the weapons streaming into Cuba were purely defensive.

The Kremlin was informed on October 22 just before President Kennedy went on television and announced the crisis to the world. In his speech to the American people that day, Kennedy virtually ignored Castro and the Cuban role in the crisis. He announced that "it shall be the policy of this nation to regard any nuclear missile launched from Cuba against any nation in the Western Hemisphere as an attack by the Soviet Union on the United States, requiring a full retaliatory response upon the Soviet Union." He then announced a full quarantine of Cuba and insisted that Khrushchev "halt and eliminate this clandestine, reckless and provocative threat to world peace."

On the same day, Kennedy personally briefed seventeen congressional leaders from both parties. Kennedy was unprepared for what followed. The leaders were extremely emotional and sharp in their criticism. They felt that a blockade was too weak a response and they urged the president to attack Cuba immediately.

Also on October 22, Kennedy moved to inform his allies. Top secret messages were transmitted to all U.S. ambassadors around the world, outlining the proposed course of action. Special emissaries were dispatched to convey the same message to America's key allies—the French, the British, and the Germans, among others. In each case, allied support was requested and, without exception, received. At the same time, the countries of the OAS took the Soviet challenge very seriously and unanimously condemned it. They also expressed their willingness to follow the leadership of the United States and called for the removal of the missiles, thus giving a legal basis to the quarantine.

At the hour that Kennedy began his address to the nation, he placed all U.S. military forces on Defense Condition (DEFCON) 3 alert. The B-47 medium-bomber force was dispersed to some thirty-three civilian airports, and the B-52s in the Strategic Air Command were loaded with nuclear bombs and placed on

DEFCON 2, the highest alert level short of war. DEFCON 2 had never been instituted before. The world stood close to nuclear war for the first time in the Cold War.

In placing the air force bombers on alert, the commander-in-chief of SAC, General Thomas Powers, decided to show the Russians just how prepared and determined the United States was to see the crisis through. On his own authority he informed his senior commanders about the gravity of the crisis, and assured them that the alert was going smoothly and that SAC plans were well prepared. Powers flaunted U.S. power by not encoding the message, but sending it "in the clear." That the Russians were alarmed by this unprecedented action was recently confirmed by General Dmitri Volkogonov.[31]

The buildup for a possible invasion of Cuba gradually took shape. A military force of some 250,000, including infantry and armored and airborne units, as well as a marine division, were already on the move into Florida. The Guantanamo Naval Base on the east coast of Cuba was strengthened, as the U.S. Navy deployed over 180 ships to the Caribbean. On October 23 when six Soviet submarines were tracked entering the Caribbean, Kennedy ordered the U.S. Navy to give the "highest priority to tracking the submarines and to put into effect the greatest possible safety measures to protect our own aircraft carriers and other vessels." The submarines were followed and harassed and all were forced to surface in the presence of U.S. ships of war.[32] These aggressive measures, as much as anything else in October, helped to convince Moscow that the United States not only enjoyed hegemony in the region but also indicated how serious the American resolve was during the crisis.

While this enormous U.S. military effort was being carried out, the Soviet Union was, for its part, not making preparations for war. Even late in the crisis it was not significantly redeploying its forces. It did not even put its air force or missile crews on alert. Knowing that the United States enjoyed regional hegemony in the Caribbean and keenly aware that it also held a decisive nuclear advantage over the Soviet Union, the Kremlin seemed to back away from a strategy of bluff leaving the United States with the bargaining edge. According to Marc Trachtenberg, the Russians were sensitive to the American emphasis on the logic of preemption. The Soviet authors of a key book on strategy that appeared in 1962 before the crisis (*Soviet Military Strategy*, edited by Marshal Sokolovskii) understood that "the one who strikes first will undoubtedly gain an important advantage." This was why the United States was so obsessed with a surprise attack. The Americans thought that they might have to launch an attack simply because they felt the Russians were about to strike. "A preemptive blow," the Soviet strategists argued, "is defensive, according to American military theorists, since it is dealt to an enemy who is ready to attack. . . . It is considered to be the final and only means of avoiding disaster." The Russians also understood the American idea of "damage limitation"; that is, if there was a warning of preparations for a Soviet strike, the U.S. missiles would automatically be launched against Soviet missile sites and airfields, thus limiting the amount of damage. Given all this, Trachtenberg concludes, "The Soviet leaders might have viewed war preparations as very dangerous."[33]

According to Russian historian Roy Medvedev and confirmed by Sergo Mikoyan, Khrushchev's first angry reaction to the quarantine was to order the construction of the missiles accelerated, and to instruct the Russian ships bound for Cuba to force the blockade. Only the intervention of Anastas Mikoyan made Khrushchev cool down and prevented a clash from occurring at sea. At this point Khrushchev sent Kennedy a letter in which he denounced the blockade of Cuba but assured the president that the Russian missiles were in Cuba to defend the island and nothing more. He asked Kennedy to exercise caution and avoid taking actions that might lead to war. On the same day, Kennedy pulled back the quarantine line—over the protests of the navy—from 800 miles to 500 miles. But the war of nerves continued as the Soviet vessels sailed toward the blockade. As the tension mounted, the word came that the Russian ships stopped at the 500 mile limit or, in some cases, turned back. In fact, those ships actually carrying the missiles turned back, while other ships kept coming. Kennedy allowed oil tankers to get through the blockade and sail on to Havana. The first ship to be stopped was under Russian charter but owned by a Panamanian. It had been carefully selected by Kennedy to be the first one boarded on October 26. He wanted to show Khrushchev that he meant business, but since it was not Russian-owned, it would not represent a direct affront requiring a response by the Russians. In fact, the ship was notified the night before that it would be boarded the next day. The ship was indeed boarded, inspected, and allowed to proceed.

On the 26th, the day the first ship was boarded, a Soviet agent contacted correspondent John Scali of the American Broadcasting Company and offered to disengage the missiles from Cuba if the United States promised publicly not to invade Cuba in the future. Khrushchev was, in a highly irregular way, floating a trial balloon. It seems clear that by that date Khrushchev realized that his position was untenable and that an American attack on Cuba was probably imminent. According to Anatoly Dobrynin, Soviet intelligence sources received information that bombing raids were set for October 29 or 30. "Comrades," said Khrushchev in addressing the Politburo, "Now we have to look for a dignified way out of this conflict."[34] Believing that time was quickly running out, he sent Kennedy a long and rambling letter. He assured Kennedy that Russia's intentions were not hostile and that the Soviet Union did not want war. He therefore asked Kennedy to lift the blockade and not force the issue to war. He also proposed a solution to the crisis: he indicated that he would be willing to dismantle the missiles in Cuba in return for Kennedy's pledge never to invade Cuba. While the White House was preparing an answer to the letter, another note arrived from Khrushchev twelve hours later. The new letter called for the removal of American missiles from Turkey in exchange for the removal of the Soviet missiles in Cuba. The tone was more formal and demanding in the second letter. Kennedy reacted angrily to it, since removing the U.S. missiles from Turkey would, he felt, give Khrushchev the victory in the crisis. Members of Excom were confused by the two letters and thought of asking

Moscow for clarification.[35] There was also a suspicion that Khrushchev was not really in complete control and that he was under tremendous pressure from his military. Actually, on the night of the 26th Robert Kennedy paid a secret visit to Anatoly Dobrynin (only the president knew about it) and suggested making the Turkish missiles part of the deal. A few hours later Khrushchev wrote his second letter making the Turkish missiles central to the settlement.[36]

At this point, the tension rose another notch when a U-2 reconnaissance plane was shot down over Cuba and its pilot killed. At the same moment, one of the Soviet tankers resumed its forward movement toward the blockade line, as Soviet technicians were photographed moving Russian warheads closer to the missiles, possibly in preparation for a first strike. It briefly looked to Excom that the moves were coordinated and that the Russians might be escalating the crisis. As it turned out, none of these moves were coordinated. The decision to fire a SAM missile at the U-2 was made by a local commander in violation of his standing orders and without the Kremlin being informed. According to General Volkogonov, when the Kremlin was informed Khrushchev became furious and had Marshal Malinovsky reprimand the officer. These were very tense hours, perhaps the most dangerous moments of the missile crisis, when one wrong move might have sent the whole situation spinning out of control. Fidel Castro was so worried about the imminence of an American attack that he spent the night of the 26th in a Soviet bomb shelter. He even, according to Khrushchev, urged Moscow to launch a preemptive nuclear strike against the United States.[37]

According to Robert Kennedy, the president was under great pressure to retaliate and at least destroy the SAM site. He told Anatoly Dobrynin that a lot of people in Washington, and not just the generals, were "spoiling for a fight."[38] What is clear is that Kennedy was under enormous pressure to act militarily, but was extremely reluctant to do so.

To break the deadlock and defuse the crisis, President Kennedy accepted a suggestion from his brother to ignore Khrushchev's second note and accept the first letter of October 26. At the same time, Robert Kennedy assured the Russians in private that American missiles would be withdrawn from Turkey, but he warned that if Moscow revealed this part of the settlement, Washington would disavow it. If Khrushchev had hesitated or rejected the settlement, Dean Rusk had secretly arranged for U Thant, the Secretary-General of the U.N., to propose a similar arrangement. Khrushchev made it clear in his memoirs that he understood that the balance of forces and Washington's resolve favored the United States in any military showdown. An invasion of Cuba by the United States would lead to a general war in which, strategically speaking, the Soviet Union would fight under a disadvantage. It was clear to Khrushchev that, unless something was done, the United States would almost certainly invade Cuba at the end of October. This put pressure on the Kremlin to head off the invasion and on October 28, Khrushchev accepted Kennedy's terms. In the end, both men felt that the missiles were not worth a world war.

Khrushchev called the missile crisis a "great victory" because it resulted in an

American no-invasion commitment and therefore a preservation of the Castro regime and its revolution. But Khrushchev was putting the best possible face on it. Actually, everyone in the Kremlin knew that he had lost the crisis; that he had put the Soviet Union in an untenable position and then called for a shameless retreat. The country had suffered a humiliation because of it and had sustained a serious blow to its prestige. Khrushchev admitted several months later that the Soviet military had opposed the missile withdrawal. They had regarded him "as though I was out of my mind or, what was worse, a traitor."[39]

Beijing also called him a traitor to world communism and mocked him for moving from "adventurism to capitulationism" and inflicting "unprecedented shame and humiliation on the international proletariat." But the most telling comment came from the Soviet diplomat, Vasilii Kuznetsov, in an exchange with John McCloy: "You will never do that to us again."[40] Indeed, the great Soviet arms buildup toward strategic parity with the United States was accelerated right after the missile crisis.

Khrushchev's power never really recovered from the missile crisis. By 1963 the virgin lands campaign, launched with such high hopes during the 1950s, had turned into a disaster. The harvest that year was the worst in many years. The result was large-scale purchases of grain on international markets, something quite unprecedented in modern Russian history. As the Sino-Soviet split widened, and Soviet-Cuban relations worsened, the criticism of Khrushchev's personal role in creating the missile crisis became more widespread, especially in the Central Committee. In October 1964, the Politburo finally removed him from power and replaced him with a group led by Leonid Brezhnev and Aleksei Kosygin.

The Kennedy White House felt triumphant about the way things worked out. But here too there were lots of dissenting opinions. As late as October 28, 1962p, General LeMay had argued for an air strike, and Admiral George Anderson, the chief of Naval Operations, complained that "we had been had." Kennedy also came under strong attack from some of the leading Republicans in the Congress, who accused him of ripping up the Monroe Doctrine and allowing a communist regime to remain in the western hemisphere just ninety miles from Florida.

Some of America's allies were not happy either with Washington's performance during the crisis, since they had been merely informed about developments during the critical weeks and not consulted. There was a general feeling throughout the Western alliance that Kennedy's brand of brinkmanship had been too dangerous.

When the missile crisis was over, Kennedy made it clear that there must be undivided control over the West's nuclear deterrent. But President De Gaulle of France was demanding nuclear sharing. Believing that France should not rely on the United States for its defense, De Gaulle announced that France would formally leave NATO by 1966. The Western alliance would never be the same again.

If there was a winner in the missile crisis it was Cuba. The Castro regime was preserved along with its revolution, and it received assurance against any future American invasion. But Castro did not see this at first. He was actually quite bitter about the removal of the missiles, refusing at one point to even receive the Soviet ambassador to Cuba. Khrushchev ascribed this to Castro's inexperience as a statesman.

Kennedy and Khrushchev came away from the crisis sobered by how close their countries had come to nuclear war. They did not believe that war was inevitable and they felt that political action by the superpowers could reduce the level of confrontation. Soon after the crisis ended, Kennedy announced a United States moratorium on atmospheric testing, which Khrushchev described privately as "courageous." The first Limited Test Ban Treaty was signed in July 1963, which prohibited atmospheric and underwater nuclear testing. Finally, the two sides agreed to install a "hot line," providing for a telephone communication between the White House and the Kremlin in the event of an international crisis.

In 1963 the United States was at the apogee of its power. In military and economic terms she was unrivalled anywhere in the world. Buoyed by this and by an unquestioned belief in itself, and led by a dynamic presidency, the American leadership formed an exaggerated estimate of the strength of the nation. This led in the latter half of the 1960s to an extension of American power abroad, as the United States began its steep descent into the Vietnam War.

Notes

1. Richard M. Nixon, *The Memoirs of Richard Nixon* (New York: Grosset and Dunlap, 1978), 201-2.

2. G.J.A. O'Toole, *Honorable Treachery: A History of U.S. Intelligence, Espionage, and Covert Action from the American Revolution to the CIA* (New York: Atlantic Monthly Press, 1991), 475-76.

3. Barton J. Bernstein, "Kennedy and the Bay of Pigs Revisited Twenty-Four Years Later," *Foreign Service Journal*, 62 (March 1985), 535-56.

4. Quoted in Lucien S. Vandenbroucke, "The 'Confessions' of Allen Dulles," *Diplomatic History*, 8 (Fall 1984), 369.

5. Michael R. Beschloss, *Mayday. Eisenhower, Khrushchev and the U-2 Affair* (New York: Harper and Row, 1986), 303.

6. Michael R. Beschloss, *The Crisis Years. Kennedy and Khrushchev 1960-1963* (New York: HarperCollins, 1991), 168.

7. Donald Kagan, *On the Origins of War and the Preservation of Peace* (New York: Doubleday, 1995), 550-51.

8. Beschloss, *The Crisis Years*, 145.

9. Beschloss, *The Crisis Years*, 146.

10. A.N. Shevchenko, *Breaking with Moscow* (London: Cape, 1985), 110.

11. Fyodor Burlatsky, *Khrushchev and the First Russian Spring*, trans. D. Skillen (New York: Scribner's, 1991), 162.

12. Anatoly Dobrynin, *In Confidence: Moscow's Ambassador to America's Six Cold War Presidents (1962-1986)* (New York: Random House, 1995), 44.

13. Quoted in Beschloss, *The Crisis Years*, 196.

14. Quoted in Beschloss, *The Crisis Years*, 196.

15. Arthur M. Schlesinger, Jr., *A Thousand Days. John F. Kennedy in the White House* (Boston: Houghton Mifflin Company, 1965), 366.

16. Dobrynin, *In Confidence*, 45.

17. Richard Reeves, *President Kennedy. Profile of Power* (New York: Simon and Schuster, 1993), 166, 172.

18. James G. Blight and David A. Welch, *On the Brink. Americans and Soviets Reexamine the Cuban Missile Crisis* (New York: Hill and Wang, 1989), 236.

19. Beschloss, *The Crisis Years*, 286.

20. Nikita Khrushchev, *Khrushchev Remembers*, trans. Strobe Talbott (Boston: Little Brown and Company, 1970), 493.

21. Khrushchev, *Khrushchev Remembers*, 493-94.

22. Raymond L. Garthoff, *Reflections on the Cuban Missile Crisis* (Washington, D.C.: Brookings Institution, 1989), 13.

23. Walter Laqueur, *A World of Secrets. The Uses and Limits of Intelligence* (New York: Basic Books, 1985), 141.

24. Blight and Welch, *On the Brink*, 248.

25. Blight and Welch, *On the Brink*, 28.

26. Kagan, *Origins of War*, 511.

27. Reported by Michel Tatu in Kagan, *Origins of War*, 505.

28. Robert F. Kennedy, *Thirteen Days. A Memoir of the Cuban Missile Crisis* (New York: W.W. Norton and Company, 1971), 97, 126.

29. Kennedy, *Thirteen Days*, 9.

30. Kennedy, *Thirteen Days*, 27.

31. Garthoff, *Reflections*, 61-62.

32. Kennedy, *Thirteen Days*, 55.

33. Marc Trachtenberg, *History and Strategy* (Princeton, N.J.: Princeton University Press, 1991), 256.

34. Dobrynin, *In Confidence*, 88, 89.

35. Kennedy, *Thirteen Days,* 73-74.

36. B. J. Allyn, J. G. Blight, and D. A. Welch, *Back to the Brink* (Cambridge, Mass.: Harvard University Press, 1992), 143.

37. Nikita Khrushchev, *Khrushchev Remembers. The Glasnost Tapes*, trans. J. L. Schecter with V. V. Luchkov (Boston: Little, Brown and Company, 199), 177.

38. Dobrynin, *In Confidence*, 87.

39. Garthoff, *Reflections*, 77.

40. Charles Bohlen, *Witness to History 1919-1969* (New York: W.W. Norton and Company, 1973), 495.

17

The Congo Crisis

Since the end of the Korean War the Soviet Union pursued a much more dynamic and aggressive foreign policy in regions of the world from which her influence had been completely absent. She had backed Nasser's Egypt throughout the Suez Crisis and after; she had intervened in Cuba's quarrel with the United States; she had backed North Vietnam's attempt to gain control over all of Vietnam; and she had backed the left-wing leader, Patrice Lumumba, in the civil war in the recently independent Belgian Congo.

The Eisenhower administration had relied on the threat of "massive retaliation" to deter Soviet adventurism outside its own borders. The Kennedy administration had criticized this strategy as unrealistic at best and dangerous in the extreme. It certainly was not a credible strategy to cope with so-called brush fire wars. Kennedy's alternative strategy was called "flexible response." This approach was designed to meet the communist challenge in the increasingly volatile third world.

When President Kennedy came to office he ambitiously proposed to "deter all wars, general or limited, nuclear or conventional, large or small." The United States, he felt, must demonstrate the will to take up arms in a nuclear age. His doctrine called for the development of an array of options, conventional and unconventional, as well as nuclear. This would give the United States the chance to project its power across the world, and the option to tailor its response to the requirements of each problem as it might arise. It seemed imperative to do this when Khrushchev in January 1961 raised the stakes in the colonial world by pledging to support wars of liberation. When Kennedy was sworn into office two weeks later, he concluded that a new communist global offensive was about to begin.

Like all presidents since Harry Truman, Kennedy had to deal with the problem that arose from European imperial states relinquishing control of vast tracts of the colonial world. What complicated the problem was that common patterns of colonial rule, be they British, French, Portuguese or Belgian, were breaking up almost everywhere in Asia and Africa at once, and that this movement toward independence came at a moment when the superpowers were embarking on new efforts to gain influence in the third world. The influence of the colonial period was never obliterated, but each newly independent nation developed along its own path.

The Belgian Congo (Zaire) and Vietnam were two examples of African and Asian nationalism, which, albeit it in different ways, became the focus of international Cold War rivalry.

Nationalism in the Congo was a comparatively late development, and not a very mature one. When it emerged in the mid-1950s it was strongly tribal, regional, and extremely divisive. It was basically the nationalism of the African village and directed at the foreigners who ran the country. By 1960 voices were increasingly raised demanding Congolese independence as disturbances within the country mounted in frequency. The Belgian government realized that it lacked the resources to deal with the growing problem, and reacted by abruptly abandoning the country. When independence was granted on January 27, 1960, for implementation on June 30, 1960, the Congo was left with no constitutional or administrative structure to replace the colonial administration. In the five months before June 30, a constitution was hastily devised and some semblance of government was thrown together calling itself the Republic of Congo. The new republic boasted a bi-cameral legislature, a cabinet and a president. The highest positions of state, however, were filled by men of only partial education (the first African graduated at a Belgian university only in 1956) and no political experience.

Almost from the moment independence was proclaimed on June 30 the country began to fall apart. Tribal fighting broke out the next day in the capital, Leopoldville, and a few days after that the Congolese army mutinied. The soldiers ran wild, pillaging and burning, murdering and raping the Europeans who were left in the country. Troops were rushed from Belgium to protect the Europeans and repel the mutineers. On July 11 the mineral-rich province of Katanga under Moise Tshombe seceded and erected a rival center of power. The Congo's prime minister, Patrice Lumumba, a former clerk in the tax and postal administrations, wished to quell the army mutiny and recover control of Katanga. He appealed at first to the U.N., which promptly sent a peacekeeping force to the Congo on July 15, that soon numbered 20,000 troops. At the same time, paramilitary troops and mercenaries entered the Congo to defend Katanga and its European mining interests.

With the Congo sliding deeper into chaos, Foreign Minister André Gromyko of the Soviet Union accused the West of armed aggression against that unfortunate country, for the purpose of liquidating its independence. On the very day the U.N. troops arrived in the Congo, Khrushchev announced the receipt of a note from Lumumba requesting Soviet aid. Khrushchev replied positively. Like Mosaddegh, Arbenz, and Castro, Lumumba had made a fatal mistake. According to one historian, this was "the critical blunder of his brief career. . . . By inviting the Soviet Union to intervene, Lumumba became a pawn—and ultimately a victim—of the Cold War."[1] Once again a third world leader had made an appeal for outside help and once again a larger crisis broke out over conflicting positions in the Cold War. What began as a civil war quickly became another chapter in the Cold War.

In the U.N. the United States promised to do "whatever may be necessary to prevent the intrusion of any military forces not requested by the United Nations."[2]

In conditions of growing anarchy, the second-richest province in the Congo,

Kasai, also announced its secession. Lumumba now, somewhat hysterically, sought U.S. aid. He was turned down by John Foster Dulles for being a client of the Kremlin (despite the fact that his brand of socialism had little in common with Soviet communism).

Under its ambitious and energetic Secretary-General, Dag Hammarskjold, the U.N. sought to restore order in the Congo. It began to do this by closing the airports in the country to all but U.N. flights, which had the effect of barring Soviet planes from making arms deliveries to Lumumba. This amply confirmed Khrushchev's view that the U.N. represented Western interests in Africa. Khrushchev then appeared before the U.N. in the fall of 1960 to propose that the office of Secretary General be replaced by a three-man commission, with one each "from the capitalists, the socialists, and the nations in between which had liberated themselves from the colonialists but were still nonaligned or neutral. . . ." When his idea for a "troika" failed to attract much support, during a speech by Britain's Harold MacMillan, Khrushchev removed his shoe and banged it on his desk; other members of the Soviet delegation quickly followed suit. Khrushchev's crude attack on Hammarskjold and the U.N. was joined by Lumumba, who decided to break with the world organization.

Despite the obstacles placed before it by the U.N. the Russians still managed to send Lumumba some planes and trucks for troop transport. At the same time, hundreds of Soviet agents streamed into the Congo disguised as diplomats and technicians. Moscow also expressed its willingness to send "volunteers" to help Lumumba against the imperialists.

The United States now became convinced that the radical Lumumba should be removed from power. Joseph Kasavubu, the president of the Congo, and his chief of staff, Colonel Sese Mobutu, had from the beginning of the crisis decided to rely on Western help, and they now agreed to remove Lumumba. Lumumba was then dismissed from office and replaced with Col. Mobutu. In December 1960, following Lumumba's arrest, the pro-Lumumba region rebelled and set up a rival government headed by Antoine Gizenga, a former supporter of Lumumba. By the middle of 1961, besides the secessionist Katanga under Tshombe, two governments claimed rule over the whole of the country: Mobutu's in Leopoldville, and Gizenga's in Stanleyville. With the Congo trembling into anarchy and civil war, Mobutu had Lumumba assassinated.

Until he was killed in an airplane crash in September 1961, Dag Hammarskjold's policy was to exert strong military and diplomatic pressure on Katanga to end its secessionism. In this he was aided by the United States, which helped a U.N. mission quell the Katanga insurrection and, at the same time, suppressed Gisenga's claims to leadership in the Congo.

Soon after Lumumba's death, the entire staff of the Russian embassy was expelled by Mobutu, who had succeeded in establishing his personal rule over the country. He also liquidated the Russian presence throughout the Congo. In other words, Khrushchev had once again embarked on a gamble with a low investment and the possibility of great rewards. But driven from the Congo, the Soviet Union was once again humiliated.

Leading African nationalists also felt humiliated by the Western intervention and their criticism of the role the United States had played in the Congo crisis was a bitter one. By backing the pro-Soviet groups in the Congo, the Soviet Union won itself some friends in Africa—like Ghana, Morocco, Algeria, and Egypt—but it also alienated others. Both superpowers seemed to be on alien terrain in Africa, and both were trying to nullify the possible gains made by the other. Fortunately, for the inexperienced Kennedy administration, the Russians did not press the issue, and the U.N. for awhile was under a strong and ambitious leader who used the world organization in a creative way. Washington, however, had no such advantages in Southeast Asia.

Notes

1. R. Mahoney, *JFK: Ordeal in Africa* (New York: Oxford University Press, 1983), 45-46.

2. Mahoney, *JFK*, 45-46.

18

The Vietnam War

With the outbreak of the Second World War the various nationalist forces in Indochina saw a golden opportunity to free themselves from French colonial rule. The defeat of France in 1940 raised their hopes even higher. Since the Vichy government of France followed a policy of collaboration with the Japanese, the Indochinese Communist Party (PCI) tried to build its own government in North Vietnam, one that was ready to replace the French administration when the opportunity arose.

The wartime strategy of the PCI was based on Mao Tse-Tung's "protracted war" in three phases. During the first, revolutionary stage the PCI organized a broad coalition of workers, peasants, and the liberal wing of the bourgeoisie to defeat the Japanese and the French, and establish an independent liberal-democratic republic. Like the Chinese and Yugoslav Communist parties during the war, the PCI was trying to ascend to power during an intense national struggle to repel the invaders. The non-communists in the coalition never realized until it was too late that the PCI was following a strategy of deception; that it never intended to form a democratic republic and share power, but rather intended all along to rule Vietnam alone. In the meantime, while the war moved to its eventual conclusion, the PCI steadily formed front groups and secured rural bases, while its guerrillas were infiltrated into government-held areas.

In phase two, control was extended over the rural population by propaganda and political struggle, by terrorism when the party deemed it necessary, by the sabotage of government services that were not under direct communist control, and by raids on government posts. There was to be no "people's democracy" stage in the Vietnam revolution. When the PCI was sufficiently strengthened and a regular armed force ready, the party would launch phase three, which would carry the communists to power.

After 1942 the PCI in the north of Vietnam quickly established a widespread underground throughout the country. Under its leader, Ho Chi Minh, the party in 1944 was able to proclaim its first "liberated zone" in much of the North. In August 1945 and right after Hiroshima, the guerrilla forces constituted themselves into a "liberation army." At that point, the party called for a general insurrection and demanded that the Japanese surrender to them. When the Japanese retreated from the country, they left the hereditary emperor, Bao Dai, on his throne. Bao Dai then promptly declared Vietnam independent from France. But the communists had come too far to reconcile themselves to a conservative regime, and on September 2, 1945, Ho Chi Minh proclaimed the Democratic Republic of Vietnam (DRV). Bao Dai, unable to gain popular support, abdicated his throne and recognized the DRV as the only governmental authority in Vietnam. A British force was then sent by the Allies to accept the Japanese surrender and to briefly administer Indochina south of the 16th parallel. At the same time, a Nationalist Chinese army entered the country and was prepared to administer the North. This represented the first postwar division of Vietnam.

With the help of the British, the French forces once again reoccupied sections of the South and reasserted control. The attempts of the Chinese to force the communists and their rivals into a coalition government failed, as did the French policy of divide and rule. Vietnam quickly slid into chaos and civil war.

Better organized than their enemies and more ruthless, communist assassination squads eliminated thousands of their nationalist enemies even as they replaced the old bureaucracy with people's councils and consolidated their control.

From 1946 to 1949 the communist forces in Indochina waged a guerrilla war that avoided large-scale ground combat, yet had the ability to wear down the resolve of the occupying power. To better resist this, the French in 1948 succeeded in forming a provisional government in the South under the Emperor Bao Dai. In 1949 France granted Vietnam, Laos, and Cambodia limited independence within the French Union. To the end, however, it refused to grant the real independence that might have attracted enough popular support to defeat the DRV.

In 1948-1949 the power equation in Asia was sharply altered when Chinese communism triumphed on Vietnam's doorstep. In January 1950 Ho Chi Minh, bolstered by this historical development, proclaimed that the only legitimate Vietnamese government was his own in Hanoi, and he invited diplomatic recognition. This he quickly received from other communist countries. At this point, Chinese and Russian advisors and technicians swarmed into the country, as the DRV intensified political indoctrination and enlarged its army. Beginning in 1950, the large-scale military aid from China and the Soviet Union began to arrive in the country.

Until 1948, it was the official American view of the situation that France was trying to crush a nationalist revolt and regain a vital piece of her empire. By the time Mao Tse-Tung won the Chinese civil war, the Truman administration redefined the conflict as a struggle against the spread of communism. By 1954, 70 percent of the French financial cost of the war was underwritten by the United States. Nevertheless, by the end of 1953 the communists controlled most of the country and the French military effort neared total collapse. The DRV's offensives gradually increased in size and by 1954 the struggle became a conventional war. In the spring of 1954, the communist forces besieged a French and Vietnamese army of 12,000 in the fortress of Dien Bien Phu. It was clear that unless the United States extended direct military aid to the French, all of Indochina might be lost.

Throughout the crisis, Eisenhower received no encouragement from his allies. He also discovered that the U.S. Congress had no stomach for another Korean War, especially one in which the United States might have to fight alone. Dulles then made it perfectly clear that the United States would not sent ground forces to Indochina and would not take any actions without congressional blessing. At the same time, the national security bureaucracy was divided in its views, as it often was during the Cold War. For example, in 1954 the U.S. Navy and Air Force (backed by Vice-President Nixon) favored bombing targets in Vietnam using carrier-based aircraft. This was to be a minimum response to the crisis, but the U.S. Army, forcefully represented by Generals Ridgeway and Gavin, opposed intervention of any kind and carried the day. They won their point not only because of the lack of consensus in Washington for intervention but also because the professed policy of massive retaliation and brinkmanship emanating from the White House was nothing more than blustering rhetoric designed to give a patina of respectability to what the administration could not really do in the Cold War. Designed for popular consumption, it seemed to reassure the American people generally about the direction of the Cold War but specifically it was not, and could not be, a truly operative policy in Asia. Eisenhower in 1954 likened the nations of Southeast Asia to a row of dominoes ("Where in hell can you let the Communists chip away any more? We just can't stand it."),[1] but he did little to help the French end their predicament. There was no massive retaliation and Dien Bien Phu fell on May 7, 1954.

In early 1954, several months before the end at Dien Bien Phu, a conference had been called at Geneva allegedly to study the Korean situation, but actually as a convenient way to deal with the Indochina problem. That problem came up the day after the French surrendered the fortress. The two Vietnamese sides were at the table, as were the representatives of communist China, the United States, Britain, France, and the Soviet Union. France was represented by Pierre Mendès-France, who on assuming office dramatically announced that if he had not achieved a satisfactory solution to the Indochinese problem within one month, by July 20, his government would resign. In just a few weeks he indeed reached an agreement with the North Vietnamese, Red China and the Soviet Union.

The Geneva Accords provided for armistices in Laos, Cambodia, and Vietnam. Most important for subsequent Cold War history, they provided for the partitioning of Vietnam at the 17th parallel. It divided Vietnam into a communist North under Ho Chi Minh and a non-communist South headed by the Emperor Bao Dai. Moreover, it was agreed that there would be no foreign bases in either North or South; that neither country would join a military alliance; and that elections were to be held in both states leading to the unification of the whole country by July 20, 1956.

The American role at the conference was that of passive observer. To Dulles, who believed that one should not negotiate with communist countries but rather destroy them, Geneva was a nightmare. The administration, which had spent years attacking Truman and Acheson for "losing" China, now stood by without dropping a single bomb to save a region it had deemed vital to American security and allowed half of Vietnam to sink into the communist bloc. The U.S. nuclear bluff of massive retaliation was now obvious to everyone on both sides. When the accords were completed on July 21, the United States refused to sign them, although it promised not to oppose the settlement with force. In June 1955 Dulles asserted that the United States was not "a party to the Geneva armistice agreements," and that it supported Saigon's refusal to consult with Hanoi about elections on the grounds that elections could never be free in the North.[2]

Despite the call for elections, the prime minister of the southern half of Vietnam, Ngo Dinh Diem, organized a plebiscite that deposed Bao Dai and created the Republic of South Vietnam. Proclaiming the sovereignty of his country, he then sought to establish links with the United States.

John Foster Dulles had already reacted to Geneva by coming up with the idea of a new security organization for the Far East. On September 8, 1954, the United States, France, Australia, New Zealand, the Philippines, Thailand, and Pakistan agreed to form the Southeast Asia Treaty Organization (SEATO). Less a military organization like NATO, than a loose pact for economic and military aid, it did not include Vietnam, Laos, or Cambodia, who were banned from joining by the Geneva Accords, or India, Ceylon, Burma, and Indonesia, who wished to remain neutral. Ineffectual as the organization proved to be, the United States in its name pledged to defend South Vietnam. When the United States then told Paris that it would extend grants and subsidies to Vietnam, Laos, and Cambodia, the French for all practical purposes withdrew from Southeast Asia. The United States had thus taken a significant step toward assuming responsibility for the region and, of course, towards the Vietnam War a decade later.

The Eisenhower administration regarded the Geneva Accords as the appeasement of communism and as a setback to the democratic cause in Asia. Eisenhower wanted a firmer line to be drawn in Southeast Asia against further communist expansion. From his standpoint in 1954 the real key to Southeast Asia was Laos rather than Vietnam. Indeed, Eisenhower considered the independence of Laos so crucial that he was prepared to "fight . . . with our allies or without them."[3]

Outwardly a united kingdom of two and a half million people, Laos was torn by regional, tribal, and factional strife. The country was increasingly controlled in the north by the communist Pathet Lao, while an anti-communist army faction in the south was backed by the Americans. A third and neutralist group tried in vain to create a semblance of unity in the country by constructing a coalition of all parties and factions.

The Pathet Lao were an important part of the overall strategy of Ho Chi Minh. Hanoi realized that it was impossible to insulate South Vietnam against penetration from the North. And so it therefore made excellent use of the jungle trails of Laos known as the "Ho Chi Minh Trail" to infiltrate arms, men, and supplies into South Vietnam. The Eisenhower administration was therefore determined to maintain a pro-American regime in Laos strong enough to keep both the communists and neutralists at bay.

Three years after Laos was granted independence, the nationalist Souvanna Phouma organized a coalition government of neutralists, Pathet Lao, and the American-supported General Phoumi Nosavan. A neutralist solution for an Asian trouble spot that bordered on China, Burma, Thailand, Cambodia, as well as the two Vietnams, and was racked by civil war was, Eisenhower felt, simply unrealistic. Washington therefore opposed the Phouma government and initiated a major military aid program to build up Phouma's rivals in the rightist Laotian army. In 1958 the rightists succeeded in forcing Phouma out and replacing him with a pro-American government. Phouma returned to power after a coup in August 1960 and, bitter at his treatment by the Americans, he sought assistance from Moscow and North Vietnam. This was enough to damn him in the eyes of Washington. With American encouragement, the rightists once again brought pressure to bear on the regime and in December Phouma was forced to flee his country. "The Americans say I am a communist," he now said. "All this is heartbreaking. How can they think I am a communist? I am looking for a way to keep Laos non-communist."[4]

To Eisenhower, the neutralists and the Pathet Lao were linked to the same Asian communist surge toward power as Red China and North Vietnam. When he left office at the end of 1960 he still viewed Laos as the linchpin of the domino theory:

> the fall of Laos to communism could mean the subsequent fall—like a tumbling row of dominoes—of its still-free neighbours, Cambodia and South Vietnam and, in all probability, Thailand and Burma. Such a chain of events would open the way to Communist seizure of all Southeast Asia.[5]

The incoming Kennedy administration viewed the Laotian problem in a similar way. As Arthur M. Schlesinger, Jr., later explained: "If Laos was not precisely a dagger pointed at the heart of Kansas, it was very plainly a gateway to Southeast Asia." Kennedy believed, as had Eisenhower, that preventing a communist victory in Southeast Asia was a vital American interest. Like the previous administration, Kennedy believed that the containment policy could be successfully applied to the region.

As American influence spread to Laos, so did the North Vietnamese and Soviet support for the Pathet Lao. By 1961 Laos was effectively in a state of civil war, with the Pathet Lao threatening to take over the whole country. When Kennedy asked the Joint Chiefs of Staff if a large conventional force could succeed in putting down the communist guerrillas, they replied yes, but only if it was accompanied by the use of nuclear weapons on Hanoi, and even Beijing. "If we are given the right to use nuclear weapons," replied General Lyman Lemnitzer, "we can guarantee victory."[6] Nevertheless, Kennedy was prepared to undertake limited intervention in Laos. Eisenhower, he felt, was able to take the political fallout after Dien Bien Phu, but "I can't take a 1954 defeat today."[7] In April 1961 in the middle of the Bay of Pigs operation, Kennedy placed U.S. forces in the Pacific on alert, ordered the Seventh Fleet into the South China Sea, and moved hundreds of marines and helicopters into Thailand. At Okinawa he had another 10,000 marines on stand-by. The Russians knew about the preparations and were not eager for a confrontation with the United States over Laos. In April 1964 they endorsed Kennedy's appeal for a cease-fire.

In May 1961 a conference opened on the Laotian problem at Geneva and produced an outcome that succeeded in neutralizing the country. It was agreed that Laos would become neutral; it could not enter military alliances or permit foreign military bases on its soil. The new government would be headed by the durable Souvanna Phouma. With Laos effectively neutralized Vietnam became the focus of Washington's crisis management.

John Kennedy had long been interested in Vietnam. As a senator in 1956 he had declared that country to be the "cornerstone of the Free World" and "the finger in the dike." In a rush of paternalism that could only be resented by the Vietnamese leadership, Kennedy said:

> Vietnam represents a proving ground for democracy—a test of American responsibility and determination in Asia. If we are not the parents of Vietnam, then surely we are the grandparents. We presided at its birth, we gave assistance to its life, we have helped to shape its future. . . . This is our offspring—we cannot abandon it, we cannot ignore its needs.[8]

These views had not changed when he assumed office in 1961. He still believed that geopolitically Vietnam was crucial in the whole American attempt to contain the communist advance. And he was solidly backed by his secretaries of state and defense. He also felt that Vietnam was the place to restore his own personal credibility after the Bay of Pigs disaster and Khrushchev's successfully bullying of him at the Vienna summit. He told James Reston of the *New York Times*, "Now we have a problem in trying to make our power credible, and Vietnam looks like the place."[9]

In Vietnam the communists firmly believed as a article of faith Lenin's doctrine that wars to advance communism are "holy" and "just," while any efforts to oppose them were by definition, "unjust." On January 6, 1961, just two weeks before Kennedy's inauguration, Nikita Khrushchev declared that Moscow would support "wars of liberation" because they were "sacred." Kennedy and his advisors concluded that a new global and coordinated communist offensive was about to begin. Kennedy then summoned his countrymen to be "watchmen on the walls of freedom."

On April 19, 1961, the Bay of Pigs invasion collapsed, and on the following day Kennedy ordered that a military study be made of what kind of action—overt and covert—would be needed to prevent the communist victory in South Vietnam. Kennedy was informed by the military mission conducting the study that Ngo Dinh Diem, the president of South Vietnam, only controlled 40 percent of his country.

Kennedy then increased the size of the American advisory mission in South Vietnam, dispatched hundreds of Special Forces troops to the country, and underwrote an expansion of the South Vietnamese army from 150,000 to 170,000 troops. In a few short weeks Kennedy had committed the United States to save South Vietnam.

At this point, Kennedy sent Vice-President Johnson to Saigon on a fact-finding mission. Casting a critical eye on the situation, Johnson called Diem the "Churchill of today" but felt that he was too detached from his people. The real problem in the country, he felt, was hunger, poverty, and disease. America's only choice, he said, was between backing the Diem regime and withdrawing altogether. If South Vietnam was to be saved, the United States would have to move quickly and decisively.

In October 1961 Kennedy, seeking additional advice, sent Walt W. Rostow, the head of the State Department Policy Planning Bureau, and General Maxwell D. Taylor, the president's top military advisor, to South Vietnam to assess the situation and develop an appropriate policy. Like Johnson, they returned with a report of a deteriorating situation and a recommendation to massively increase support for South Vietnam. Taylor and Rostow and virtually the whole of the president's senior staff were convinced that the United States must deny the communists a victory in Vietnam. Taylor and Rostow recommended "the dispatch of an 8,000-man logistic task force comprised of engineers, medical groups and the infantry to support them." Their report made it clear that these were "minimal steps."[10]

The momentum was now clearly on the side of expanding the American commitment in the war. In doing so, Kennedy ignored Charles De Gaulle's warning that "we failed and you will fail." The Americans in 1961 had made the same error of judgment as the Japanese and the French before them. They all had miscalculated the strength of Vietnamese nationalism, the effectiveness of communist strategy, and the disciplined resolve and sheer ruthlessness of the communists to see the struggle through to the bitter end. Dean Rusk later acknowledged that he made two mistakes as secretary of state. "I underestimated the tenacity of the North Vietnamese and overestimated the patience of the American people."[11] More recently, Robert McNamara has acknowledged that the Kennedy administration lacked the experts on Southeast Asia it should have relied upon, and that consequently it underestimated the nationalist aspect of Ho Chi Minh's movement.[12] Almost to the end of the war, Washington remained ignorant about its adversary. The North Vietnamese, who always remained optimistic about their eventual victory, drew their confidence from many sources: their previous victory over the French; their conviction that in the armed struggle being waged they were part of a global movement predestined by the forces of history to win; their belief that the revolutionary will of a determined and disciplined group of people could prevail over a technologically superior superpower like the United States; and their understanding that their adversary in South Vietnam was inherently flawed and no match for a united and politically motivated communist state. North Vietnam since 1954 had achieved a political synthesis written in blood.

Hanoi had liquidated thousands of its enemies, including hundreds of village chiefs, French sympathizers, and landlords, while others had been sent to reeducation camps. The communist revolution was then gradually extended to each liberated area. By contrast South Vietnam lacked the political synthesis achieved by the North. Unlike the North, the peoples of South Vietnam did not clearly see the consequences of defeat. The North could always think of both victory and a political program; the South just thought in terms of hanging on and hoping for the best.

Despite American attempts at nation-building in South Vietnam, it was in the long run unable to reshape what one hundred years of French colonial rule had created. By 1954 South Vietnam was a deeply divided society with little basis for democracy.

In 1954 Ngo Dinh Diem accepted the premiership of Bao Dai's government, after being granted sweeping powers. The scion of an old, Catholic family, Diem was enormously popular in South Vietnam. In 1955 he won a nationwide referendum by a sizeable margin. He then proclaimed himself as president and was immediately recognized by the United States.

The problems Diem faced when he came to power were enormous. Almost all institutional life in the country had ceased functioning, the financial system barely existed, much of the political power was in the hands of paramilitary sects that held nearly autonomous areas, and the countryside suffered serious war damage.[13] Because of this chaos, Diem refused to participate in the Vietnamese elections scheduled for 1956 under the Geneva Accords. He understood that the communists of the North would vote as a bloc and that along with the volatile groups of the South they might capture a majority. That view was shared by Washington, which counseled a postponement of the election until things settled down.

While Diem consolidated his power, his government settled over 900,000 refugees from the North (most of them Catholics fleeing communist tyranny) while some 100,000 communists moved to the North. In many ways the exodus into South Vietnam was regarded as an alien intrusion by a population predominately Buddhist. To make matters worse, Diem was not sensitive to this problem. Rather than recognize the social equation, the Diem government silenced Buddhist dissent, often brutally, and continued to discriminate in favor of his coreligionists who held a disproportionately high number of official positions in the government. With Diem's contrivance, a Catholic oligarchy came to dominate South Vietnam. As Diem concentrated more power into his own hands, and as large sections of the population drew attention to the high-handed treatment of his own generals (he had tried to take personal charge of the war), to the venality of the Diem family, and to the widespread corruption, the Buddhist leaders increasingly identified Buddhism with the national cause. As one Buddhist monk put it:

> The campaign to overthrow the Ngo Dinh Diem regime in 1963 not only succeeded in mobilizing the people to the defense of Buddhism but also awakened the nationalist consciousness of the masses. In every Buddhist the idea of Buddhism and nationalism are intertwined and

cannot be easily separated. Many non-Buddhist elements also took part in the Buddhist campaign, not because they wanted to support the Buddhists but because they realized that the Buddhist campaign was consistent with the people's aspirations.[14]

The political goal of the Buddhists was the removal of Diem from office, and the creation of a coalition government that would eliminate corruption, establish national harmony, and eliminate American influence.

In 1962 Diem instituted the Strategic Hamlet Program. Designed to cut off the Vietcong (the southern communist guerrillas) from the food, supplies and recruits it needed to survive and fight, the government fortified villages and isolated them from enemy influence. In practical terms it often meant relocating entire rural communities on which the Vietcong relied for support. Peasants were ordered to move their hamlets without compensation or incentives and with no promise of land reform to follow. Indeed, the Saigon government lacked the resources to protect the new communities. The program was enormously unpopular and aroused deep resentment among the peasants and permitted the Vietcong to pose as saviors.

In May 1963 the situation came to a head when Diem's troops opened fire on a large Buddhist protest demonstration killing nine. In response several Buddhist monks set themselves on fire. Diem's sister-in-law, Madame Nhu, dismissed these acts as "monk barbecues."[15] During the late summer and fall the protest movement grew, as did Diem's attempts to suppress it. The United States urged the Saigon government to make concessions but Diem's family insisted that the Buddhists were communist-led and should be crushed. Government attacks were then launched on unarmed pagodas, and thousands of students were arrested as high schools and colleges were closed. The repression disturbed many officials and military officers and many thousands of loyal citizens who felt that the government should be directing its violence against the Vietcong and not against innocent Vietnamese. When Washington threatened to withdraw some support the Vietnam army whispered of revolt. At this point, Defense Secretary Robert McNamara sent marine general Victor H. Krulak and State Department officer Joseph Mendenhall to Saigon on a quick study mission. Krulak played down the Buddhist trouble and insisted that the war was going well, while Mendenhall argued that the South Vietnamese people hated the Diem regime even more than they hated the Vietcong. A puzzled Kennedy asked: "You two visit the same country, didn't you?"[16]

On November 1, 1963, a military coalition—with the distant blessing of Washington—staged a coup in Saigon, seized Diem and his brother, Ngo Dinh Nhu, and executed them. The generals followed their coup with a purge of "Diemists" from the bureaucracy and took reprisals against their rivals. All of this only served to paralyze government initiative, ignite urban discontent, and encourage the Buddhist movement to grow and demand more political influence. Taking advantage of this domestic chaos, the Vietcong insurgency escalated. Infiltration from North Vietnamese guerrillas grew substantially and was matched by local recruitment in the South. At the same time, large quantities of communist-bloc weapons arrived to spur the insurgency on.

When Kennedy took office in 1961 there were only 900 American military personnel in South Vietnam. By November 1963 when he was assassinated, the figure had risen dramatically to over 16,000. In response to the chaos of 1963, the new president, Lyndon Johnson, increased that number to 22,000.

When Lyndon Johnson became president he retained most of Kennedy's advisors and shared the Cold War assumptions of his predecessor. He insisted on nothing less than total victory to prevent a "communist takeover" of Southeast Asia. To pull out of Vietnam was to him unthinkable, since it would inform both allies and enemies alike that the United States was not dependable and would make similar retreats elsewhere. Clark Clifford found Johnson to be the most complex man he had ever met. A man of boundless energy and ambition, and one of the giants of the U.S. Senate, he reminded Clifford of "a powerful old fashioned locomotive roaring unstoppably down the track." "I am not going to be the President," Johnson declared, "who saw Southeast Asia go the way China went."[17]

Kennedy, and to a certain extent Johnson, viewed the Vietnam struggle as *the* testcase for confronting guerrilla wars of liberation. Massive retaliation was useless in this context. What was needed was a new, imaginative application of the idea of "flexible response" to the problem of third world emergencies. The idea of "counterinsurgency" was developed to deal with the problem. Kennedy always took a personal interest in the creation of the Special Forces, an elite group trained to wage war against insurgent guerrillas by irregular means. The mission of the Green Berets, as they were called, was to seek out the Vietcong on their own terrain and destroy them. At the same time, combat troops would encounter the enemy's regular army in just sufficient strength to defeat them. This would enable the U.S. military to meet force with counterforce in the "brushfire" sort of war without resorting to the nuclear option. But in practice what it meant was that the United States was drawn into an ever increasing military commitment. Every increase of U.S. combat troops was matched on the other side. What therefore began as a strategy of flexible response would end as a war of attrition without any foreseeable end. Khrushchev made some of this clear to Dean Rusk in 1963. "Go ahead and fight in the jungles of Vietnam," he said. "The French fought there for seven years and still had to quit in the end. Perhaps the Americans will be able to stick it out for a little longer, but eventually they will have to quit too."[18] A year later, a senior U.S. military advisor was to write that "the South Vietnam government could not prevent the enemy from taking over the country."

In the aftermath of Diem's removal, the Saigon government was even more unstable and unpopular than it was before, and less legitimate. It was also unmotivated to enforce the hard decisions to deal with its communist enemy. In 1964, for example, 73,000 men deserted the South Vietnamese army and thousands more from the paramilitary and auxiliary units went over to the Vietcong. By mid-1964 it became obvious in Washington that the initiative in the war had passed to the Vietcong and that the United States must be prepared to introduce a substantial number of ground troops to the struggle. An incident a few months later gave Washington the excuse to do this.

On August 2, 1964, North Vietnamese torpedo boats opened fire on an American destroyer some eight nautical miles offshore. The vessel was on an intelligence mission gathering information on radar and coastal defenses. The attackers were driven off by U.S. aircraft. Two days later another U.S. ship reported a similar incident, although the attack was never confirmed. The incidents produced a strong reaction in the White House. Charging North Vietnam with deliberate aggression, President Johnson ordered air strikes on the North. He also seized on the incidents as a pretext to extract special war powers from the U.S. Congress. The Gulf of Tonkin Resolution passed by the Congress granted Johnson the widest discretion to repel armed attack on U.S. forces and "to prevent further aggression;" furthermore Johnson was now given the power to use armed force to come to the aid of any nation belonging to SEATO and fighting for its freedom, if it asked for it. It gave Johnson the power to wage war in Vietnam without formally declaring war, or even requesting support from Congress for war. The resolution, said Johnson, was "like grandma's nightshirt—it covered everything." The resolution was passed in both houses of Congress by overwhelming majorities. And when Johnson's "approval ratings" rose dramatically from 42 percent to 72 percent he confidently claimed to have the support of the American people and their representatives.

The U.S. Army had no experience with guerrilla warfare and had never accepted the ideas about unconventional warfare that were the rage in the Kennedy White House. Their most recent war experience had come in Korea. There they had fought a conventional war out of the sanctuary of South Korea and were aided by thousands of highly motivated Korean troops. In Vietnam the battlelines were everywhere, the native population was hostile, and the enemy dedicated and supplied from Hanoi. The U.S. Army and its Vietnamese allies won lots of skirmishes against an enemy who constantly renewed himself. The U.S. Army leadership never really adjusted to this kind of warfare; instead, it relied on what it knew and did best—a war of attrition with its emphasis on mobility and firepower, mechanization, and rising levels of troop commitments. These were, as it turned out, the wrong tactics for this kind of war.

The man who best exemplified this traditional approach to warfare was Lt. General William C. Westmoreland, the commander-in-chief of the U.S. armed forces in South Vietnam. Westmoreland's strategy was to introduce a large enough force to seek out and destroy the communist main force units, especially in the remote areas of the country. At the same time, the South Vietnamese army would concentrate on the pacification of the more densely populated lowlands. Westmoreland predicted that the North Vietnamese regulars would retreat and the Vietcong could then be crushed. The general assured President Johnson that U.S. troops could begin to be withdrawn by late 1967.

On February 7, 1965, the Vietcong attacked a U.S. airfield at Pleiku and killed eight Americans. Johnson then retaliated with a series of U.S. bombing raids against carefully defined military targets in the North. Operation Rolling Thunder, as it was called, was expected to bring victory without costly American losses. By

July 80,000 U.S. troops were operating in the South. In fact, the American troop commitment in South Vietnam seemed to grow incrementally as Westmoreland increasingly militarized the conflict. By 1969 the troop level of 1965 had risen to 543,000. Supporting that force was all the modern technology of a great power: thousands of planes, tanks, trucks, artillery pieces, and all stretched out from Guam and the Phillippines to Thailand.

Like so many of his predecessors, Johnson made simple analogies to the historical past he had either lived through or studied, to justify his foreign policy. "Just like FDR and Hitler, just like Wilson and the Kaiser," he said, "the United States had to stop "aggression.""[19] Johnson was persuaded that a combination of military force on the ground and air raids on the North, coupled with peace offers, would force Hanoi to call off the conflict and accept the status quo in Vietnam. He was also persuaded that America's standing in the world would suffer if the country cut its losses and departed the scene. As far as the U.S. military effort went, the heavy bombing had little impact on the enemy's ability to resist, and the North matched every American escalation of the war.

Johnson's gradual escalation of the war was carried out with one wary eye on the Red Chinese and the other on domestic opinion. He would go just so far to defeat communism in Vietnam and no further, especially if it meant risking an all-out war with the Chinese. He did not want a repetition of the Korean War. And as far as the domestic consensus went, it began to erode sometime in 1967. By that year the American public had been fed a steady diet of optimistic reports about the progress of the ground war, which emanated originally from the military and intelligence services. The government consistently assured the American people that all was going well with the war. Indeed, 1967 was supposed to have been the year of victory. But the number of U.S. ground troops in South Vietnam passed the 500,000 level that year and still General Westmoreland was asking for further reinforcements. People increasingly began to realize that Vietnam was to be no short war with a minimum of casualties. This clash between the illusions and realities of the war at first produced an irritation among the American people, but by the Tet offensive of 1968 the irritation hardened into an anger directed at the government responsible.

Both sides in the war had normally observed an annual truce during the celebrations surrounding the lunar new year in Vietnam, or Tet as it was called. In an attempt to achieve total surprise, the Vietcong on January 31, 1968, broke the truce and mounted a huge offensive against South Vietnamese provincial capitals. The attack was mounted on such a broad front so as to neutralize American firepower. The Vietcong seized not only the ancient capital of Hue, but at one point actually penetrated the grounds of the U.S. embassy in Saigon. For the first time in the war the Vietcong surfaced and fought on conventional battlefields. The Vietcong were doing more than carrying the armed struggle to the heretofore inviolable cities; they were also, according to Bui Tin, a former colonel in the North Vietnamese army, trying "to weaken American resolve during a presidential election year." It was the senior commander of the Vietcong in the South, General

Nguyen Chi Thanh, who proposed the Tet offensive. Thanh's whole philosophy of war, says Tin, was that "America is wealthy but not resolute," and "squeeze tight to the American chest and attack." Tin also quotes Ho Chi Minh as saying, "We don't need to win military victories, we only need to hit them until they give up and get out." Tet was therefore designed to influence an American public opinion whose support they understood to be critical to the whole American war effort. That particular moment was chosen to launch the attack because as Tin says,

> Johnson had rejected Westmoreland's request for 200,000 more troops. We realized that America had made its maximum military commitment to the war. Vietnam was not sufficiently important for the U.S. to call up its reserves. We had stretched American power to the breaking point. When more frustration set in, all the Americans could do would be to withdraw; they had no more troops to send over.[20]

If one examines the Tet offensive in strictly military terms, then the battle was a staggering North Vietnamese defeat. Their losses were so heavy (upward of 50,000 men killed) that virtually their entire guerrilla superstructure in the South was liquidated. According to Bui Tin, it took the North Vietnamese until 1971 to reestablish its presence in South Vietnam, and it only did so by substituting North Vietnamese regular army troops for local guerrillas. Nevertheless, Hanoi was able to turn Tet to its great psychological and political advantage. The graphic scenes of bloody warfare shown each day on American television screens convinced many Americans that their soldiers should be brought home. The public support for the war fell in response to the rise in casualties and the apparent inconclusiveness of the fighting. The president's assurances that Tet was a great American victory were perfectly true, but fell on deaf ears. General Westmoreland also publicly claimed a great victory for American arms, but it was soon learned that he had also asked the president for 200,000 more men. What Tet did in the long run was ruin the credibility of government officials from the president down, who had all along claimed progress in the war and a "light at the end of the tunnel."

Henry Kissinger argues that only a small but vocal section of the American people turned hostile to Washington's commitment to Vietnam. He cites public opinion polls taken just after Tet that showed that 61 percent of the American people considered themselves "hawks," and 23 percent "doves." No less than 70 percent of those polled favored the continuation of the bombing.[21] The vocal opposition was mainly confined to the intellectual and non-union left, located in Congress, the media and on university campuses. This was still important, of course, and served to undermine the administration, which was bombarded constantly by the growing anti-war movement that, as never before in American history, openly questioned American participation in a major war. The American national consensus on foreign policy, intact since 1941, now collapsed.

His confidence a bit shaken, Johnson assembled a group of men from previous administrations to advise him on what steps should be taken next. Former "hawks" like Dean Acheson, John McCloy, McGeorge Bundy, Douglas Dillon, and Clark

Clifford convinced Johnson that the United States could no longer win the war. They recommended that no more troops be sent to Vietnam and that negotiations to end the war begin at once. Caught between the anti-war movement and the challenge mounted against him in the presidential primaries of 1968 by members of his own party, Johnson felt that trying to retain his office would only divide the nation further in a losing cause. On March 31, 1968, therefore, he announced that he would not seek the nomination of his party for another term. He also declared a bombing halt over the North and called upon Hanoi to come to the peace table. Formal talks to end the war opened in May 1968.

It was Richard M. Nixon who inherited the thankless task of ending the Vietnam War on something like honorable terms. One of the few presidents to come to office in this century with a wide knowledge of international affairs, he was convinced that victory in Vietnam was no longer possible. To an aide, he said: "I'm not going to end up like LBJ, holed up in the White House afraid to show my face in the street. I'm going to stop that war fast."[22]

Along with his national security adviser, Henry Kissinger, Nixon was determined to break the negotiating deadlock in terms that could not be construed as a defeat. It was Nixon's and Kissinger's belief that military operations should be geared solely to negotiating objectives, and that the responsibility for the conduct of the war should be returned to the South Vietnamese government. But Nixon's campaign promise to reduce the number of U.S. combat forces in Vietnam eroded America's bargaining position at the Paris peace talks. In June 1969 at a meeting with President Nguyen Thieu (who had come to power in South Vietnam in 1967), Nixon announced the first withdrawal of 25,000 troops, with others to follow. The prime aim of Hanoi was to reach an agreement that would force the United States out but leave North Vietnam able to continue the armed struggle until the whole country was theirs. According to Kissinger, Nixon, like his predecessors, "had underestimated the tenacity and the determination of Hanoi. Ho Chi Minh had become increasingly certain that, given the inept Saigon leadership and faltering American commitment, Hanoi's forces could win an unconditional victory. A practitioner of *Realpolitik*, Ho was not about to concede at a negotiating table what he expected blood and bullets would win him on the battlefield."[23]

In July the president enunciated what became known as the Nixon Doctrine. In it he made it clear that the United States was willing to provide its allies with assistance, but that it was no longer willing to do all the fighting or provide all the troops. The message was clear. Washington served notice that it could no longer play the role of world policeman, and that its allies would have to defend themselves. And in February 1970 Henry Kissinger opened secret talks in Paris with representatives of North Vietnam.

Almost from the day Nixon was sworn in as president evidence began piling up that indicated that Hanoi was infiltrating more troops into the South in preparation for a new offensive. A resumption of the bombing of the North would only have rekindled the anti-war movement, and Nixon looked for a retaliatory response against the communist sanctuaries in Cambodia.

The geography of Southeast Asia had always made it impossible to insulate South Vietnam from its neighboring states. In the 1960s the North Vietnamese had established a series of sanctuaries inside Cambodia—thirteen in all—just across the border from South Vietnam. They included staging areas, supply-dumps, and rear-echelon headquarters from which Hanoi could launch large attacks against American and South Vietnamese positions. The sanctuaries were supplied through the Ho Chi Minh trail. Prince Norodom Sihanouk, the leader of Cambodia, reluctantly allowed this blatant violation of Cambodian neutrality because he wished to prevent his country from being engulfed by the war, and because he was resigned to a communist victory in South Vietnam.

Well before the Tet offensive, General Westmoreland recommended ground attacks across the border to eliminate the sanctuaries. But Nixon preferred to rely on air power, since this would allow him to attack the sanctuaries without altering his plans for bringing U.S. combat forces home. The president ordered the bombing to begin in March 1970. Originally the bombing was to be short-term and secret. But what the air raids really succeeded in doing was embedding the North Vietnamese even deeper into Cambodian territory. It also resulted in getting Hanoi to arm the Cambodian communists, the Khmer Rouge, who then were able to launch a new attack against the capital, Phnom Penh, in 1968. The regular Cambodian army wanted to ask the United States for aid, but Sihanouk preferred to rely on diplomacy. In March 1970, General Lon Nol, who was also the prime minister, staged a coup that removed Sihanouk from office.

In April 1970 Nixon committed the administration to bringing home another 150,000 troops. But in the same month he admitted to the American public that the United States and South Vietnamese troops crossed into Cambodia and that, backed by B-52s, they were trying to destroy the communist sanctuaries. Described by the administration as an "incursion," the attack never achieved its goal of driving the communists out of Cambodia. The attack only succeeded in widening the Indochina conflict, and reactivated the anti-war movement in the United States as never before. It also had a profound effect upon military morale. Desertions now became common within the U.S. Army, and outside the military many more thousands sought to avoid the draft by fleeing to foreign countries.

In April 1971 the administration announced another troop withdrawal of 100,000 and this helped to contain the anti-war movement. By 1972 there were only 6,000 U.S. combat troops in South Vietnam, while there were one million South Vietnamese troops at Saigon's disposal. Nevertheless, the South Vietnamese army was thinly spread across the country. In March 1972, 120,000 North Vietnamese and thousands of Vietcong launched a new campaign against South Vietnam. The United States responded by renewing the bombing of the North, including Hanoi and the harbor of Haiphong, and mining the country's ports and harbors, a step that Lyndon Johnson had never dared to take.

As Nixon's outward approach became more combative with the renewed bombing of the North, so he became more belligerent at home. He publicly blamed the anti-war movement for the lack of progress in peace negotiations, and he appealed for support to the "silent majority" of the American public. Opinion polls taken in 1970 seemed to show that the majority of the American people believed that the introduction of U.S. ground troops into the war had been a mistake, but the approval for Nixon's handling of the crisis rose dramatically in January 1970 to 65 percent of those polled. Nixon therefore felt confident that the public wanted an end to the war, but on the terms Nixon had insisted on.[24]

The bombing of the North was moderately successful in producing a shift in the negotiations at Paris. But it was really the pressure from China and Russia that produced the breakthrough.

Since Nixon came to the presidency, he had made known his desire through secret channels to improve his relations with Moscow—if Moscow reciprocated by pressuring Hanoi to become more pliant at the peace table. Actually, secret contacts had been made between Washington and Hanoi through various intermediaries intermittently since 1964, but the contacts had always come to nothing.

Since the Korean War, Mao Tse Tung had always taken care to avoid a direct confrontation with the United States, even when China was urged to intervene in Vietnam when the Americans were escalating their role in the war. Earlier in 1962 when he feared that the United States would back a nationalist invasion from Taiwan, he was only reassured when a hastily arranged contact was made between the Chinese and American embassies in Warsaw. For all his rhetoric about the dangers of American imperialism Mao was a very cautious man, worried more about maintaining his country's independence than he was about extending the communist revolution.

One of Mao's biggest fears was that Khrushchev's "errors" in attacking the Stalin cult might be repeated in China, since Beijing had a cult of its own. Mao felt the need to protect himself from the noxious charge that he was following in Stalin's footsteps, and from the possibility that opposition groups in his country might be tempted to take the capitalist road. Mao's answer to this was a deliberate attempt to arouse the revolutionary spirit in China by pitting the Chinese masses against the party functionaries and bureaucracy, who, he felt, were conservatively attached to maintaining the status quo. After levelling an attack against one of Deng Xiaoping's protégés, he declared his intention to launch the Great Proletarian Cultural Revolution. The resulting domestic turmoil produced an explosion in Chinese society that wrecked millions of lives. From 1966 to 1968 the struggle assumed the dimensions of a civil war all over the country.

The convulsion of the Cultural Revolution in China began with dissident students organizing themselves spontaneously into "Red Guards" to carry out Mao's will. Raising Mao's teaching to an extraordinary personality cult, the guards attacked the party elders who seemed to stand in the way of the fulfilment of the Chinese Revolution. Mao encouraged these attacks to root out Chinese traditions and "bourgeois revisionism," and the party members who best represented them. Actually, the targets grew to represent anyone in authority. Hundreds of thousands died in the onslaught. China's cities became for awhile ungovernable, as local authorities became paralyzed by the wave of attacks. Even Mao for a time lost control of the movement. Wherever it could, the army restored order and by 1967 became the dominant force in the country.

Mao now tried to curb the power of the army and summoned up another wave of violence against the military. At the same time, whole groups split over the course of the revolution—peasants, soldiers, and Red Guards—and all fought each other. The turmoil was so extensive it threatened to destroy the country. By 1968 the anarchic violence began to subside, the Red Guards were gradually discredited, and the army was credited with imposing revolutionary discipline. Behind the scenes, Lin Biao, the army chief, was taking charge.

Ho Chi Minh had always pursued policies and military strategies designed not to alienate either of the communist superpowers. He had always been careful to maintain his country's neutrality in the Sino-Soviet split and he had cleverly allowed both of his allies to sponsor Hanoi's cause.[25] The Soviet Union, after all, supplied North Vietnam with most of its heavy equipment, but the main supply route for Soviet arms deliveries to North Vietnam lay through China. But Hanoi's neutrality soon became a precarious balancing act between her allies. For example, on the question of tactics in the war, the Chinese urged Hanoi to pursue guerrilla warfare in a protracted war, while Moscow emphasized a more conventional strategy and, at the same time, pressed Hanoi to end the war by seeking a political settlement.

Much of the friction in the Sino-Soviet conflict rose in the aftermath of the Soviet invasion of Czechoslovakia in 1968, which coincided with the peak of the Chinese Cultural Revolution. The Chinese supported the Dubcek regime in Prague as they had supported the Gomulka regime in Warsaw in 1956. In both cases they accused the Russians of "Great Power Chauvinism" in trying to subdue communists by force. What especially worried Beijing about the Czech repression was the Brezhnev Doctrine. The doctrine held that the Soviet Union had the right to unilaterally invade any communist country when, in the judgment of the Soviet leadership, communist domination of that country had been threatened. For China, the implications of the Brezhnev Doctrine were obvious. The Chinese were bitterly opposed to this policy since Moscow was really trying to displace a communist government in Prague that was not of its liking; might Moscow take advantage of the chaos in China and interfere by supporting political factions ready to "take the fortress from within"? In October 1968 Mao is supposed to have referred to the Soviet Union for the first time as China's primary enemy and in the following month Beijing proposed private talks with the United States on the subject of peaceful coexistence. The Chinese leadership was now compelled to seek ways out of China's diplomatic isolation.

In March 1969 pitched battles were fought on a daily basis between units of the Chinese and Soviet armies on their common border. In both countries the outbreak of fighting produced new nationalist fervor, a closing of ranks, and a determination to fight to the bitter end. The Russians compared Mao to Genghis Khan and the Chinese compared Brezhnev and his comrades to the old tsars. The battles went on for months with Russia stationing her best air and military units on the Chinese border and in Mongolia, and with the Chinese working to build underground air raid shelters everywhere in the country. The friction with the Soviet Union was the major reason why the Chinese chose to improve their international situation after 1969.

When Aleksei Kosygin, the Soviet prime minister, sought to negotiate the quarrel, he was treated with deliberate rudeness, the Chinese hot line operator declaring, "You are a revisionist, and therefore I will not connect you."[26]

In the summer of 1969 while the United States sent messages of goodwill to China and began its troop withdrawal from South Vietnam, the Soviets constructed a large air base in Mongolia and made aggressive speeches designed to intimidate the Chinese. They even went so far as to leak the information that Moscow was considering a preventive attack on Chinese nuclear installations. Chou En Lai, the Chinese foreign minister, certainly took this threat seriously (as did Nixon) and gave an account of this to the journalist Joseph Alsop.[27] When Kosygin finally met with Chou En Lai, the Chinese accused the Russians of flaunting Soviet superiority and went so far as to declare that the enmity between the two countries would likely last for a thousand years.

From 1969 to 1973 the Nixon administration secretly pursued detente with both communist superpowers, aiming to exploit the Sino-Soviet split without alienating either. This triangular diplomacy yielded brilliant results.

The Nixon administration's determination to conclude the war in Vietnam was the most important factor in the pursuit of detente. For Nixon it meant abandoning the idea that North Vietnam's belligerence was merely an expression of Chinese and Russian expansionism. It also meant that Nixon had concluded that the United States was overcommitted and that its foreign policy was too ambitious. He understood that the United States had made itself responsible for Asia and that for years it had acted without real conviction or consistency in the region, and that its military power was relatively ineffective in the area. Nixon had come to believe that the United States had no vital interest that could be immediately threatened by Asians. Why then play the role of policeman? Nixon was therefore anxious to recover the diplomatic freedom of maneuver by ending the long-standing quarrel with China. "We needed China," Kissinger said, "to enhance the flexibility of our diplomacy."[28] Nixon made this clear in an interview soon after gaining the Republican nomination in 1968. "We must always seek opportunities to talk with China," he said. "We must not only watch for changes. We must seek to make changes."[29] In pursuing this policy Nixon understood that he was operating under a clear advantage. Being a keen student of power politics he appreciated that the Sino-Soviet conflict had become so intense that Moscow and Beijing were anxious to improve relations with the United States and that Hanoi had every reason to fear that their support for the war in Indochina might, as a consequence, slacken. Nixon also came to believe that the reality of communist China as a world power could no longer be ignored. He also understood that as a hard-line American conservative pursuing this policy he would encounter much less opposition at home than would the leader of the Democratic Party. Even before his election he had made use of

Nikolai Ceausescu, the Romanian leader, who enjoyed close relations with China, to approach Beijing about normalizing relations. For Beijing, despite its public pronouncements, the private channels of communication had been opened to Washington ever since Nixon took office in 1969. In China's case, the leadership had become convinced that American troop withdrawals meant that the United States was serious about withdrawing from Vietnam. The Americans also scaled back U.S. Seventh Fleet operations in the Taiwan Straits and relaxed trade restrictions with China. Beijing certainly picked up the signals. By January 1970 Chou En Lai was hinting that Washington should send a top official to Beijing for exploratory talks. The U.S. invasion of Cambodia in April delayed this meeting, but in July 1971 Henry Kissinger paid the first secret visit to China, which led to the eventual diplomatic visit of President Nixon himself.

Nixon's visit to China almost coincided with a power struggle in Beijing. The struggle was between Mao and his powerful army chief, Lin Biao, as well as the nominal head of state Liu Shaoqui. Survivors of the Cultural Revolution, they attempted to assassinate Mao in September 1971 and take over the government. The plot failed and Lin Biao fled toward the Soviet Union, only to be killed in a plane crash on the way. After his death he was accused of being in collusion with the Soviet Union whose intervention he had requested. He was also accused of resisting Mao's turn from the Soviet alliance toward a normalization with Washington. While there must have been a certain amount of hyperbole in these accusations, nevertheless, a purge did follow the Lin Biao episode—Taiwan reported no less that 37,000 arrests in the army alone—all of which had the effect of aiding Mao's tilt toward Washington.

President Nixon paid his historic visit to China on February 21, 1972. Much more pragmatic than ideological, the opening to China followed from his own initiative. "Kissinger," writes Walter Isaacson, "was at first sceptical about any quick opening to China and it was Nixon's dogged vision that propelled the initiative."[30]

From the beginning of the trip Nixon was conscious of the fact that he was making history. The American delegation numbered thirty-seven and they were accompanied by eighty-seven members of the press corps. They were all greeted graciously by their Chinese hosts. Mao praised Nixon's book *Six Crises*, and the two leaders toasted each other warmly as a Chinese military band played "Home on the Range." Borrowing a page from Chinese communist history, Nixon called for a "long march together." He also quoted Mao himself: "Seize the day, seize the hour. This is the hour."

The outcome of the discussions and negotiations with the Chinese were incorporated in the Shanghai communiqué of February 27 in which both sides declared their intention to normalize relations. The communiqué was indeed a turning point. The two countries agreed to broaden their relations through scientific, cultural, and economic exchanges as well as some political ties. Both declared that they wished to reduce the danger of international conflict and did not seek hegemony. In an oblique reference to the Soviet Union, they declared that they would oppose anyone trying "to establish hegemony" in "the Asia-Pacific region." For their part, the United States reaffirmed its friendly relations with South Vietnam, South Korea, and Japan. The Chinese, on the other hand, declared their continued support for "the struggles of all oppressed people" against all bullies, real and potential. The stickiest issue was not Vietnam, but Taiwan. The Chinese maintained that "Taiwan is a province of China," and that its liberation was a domestic Chinese affair. It also called for the withdrawal of all U.S. forces from the island. For its part, the United States. "Acknowledges that all Chinese on either side of the Taiwan Straits maintain there is but one China and that Taiwan is part of China." The United States would not challenge that position. Washington called for "a peaceful settlement of the Taiwan issue by the Chinese themselves," and it declared its "ultimate objective was the withdrawal of all U.S. forces and military installations from Taiwan." The last line in the communiqué reflected the American expectation that the Chinese would come to play a pivotal role in ending the Vietnam War. The United States, the document stated, will reduce its commitment in Taiwan "as the tension in the area diminishes."[31]

While the discussions and agreements fell short of full normalization of Sino-American relations (full diplomatic recognition came only in 1978), "the bipolarity of the postwar period," Kissinger concluded, "was over."

The American efforts in Beijing were certainly rewarded. According to Raymond Garthoff, the Chinese made "a concentrated effort to persuade the Vietnamese to compromise."[32] Certainly North Vietnam's room for maneuver was seriously limited by detente between the United States and China. It was limited even further by detente between the United States and the Soviet Union.

At the Salt I talks of 1972, Nixon warned the Soviet leaders that an arms agreement could not be concluded while the Vietnam War continued. Moscow therefore helped convince North Vietnam to conclude a truce in the war with South Vietnam. The secret talks between Henry Kissinger and Le Duc Tho of North Vietnam then resumed in the summer of 1972 and by the end of the year they had come to the basis of an agreement.

The agreement to end the Vietnam war was signed on January 27, 1973, and left the opposing Vietnamese forces in control of their own areas of South Vietnam. This gave a decided advantage to the North since they did not have to withdraw north of the 17th parallel. This latter concession made the agreement possible. There was also to be a cease-fire between the United States and North Vietnam. American troops would withdraw and U.S. prisoners of war would be repatriated. All political problems associated with the future of the country were to be left to the Vietnamese themselves. A coalition would conduct elections in the South. For the Americans it was a chance to bail out of its long nightmare; for the North Vietnamese it was a chance to get rid of the Americans.

The United States and North Vietnam had all along negotiated in secret. For the president of South Vietnam, General Nguyen Van Thieu, the Americans had bargained in bad faith. Bitterly resentful, Theiu at first refused to sign the Paris Accords. "I wanted to punch Kissinger in the mouth," he later recalled.[33]

Thieu really had little choice in the matter. The Americans told him bluntly that they were leaving, and that if he did not sign the Paris Accords he would suffer a cutoff of U.S. aid. Thieu finally gave in. "Ah, these great powers who divide the world among themselves!" he commented. "They have an open market everywhere and what does it matter if this market costs the life of a small country?"[34]

The last of the U.S. forces withdrew from South Vietnam in March 1973. The Americans handed over their installations to the South Vietnamese army and supplied them with vast quantities of equipment. As a result, Saigon acquired the world's fourth-largest air force and, at least on paper, presented a formidable military threat. It was now up to the Saigon government to defend itself.

Neither side had any intention of honoring the cease-fire. By the autumn of 1973 the fighting resumed as Richard Nixon found himself being consumed by the Watergate scandal. In January 1975 a new North Vietnamese offensive broke out and the South began to collapse. A reentering of the war by the United States, at this point under Nixon's replacement, was unthinkable. On April 30, 1975, the communists marched into Saigon and renamed it Ho Chi Minh City in honor of their leader who had died in 1969.

Most of Indochina buckled as well. Communist insurgents triumphed in Cambodia and Laos in the same year. Indeed, the Khmer Rouge came to power in Cambodia and instituted a program that killed millions of people.

Vietnam was the site of America's biggest war since Korea. The U.S. Air Force dropped three times the amount of bombs on North Vietnam as it dropped in all the theaters of the Second World War combined. Three million Americans came to serve in the region, as the number of U.S. military personnel grew generally throughout the world to nearly nine million men and women. Roughly 58,000 Americans were killed in the war along with one and a half million Vietnamese.

The war cost the United States between $150 billion and $170 billion. This had a lasting impact on the American economy. War costs began to rise significantly in the mid 1960s. In 1966, for example, Washington spent $8 billion to fuel the struggle, but in 1967 as the war escalated, it jumped to $21 billion. As the expenses for the war steadily mounted, the Great Society domestic program of President Johnson began to sink. For years the administration had kept up the fiction that the country could have "both guns and butter." But without imposing new taxes (which Johnson avoided for political reasons) he only managed to create severe weaknesses in the economy as the debt rose. The nation's export trade began to lag and for the first time the United States began to feel the pinch of competition from the German and Japanese economies. As early as 1963, when the United States was at the zenith of its power, President Kennedy tried to discourage the export of capital from the United States and to ease the pressure on the balance of payments. From 1968 to 1972 there occurred the longest and largest postwar deficit in American history. Estimates showed that the dollar outflow and the shifting trade balance, along with the costs of the war, caused the balance of payments deficit to rise dramatically. Foreign holdings of dollars grew enormously and the inflation grew significantly. The real income of workers rose in the postwar period until the early 1970s, and then declined in a manner unprecedented in this century.

By 1971 the gold reserves of the United States had dropped 50 percent since 1949. In response to growing speculation against the dollar—the New York Federal Reserve Bank had during the spring actually cautioned Washington that the dollar might collapse—Nixon broke the Bretton Woods exchange rate system. The end of the gold exchange standard signalled the end of American predominance in the economic world. Since 1945 the United States had played the central role in the restoration of the "free world" economy. The period of recovery for its allies had drawn to a close and the world returned to economic multipolarity.[35]

The United States had since NSC #68 and the Korean War borne the costs of waging the Cold War and providing its allies with a *Pax Americana*. In doing so it had consciously subordinated its economic interests to its geopolitical needs. The United States after 1971 still possessed the greatest economic strength in the world, and the weakened dollar still remained the basis of world trade and finance, but in relative terms the country began its long economic slide, accelerated by the costs of the worst war in its history.

Notes

1. Quoted in John Lewis Gaddis, *Strategies of Containment: A Critical Appraisal of Postwar American National Security Policy* (New York: Oxford University Press, 1982), 131.

2. Quoted in Allen W. Cameron, ed., *Viet-Nam Crisis: A Documentary History, Vol. I: 1940-1956* (Ithaca, N.Y.: Cornell University Press, 1971), 378.

3. Dwight E. Eisenhower, *Waging Peace: The White House Years, 1956-1961* (Garden City, N.Y.: Doubleday, 1965), 610.

4. Quoted in Arthur M. Schlesinger, Jr., *A Thousand Days. John F. Kennedy in the White House* (Boston: Houghton Mifflin Company, 1965), 330.

5. Eisenhower, *Waging Peace*, 607.

6. Schlesinger, *A Thousand Days*, 338.

7. Schlesinger, *A Thousand Days*, 339.

8. Quoted in David L. Di Leo, *George Ball, Vietnam, and the Rethinking of Containment* (Chapel Hill: University of North Carolina Press, 1991), 54.

9. Quoted in David Halberstam, *The Best and the Brightest* (New York: Random House, 1972), 76.

10. Maxwell D. Taylor, *Swords and Ploughshares* (New York: W.W. Norton and Company, 1972), 239-41.

11. Quoted in Thomas G. Paterson, J. Gardy Clifford, Kenneth J. Hagan, *American Foreign Relations: A History since 1895*, 4th ed. (Lexington, Mass.: D.C. Heath and Company, 1995), 386.

12. Robert S. McNamara, *In Retrospect* (New York: Random House, 1995).

13. Chester A. Bain, *Vietnam: The Roots of Conflict* (Englewood Cliffs, N.J.: Prentice-Hall, 1967), 118.

14. Thich Nhat Hanh, *Vietnam: Lotus in a Sea of Fire* (New York: Hill and Wang, 1967), 45.

15. Quoted in Michael R. Beschloss, *The Crisis Years: Kennedy and Khrushchev 1960-1963* (New York: HarperCollins, 1991), 651.

16. Quoted in George C. Herring, *America's Longest War*, 2nd ed. (New York: Alfred A. Knopf, 1986), 100.

17. Quoted in James Barber, *The Presidential Character*, 4th ed. (Englewood Cliffs, N.J.: Prentice-Hall, 1992), 25.

18. Quoted in *The Crisis Years*, 649.

19. Quoted in Doris Kearns, *Lyndon Johnson and the American Dream* (New York: Harper and Row, 1976), 329.

20. "How North Vietnam Won the War," *Wall Street Journal*, 3 August 1995.

21. Henry Kissinger, *Diplomacy* (New York: Simon and Schuster, 1994), 671.

22. Quoted in H. R. Haldeman, *The Ends of Power* (New York: Times Books, 1978), 81.

23. Kissinger, *Diplomacy*, 678.

24. Tad Szulc, *The Illusion of Peace* (New York: Viking Press, 1978), 158.

25. Donald S. Zagoria, *The Sino-Soviet Conflict 1956-1961* (Princeton, N.J.: Princeton University Press, 1962), 102-4.

26. Richard M. Nixon, *The Memoirs of Richard Nixon* (New York: Grosset and Dunlap, 1978), 568.

27. Joseph Alsop, "Thoughts Out of China . . . Go versus No Go," *New York Times,* 11 March 1973, Magazine 31, 100-2.

28. Henry Kissinger, *White House Years* (Boston: Little, Brown and Company, 1979), 1049.

29. Kissinger, *White House Years*, 164.

30. Walter Isaacson, *Kissinger* (New York: Simon and Schuster, 1992), 336.

31. The full text of the Shanghai Communiqué are in *White House Years*, 1490-92.

32. Raymond Garthoff, *Détente and Confrontation: American-Soviet Relations Nixon to Reagan* (Washington, D.C.: Brookings Institution, 1985), 255.

33. Quoted in Nguyen Tien Hung and Jerrold L. Schecter, *The Palace File* (New York: Harper and Row, 1986), 88.

34. Quoted in Oriana Falacci, *Interview with History* (Boston: Houghton Mifflin Company, 1976), 56.

35. Joseph S. Nye, Jr., *Bound to Lead: The Changing Nature of American Power* (New York: Basic Books, 1990), 94.

19

The Road to Detente

In the early 1960s the Soviet Union briefly held the initiative in world politics. As the decade opened it came close to shattering the U.N. over the Congo crisis. In 1961 communist forces were on the move all over Indochina. In the same year Khrushchev succeeded in intimidating Kennedy at the Vienna summit and supported East Germany in the building of the Berlin Wall. At the same time, the Russians tested a whole series of enormous nuclear weapons. To be sure, the Russian actions in no small way concealed a strategic inferiority. But nevertheless, the Russians obtained the maximum psychological advantage from their aggressive stance because they always used their own military judiciously, and because they were able to successfully test Western timidity.

But the Cuban Missile Crisis exposed Khrushchev's technique of bluff and Soviet prestige suffered a humiliating blow. By the time Brezhnev replaced Khrushchev the Sino-Soviet conflict had already signalled the end of formal unity in the world communist movement. The war of words that helped to poison relations between the Soviet Union and China enabled other bloc members like Albania, Romania, North Korea, and North Vietnam to utilize the quarrel to carve out positions of autonomy within the world movement. Pro-Soviet and pro-Chinese factions emerged in virtually all Communist parties, and "polycentrism" appeared as a permanent factor detrimental to Soviet world power. In the competition with Beijing, Moscow tried to lean on communists everywhere to obtain a general condemnation of China. The results were mixed. For example, in Cuba's case its inclination toward the Chinese side was stopped cold by Russia's use of economic and military aid. In fact, it was the promise of such aid that kept most communist states in the Soviet fold. These were weapons that China could not match. Outside of Albania, the only ruling party to choose China's side was the genocidal Khmer Rouge in the 1970s.

Albania was actually the first communist bloc nation to get caught between China and the Soviet Union when the Sino-Soviet conflict flared into the open in 1960. Feeling threatened by Yugoslavia, the Albanians may have found the anti-Yugoslav rhetoric of Beijing attractive. The Albanian Communist Party came out on the Chinese side in 1960 and as a consequence was exposed to Soviet economic pressure and the threat of a Soviet-backed coup attempt. In 1961 China supplied

Albania with money and grain and later that year the Albanians evicted the Russians from the naval base at Vlone on the Adriatic. In October 1961 Khrushchev denounced Albania at a world communist meeting in Moscow for opposing his de-Stalinization campaign. At the same meeting Chou En Lai chided Moscow by observing that "open unilateral condemnation of a fraternal party does not make for unity," and then to rub it in he laid a wreath on Stalin's tomb. Khrushchev replied to this by disinterring Stalin's body from the Lenin Mausoleum in Red Square and reburying it elsewhere.[1]

In Italy the Russian pressure only succeeded in accelerating the Communist Party's drift into revisionist "Eurocommunist" unorthodoxy. In Romania the leadership began to disengage itself from Moscow. It refused to be integrated into Comecon and managed to establish an independent role within the Eastern bloc. It maintained formal, but distant ties, with Moscow.

There were many shifts taking place across the Iron Curtain in the 1960s and Moscow was unwilling to tolerate any satellite's bid for out-and-out independence. Unlike Albania and Romania where nothing like internal liberalization was taking place, Czechoslovakia was in the throes of a genuine reform movement. And it was here that the limits of political and economic change were severely restricted.

Like the revolutionary developments in Poland and Hungary in 1956, the impetus for reform in Czechoslovakia came from the top policy-makers who were concerned about the declining rates of growth in their country. Czechoslovakia's national income fell in 1962-1963, and so market socialism gained a hearing in Prague. By 1966 the government under the leadership of Antonin Novotny took the first steps toward decentralization, instituting a system of profit accountability and giving priority to consumer goods. The reforms were half-hearted and the spark for revolt was provided by students in November 1967 when thousands of them demonstrated in Prague against the government's half-way measures. This was brutally suppressed by the police and this in turn triggered a wide sympathy movement. The episode coincided with an acute crisis in the party leadership—the reformers versus the Novotny faction—over the amount of internal party democracy there was to be in the country. All of it seemed to exacerbate a worsening economic situation.

In January 1968 a new reforming leadership emerged under Alexander Dubcek. A compromise candidate approved of by Novotny, Dubcek now called for a greater democratization of public life and an easing of the censorship. This call was echoed throughout Czech society. In June, most Czech newspapers published "the two thousand words," a manifesto issued by writers and intellectuals that advocated democratic reforms while promising support for Dubcek in the event of a Russian intervention. Of all the bloc countries the Western tradition beat strongest in Czechoslovakia. That tradition had been suppressed in 1948, but it was now clear that it had not been uprooted.

Dubcek was a cautious man and, while he promoted the decentralization of the economy, he made it clear that there would be no retreat from socialist principles in industry and agriculture. He was willing to explore links with the West, but he made it clear that Czechoslovakia's foreign policy was still oriented toward the Soviet Union and that it would remain in the Warsaw Pact. Dubcek had read the history of 1956 and he was determined not to repeat it.

Nevertheless, the satellite leaders were afraid that the democratic movement would grow within Czechoslovakia and spread to other countries in the bloc. In July the Soviet Union and its allies in Eastern Europe issued the "Warsaw Letter," which called for the preservation of one-party rule. Dubcek maintained that the Czech people had the right to manage their own affairs without outside interference, but, at the same time, he continued to profess his loyalty to the Communist Party and to the Warsaw Pact.

Nevertheless, Dubcek made a tactical error that helped shape perceptions in the Kremlin toward his program. At a time when separatist tendencies were evident in Communist countries like Albania and Romania, Dubcek welcomed Ceausescu and Tito to Prague for official visits. Suspecting that Czechoslovakia might return to the bourgeois republic of Masaryk and Benes, it now seemed imperative to Moscow and its allies that they take immediate action against the further disintegration of the Soviet bloc.

On August 20, 1968, 500,000 Warsaw Pact troops invaded Czechoslovakia. In marked contrast to Hungary in 1956, there was a great deal of passive but little overt resistance to the invaders. The Prague government had simply asked its people not to resist. Dubcek's comment about the intervention was, "So they did it after all—and to *me*!" Dubcek and his cabinet were arrested and taken to Moscow, where they were forced to accept the end of Czech democratization. When demonstrations against the Soviet Union broke out in March 1969 they were quickly put down and Dubcek was replaced with Gustav Husak, a former reformer who was willing to do the bidding of Moscow. The "Prague Spring" was at an end.[2]

Once again it was clear that the Soviet Union had to resort to force to safeguard its position in the bloc. If reform was to come one day and alter the character of any communist regime, it could only originate in Moscow.

By the late 1960s the Soviet Union had lost its image as a dynamic revolutionary superpower. It even withdrew from the space race to the moon and allowed the United States to once again demonstrate its technological superiority. Instead, it appeared to be a clumsy giant at great pains to maintain stability and discipline within its own core bloc. Furthermore, it came to be viewed by radical forces across the developed world as an essentially conservative political system. At a time when the Chinese communist leadership was arguing for violent struggle across the underdeveloped world, Moscow was arguing that a peaceful and constitutional evolution to socialism was possible. The Soviet Union failed to expand its influence in the third world, especially in sub-Saharan Africa where it made the mistake of assuming that newly emerging nations would naturally tend toward socialism. This was also true of the Middle East during and after the Arab-Israeli War of 1967.

With the proclamation of the Eisenhower Doctrine in 1957, the United States had committed itself to assisting any nation in the Middle East that was judged to be threatened by communist aggression. Applying it in 1958 the United States had intervened to rescue the pro-Western regimes of Jordan and Lebanon from the threat of a pro-Nasser coup. By the 1960s the United States and the Soviet Union had become embroiled in the bitter dispute between the two sides of the Arab-Israeli dispute. Gamel Abdel Nasser's principal reason for cultivating Russian friendship was the hope that diplomatically and militarily the Soviet Union would provide Egypt with a counterpoise to Western influence in the region, and help him in removing his chief enemy: the state of Israel.

While the Soviet Union furnished military assistance to Egypt and the pro-communist regime in Syria, the United States supplied arms to Israel, Turkey, Jordan, and Lebanon. When the links with Moscow failed to produce the breakthrough the Egyptians and Syrians had hoped for, they took matters into their own hands and sought a military solution to the problem.

Nasser began by demanding and receiving the removal of the U.N. peacekeeping force that had acted as a buffer between Israel and Egypt since 1956. On May 22, 1967, he blocked Israel's access to the Red Sea by closing the Straits of Tiran and thus the Gulf of Aqaba to Israeli shipping. At the same time, he reinforced the Egyptian garrisons in the Sinai Peninsula. The Israeli prime minister, Levi Eshkol, responded very hesitantly, not certain about Nasser's ultimate intent. Washington urged caution, while working behind the scenes to keep the Gulf of Aqaba open. Encouraged by what appeared to be Israeli and American timidity, Nasser concluded that he might hope for more.

On May 28 the Russian premier, Aleksei Kosygin, assured Nasser that if war broke out in the Middle East his country would check the United States.[3] This very unwise assurance came after a massive Russian diplomatic and propaganda campaign beginning in the mid-1960s, which sought to draw the Arabs together by exploiting the specter of a common enemy, namely Israeli Zionism backed by Western imperialism. Kosygin's assurance, however vague, was all the encouragement Nasser needed to escalate the matter into a major crisis. On May 29 he raised the Palestinian question in such a way as to make it clear that he was out to destroy Israel completely. The whole Arab world rallied to Nasser's side, and on the next day King Hussein of Jordan placed his entire army under Egyptian command. Iraq followed suit a few days later.

Believing these moves to be but the prelude to an attack, Israel launched a preemptive strike against Egyptian and Syrian positions on June 5. The Israeli attack carried all before it. In a matter of days it succeeded in wresting the Golan Heights from Syria, the entire Sinai Peninsula from Egypt, and the West Bank of the Jordan River, including the Jordanian sector of Jerusalem. The Arab nations had enjoyed superior numbers and fought with Soviet weapons, but still suffered a humiliating defeat. Despite the Kremlin's earlier assurances of support it had been unable to lend any practical assistance to its Arab allies. The Soviet Union seemed to have been beaten by proxy and suffered a defeat almost as humiliating as the Arabs.

The result of the Arab-Israeli War of 1967 was to give the Israelis for the first time some bargaining power over the Arabs. Israel, after all, had taken control of large territories and now hoped to use them to negotiate a settlement to resolve the Arab-Israeli dispute. At the very least, Israel wanted a formal Arab recognition of its right to exist. They had to wait in vain—at least for another quarter century—since Arab leaders felt that a peace that meant solving the Palestinian question at their expense and not at Israel's was too high a price to pay. With the continuance of large Russian military aid the Arabs felt that they could afford to wait, rebuild their armies, and renew the recent war on more favorable terms. The Americans replied to the Soviet arms buildup by extending more aid to Israel, and the arms race in the Middle East began once again.

In 1970 the Soviet Union supplied Egypt with 300 surface-to-air (SAM) missiles to aid in its defense, along with thousands of Soviet advisors and technicians to man the missile sites and reorganize the Egyptian army. In exchange Moscow obtained the use of Egyptian airfields and naval facilities at Alexandria and Port Said for its Mediterranean fleet. In 1971 Anwar Sadat, who succeeded Nasser as president of Egypt, concluded a fifteen-year treaty of friendship with Moscow in the hope of continuing the arms supply.

By that same year at the Communist Party Congress in March Brezhnev had emerged as the undisputed leader of the Communist Party of the Soviet Union. It was at this point that he took over the conduct of foreign affairs from Kosygin. Understanding that a softening in the Cold War with the West would do much to enhance the prestige of his leadership and help shore up Russia's international position, Brezhnev in October 1971 invited President Nixon to come to Moscow. "We proceed from the assumption," Brezhnev said, "That it is possible to improve relations between the USSR and the USA."

This shift in the foreign policy of the Soviet leadership toward the world was shaped by fear and power: fear that the arms race was becoming an onerous burden, fear about a German resurgence, fear about a repetition of the Cuban Missile Crisis, fear about the future of the third world, and fear that communist China and the United States might exploit these potentialities and ultimately challenge Soviet security itself; and power in the knowledge that the missile gap with the United States had been closed, that she was building a world class navy to rival the American, and that diplomatically she was able to hold most communist-led states in the Soviet column and normalize relations with West Germany and the United States. Above all, the U.S. opening to China posed a major danger for the Soviet Union which now faced a nuclear China and a unified Western Europe backed by the United States and Japan. According to Anatoly Dobrynin it was the crisis in Sino-Soviet relations that prompted the Kremlin to alter its foreign approach "to neutralize any collusion between Washington and Beijing." The appeal of detente, he argues, was further enhanced by the failure of the Russian grain harvest of 1972. Enormous purchases of grain had to be made in the West and most of it from the United States.[4]

The decisions subsequently made in the Kremlin to improve relations with West Germany and the United States indicated that in Soviet eyes the United States was no longer viewed as the primary danger in the world, but that its communist rival in Asia was.

When the Social Democrats swept to power in the West German elections of 1969, Premier Willy Brandt began to seek closer ties with East Germany and to normalize relations with Moscow. The Sino-Soviet conflict coincidentally peaked at this moment and so Moscow proved amenable to Brandt's *Ostpolitik*.

On August 12, 1970, the Soviet Union and West Germany concluded the Treaty of Moscow, which for all practical purposes amounted to a European peace treaty. Brandt recognized the existence of the East German government and signed pacts that finally accepted eastern European boundaries, including the Oder-Neisse line drawn by the Red Army in 1945. These were to remain "inviolable now and in the future."[5] At the same time, Bonn preserved Germany's right to eventual unification.

In December the Treaty of Warsaw between West Germany and Poland marked the logical continuation of the Treaty of Moscow. The treaties were a landmark in creating greater security for the Soviet Union and Poland, and a turning point in their relations with West Germany.

Nixon and Kissinger were at first cool to *Ostpolitik,* believing that reunification of the two German states was simply not realistic, and because "a unified Germany raised in many West European and some American minds the spectre of new German hegemony."[6] But they also believed that new, creative ways had to be found for dealing with the communist world. "[Woodrow] Wilson had the greatest vision of America's world role," Nixon once remarked. "But he wasn't practical enough."[7] Kissinger understood that the United States was in "a period of painful adjustment to a profound transformation of global politics" and that a statesman's duty to his people was to strive and create since "history knows no resting places and no plateaus." As he saw it, part of the answer lay in changes in the international order. Detente for Kissinger and Nixon meant cooperating with Red China and the Soviet Union in a limited way within a general environment of competition. It was a means of reducing international tensions and, at the same time, maintaining American leadership in world politics.[8]

The road to the Nixon-Brezhnev Summit of May 22, 1972, was not a smooth one. Not only did the United States mine Haiphong harbor that month, where Soviet ships were anchored, but there was friction between the two superpowers arising from the rebellion of the Bengalis in East Pakistan against their rulers in West Pakistan. The Bengalis declared the independent nation of Bangladesh, and the Pakistani government tried to crush it by slaughtering thousands of people. India, which had just signed a treaty of friendship with the Soviet Union and which saw an opportunity to break up Pakistan, intervened on behalf of the Bengalis.

The White House tended to view the Indo-Pakistani rivalry in Cold War terms, since Pakistan was an American ally. As Kissinger remarked at the time, "We don't really have any choice. We can't allow a friend of ours and China's to get screwed in a conflict with a friend of Russia's."[9]

Indian troops invaded East Pakistan in November 1971. The fighting soon grew when the president of West Pakistan launched air strikes against the rebels and their allies. There was certainly some potential for a wider crisis: China put thousands of its troops near the Indian border on alert; the Soviet Union blocked all attempts in the U.N. to achieve a cease-fire; and the United States ordered an aircraft carrier group into the Bay of Bengal. Believing that India was acting as a surrogate of Moscow, the United States pressed the Russians to restrain the Indians. In December 1971 the Russians offered Washington private assurances that it would, and the crisis ended when Pakistan's forces in the east surrendered. India then helped to reconstitute Bangladesh as an independent country.

Although some tough talk had been exchanged between the superpowers during the crisis, detente still remained the goal of both. On May 22, 1972, Nixon travelled to Moscow for a productive summit meeting, which laid the foundation for detente. He went there to strike a deal with a Soviet Union much different from the one Eisenhower made long before at Camp David. The Soviet Union was now a formidable nuclear power on a par with the United States and far ahead of its rival in conventional arms; the United States was still mired in Vietnam and facing serious social and economic problems at home, and Nixon hoped that Moscow could help the United States extricate itself from the Vietnam problem gracefully. More distantly, Nixon wished to consolidate his reelection chances that year with a dramatic foreign policy success. "My reputation is one of being a very hard-line, cold-war-oriented, anti-communist," Nixon told Brezhnev, but he now believed that the two systems could "live together and work together."[10]

Brezhnev made it clear from the start that he was anxious about the growth of Chinese power in Asia. He actually tried at one point to convince Nixon that "we are whites" and "we Europeans" should control the Chinese before they become "a superpower." Nixon would have none of it but, of course, used the Sino-Soviet rivalry as a negotiating card.[11]

The two sides quickly came to agreements in the fields of medicine and public health, space exploration (culminating in a joint space venture in 1975), and scientific and technological research. These agreements, while certainly a beginning, were only symbolically important and could easily be dismissed when relations between the superpowers cooled. Of far more importance were the agreements over trade relations and the arms race.

Central to the summit was the Strategic Arms Limitation Talks (Salt I). When Nixon entered office he fell heir to a collection of doctrines that had defined nuclear strategy for his predecessors. In the previous decade the doctrine of "massive retaliation" evolved into the concept of "mutual assured destruction," or MAD. Its feasibility depended on each side's "second-strike capability," that is, the capacity of the United States to absorb a nuclear attack and still retaliate with enough missiles to destroy the attacker. By 1969 the United States had 1,054 ICBMs to the Soviet's 858 and it ranked first in total nuclear warheads, roughly a four-to-one edge. But Nixon understood that the Soviets were building them at a much more rapid pace and that parity between the two sides was only a matter of time. The moment to limit that growth was now.

In the Salt I agreements the number of offensive ICBMs were limited to 1,410 land-based missiles and 950 submarine-launched missiles on the Soviet side, and for the United States, 1,000 land-based missiles and 710 submarine-launched weapons. The United States still held an edge through her superiority in bombers—450 to 150 Soviet planes, and with her MIRVs (Multiple Independent Re-Entry Vehicles). Nixon refused to accept any limits in this latter category, in which the United States was well ahead. In fact Nixon had seriously underestimated the Russians who were soon producing MIRVs on their own.

The two sides also came to an agreement on defensive antiballistic missile systems (ABMs). Because ABMs theoretically protected offensive weapon's from attack, the United States had warned the Soviets ever since the Salt talks began in 1969 not to continue to deploy such systems because it would force the United States to construct more and better nuclear weapons to overcome their defenses. In other words, the ABMs would stimulate the arms race. In 1972 Brezhnev accepted this argument and both sides agreed to limit themselves to one defensive system for their capitals and a second to defend an area containing ICBM launchers.

What the agreement did not cover was just as important as what it included. Salt I did not prohibit the development of new weapons. The United States therefore went ahead and built the Trident submarine, the B-1 bomber, and the cruise missile. As Kissinger said: "The way to use this freeze is for us to catch up."[12]

The two countries also struck an important agreement over trade. A joint American-Soviet Commercial Commission was set up to work out a normalization of trade relations. The two sides agreed on a settlement of Soviet debts to the United States stemming from the lend-lease program of the Second World War, in return for which the Soviet Union was to receive credits for purchases of U.S. technology and agricultural products. Along with the extension of most favored nation (MFN) status to the Soviet Union, the trade agreements "would be," said Kissinger, "a carrot for restrained [Soviet] political behavior."[13] This quickly became known as "linkage," the idea that if the Soviet Union proved accommodating in certain areas of diplomacy it should be allowed what it wanted in others. Nixon also understood that Congress was unlikely to support an expanding economic relationship with the Soviet Union if that country continued to follow an aggressive foreign policy.

It was the American grain sales to the Soviet Union that provided the first test-case for detente. Because of the disastrous crop failure of 1972 the Soviets entered the U.S. grain market for the purchase of large quantities of wheat that U.S. taxpayers had paid farmers high subsidies to produce. Aided by generous credit terms the Soviets purchased virtually the entire American grain surplus at well below world prices. The U.S. grain dealers made money, but U.S. bread prices increased and Congress accused the Nixon administration of having been duped by the Russians. Congress struck back at the administration on the issue of granting MFN status to the Soviet Union. Thereafter, Congress imposed its own linkage on U.S.-Soviet relations in 1974 through the Jackson-Vanick Amendment to the reciprocity treaty. The amendment stated that MFN would only be extended to the Soviet Union when it eased the restrictions on the emigration of Jews from the Soviet Union. Senate liberals and conservatives had joined together to pass this bill, which Kissinger called "a rare convergence, like an eclipse of the sun."[14] He was bitter about the amendment because it meant intervening in Soviet domestic policy. And it had the opposite effect. The level of Jewish emigration from the Soviet Union rose from 400 annually in 1968 to 35,000 in 1973. In that year Brezhnev imposed a tax making emigration more difficult. Senator Jackson now linked this with the MFN. Anatoly Dobrynin acknowledges that it was a mistake and Brezhnev soon lifted the tax. But Jackson demanded assurances for the future. Brezhnev, says Dobrynin, could not accept the Jackson-Vanick Amendment because of the strident campaign that accompanied it. It would have meant yielding to American pressure on an issue of internal importance for the Soviet Union. All the Jackson campaign succeeded in doing was getting the Soviets to angrily denounce the reciprocity treaty and slow Jewish emigration from the Soviet Union to a trickle. The vulnerability of detente to domestic pressures was now obvious.

Salt I slowed the arms race only temporarily, as both sides eventually forged ahead building new submarines, bigger bombers, and better missiles. While Brezhnev cracked down on internal dissent, he continued to modernize his armed forces in what was already the largest peacetime buildup since the German rearmament of the 1930s.

Despite the tensions that helped to dilute Salt I, other summits followed—at Vladivostock in 1974 and Vienna in 1979—that built upon the initial agreement. If the Salt talks bogged down it was over which types of weapons were to be included in the agreements, and because of the paranoid feelings on both sides that the other was secretly building toward superiority. As Brezhnev acknowledged, detente, even if it did not live up to the original expectations of its architects, was still an enormously helpful addition to Cold War crisis management. And he had in mind the resolution of the Arab-Israeli War of 1973.

After the disaster of 1967, Moscow played a cautious game in the Middle East. The Soviet goal was to keep the region unsettled, but not to be drawn into a conflict with the United States. In November 1967 Moscow intervened in the civil war in Yemen and in 1968 it agreed to provide military and technical aid to the new pro-Soviet government of South Yemen, formed after the British withdrawal from Aden. But at the same time, Moscow resisted all of Nasser's attempts to draw the Soviet Union more closely into the actual fighting in the region. Moscow therefore rejected his suggestion for a defense treaty with the Russians, or his other idea to have the Russians take control of the Egyptian air force. Moscow was willing to send arms to its allies in the Middle East but not actually defend them. The latter road, of course, led to a possible direct confrontation with the United States. The Russians therefore, extended lots of aid to Nasser with the understanding that he seek a political solution to the region's problems. Nasser, on the other hand, was more intent on resuming the military struggle with Israel.

A war of attrition between Egypt and Israel replaced their clash of 1967. This lasted until 1970 when Nasser suddenly died. His successor, Anwar Sadat, was always sceptical about the Soviet role in the Middle East and he doubted that Moscow's intentions were all that sincerely pro-Arab.

To deal with the war of attrition that had turned against Egypt, Sadat travelled to Moscow in 1972 to procure offensive arms. When he failed to get the aid in the amounts he needed to give Egypt military superiority over Israel, he expelled all 20,000 Soviet technicians and advisors from Egypt on July 18, 1972. This came shortly after the Nixon-Brezhnev talks in Moscow and appeared to confirm the Kremlin's commitment to East-West detente at the expense of its clients in areas like the Middle East.

Sadat and his allies in Syria remained convinced that, even without the sophisticated weaponry withheld by Moscow, they could recapture some of the land seized by Israel in 1967. He also came to believe that some involvement of the superpowers was necessary to produce a lasting Middle East peace settlement. He therefore invoked the war option as the only alternative to break the deadlock with Israel and force the superpowers to act, and especially make the United States press Israel for a settlement. Before he went to war, Sadat obtained the support of the Saudis for an oil embargo against the West, and other Arab producers followed suit.

On Yom Kippur Day, October 6, 1973, the holiest day in the Israeli religious calendar, the Egyptians and Syrians launched a surprise attack. While Egyptian troops attacked the Israeli defense positions in Sinai, Syrian armored divisions swarmed onto the Golan Heights. Despite heavy losses, the Arab armies did extremely well in the first days of the war. The Soviets, despite the strain in relations with Egypt, poured arms and supplies into the Arab armies but also urged Sadat to seek a truce while he was winning. Instead, smelling victory, Sadat forged ahead. On October 12 Israeli Prime Minister Golda Meir seemed to recognize the inevitable when she notified Washington that the war was going very badly and that the existence of her country was at stake. She then urgently requested aid and, at the same time, cryptically conveyed a more ominous message: that in defending her country she was determined to employ whatever means were required to win. This was taken in the Nixon White House as a thinly veiled threat to use nuclear weapons to stem the Arab tide. The United States sent aid immediately.

By mid-October, after two weeks of the largest and fiercest tank battles since the Second World War, the tide turned and Israel gained the upper hand. While an Israeli force counterattacked into Syria, a brilliant flanking maneuvre brought an Israeli armored force to the west bank of the Suez Canal and encircled an entire Egyptian army on the east bank in Sinai.

The superpowers were reluctant to become involved in the war, especially since it could destroy the detente between them before the ink was dry on the agreement. On the other hand, they were reluctant to allow their clients to be defeated. Both sides therefore armed the belligerents in what became, in one sense, a war of proxies. Each side did this but their aid was balanced by a determination to prevent a breach with each other over it.

By October 16 it was obvious to the Kremlin that the Arabs were facing total defeat. Aleksei Kosygin secretly flew to Cairo and persuaded Sadat to accept a cease-fire. On the same day, the Kremlin endorsed Sadat's request that the superpowers jointly intervene to separate the belligerents. However, Nixon recoiled at the idea since it would introduce Russian troops into the Middle East for the first time, a region of great strategic and economic importance. Moscow, which had already placed three airborne divisions on alert, thereupon declared its intention to introduce Soviet forces into the region unilaterally. In response, Nixon placed U.S. forces on worldwide nuclear alert, and the Russians promptly followed suit. For a brief moment it looked like the superpower confrontation had totally eclipsed the understanding of detente.

On October 20, Secretary Kissinger agreed with the Soviet leaders to press for a cease-fire in the U.N. A U.N. resolution calling for a cease-fire was adopted on October 22, but the Israelis were still determined to press their advantage. Sadat now realized that Moscow's guarantees were not worth much, and so he turned desperately to Washington to end the war. Seeing this as a major diplomatic turn in the crisis, Nixon and Kissinger secretly notified Cairo that the United States would not permit Israel to destroy the Egyptian army in Sinai. Kissinger could now exploit Sadat's loss of faith in the Soviet Union to not only end the war, but to also broker a permanent peace between Egypt and Israel. Egypt and Israel signed an agreement to end the war on November 11, 1973.

The United States had now cast herself in the role of mediator in the Middle East, the friend of both Egypt and Israel. Very carefully Kissinger managed to freeze the Russians out of the peace process where their role could potentially complicate the resolution of regional problems. Kissinger was able to do this when both Israel and Egypt asked Kissinger to mediate the quarrel between Jerusalem and Cairo. Using "shuttle diplomacy," Kissinger was able to get Egypt and Israel to initial an historic agreement on September 1, 1975, which provided for an eventual Israeli pull back from part of Sinai, turning over a buffer zone to the U.N. and American patrols, and placing U.S. military personnel in "early warning" stations to detect military activities. Washington agreed to underwrite the process by providing substantial foreign aid to both Israel and Egypt.

The Russians had been decisively cut out of the peace process and had once and for all lost Egypt, the largest country in the region, as an ally. Although Moscow did not recognize this American-sponsored solution to the Arab-Israeli conflict, it refrained from interfering with it. This lessened the chance of superpower conflict and allowed detente time to grow. In this sense, the Soviet Union was more than a passive spectator, since it could have interfered with the peace process at any time. In fact, Brezhnev made it clear after the war that without detente "the situation would look entirely different. If the current conflict would explode in an environment of general international tensions . . . , the confrontation in the Middle East could become far more dangerous and be on a scale threatening the general peace."[15]

Both Moscow and Washington credited detente for resolving the worst crisis between them since the Cuban missile crisis, but both nevertheless continued to hope that detente would promote the type of international order they preferred. For years detente would remain vulnerable to the eruption of regional conflicts in the third world, because it was the long-established tendency of the superpowers to view each problem that arose through the lenses of the Cold War. This was one of the reasons for the myopia about the arms race—the paranoid belief that the other side was secretly building weapons for superiority and not just parity. This was especially true on the Soviet side. Military spending in the Soviet Union probably doubled between 1960 and 1976. Central to this surge was the development of a vast nuclear arsenal, which by Salt I allowed the Russians to pull abreast of the United States. In any future missile crisis the Soviet Union would not labor under a strategic and therefore political disadvantage as it had in 1962. The Kremlin had learned from that crisis that nuclear war was not an acceptable option, but achieving at least parity gave them the possibility of bargaining from strength. This also reflected a more fundamental ideological shift in the leadership's thinking; where only a generation before, the Soviet rulers thought more in terms of spreading the revolution, now in Brezhnev's day they were more concerned with enhancing the security and prestige of the Soviet Union. "Cold warriors" like Nixon and Kissinger understood this when they signed Salt I; they realized that Soviet power was now a far greater danger than communist ideology, and that the real determinant of international politics was the struggle for power and diplomatic efforts to establish a balance among competing states. The arms race was not matched by the United States in the 1970s because it was still burdened by the Vietnam War, and its leadership demoralized by the Watergate scandal. The arms buildup in the Soviet Union served to give the leadership of that country what it had striven for since the days of the tsars: military security. What it did not give them, at least until the mid-1970s, was political security.

Detente may have worked imperfectly from the beginning, and the Salt II talks may have bogged down, but in Europe detente worked successfully to ease tensions. As early as 1950 and the Korean War, the frontiers of the Cold War had solidified in Europe and the major struggle had shifted to Asia, the Middle East, and Africa.

The European status quo was now formalized in 1975, when thirty-five nations assembled in Helsinki, Finland, for the Conference on Security and Cooperation. The United States and Canada attended, as did all the nations of Europe (except Albania). Often thought of as the peace conference that officially ended the Second World War, the Helsinki Conference was a more representative convocation of European heads of state than the Paris Peace Conference of 1919.

When delegates signed the Helsinki Accords they committed themselves to three areas, or "three baskets" as they were called at the conference: security, economic cooperation, and humanitarian cooperation. The second basket provided for an increase in economic aid and cultural relations between the two blocs and produced no controversy at all. The other two baskets did. In the first, the delegates accepted the existence of the political boundaries of Europe, which had for a generation divided East and West, and the commitment not to change any of them by force. The agreement pertained to the most sensitive territorial adjustments since the war, including the border separating the two Germanies from each other and from Poland. This amounted to nothing less than an implicit acknowledgement of Russian domination of Eastern Europe and therefore a major political victory for the Soviet Union. It was this which gave the Russians the political security they had sought since 1945.

But it was the third basket that caused the most trouble in Moscow. According to this agreement, the signees would agree to guarantee respect for human rights, political freedoms, freedom of movement, and the free exchange of ideas. The accord was strongly reminiscent of the Yalta Declaration on Liberated Europe. The second basket represented a major concession by the West, but in the third the Soviet Union had to reciprocate with major concessions of its own.

When the treaty was ready and laid before the Politburo, they were, says Anatoly Dobrynin, stunned. The hard-liners, like Mikhail Suslov and Yuri Andropov, strongly objected to the proposal on the grounds that humanitarian issues were really domestic matters and therefore no one else's business. The West, of course, felt them to be extremely important international issues. Andre Gromyko, who supervised the long set of Russian negotiations leading up to Helsinki, argued that on balance Russia had received something substantial at the conference—the recognition of the permanence of European borders and the tacit recognition of Soviet overlordship of Eastern Europe, everything the Kremlin had worked and hoped for since Stalin's day. The final act of the Helsinki Accords was a political statement of intent and not a legally binding document, and as far as human rights went, Gromyko pointed out, "We are masters in our own house." The Soviet government still had the power to decide what constituted interference in Russian domestic affairs. According to Dobrynin, this argument won over Brezhnev and the Politburo.[16]

In the short run the Helsinki Accords represented a major political victory for the Soviet Union. But in the long run "basket three" became a rallying point for dissidents all over the Soviet bloc, and a focus point for Western pressure. None of this happened overnight but, as Dobrynin acknowledges, dissidence inside and outside the Soviet Union was directly encouraged by this document. As he points out, "its very publication in *Pravda* gave it the weight of an official document. It gradually became a manifesto of the dissident and liberal movement, a development totally beyond the imagination of the Soviet leadership."[17] Dozens of "Helsinki groups" sprang up across the Soviet bloc pressing their governments to honor their commitments made to human rights at the conference. One such group was Chapter 77 headed by Vaclav Havel in Czechoslovakia, and another was the union, Solidarity, led by Lech Walesa in Poland. Eventually these groups became revolutionary vehicles for the transition to democracy.

In the days following Helsinki the Kremlin clamped down severely at home and arrested hundreds of Soviet intellectuals who were demanding freedom of speech. In the long run the repression was ineffective. Ultimately, admits Dobrynin, the Helsinki Accords played "a significant role in bringing about the long and difficult process of liberalization inside the Soviet Union and the nations of Eastern Europe. This in the end caused the fundamental changes in all these countries that helped end the Cold War."[18]

The political and military detente of the 1970s was followed by an economic loosening up of the commercial arteries between East and West. By the mid-1970s there was a notable increase in trade and investment between the two economic blocs. Western banks extended loans to Eastern European states which enabled them to purchase Western consumer goods and industrial products in large quantities. In some cases industrial plants were opened in the bloc, and the United States became the Soviet Union's principal supplier of grain. Less clear at the time was the growing indebtedness of the more backward nations of the communist East to Western states, which in the 1980s would have dramatic consequences.

Notes

1. Joseph Rothschild, *Return to Diversity: A Political History of East Central Europe* (New York: Oxford University Press, 1989), 174.

2. Z. A. B. Zeman, *Prague Spring* (New York: Hill and Wang, 1969).

3. Nadav Safran, *Israel: The Embattled Ally* (Cambridge, Mass.: Belknap Press, 1978), 399-401.

4. Anatoly Dobrynin, *In Confidence: Moscow's Ambassador to America's Six Cold War Presidents (1962-1986)* (New York: Random House, 1995), 193.

5. Quoted in Robin Edmonds, *Soviet Foreign Policy 1962-1973: The Paradox of Super Power* (New York: Oxford University Press, 1975), 94.

6. Henry Kissinger, *White House Years* (Boston: Little, Brown and Company, 1979), 409.

7. Quoted in Gary Wills, *Nixon Agonistes* (Boston: Houghton Mifflin, 1970), 20.

8. Kissinger, *White House Years*, 55, 57-58.

9. Quoted in Richard M. Nixon, *The Memoirs of Richard Nixon* (New York: Grosset and Dunlap, 1978), 527.

10. Nixon, *Memoirs*, 527.

11. C. L. Sulzberger, *The World and Richard Nixon* (New York: Prentice Hall, 1987), 199-200.

12. Kissinger, *White House Years*, 1245n.

13. Kissinger, *White House Years*, 1250.

14. Quoted in John Newhouse, *War and Peace in the Nuclear Age* (New York: Alfred A. Knopf, 1989), 241.

15. Quoted in D. K. Simes, "The Death of Détente?" *International Security* 5 (1980), 3.

16. Dobrynin, *In Confidence*, 346.

17. Dobrynin, *In Confidence*, 346.

18. Dobrynin, *In Confidence*, 347.

20

The Erosion of Containment
and the End of Detente

The long ordeal in Vietnam and the Watergate scandal that destroyed the Nixon presidency had wounded American pride and diminished its prestige abroad. The American foreign and domestic performance succeeded in raising serious questions about America's ability to lead the Western alliance in the future. The slippage of power that the American people had begun to sense was reflected in the relative decline of the U.S. economy since the early 1960s. Between 1968 and 1978, for example, U.S. prices doubled, not only driving up the price of foodstuffs but making American goods less competitive in world markets. Key industries like steel and automobiles began to deteriorate as thousands of workers faced unemployment. West German Chancellor Helmut Schmidt went so far as to declare that the Americans had abdicated their economic leadership in the early 1970s. Schmidt seems to have communicated his concern to President Carter who has written that in a particularly bitter discussion of economic issues between the two men, Schmidt "got personally abusive toward me."[1]

Foreign affairs offered no respite for Washington, as many countries in Africa and Latin America drifted inexorably toward revolution. By the late 1970s the United States had lost any real initiative in the Cold War.

The moment called for a vigorous president who was willing to break with the past and who was able to supply the necessary leadership to stimulate national renewal. Gerald Ford, who had been sworn in as president in 1974 to serve out Nixon's term, was an honest man who did much to restore the integrity of the presidency. But being both a virtual unknown and an interim president left him unable to cope with America's domestic problems and the Cold War in a vigorous way.

Jimmy Carter was a Washington "outsider" who like Gerald Ford had emerged from obscurity to take advantage of the Watergate scandal and capture the White House. Because of his narrow election victory in 1976 Carter lacked the broad base of national support that might have overcome his lack of charisma. Carter carried a high moral tone to his office and he seems to have understood that some sort of national redemption was needed,[2] but unfortunately he lacked the experience and the personal qualities of leadership to shape American politics in the 1970s.

This interlude between the Nixon and Reagan presidencies coincided dangerously with a period when the Soviet Cold War offensive reached its apogee, and when the Kremlin seemed poised to dictate the Cold War's outcome. It even appeared that with the Russian assertion of global strength, coming as it did on top of a period of American drift and weakness, the moment seemed ripe for an historical turning point.

Like Gerald Ford, Jimmy Carter came to the White House basically ignorant of foreign affairs. As his secretary of state Carter selected Cyrus Vance, a lawyer who had held top posts in the Department of Defense in the 1960s. Like Carter he hoped to reduce armaments and military expenditures and he was reluctant to prop up regimes that had proven unpopular with their people. Like Carter he believed that the country had turned a corner after Vietnam and that there were no longer American solutions to every problem. Moreover, he did not believe in the Soviet blueprint to foment conflicts across the world and he felt that the pursuit of quiet diplomacy would sooner or later pay large dividends in Soviet-American detente.

The influence Vance exerted on the president was to a certain extent balanced by Carter's national security advisor, Zbigniew Brzezinski. Like Henry Kissinger, Brzezinski was a brilliant student of power politics recruited to Washington from one of the nation's great universities. An advisor who might have been more at home in the Nixon or Truman administrations, Brzezinski made his geostrategic considerations and policies on the record of what the Russians actually did in the world since 1945, and not on the basis of what they promised to do. When he looked at Soviet motivations and designs he concluded, unlike Vance, that there indeed was a calculated Soviet bid for European domination, and beyond that to an alteration of the correlation of forces in large parts of the third world. He therefore felt that the United States must maintain its side of the arms race and, like Kissinger, he worked to play China off against the Soviet Union. To Vance, the Soviet Union was a great power in an international system of states and as such worthy of respect. Moreover, a sustained effort at innovative statecraft could succeed in accommodating it in the family of nations. To Brzezinski, on the other hand, the Soviet Union was the enemy par excellence, an aggressive state whose enmity was a fact of recent, present, and future history. A Pole by background, Brzezinski was committed to winning the Cold War and obsessive about the Russians. At one of the initial Pentagon briefings on nuclear war, Brzezinski asked the question: "Where are the criteria for killing Russians?" The briefer misunderstood the thrust of the question and replied that a nuclear barrage against Soviet industrial centers would kill roughly 113,000,000 people. Brzezinski retorted, "No, no, I mean *Russian* Russians." To Brzezinski the ethnic Russians bore the responsibility for the Cold War because they were the core group within the Soviet Union. This was the group you had to "deter," or, if it came to war, kill. The briefer "felt that he was listening to the voice of 600 years of Polish history."[3]

It soon became obvious that two men like Vance and Brzezinski could not possibly get along. President Carter was both unable and unwilling to end the infighting between the two men and he never succeeded in taking charge of foreign policy. Because of this, his foreign policy appeared vacillating and inconsistent.

In the first few years of his presidency Carter leaned to the Vance view of foreign relations. This meant that his administration avoided the reactive foreign policy called for in the policy of containment. Instead, it pursued a reduction in nuclear arsenals, worked toward an economic stability in the world, and sought solutions to environmental problems. "The soul of our foreign policy," said Carter in a Wilsonian flourish, was human rights, and he insisted that dictators must respect human rights if they wished to continue receiving U.S. foreign aid. This included human rights within the Soviet Union. Carter took the Helsinki Accords seriously. When, for example, Moscow jailed Russian dissidents, Brzezinski got the White House to temporarily stop the sale of computers to the Soviet Union. The human rights program served to intensify the crisis within the Soviet political and social system itself.

The Carter administration also relied on preventive diplomacy to advance the peace process in the Middle East and mediate quarrels in the third world. The policy had mixed results, especially in the third world.

One of the places where Carter's activist diplomacy worked successfully was in the settlement of the Panama Canal problem. From the opening of the canal in 1903 the Panamanians had tried unsuccessfully to gain control of the waterway that bisected their country. "What nation of the world," asked Panamanian General Omar Torrijos, "can withstand the humiliation of a foreign flag piercing its own heart?"[4]

Violent anti-American riots in the mid-1960s prompted the Johnson administration to take a serious look at the problem, although little was actually accomplished. In 1974 Henry Kissinger agreed in principle to a future transfer of the canal to Panama. But it was Jimmy Carter who decided to solve the problem once and for all. Bringing the negotiations begun years before to a conclusion, he signed two treaties with Panama in 1977. The first treaty abrogated the 1903 agreement and provided for the gradual transfer of the canal's sovereignty to Panama over the following twenty-two year period. The United States, at the same time, agreed to give Panama a greater percentage of the canal's revenues. The second treaty stipulated that the United States had the right to defend the "neutrality" of the canal in perpetuity. Conservatives in Congress attacked the treaties as so much appeasement of petty dictators, and as yet another indication of American decline. They were worried about turning a key artery over to a foreign regime. When asked by a committee of Congress what Washington's response would be if the Panamanian government closed down the canal for "repairs," Brzezinski replied, "we will move in and close down the Panamanian government for repairs."[5] Despite some bitter opposition in Congress, the treaties were ratified on March 16, 1978. Not since the Roosevelt administration in the 1930s had Washington scored such a diplomatic victory in Latin America.

Carter was less successful in Nicaragua. The Nicaraguan revolution of 1978-1979 received much less attention than the Panama Canal problem, although it had a longer-term significance. Since 1936 the Somoza family had ruled Nicaragua with a corrupt and iron hand, able to draw support from Washington because it was a reasonably stable and anti-communist regime. The formation of a major resistance group against the regime was almost a foregone conclusion.

In the 1960s an alliance of the left formed the first guerrilla groups led by the Sandinista National Liberation Front (FSLN). It recruited its support initially from peasants and students. The government's mishandling of the relief aid during the Managuan earthquake of 1972 broadened the opposition. When a rebellion broke out in 1978 the Carter administration tried to broker a government that stood somewhere between the Sandinistas and the Somozas, but failed. As Carter vacillated, the Sandinistas launched their final offensive in the spring of 1979. When Carter asked the O.A.S. to intervene and establish a moderate government, not one Latin American state supported the plan. On July 17, 1979, the Sandinistas marched into Managua and Somoza fled into exile in Paraguay (with most of the national treasury).

Latin America now had its second Marxist-Leninist government. The junta that had seized power was more pragmatic than, for example, Cuba, permitting some degree of plurality in the government and society, and some private ownership. Nevertheless, it did not honor its original promise in 1979 to hold elections. It still wanted to retain power in its own hands to build a socialist society on the Soviet model. Through the army and the security services, the government under Daniel Ortega was able to exercise firm control over the country. But by the early 1980s the dissidents who had fled the new regime along with remnants of Somoza's National Guard formed guerrilla bands on Nicaragua's borders. Contras, as they were called, enjoyed the backing of the new Reagan administration and waged a determined war against the Sandinista regime. At the same time, the Ortega government was able to draw upon Moscow's support to keep its balance. But by the mid-1980s Moscow began to feel the economic pinch that ultimately sank her own economy, and so cut back on aid to Managua. At the same time, the Democratic Congress chose to starve the Contras for aid and the civil war reached a stalemate.

By 1990 it was apparent that the revolution in Nicaragua had gone nowhere and Daniel Ortega decided to hold a free election. The opposition under Violeta Chamorro won and the civil war ended, certainly the first time a Marxist-Leninist regime surrendered power willingly after a free election.

In the Middle East Carter's diplomacy seemed to stumble into a showy success. The Arab-Israeli dispute was more complex and geopolitically more important than the question of who ruled in Managua. On March 15, 1976, President Sadat cancelled Egypt's treaty of friendship with Moscow, inflicting a major setback on Soviet policy in the Middle East. The defection of the area's strongest state deprived the Soviet Union of much of its leverage in the region. After the break with Moscow Sadat drew closer to the United States and hinted that it might be time for Egypt and Israel to settle its long-standing grievances.

Carter responded to this suggestion by departing from the shuttle-diplomacy of Henry Kissinger in favor of a more comprehensive peace treaty. Not thinking his next move through carefully, he struck out clumsily in two directions: he decided it was time to call for a Palestinian homeland, which, of course, angered Israel, and he agreed with the Russians to sponsor a Middle East peace initiative and reconvene the Geneva Conference. This latter initiative alarmed Anwar Sadat because it would give the Soviet Union the chance to fish in troubled waters by supporting other clients in the region, while the United States would support Israel. Egypt would therefore be isolated as never before. Realizing that an unhealthy stalemate might ensue, and convinced that continued American support for Israel gave Jerusalem the military advantage in any future war, Sadat elected to head off the Geneva conference by making his famous trip to Jerusalem in November 1977.

While Sadat had seized the initiative from Carter, it was ironically the failure of Israel and Egypt to come to an agreement which brought the United States back to the peace process. Worried about the spreading crisis in Iran, Carter saw that he must scrap his original idea for a comprehensive peace and quickly explore what was politically possible to stabilize the Middle East. Working now toward more limited goals, Carter persuaded Sadat and Menachem Begin of Israel to come to the United States for direct negotiations. On September 17, 1978, after thirteen days of discussion, the Camp David Accords were signed. A diplomatic amateur at the best of times, Carter's role was nevertheless pivotal. He had alternately cajoled and threatened both sides with either a cutoff or a promise of aid; he had even spent long hours discussing the Bible with Begin. But he succeeded in getting them to at least partially compromise.

In the accords, Sadat agreed to recognize Israel's government and the two countries exchanged ambassadors in 1980. For the first time an Arab state had formally acknowledged Israel's right to exist. For his part, Begin agreed to turn the Sinai Desert back to Egypt in a phased withdrawal to be completed in 1982. They both agreed to the stationing of a U.N. force along the Egyptian-Israeli boundary to monitor the agreement. They also agreed to the establishment of full economic relations and the opening of negotiations on Palestinian rights in the occupied West Bank and Gaza (although Begin put a slightly different spin on this latter point). Carter called the treaty "the first step of peace . . . there now remains the rest of the Arab world."

The Camp David Accords were denounced in Moscow, no less than in the Arab world, as the product of Israeli and American imperialism. The Russians were particularly incensed not only because they had been cut out of the peace process but also because the rupture in relations between Egypt and the Soviet Union was now complete. Moscow had extended vast amounts of aid to Egypt over the previous dozen years and now had nothing to show for it. Furthermore, the defection of the most powerful Arab state from this relationship insured against a renewed eruption of the Arab-Israeli conflict. As General Moshe Dayan once put it, "if you take one wheel off a car, it won't drive. If Egypt is out of the conflict, there will be no more war."[6] All that was left for the Soviet Union to exploit in the Middle East was the unresolved Palestinian issue.

One of the problems the superpowers had with regard to each other's intentions was a shared mentality of globalism. Each side in pursuing its security interests almost naturally saw the manipulative hand of the other in each new crisis as it arose; they then took steps that aroused the apprehensions of the other side thus exacerbating the problem that may in origin have only followed from local circumstances. And there were lots of opportunities in the third world for the superpowers to exploit and clash over. The third world was backward and, at the same time, strategically and economically valuable. Africa is the best case in point.

The states of Africa made up at least one-third of the General Assembly of the U.N., giving them a certain political importance. But the continent was also a vast reservoir of some of the most vital raw materials—like cobalt, oil, uranium, manganese, and chromium. Moreover, it lay astride some of the major sea lanes and commercial arteries like the Persian Gulf, the Indian Ocean, and the Atlantic Ocean. And because the continent was so backward its instability tempted the United States and Soviet Union to dabble in the politics of many of its countries.

By the mid-1970s the Soviet Union aggressively sought to extend its influence into Africa and the northwest littoral of the Indian Ocean. In 1968 when Britain began a drastic reduction of its naval forces in the waters "east of Suez," it afforded the Soviet Union the opportunity to play a more active role in the region. The appearance of a Soviet naval squadron in the Indian Ocean that year highlighted the Kremlin's need to acquire naval facilities to accommodate its vessels.

What were the motives behind the Russian attempts to penetrate into Africa? There was, of course, the great power desire to increase its influence into a key region of the third world commensurate with its sense of growing military power. Second, there was the quest for dominant control of the resources indispensable to the Soviet future, and just as important, denying them to the West. Third, there may also be some substance to the argument advanced by Richard Pipes that placed Soviet behavior in Africa and the Middle East within the framework of a "Grand Strategy" (rather than a "Grand Opportunism"), which coveted a control of those countries that lay astride the key supply routes to the West. Among these strategic points were the southern entrance to the Red Sea, giving access to the Suez Canal, and the Strait of Hormuz, giving access to the Persian Gulf.[7]

In the push into Africa the Soviet Union was able to exploit the collapse of the Ethiopian monarch Haile Selassie's forty-four-year-old regime in 1974. In its place it helped to establish a Soviet client state on the Horn of Africa. In the same year it was able to take advantage of the overthrow of the dictatorship in Portugal to extend its influence into the Portuguese colony of Angola on the west coast of Africa. To help them to this, the Soviet Union in 1975-1976 introduced 20,000 Cuban troops together with tanks and armored personnel carriers to the country to tip the balance in the Angolan civil war. The struggle was between the Marxist-oriented Popular Movement for the Liberation of Angola (MPLA) and its two rivals, the National Front for the Liberation of Angola (FNLA), and the Union for the Total Independence of Angola (UNITA), backed by 5,000 South African troops.

The Soviet Union was able to exploit the indecision in Washington following the collapse of the Nixon presidency. The White House under Gerald Ford responded only weakly to Moscow's initiatives in Africa; nor could it do otherwise given the mood in Congress following the Vietnam War. Anxious to avoid foreign military entanglements like the Asian war that tore the country apart, Congress cut off American aid to the FNLA and UNITA, thus allowing Russia's clients to win the struggle and form a Marxist government in Angola.

Like many of its victories in the third world, the Soviet gains in Angola were not complete. They were still deprived of the naval facilities on Angola's coast they had coveted, and if anyone looked closely they would have seen the same old Western multinational corporations doing business-as-usual in the country. Nevertheless, the Soviet Union managed to acquire an important influence in a strategically located and resource-laden country previously denied to them.

There can be no doubt that developments in Africa in the latter half of the 1970s gave the Soviet leadership every reason to be geopolitically optimistic about the future. Not only were Soviet troops deployed in Ethiopia, Yemen, and Cuba, but Soviet surrogates were active in Angola, Mozambique, and elsewhere. In Angola, Mozambique, the Congo Republic, and Benin (formerly Dahomey), Marxist regimes were established with Soviet-bloc assistance. In addition, the radical regime of Col. Muammar el-Quaddafi in Libya, which had toppled a pro-Western regime in 1969, generally followed Moscow's foreign policy goals until the 1980s.

The American response to the escalating Soviet involvement in Africa underwent a gradual change in the latter half of the 1970s. The Angolan civil war produced in Washington the growing belief that the Soviet Union had reneged on detente. What alarmed Washington even more was the Soviet-Cuban collaboration in supporting liberation struggles in Africa. Behind all these anxieties lay a deeper American concern: That if the Soviet Union continued to move unimpeded through the continent, the remainder of the pro-Western regimes might be undermined and the United States might conceivably face an eventual cutoff of strategic minerals. Moreover, Russian activities in Africa attested to the transformation of the Soviet Union from a Eurasian land power to a superpower with global reach, accompanied by an awesome military establishment. The ring of states that were created to contain the Soviet Union after 1945 were now rendered almost irrelevant by a Russian colossus able to swerve around them into Africa.

The Carter administration's intention was to toughen up its foreign policy in Africa. But all it actually did was refuse to recognize the Angolan regime, and furnish a little logistical support to French and Belgian troops who were helping the Mobutu regime repel Cuban-trained rebels from Zaire. This discrepancy between Washington's intentions in Africa and its lack of will to commit any real assets to the region was most evident in its handling of the problems in East Africa.

In February 1977 Colonel Haile Mengistu came to power in Addis Ababa and Ethiopia assumed all the trappings of a Marxist people's republic. As a result of Somalian support for the independence movement in Ogaden, an Ethiopian province but ethnographically Somalian, the area tumbled into a long and vicious war. A curious exchange of partners quickly followed. Ethiopia had received support from the United States for years, but Washington was now, for ideological reasons, very cool to the Mengistu regime. When Mengistu reached out for Soviet support, Somalia, which had been aligned with the Soviet Union, now sought closer relations with the United States. In July the United States agreed to dispatch defensive arms to Somalia to sustain the guerrilla war in the Ogaden, while the Soviet Union supported Ethiopia. But when the Somalis invaded the Ogaden, Washington withdrew its promise of arms. At the same time, in November 1977 the Soviet Union and Cuba agreed to intervene with troops on the side of Ethiopia. Like its weak performance in the Angolan civil war, the Carter administration lacked the political will to match the military effort of the Russians and Cubans and so ended up backing the losing side in East Africa. Sensing weakness in Washington, Moscow then went on to extend even more support to Mengistu to crush a rebellion in Eritrea, also a province of Ethiopia.

The performance of the Carter administration in Africa was, at best, a flaccid one. By 1979 the American containment policy was in disarray and undermined even further by developments in Iran and Afghanistan.

Iran is far more important geopolitically than most countries of the Middle East. Lying between the Caspian Sea and the Persian Gulf, it borders on the Soviet Union, Turkey, Iraq, Afghanistan, and Pakistan. The Soviet interest in Iran went back to the days of the Russian empire. Its strategic location was always of geopolitical interest to Moscow, as was the number of ethnic minorities who lived on both sides of the border and who comprised much of the Islamic belt of the Soviet Union. It is oil, of course, that gives Iran its significance, supplying much of the needs of Western Europe and Japan. From the days of the tsars to Brezhnev, Moscow had viewed Iran in two ways: first in an expansionary way, as the road to warm water ports and the Indian Ocean; and second, in a defensive way, seeing it as yet another invasion route to Russia itself, and therefore a country to be neutralized into a buffer zone. The serious problems between Moscow and Teheran sprang from two sources as well: from Iran's deepening relationship with the United States, and its constant friction with Iraq; and its own aspirations as a Persian Gulf power.

Ever since 1953 when the CIA helped restore him to his throne, the Shah sought to establish a positive relationship with Moscow. But when the Soviet Union established close links with Nasser's Egypt and when a revolution broke out in Iraq in 1958, the Shah signed a mutual defense agreement with the United States in 1959, which allowed for U.S. bases in Iran. This was exactly the sort of thing that Moscow feared. The ill-feeling between Moscow and Teheran continued when Iraq became a client state of Moscow. In the perennial rivalry between Iran and Iraq that flared up intermittently in the 1960s and 1970s, and which erupted into a major war in 1980, the Soviet Union increasingly tilted toward Iraq, while trying to remain outwardly neutral.

Moscow was also alarmed at Iran's attempts to enhance its power in the Gulf.

Given the once great imperial past of Iran and its present economic importance, it was understandable that the Shah wanted to assert the independence of his country and create a new military base for a new modern greatness.

The Russians were particularly concerned by the Iranian arms buildup, which it felt was helping to destabilize the area right on Moscow's doorstep. The more it was armed by the United States the more Iran acted like an independent power in the Gulf. For example, in 1971 it unilaterally took control of some islands it had laid claim to in the Straits of Hormuz, and it took it upon itself to act as a guard at the mouth of the straits. At the same time, Teheran directed its activities against radical and national liberation groups in Oman and South Yemen and established working relationships with pro-Western Gulf states like Saudi Arabia, Bahrain, the United Arab Emirates, Qatar, and Oman. After Vietnam, Washington looked to regional powers like Iran to assist the United States in maintaining stability. At the same time, the United States hoped that Iran would function as a replacement for Great Britain as the principle peacekeeping force in the Persian Gulf.

Both the United States and the Soviet Union failed to anticipate the revolutionary wave that engulfed the country in the 1970s. It is not hard to see why. The Shah's regime seemed to be an enlightened autocracy dedicated to the modernization of his country. His economic program seemed to resolve class conflicts; there seemed to be a genuine lack of enthusiasm for socialism in a traditional Islamic society; and the Iranian Communist Party was riddled with dissension and penetrated by the Shah's secret police. Both Washington and Moscow failed to see any revolution in Iran's future.[8]

But the Shah's modernization program only served to widen the gap between rich and poor and alienate a people more committed to Islamic than to Western or secular traditions. At the same time, the Shah had been extending his dictatorial rule. He was able to keep a tight grip on the country by appointing Iran's parliament and by establishing a security police (SAVAK), which was invested with the power to arrest, imprison, torture, and sometimes even murder enemies of the regime. White House attempts to get him to soften and democratize his regime met with little response. From the point of view of the West, the Shah was the best political bet in a backward society, and since Moscow had already established client states in Iraq, Syria, and Yemen, the Western leaders allowed themselves to accept the Shah's view of himself as the bulwark of the region against the encroachments of communism.

In 1977 the opposition movement, which had been held to a murmur for years, began to roar. The pace of events quickened that year when an inflationary spiral forced the government to institute cutbacks. Sporadic guerrilla attacks throughout the country, inspired and led by the Islamic clergy, indicated that the Shah's rule was inspiring popular resistance. Moreover, when President Carter announced his new human rights policy in 1977, it was taken in Iran as a signal that Washington would no longer tolerate repression in that country and that it wanted a new government in Teheran with a broader base of support. For the first time hostile demonstrations broke out in Teheran itself, at a moment when the Shah was visiting Washington in November. A factor in the Shah's lack of vigorous response, and one hidden from public view, was his deteriorating physical condition. He was suffering from cancer and it was his wish to buy time to insure his dynasty for his son.

Slow to react to the changing climate in Iran, President Carter could only say that "Iran is an island of stability in one of the more troubled areas of the world. . . . This is a great tribute to you, your Majesty, and to your leadership and to the respect, admiration and love which your people give to you."[9] Remarks like this would cost the president dearly when the Shah's opponents eventually came to power.

Of all the opposition groups facing the Shah, the religious group was the most important in bringing about a revolutionary change in Iran. Led by the Muslem clergy inside the country, and by the Ayatollah Ruhollah Khomeini, who had been exiled in 1964 from the holy city of Qom, the Iranian people gradually learned to base their opposition to the regime on Islamic principles. Throughout 1978 fierce opposition to the regime developed among a broad-based Muslem-led coalition, which hated both the growing secularization of society, the Western-style modernization program, and the repressive measures of SAVAK.

In 1978 large demonstrations and riots shook Iran. There were over a million participants in Teheran alone. The Shah responded by declaring martial law. "Hang firm . . . count on our backing,"[10] Carter told him. At this point, the split within the White House took its toll. Brzezinski argued for a vigorous response from the Iranian army, which, he felt, should stage a coup and rule in place of the Shah. But Secretary of State Vance countered that such a plan would repudiate the president's own foreign policy, and would not work anyway. In a face-off between the two men, Vance argued that saving the Shah's throne would produce bloodshed with nothing gained. Brzezinski made sure that Vance and the president knew that "world politics was not a kindergarten."[11]

In January 1979, massive street demonstrations once more erupted in Iran and this time the Shah was forced into exile. A month later power was passed to the fundamentalist Islamic movement loyal to Khomeini. A wave of anti-Americanism now broke over the country. Pro-American elements in the army and government were purged; American holdings in the country were confiscated; and American military installations, which monitored Soviet military movements across the border, were closed down. But the most extreme form of anti-Americanism was yet to come. When the Shah was allowed into the United States to be treated for cancer in October 1979, a few days later on November 4 militant university students seized control of the American embassy in Teheran taking sixty hostages. They were eventually released on January 20, 1981, but not until the United States was thoroughly humiliated and rendered impotent, and its president voted out of office.

Throughout the Iranian crisis, the Soviet Union and the small Iranian Communist Party had played an insignificant role. Nevertheless, the anti-American character of the Iranian revolution dealt a devastating blow to Western interests in a strategically important part of the world. The United States had lost a strong ally with a large army, easy access to oceans of oil, listening posts near the enemy, and a steady customer that bought enormous amounts of American arms. Instead of a loyal island of stability, Iran was quickly transformed into a center of anti-American agitation in the Muslim world. Moreover, American prestige, which was so frayed after Vietnam, was now virtually destroyed, raising real questions among its allies about the country's ability to lead. The United States appeared to reach its nadir in the Cold War.

While the Soviet Union played little or no role in the crisis, Washington persisted in worrying about it, especially after it invaded Afghanistan. The possibility of a Soviet military intervention in Iran, a country whose oil Moscow had coveted since Stalin's day, was considered very seriously by the Carter White House.[12] In the final analysis, the crisis in the short run helped shift the correlation of forces in the Soviet Union's favor, and in the long run it produced a marked upsurge of Muslim fundamentalism, which has spread to other countries of the Middle East and that has only grown stronger with time.

As the balance of power seemed to shift against the United States, the Soviet Union embarked on its first overt military operation across its border since the Second World War.

Like Iran, Afghanistan had been the scene of intense rivalry between tsarist Russia and Great Britain before 1914, and like Iran it experienced a revolution in the late 1970s. Despite a long record of British influence in the country dating back to the nineteenth century, Afghanistan was more in the Soviet than in the Western orbit since 1945.

Afghanistan was a remote, backward rural society whose various tribal and linguistic groups were governed less by the regime in Kabul than they were by the rhythms of their Muslim faith and the authority of the village headman. In 1973 Mohammed Daud Khan seized power, abolished the monarchy, and tried to move his country away from the influence of Moscow. He thereafter modelled his regime upon that of the Shah of Iran.

In 1978 a small left-wing movement, the People's Democratic Party of Afghanistan (PDPA) overthrew Daud and took power. The secretary-general of the PDPA, Nur Mohammed Taraki, became prime minister and established an openly pro-Soviet government. In the same year, the PDPA launched a program of radical reforms involving land tenure and education, even dowries and arranged marriages. The reforms were designed to overturn traditional and economic relationships in the countryside. The PDPA soon faced a massive fundamentalist Muslim insurgency against its rule. Under this pressure, the PDPA split along ideological and tribal lines. In September 1979 Taraki was arrested by Hafizullah Amin, the leader of a more radical faction within the PDPA, and executed. With Afghanistan aflame with rebellion and with the ruling Marxist party in disarray, Amin was strongly suspected in Moscow of tilting to the United States. In December 1979, the Russians decided to intervene militarily in Afghanistan.

The Kremlin decision to intervene was not an easy one. According to Anatoly Dobrynin, the Politburo felt that the chaos in Afghanistan threatened the southern borders of the Soviet Union. "All this could be used against us by the United States, China, or Iran through the creation and support of an unfriendly Afghan regime."[13] Originally the Kremlin rejected the military option because it might wreck the preparations for the Brezhnev-Carter summit that was not far off. But by December the Politburo felt that their relations with Carter had cooled. American input was not taken that seriously anyway, since the Politburo considered Afghanistan to lay within its own sphere of influence, and security factors outweighed all other considerations. Dobrynin also adds that the KGB played a central role in the decision to intervene, and that it enjoyed strong support from the international department of the central committee of the party. Furthermore, because Brezhnev's health was so poor, the ultimate decision to intervene was made by Yuri Andropov, the KGB chief, and General Dmitrii Ustinov, the minister of defense.[14]

The Soviet invasion of Afghanistan from the Kremlin's perspective represented the logical extension of the Brezhnev Doctrine to a neighboring state whose communist regime had to be maintained against the revolt of anti-Soviet Muslim fundamentalists, despite the fact that they seemed to enjoy popular support. What the Kremlin had originally in mind in its intervention was something along the lines of a palace coup in Kabul backed up by a few Soviet tanks. What they got was their own version of Vietnam. By the spring of 1980 almost 100,000 Soviet soldiers had spilled into Afghanistan to deal with a religiously fuelled mass movement they had little chance of defeating. For almost ten years the Soviet army would remain in the country, gradually yielding the countryside to the rebels, until its only solid point of occupation was in Kabul. By the time it was over, the war had killed one million Afghan civilians and military personnel, and produced five million refugees who fled to nearby Pakistan and Iran. The war also cost the Soviet Union over 14,000 combat deaths and, according to some reports, roughly the same number of non-combat deaths. At least 37,000 Russian soldiers were wounded in the war.[15]

There was, says Anatoly Dobrynin, no geopolitical intention in the decision to invade Afghanistan, no "grand strategic design" to seize a key country and then penetrate down to the oil riches of the Middle East to alter the global balance of power once and for all. The invasion was merely "a Soviet reaction to a local situation."[16] Nevertheless, the mounting costs of the war weighed heavily in the growing economic crisis the Soviet Union found herself in the 1980s. And at the same time, with millions of Soviet Muslims susceptible to an Islamic resurgence, both the ideology of the Ayatollah Khomeini and the victorious struggle of their co-religionists in Afghanistan posed a new threat to Soviet stability. In the short run, however, the invasion of Afghanistan had the greatest impact on the relations between the Soviet Union and the United States.

After taking office in January 1977, the Carter administration sought to conclude a new strategic arms limitation agreement before Salt I expired in October. Washington was chiefly concerned with the recent Soviet development of multiple-warhead weapons and by the advanced backfire bomber, which took to the skies in 1974. On their side, the Soviets were worried about the new American cruise missile. The Salt II talks were opened in Geneva on May 18, 1977, and soon Gromyko proposed a Carter-Brezhnev summit.

During 1978 a controversy developed over the American plan to build a neutron bomb, a weapon with great destructive power but with no radioactive fallout. Moscow denounced it as an inhuman weapon and Brezhnev warned NATO not to install it in Europe. At the same time, the Russians were improving their own tactical nuclear weapons and installing SS-20 mobile multiwarhead missiles that could reach any part of Europe. By the end of 1978 the negotiators at Geneva had done their work and submitted a plan for Salt II for approval. On many of the issues in the final document, the Soviet interpretation seemed to prevail. Worried by the political fallout at home, Carter tried to force Soviet concessions on Salt II by announcing that full United States diplomatic relations would be extended to communist China and that its new leader, Deng Xiao-Ping, would visit Washington in late January 1979. Brezhnev reacted angrily at the U.S.-Chinese discussions that produced this, and he was especially critical of the joint Sino-American statement which obliquely attacked the Soviet Union for seeking "hegemony" in Asia and elsewhere. Brezhnev promptly broke off the Geneva negotiations.

The Geneva talks soon got back on track and a Salt II agreement was signed in June 1979. Salt II capped strategic nuclear launchers at 2,400 (with a future reduction to 2,250) and no more than 1,320 were to be MIRVed. But Salt II did not really deal with the backfire bomber and it allowed the Soviets to keep missiles and warheads that were much larger and had more "throw weight" than the American weapons. Like Salt I the verifications were left to each nation to conduct.

The Salt II agreement came under immediate attack from members of both parties in and outside of Congress. Much of the criticism came from the Committee on the Present Danger, which included such "hawks" as Paul Nitze, Dean Rusk, and George Schultz, the future secretary of state under President Reagan. Nitze, the original architect of NSC-#68, argued that Salt I had not produced strategic stability: "on the contrary, there is every prospect that under the terms of the Salt agreements the Soviet Union will continue to pursue a nuclear superiority that is not merely quantitative but designed to produce a theoretical war-winning capability."[17] Nitze also meant that because the verification procedures were so flimsy, that the Soviet Union could and would continue to build for superiority. They therefore advocated scrapping Salt II and enlarging the military.

The Salt II treaty therefore faced serious trouble in the U.S. Senate even before Afghanistan. Critics in the Senate reflected the same concerns that Nitze had but with one difference; they also felt that nuclear arms control should be linked to Soviet behavior on other issues, such as human rights, Africa, and the Middle East. Many senators felt that Angola and Afghanistan showed that the Soviet Union had reneged on detente. With the invasion of Afghanistan in December 1979, it became politically impossible to win ratification. In January 1980 Carter himself requested that a vote on the treaty be delayed.

President Carter seems to have been shocked by the invasion. Not only did he feel that the Russian action represented a "quantum jump in the nature of Soviet behavior," but that it posed "the most serious threat to peace since the Second

World War." In early 1980 he responded punitively to the Soviet action by imposing an embargo on grain deliveries to the Soviet Union in excess of the minimum amount specified in the 1975 agreement, restricted Soviet access to American fishing waters and high technology exports, and organized a boycott of the Olympic games held in Moscow in July 1980. At the same time he increased the U.S. defense budget by 5 percent in real terms. The Pentagon budget now jumped from $170 billion in 1976 to $197 billion in 1981.

The most dramatic step Carter took was the announcement of the Carter Doctrine in his State of the Union Address of January 1980. Anxious about a possible future Soviet thrust down to the Persian Gulf and Indian Ocean, and becoming more hard-line in his views about the Cold War, Carter declared the Persian Gulf vital to the U.S. national interest and that "an attempt by any outside force to gain control of the Persian Gulf region" would "be repelled by any means necessary, including military force."[18] U.S. military and medical aid now began flowing directly to the Afghan rebels. At the same time, Carter put together a coalition embracing Pakistan, China, Saudi Arabia, Egypt, and Britain on behalf of the Afghan resistance. Washington recognized at once that Pakistan represented the key to winning the struggle in Afghanistan. To convert Pakistan into a sanctuary for Afghan guerrillas, and an enormous arms depot to help fuel the war against the Russian occupation forces, Carter extended to Pakistan a public guarantee against any major reprisal from the Soviet Union. With this act and the supply of weapons to the guerrillas, the United States had begun to recapture the ideological and political initiative in the Cold War.

The Soviet invasion of Afghanistan and the failure of Salt II marked the definitive end of detente and Western accommodationism. It also helped usher in the last stage of the Cold War.

Notes

1. Jimmy Carter, *Keeping Faith* (New York: Bantam, 1982), 112.

2. Carter, *Keeping Faith*, 143.

3. Quoted in Robert Jay Lifton and Eric Markusen, *The Genocidal Mentality: Nazi Holocaust and Nuclear Threat* (New York: Basic Books, 1990), 31-32.

4. Quoted in Richard Hudson, "Storm over the Canal," *New York Times Magazine* (May 16, 1976), 24.

5. Zbigniew Brzezinski, *Power and Principle* (New York: Farrar, Straus and Giroux, 1985, rev. ed.), 136.

6. Quoted in William B. Quandt, *Peace Process* (Washington, D.C.: Brookings Institution, 1993), 268.

7. Richard Pipes, *U.S.-Soviet Relations in the Era of Détente* (Boulder, Colo.: Westview Press, 1981), 187-88.

8. Galia Golan, *Soviet Policies in the Middle East: From World War II to Gorbachev* (Cambridge: Cambridge University Press, 1990), 185.

9. Quoted in Cyrus Vance, *Hard Choices* (New York: Simon and Schuster, 1983), 323.

10. Jimmy Carter, *Keeping Faith*, 439.

11. Brzezinski, *Power and Principle*, 380.

12. Brzezinski, *Power and Principle*, 451-52.

13. Anatoly Dobrynin, *In Confidence* (New York: Random House, 1995), 438.

14. Dobrynin, *In Confidence*, 436, 438.

15. Marshall Goldman, *What Went Wrong with Perestroika* (New York: Norton, 1992), 198.

16. Dobrynin, *In Confidence*, 441.

17. Paul Nitze, "Assuring Strategic Stability in an Era of Détente," *Foreign Affairs* 54, no. 2 (January 1976), 207.

18. Quoted in Thomas Hammond, *Red Flag over Afghanistan* (Boulder, Colo.: Westview Press, 1984), 122.

21

The Crisis of Communism

Communism never had much time to sink deep roots in Eastern Europe. In a rather natural way it began to unravel after Stalin's death in 1953. Lescek Kolakowski, the Polish philosopher and one of the most important dissidents in the Soviet bloc, has called attention to this in his book *Main Currents of Marxism*:

> On Stalin's death the Soviet system changed from a personal tyranny to that of an oligarchy. From the point of view of state omnipotence this is a less effective system; it does not, however, amount to de-Stalinization but to an ailing form of Stalinism.[1]

The undermining of communism as an ideology began officially with Khrushchev's dramatic post-mortem of Stalinism in 1956. His speech to the Twentieth Communist Party Congress was an open admission of serious crimes having been perpetrated in the name of Marxism-Leninism. The ideology, after all, had always been used to justify control of Soviet society by the party. By admitting that the previous generation was full of political murders, deceit, and massive suppression, the party lost any credibility it may have had.

Being a Stalinist apparatchik himself, Khrushchev pulled back from dismantling the key institutions that formed the backbone of Soviet communism. His reforms in the end were half-hearted and only served to inspire serious revolts within the Soviet bloc. From 1956 the old Stalinist leaders were on the defensive against nationalistic and liberal forces both within and outside their own ranks. What the revolutions of 1956 and the Prague Spring of 1968 foreshadowed was the disintegration of the Soviet bloc and even of the Soviet Union. The lesson of these crises, which the Kremlin failed to learn, was that, when encouraged directly or indirectly, the forces of nationalism and democracy could turn into a tide that had the potential of sweeping away the last of the great empires.

There was, of course, a certain inevitability about the transformation of Marxism-Leninism as a radical ideology. When it triumphed in the Soviet Union in the early 1920s its spokesmen promised to overturn the old world and replace it with a utopian society of plenty and social justice. And that transition from one kind of society to a better one was to be forged by a party whose legitimacy was protected by the iron "laws" of history. It was the revolutionary character of Soviet culture and the idealized image of the world as it ought to be that attracted so many artists and writers in the 1920s. But it seems to be the fate of radical movements that when they come to power and rule for long without really remaking the world they undergo a process of de-radicalization. They seem to give up their messianic obsessions and transform their regimes into conservative dictatorships, still working for social change but no longer in a radical way.[2]

What the communist regimes in Eastern Europe failed to do was change the aspirations and attitudes of their citizens—people still wanted freedom, national independence, and a better material life. The Communist parties promised these things but failed to secure a decent and dignified existence for their people. This discrepancy between the regime's rhetoric and its performance was clear by the Prague Spring of 1968. The destruction of the Dubcek government dealt a severe blow to communism in Eastern Europe. It seemed to destroy any vestige of belief that socialism could evolve into anything resembling a human face. Indeed, there had been a tendency for fifty years among the European intelligentsia to accept the Soviet Union at face value—to accept what it said about its accomplishments, economically, socially, and politically. The Soviet Union was always discussed dialectically by intellectuals of the left and measured not by its achievements and failures as much as by its promises. Especially in the West, they were extremely reluctant to be critical of the failures and inadequacies of communist totalitarianism lest it benefit their enemies on the right. But in Eastern Europe most, if not all, the intellectuals were by Brezhnev's era hostile to the communist regime. They were certainly the first group in society to depart from the official view of communism's performance.[3]

The intellectuals' engagement with the world has always been a problem for entrenched regimes, precisely because as a group they are intrinsically subversive. For regimes based on an ideology this is doubly so, since its spokesmen understand that ideas have consequences touching and shaping lives in ways that we may scarcely realize. Certainly since the Enlightenment philosophes of the eighteenth century, intellectuals have held the social and political systems they have lived under up to examination, found them wanting, and constantly demanded change. The postwar communist regimes never really trusted intellectuals, even when they willingly conformed to the new orthodoxy. The leadership placed its hope in the eventual emergence of an intellectual class that not only conformed to the system but were true believers in it. That hope was never realized. Instead, from the explosive events of the 1950s there emerged an ideological crisis in the communist world, a belief that communist regimes could not rely on a real legitimacy in the traditional sense and that the whole Soviet experience should be reconsidered.

In spearheading what amounted to an ethical revolution in Eastern Europe, intellectuals began by challenging the Communist Party's monopoly of truth. From there they moved on to question the validity of Marxism-Leninism itself. For example, for Vaclev Havel, the dissident Czech writer and future president of his country, living in truth was the only human antidote to the stifling demands of communist totalitarianism. According to the Polish poet, Antoni Slonimski, "only a true democratization of public life, restoration of public opinion, and the returns from fideism to rational and unfettered thought can save us from Caesarism."[4] There was in these criticisms the general feeling that communism was inherently incapable of reforming itself. "There is no such thing as nontotalitarian ruling Communism," wrote the Polish dissident, Adam Michnik. "It either becomes totalitarian or it ceases to be Communism."[5] It was apparent to Lescek Kolakowski, who in many ways best represents his generation's transition from Marxism to a sweeping criticism of its tenets, that as early as the 1950s the ideology could no longer mobilize the population:

> Marxism both as an ideology and as a philosophy has become completely irrelevant. . . . Even the rulers have largely abandoned this notion and even its phrases. They no longer use Marxist phraseology, not even the Communists. They use it at most in ceremonial cases. When the Polish government wants to enter into any sort of communication with the public, it no longer employs sweet phrases about the glorious future of communism or about Marxist-Leninist truths, because it knows that such phrases cannot excite anyone. They now refer instead to so called geo-political arguments. This means that they want to persuade people that where we are now we cannot survive without the great Soviet Union, which is our brother; we cannot survive without the Soviet fraternal alliance and fraternal help, because we are surrounded by enemies and the like.[6]

At the same time, it was clear that Soviet troops were stationed throughout Eastern Europe to prevent the collapse of what Michnik called "the barren twilight of the old totalitarian dictatorship."

This growing crisis of confidence and the development of a "true counterculture of resistance"[7] was by no means confined to a small group of intellectuals and prominent dissidents inspired by the Helsinki Accords. Criticism of the regime and its ideological bases took place against the background of marked improvements in the educational level of the population, along with increasing cultural contacts with the West—either through the media or through travel abroad. "A new generation was coming up," writes Georgi Arbatov, the top Soviet expert on U.S. affairs in the 1980s, "literate, curious, and not as scared as its parents."[8] By the beginning of the Brezhnev era in 1972, genuine belief in the communist system had all but died in the Soviet Union and was replaced by popular cynicism and resentment. And it was this to which dissidents increasingly gave intellectual expression.

This developing crisis of confidence in the communist system also took place against a growing economic crisis. The Brezhnev years were not only marred by the absence of political idealism but also by low growth rates. This was true of all vital sectors of the economy. For example, agricultural production fell far short of the state targets. Partly because of climactic reasons but also due to the extremely inefficient and archaic distribution system, which often prevented agricultural production from reaching its markets, Soviet production sagged dramatically in the

1960s, and only got worse in the 1970s and 1980s. When it did the Kremlin was forced to turn to the West annually for huge grain imports. And all of this despite the fact that by 1970 the Soviet Union was devoting almost one-fourth of its total economic investment to agriculture. Furthermore, state subsidies rose as the collective farms were paid more for what they sold to the state, while retail prices were prevented from rising so as to help consumers. In the 1930s agriculture was made to produce the needed capital for industrialization; now it only became a huge burden on the economy. This inability of the Soviet Union to produce enough food for its population on a regular basis was a fundamental failure in economic policy.

The industrial performance was not much better. With the Seven-Year Plan of 1959 the Kremlin placed its emphasis on energy (especially oil, electricity, and natural gas) and chemicals. But too much capital needed to support this program was siphoned off to support the space race with the United States. Those funds helped to produce the first manned space flight in 1961, but the price was too high. The command economy, though successful in producing missiles, planes, and tanks, could not compete with the postwar shift in high technologies and mass consumer goods produced so effectively in small countries but not in the Soviet Union. The shortcomings in this area of the economy became especially acute in the 1980s.

The other thing that drained the country was the military expansion after Khrushchev's removal in 1964. This expansion, historically the largest peacetime program of its kind, seemed to have a momentum of its own and was almost totally unrelated to the external threat in the 1970s. The military's argument that there was an external danger from the United States and China convinced Brezhnev of the necessity of the buildup. In the military expansion it was the case of the defense strategy that determined the availability of funds, not the other way around. It was, according to Georgi Arbatov, the growing military influence in policy making that contributed to the debacle in Afghanistan in the 1980s and the killing of detente. "The military leaders of the time," he writes, "had a monopoly on the leadership's ear."[9]

Military expansion also distorted industrial production. Nearly half the output of the Soviet Union's machine industries went to feed the military machine. It has been variously estimated that at its peak spending on the military amounted to at least 25 percent of GNP (the United States spent six percent). To add to this the Soviet Union in the latter half of the 1970s began deploying new medium-range missiles (the SS-20s) in Europe. Not only was the scheme excessively costly, but it also served to unify NATO, which now took a more militant stand toward the Soviet Union. In short, the arms expansion was economically and politically disastrous. It only served to bankrupt the nation and undermine any trust the Kremlin had built up in the West since the 1960s.

The economy was, then, the larger victim. And yet among the leadership there was no sense of an approaching crisis. According to Arbatov, the most important and fundamental economic issues were rarely raised in the Politburo.[10] To maintain the popularity of the Communist Party the leadership sought to guarantee full employment and low prices regardless of the effect on output and the quality of goods produced. Factories were kept running even when the demand for their products disappeared. At the same time, the price of bread remained at the 1952 level and rents at the 1928 level. Housing, healthcare, and education were highly underfunded, while the *Nomenklatura* were left to enjoy their own special schools, hospitals and food stores.

One of the basic weaknesses of the economic system was its planning structure. The imposition of an overall plan by the State Planning Commission (Gosplan) with specific targets and quotas that coordinated the production of roughly four million different products in 50,000 factories produced only inefficiencies, unneeded and inferior products, and chaos. Factory workers lacked incentives to work ("they pretend to pay us, we pretend to work"), and shortages of essential commodities became more acute as queues at stores became longer. Sometime after 1975 the Soviet Union slipped into a position of zero growth. Grain production in 1978 was 237 million tons but then dropped precipitously to 179 million tons in 1979, seriously affecting the whole economy. The quality of life declined dramatically as well. Infant mortality began to rise and life expectancy declined from sixty-six years in 1965 to sixty-four. At the same time, chronic alcoholism rose among working-class males from 3.5 percent during the 1920s to 37 percent in the late 1970s. Between 1973 and 1983 crime nearly doubled with crimes of violence rising 58 percent. At least one-third of the Soviet people lived below the poverty line.[11] Progressively ill, Brezhnev was unable (and some would say unwilling) to address the problems of long-term restructuring. Unable to cope with even the day-to-day problems, he nevertheless clung stubbornly to power until his death in 1982. Meanwhile, the problems in Russian society and economy were allowed to deepen.

After the Yom Kippur War of 1973 and the formation of OPEC, the great oil cartel, the West had to deal with higher oil prices, shortages, and irregular deliveries. The impact on the Soviet Union was more positive. Higher oil prices coincided with the Soviet development of the Tyumen oil and gas fields in western Siberia. In the short term this helped save the Soviet economy as oil became the country's major source of foreign exchange. Its sales to the West allowed the Soviet Union to survive without substantial foreign trade. In fact, it accounted for most of the growth of the Soviet economy into the 1980s.

By the time Brezhnev died in 1982 the Soviet Union gave every indication that it was too backward to compete with the rest of the world. The feeling of drift and stagnation became more pronounced as did a certain sense of hopelessness. The Soviet Union stood on the brink of economic disaster.

As the Soviet Union unravelled economically and politically its bloc partners in Eastern Europe experienced a similar decline. Since they were locked into the same Stalinist economic model they were plagued by the same set of problems: gross mismanagement, antiquated equipment, poor quality controls, and limited opportunities for foreign trade. The result was also the same: declining industrial and agricultural production leading to near negative growth throughout the region. In the 1970s, as a way to stave off the crisis, bloc leaders borrowed heavily from the West to modernize their industries. But the centralized economic systems proved unable to adapt Western technology efficiently. All too often the money went for higher wages. As a result the bloc countries only succeeded in building up an enormous burden of indebtedness to Western banks. Like the Soviet Union, the attempts of bloc regimes to deal with their outstanding problems led to dramatic results.[12]

Poland was the Soviet Union's largest and most important satellite and it was there that communist rule was especially fragile. On December 12, 1970, Wladyslaw Gomulka introduced an austerity program to stave off the growing economic crisis. It called for an almost 20 percent increase in prices and offered new incentives to boost production. Many Poles, however, saw it merely as a scheme to make them work harder. Two days later workers in the Baltic Sea ports of Gdansk, Gydnia, and Sopot went on strike against the increases and attempted to burn down the regional Communist Party headquarters. Clashes with the police followed in which many workers were killed. The violence spread to other cities as the demonstrations grew larger. In an attempt to restore order, and worried about the danger of Soviet intervention, the Communist Party at a special meeting on December 20 deposed Gomulka and replaced him with Edward Gierek.[13] The episode was important because industrial workers had succeeded in reversing a Communist Party reform program and removing its leader.

It was Gierek's hope that he could significantly boost the Polish economy by floating loans in the West and investing them in the necessary infrastructure. In the 1970s, unable to do anything about lagging Eastern European growth but nervous about radical reforms, Moscow encouraged such links with the West. However, the loans were actually used to placate the workers through wage increases and a slight rise in the standard of living. In 1976 Gierek raised the prices on food and agricultural products, an increase even larger than the one in 1970. Once again the workers reacted angrily. There were demonstrations in many factories and there was more violence, and once again the government backed down and withdrew the price increases. But out of the rioting of 1976 emerged the first real organized opposition to the Polish government—the Workers Defense Committee, known as KOR.

KOR was set up by a group of dissident intellectuals to extend legal and material assistance to the families of workers injured or arrested during the events of 1976. Aware of their growing power, workers and intellectuals began to organize and petition the government for redress of grievances associated with violations of the rule of law and civil rights. This alliance helped to convert dissent into political power. The wildcat strikes of 1970 and 1976 had a dramatic impact but they were only of temporary importance. Real change would arise when labor unrest was allied with broader social forces. KOR demanded that fired workers be reinstated and imprisoned workers be amnestied. In 1978 KOR published a direct appeal to the Polish nation in an attempt to explain how far the breakdown of socialism had come. The authorities, it claimed, feared society and therefore were unable to give it the truth of the situation. The "Appeal of Society," as it was called, drew attention to the economic shortages, the standing in food lines, the poor state of health services, the insufficient nutrition, the poor hospital services for the people but the special facilities for party dignitaries, the deepening crisis in agriculture, the lack of coal, the violations of the rule of law, the limitations on personal freedom, the censorship, and the low state of culture, all of which threatened the country's national and cultural identity.[14] Influential members of the movement like Jacek Kuron and Adam Michnik drew attention to a remarkable development that the Communist Party was not cognizant of: the gradual coming together of the Roman Catholic Church and its supporters with former communist activists and their willingness to form a common front against the communist system and adopt an evolutionary, rather than a revolutionary, approach to social change.[15]

In the middle of this political and social ferment when Poland's indebtedness swelled and poverty became widespread, and when the country reached a situation of negative growth, Karol Woytyla was elected the first Polish Pope in the history of the Roman Catholic Church (October 16, 1978).

In 1979 Pope John Paul II paid a nine-day visit to his native land in which he spoke in six cities. Thirteen million Poles—a third of the population—turned out to hear him. In his main speech in Victory Square, Warsaw, on June 2, 1979, he likened himself to Saint Peter travelling from Jerusalem to Rome (presumably to convert the barbarians). He referred to Saint Stanislaus, the Polish patron saint—a symbol of resistance to the excesses of secular power. He called upon Poland to bear witness and he reminded his audience that their country was inseparable from the church. Along with his references to history—namely the Warsaw Rising of 1944 and other battlefields of the Second World War—he sought to evoke a common sense of patriotism in a religious direction. He made it abundantly clear that the church had deep roots in Poland. By implication, he was saying that the Communist Party did not.[16] The visit certainly produced what one observer called a "psychological earthquake."

The Papal visit had clearly revealed the power of the church in Poland. It also succeeded in raising the hopes of the Polish clergy and helped firm up their resolve to struggle with the regime. At the same time, it strengthened nationalism among all Polish classes and helped create the psychological conditions within which the Solidarity trade union emerged a year later.

On July 1, 1980, the Polish government raised meat prices by as much as 60 percent. Almost immediately workers formed representative committees and went on strike. By August some 640,000 were involved. In that month workers in the Lenin Shipyard of Gdansk not only demanded wage increases and additional benefits, but they also demanded the democratization of Polish society, the lifting of restrictions on the church, and they claimed the right to organize an independent trade union. Creating an independent trade union was unprecedented in a communist country. Once the union was created, it quickly expanded to ten million members by 1981. The name chosen for the union, Solidarity, was significant; it seemed to promise the opposite of the atomized society of individuals created by communism, a new society of millions of free people linked together in the fraternal bonds of community. Lech Walesa emerged as the union's leader and opened negotiations with the government. With the economy in a deepening crisis and faced with a genuine proletarian revolution, the government appeared on the verge of collapse and ready to grant dramatic concessions.

In the Gdansk Agreement of August 31, 1980, the government recognized the legitimacy of Solidarity. Poland thus became the first communist-led polity to recognize an independent trade union. The government also promised to relax the censorship and remove incompetent managers from factories. Solidarity at this point enjoyed the solid backing of the country's intellectuals and the Catholic Church.

The Soviet response to the Gdansk Agreement was predictably blinkered and hostile. Moscow was extremely unhappy with the agreement since it feared that if left unchecked it could lead to a Polish defection from the Warsaw Pact. They were particularly worried by a potentially revolutionary situation in which a powerful worker's body might play a role beyond Communist Party control.

In early December the Warsaw Pact convened in an emergency meeting in Moscow and insisted that Poland must remain a socialist country. A Soviet intervention on the scale of 1968 seemed imminent, as the Kremlin mobilized thousands of troops for just such a contingency. The Polish General Staff certainly believed in its imminence and apparently informed Moscow that a Soviet invasion would be resisted by the Polish army. President Carter added his own voice to the warnings given to the Kremlin:

> We were monitoring Soviet military preparations very closely. Fifteen or twenty divisions were ready to move. . . . The Soviets were surveying invasion routes, had set up an elaborate communications system throughout Poland . . . and were holding their military forces in a high state of readiness. . . . I sent Brezhnev a direct message warning of the serious consequences of a Soviet move into Poland, and let him know more indirectly that we would move to transfer advanced weaponry to China.[17]

Soviet fears about developments in Poland only increased when Solidarity called for self-management in industry and the democratization of political life. By early 1981 a series of Polish premiers sought unsuccessfully to cope with the growing crisis, as dissent grew in every sector of society. In February the Communist Party turned almost desperately to the defense minister, General Vojtech Jaruzelski, and named him prime minister. In September Solidarity held its first national congress and raised its demands. Now it called for free parliamentary elections and worker's self-management. When the government refused to accept these demands, the union called for a general strike and the overthrow of communism. Solidarity went so far as to issue an open letter urging workers all over the communist bloc to throw off the yoke of communist rule and form their own independent labor unions. Jaruzelski now became first secretary of the Communist Party. With all the top posts in Poland now in his hands, he surprised everyone on December 13, 1981, when he declared martial law, arrested thousands of Solidarity members, and forced thousands more underground. There seems to have been in Jaruzelski's action an attempt to keep the Soviet Union from trying to restore order in Poland itself. In an address to the nation on Christmas Eve he referred to the need to choose between "a greater and a lesser evil." With the declaration of martial law Jaruzelski announced that he would rule through a "Military Council for National Salvation."

The events in Poland during the period 1979 to 1981 indicated that the Communist Party as an institution, like the monarchies of the old regime, could not run a modern state. Indeed, for the first time something like a military junta had taken power in a communist state and completely superseded the party. Here was the first real sign that communism would collapse in the Soviet bloc.

Like Poland, Hungary was in the forefront of change and managed to give Moscow almost as much cause for alarm. After the 1956 revolution the regime of Janos Kadar steadily built up its policy of economic reform and open discussion. The economic reform was called the New Economic Mechanism and it included the weakening of central planning and the encouragement of private enterprise in service industries and the end of collectivization in agriculture. A number of large state enterprises were allowed to break up. The mixed economy that resulted was often referred to as "goulash communism." Hungary's commercial contacts with the West were substantial and in 1973 it acceded to the GATT agreement. Five years later it was granted "most favored nation" trading status by the United States and in 1982 it joined the World Bank and the IMF. Like other Eastern European countries, Hungary borrowed heavily from Western banks to fuel its expansion and failed to manage its debt properly. By the early 1980s its economic growth slowed substantially and living standards declined.

The steady erosion of faith in the communist system continued all over the bloc. In Czechoslovakia the regime of Gustave Husak came to power with the crushing of the Prague Spring in 1968. Like Kadar in Hungary, he tried to restore stability and win support for the regime by improving conditions for consumers. In January 1977 300 Czech intellectuals circulated a petition, "Charter 77," which condemned the regime. The group was suppressed but its leaders were not killed.[18] Husak was loyal to Moscow but anti-Stalinist. At the same time, he had some success establishing trade links with the West but the economy, like the others in the region, slowed down in the early 1980s. This was primarily due to the rising cost of energy. Czechoslovakia's chief source of supply for oil was the Soviet Union, which had doubled its price in that decade.

Among the nations of the Soviet bloc Romania was ruled by the most Stalinist regime of all and pursued the most independent foreign policy of all. The Ceausescu regime made clear its condemnation of the Soviet Union's invasion of Czechoslovakia in 1968 and its intervention in Afghanistan in 1979. In the hope of securing large development loans from the United States it forged close relations with its Western neighbors and like Hungary it became a member of GATT and the IMF. The American and Romanian leadership exchanged visits and forged a reasonably cordial relationship. Moscow allowed these contacts because it felt that they posed no long-range threat to Soviet hegemony in Eastern Europe. Romania was not as strategically important as, for example, Poland, and Moscow could take some comfort in the fact that Ceausescu had crushed almost every vestige of reformist tendencies in his country. Unlike the other countries in the bloc, the Romanian dictatorship was an intensely personal one, and repression was a hallmark of the regime. Family members were appointed to powerful state positions while Ceausescu's son was groomed to succeed his father. Like the other bloc states Romania tried desperately to liquidate its foreign debt. To do this it adopted the most severe austerity measures in Europe to reduce imports and domestic consumption and at the same time sell its oil and food abroad. The result was the most appalling working conditions in the region and its most hideous dictatorship.

If Romania was the most independent of the bloc states, Bulgaria was the most slavishly docile. Like most of its bloc partners it made an attempt to decentralize its economy in the 1960s and borrowed heavily from Western banks to promote economic development. By the 1980s it had only succeeded in rolling up a huge debt as reform came to an end. By mid-decade the regime of Todor Zhivkov seems only to have accomplished the persecution of its large Turkish minority. It forbade the use of the Turkish language in the media and insisted that Turkish citizens adopt Bulgarian names. The reaction was an angry one and the army had to be called in to restore order.

Finally, of all of the bloc states the German Democratic Republic (GDR) had the unique problem of legitimacy and identity. As events would subsequently prove, the GDR was not in the final analysis a viable state. The regime of Erich Honecker had since 1976 sought to overcome this by clinging desperately to its close association with the Soviet Union on whose bayonets it relied for survival, and by working hard for economic progress.

The GDR went against the Soviet bloc trend of decentralizing its economy. Instead it increased its contacts with COMECON and soon became Moscow's main trading partner. There was certainly growth in the 1970s and the GDR enjoyed a relatively decent standard of living in Soviet-bloc terms, but was clearly backward as an economy and society when compared to West Germany. In the early 1980s Honecker floated large loans in West Germany, but contacts like this with the West only produced greater indebtedness, especially when oil prices rose. The Soviet Union was its main supplier of raw materials and, when the price of oil rose in the 1980s, the trade deficit rose as the retail trade slowed.[19]

Like all the satellites the GDR had become a burden on the Soviet Union. Moscow had found itself impotent to solve the region's problem of economic inertia especially since it could not solve its own. For years it had subsidized the area with cheap oil and raw materials and bore the lion's share of defense spending to maintain the Warsaw Pact. All Moscow had accomplished was the draining of the Soviet treasury. Clearly, the burdens of empire had succeeded in hastening Soviet decline.

Notes

1. Leszak Kolakowski, *Main Currents of Marxism*, Vol. 3 (New York: Oxford University Press, 1980), 456.

2. Richard Lowenthal, *World Communism: The Disintegration of a Secular Faith* (New York: Oxford University Press, 1966), 39-69.

3. Abbott Gleason, *Totalitarianism: The Inner History of the Cold War* (New York: Oxford University Press, 1995).

4. Quoted in Paul E. Zinner, ed., *National Communism and Popular Revolt in Eastern Europe* (New York: Columbia University Press, 1956), 54.

5. Adam Michnik, *Letters from Prison and Other Essays* (Berkeley: University of California Press, 1986), 47.

6. Quoted in Vladimir Tismaneanu, *The Crisis of Marxist Ideology in Eastern Europe: The Poverty of Utopia* (London and New York: Routledge, 1988), 115.

7. Tismaneanu, *Marxist Ideology*, 217.

8. Georgi Arbatov, *The System: An Insider's Life in Soviet Politics* (New York: Random House, 1993), 33.

9. Arbatov, *The System*, 195.

10. Arbatov, *The System*, 208.

11. Walter Laqueur, *The Dream That Failed: Reflections on the Soviet Union* (New York: Oxford University Press, 1994), 56, 60-61, 64.

12. Karen Dawisha, *Eastern Europe, Gorbachev, and Reform: The Great Challenge*, second edition (Cambridge: Cambridge University Press, 1990), 169-73.

13. Leslie Holmes, *Politics in the Communist World* (Oxford: Clarendon Press, 1986), 303-5.

14. Jan Josef Lipski, *Kor: A History of the Workers' Defense Committee in Poland* (Berkeley: University of California Press, 1985), 474-79.

15. Gleason, *Totalitarianism*, 178-79.

16. Gale Stokes, ed., *From Stalinism to Pluralism: A Documentary History of Eastern Europe since 1945* (New York: Oxford University Press, 1991), 200-3.

17. Jimmy Carter, *Keeping Faith: Memoirs of a President* (New York: Bantam, 1982), 584-85.

18. Janusz Bugajski, *Czechoslovakia: Charter 77's Decade of Dissent* (New York: Praeger, 1987), 8-51.

19. Mike Dennis, *German Democratic Republic: Politics, Economics and Society* (London: Pinter, 1988).

22

The Struggle to Reform the Soviet Union

When Leonid Brezhnev died in 1982 the Soviet Union had already experienced almost a generation of economic decline. The moment called for vigorous leadership as well as national renewal. All strata of Soviet society therefore expected a great deal from Yuri Andropov when he took over the reins of power that same year. Like other conservatives within the Communist Party, however, he favored a cautious and disciplined approach to reform. He therefore began by launching a campaign against corruption so endemic throughout Soviet society and by favoring efficiency drives in the economy. His approach to changes in the price structure and the introduction of market methods was extremely cautious because the party leadership felt that the Soviet people would never tolerate radical changes that called upon them to make important sacrifices. He certainly had doubts about his country's military programs but he shied away from confrontation with the military-industrial complex.

Casting its shadow over the whole process of reform from the beginning was the Communist Party, which insisted on being involved in all aspects of any program of change. It was clear from 1982 on that the party was not prepared to accept a reduction of its own power. This was another reason for Andropov's very conservative approach to reform. Indeed, it raised the whole question of whether the communist system could be reformed at all. Years of steep economic decline demonstrated that the party as an institution had stumbled badly in the running of a modern state. Andropov never really faced this squarely, and by his death two years later it seemed clear that the regime was its own worst enemy.

In his brief time as party leader, Andropov had accomplished very little. He was replaced by yet another caretaker premier, Konstantin Chernenko, who was already ailing when he assumed office and who died only a year later in 1985. In that year Mikhail Gorbachev, a protégé of Andropov, became the fourth secretary-general of the Communist Party to hold office in less than three years. Gorbachev was a good deal younger than his predecessors (he was fifty-four in 1985). He had spent his whole mature life in the Communist Party, which he had joined at the age of twenty-one. He had spent the next thirty-three years working his way up the bureaucratic ladder to finally reach power in 1985. For this reason he started out believing that a major reform effort could be made using the party cadres to do so.

When Gorbachev took over the leadership of the Soviet Union in March 1985 there had been virtually no economic growth since 1978. When his friend Edvard Shevardnadze confided to him that "everything's rotten. It has to be changed," Gorbachev could only agree.[1] He began by speaking very candidly about the shortcomings of Soviet production, the shortages of consumer goods, and the decline of living standards. He understood that throughout its long history Russia had been a country with a mission; but he also understood that for most of that time Russia lagged behind economic developments elsewhere and that its history had been checkered by some enormous efforts to catch up with the West. Once again, Russia found herself in a position of economic inferiority trying to pull abreast of rivals who for long had been on the cutting edge of progress.

The program of economic recovery that Gorbachev envisaged would modernize the Soviet Union was to be called *perestroika*, or restructuring. *Perestroika* was designed to cure the economic inertia, overhaul the bureaucracy, the Communist Party, and even the military, and so make the country more competitive. The restructuring of the Soviet economy came to include a partial reduction of the central planning system, the introduction of market mechanisms, an emphasis on quality, the more efficient employment of labor, and the infusion of new investment and technologies into industry. Gorbachev began to introduce these changes with his first package of reforms in January 1988. It included a plan that tried to get state enterprises to stand on their own economic feet and pay their own way. If they failed to "self-finance" themselves, these enterprises would be merged with healthier ones or simply closed. The same reform sought to draw the workers into the process by introducing elections in factories for managerial positions. These measures, however, were too contradictory and somewhat incoherent. The reforms continued to operate under a centralized planning system and no one had the courage to radically change the price system without which market forces could not operate. Indeed, the reluctance to tamper with the price structure was symptomatic of *perestroika*'s lack of results from the beginning. For fifty years, more than 25 million prices had been set by the Soviet economic bureaucracies. Rents, for example, had been set at the end of N.E.P. in 1928 and had not been raised since. Neither was the price of bread which had been set in 1954 and meat prices in 1962. *Perestroika* seemed to be "written on the run."[2]

The problem of economic reform was compounded by the fact that Gorbachev's knowledge of economics was very weak. Reluctant to accomplish the transition from socialism to capitalism, he opted instead, he once told George Bush, for a socialism modelled on the Swedish economy. Bush had to inform him that Sweden was a capitalist country with an elaborate welfare system. At one point in their conversation, Gorbachev insisted that there was no private property in the United States. "Why," he said, "some of your firms have as many as twenty thousand shareholders."[3]

From the beginning, *perestroika* was linked to political reforms. Central to this was the introduction of *glasnost*, a policy which was meant to encourage more openness and self-criticism in Soviet society. For this reason he lifted the censorship and liberated the Soviet media and encouraged widespread criticism of Stalinism. He viewed the intelligentsia, who were the chief benefactors of this change, as primarily his strongest allies in reforming the country.

The pressing need for *glasnost* was underlined during the Chernobyl nuclear plant catastrophe in 1986, when bureaucratic paranoia and secrecy delayed the dissemination of vital information about the accident, with severe consequences for people living in the vicinity of the plant. After Chernobyl a torrent of criticism was directed toward the party, which had mishandled the emergency so badly; and even Marxism-Leninism drew strong criticism from younger party members with some of their sharper attacks reserved for Politburo members and their policies.

Gorbachev wanted to preserve the Soviet Union but he never really understood just how far his own reforming logic would take him. He believed that *glasnost*, even when extended to the full, was compatible with a communist society. Along with this mistaken notion went an even bigger one: his confident belief that the communist system could be reformed without threatening its very existence. An early sign that he was striking out on a very dangerous path came as early as December 1986, when *glasnost* was followed by riots in Kazakhstan, and then again in 1988 when there were bloody clashes between Armenians and Azerbaijanis. He at first simply did not understand that certain groups would, if given a chance, take advantage of his reforms. Moreover, the reforms not only served to produce chaos in the country but they also produced a backlash against them among bureaucrats, factory managers, the KGB, and the military. These groups felt that *perestroika* and *glasnost* threatened both their vested interests and the unity of the Soviet empire. Gorbachev correctly saw them as feudal baronies entrenched within the Stalinist system and therefore obstacles to reform and change. Political camps soon arose and in the fall of 1987 one of Gorbachev's erstwhile allies, Boris Yeltsin, quit the Politburo after denouncing *perestroika* as being inadequate for real reform. His daring inspired others to organize in opposition to the crumbling orthodoxy. At this point there seemed to be two major points of view (other than Gorbachev's) about the future of reform. One was the conservative view of gradual and disciplined reform that did not undermine the predominance of the Communist Party, and which was associated with the political figures of Egor Ligachev and Viktor Chebrikov; the other was the liberal view which argued for a headlong plunge into reform and that hoped to involve the masses more directly in the politics of the movement for change, and which expected nothing from the Communist Party. This "camp" was associated with the figure of Boris Yeltsin. Gorbachev at first used an incident to move against his conservative opposition.

On May 29, 1987, a small one-engine plane flown by an amateur German pilot violated Soviet airspace, flew by the Kremlin, and made a safe landing in Red Square. The Russian radar defense network had been unable to detect his aircraft and the Defense Ministry was unable to explain why. The next day Gorbachev called an urgent meeting of the Politburo and demanded an explanation. Both Defense Minister Sergei Sokolov and his deputy, General Ivan Lushev, admitted to a weakness in the defense system—the system could not handle low-altitude targets and there was a lack of coordination and cooperation among the defense crews. Seizing the opportunity to remove serious rivals, Gorbachev directed his attention to the army leadership who had proven themselves hostile toward *perestroika* and the "new thinking" and urged them to get on the side of reform. He demanded a change in the leadership "to increase the military establishment's sense of political responsibility," and he called for Sokolov's resignation. This was given immediately and, as prearranged, he was replaced a few minutes later by the more pliant General Dimitri Yazov. Even more important for Gorbachev, Sokolov was followed into retirement by roughly 100 generals and colonels who had opposed the direction in which Gorbachev was taking the country.[4] Later in 1988, with the army under his control, he was able to get the Politburo to reduce the armed forces by half a million men. At the same time, in April 1988 he made the decision to pull the Soviet army out of Afghanistan.

Having gained control of the military establishment, Gorbachev then moved against the other obstacle to reform, the party apparatus. Once he realized that the success of *perestroika* depended not on the rejuvenation of the party, but on its removal from any significant role in the state, he gradually reduced its power between 1986 and 1990 and, by so doing, blindly hastened the process of political disintegration of his country.

In July 1986 the Communist Party Central Committee allowed local parliaments to take more responsibility, and a year later the first experimental multi-candidate elections were held in some local districts. In the summer of 1988 Gorbachev assembled a special party conference to discuss this and other reforms. The Soviet people had not heard such heated discussions and open disagreements like these since the 1920s. According to Robert V. Daniels the confrontation resembled the nineteenth-century debates between Westerners and Slavophils:

> It was . . . an epochal confrontation between two political cultures contending for the future of Soviet Russia. One was the old secretive, conspiratorial, xenophobic Muscovite political culture shared by the Stalinist bureaucracy and the peasantry from which it stemmed. The other was the political culture embodied in the Westernized intelligentsia since the eighteenth century, committed to a free, rational, and cosmopolitan public life. It was to this culture that Gorbachev linked his fate.[5]

The debates were aired in the media in some detail and for the first time the Soviet people understood the full extent of the economic crisis.

The conference of 1988 decided on a whole range of political reforms. What it basically attempted to do was reject the political system by shifting power from the central bodies of the Communist Party to regional governments over which the party was to have limited influence. For example, it eliminated the authority of the Secretariat, the key decision-making body of the party, over the party itself and the economy. At the same time, it called for term limits for people holding major office, and for contested elections of party representatives to a new legislature, a Congress of People's Deputies. The Soviet Union had taken a large step away from totalitarianism.

In March 1989 the first real multicandidate elections held in the Soviet Union since the balloting for the Constituent Assembly in 1918 were held for the new parliament. Two-thirds of the seats were to be filled by election and one-third by nominees of bodies like the Communist Party and the official trade unions. As a result, dozens of party candidates suffered humiliating defeats in key constituencies. The party was voted out of office in Leningrad and Kiev. In Moscow, Boris Yeltsin, formerly a Communist Party chief in the region, ran on an anti-Communist platform and received 89.4 percent of the vote. Less than a year later Gorbachev asked the Communist Party leadership to give up the exclusive hold on power and he transformed the political system into a presidential form of government. He also fired all twenty-five members of the Politburo and the Secretariat except himself and Edvard Shevardnadze. The attempt to form a conservative alliance to halt this whole process was easily broken by Gorbachev. The resistance to his reforms at this point was half-hearted and disorganized, due no doubt to the popular animosity directed toward the Communist Party. Despite the fact that discontent with the reform was growing, fuelled by the inflation and the chronic shortages, it was the party that continued to draw most of the Soviet public's ire. According to a poll taken in 1989, half the Soviet people blamed the current crisis not on *perestroika* but on communism. When asked what should be the country's highest priority, the vast majority expressed their strong wish for material and moral improvement, democracy and personal freedom.[6] Meanwhile support for communism was rapidly declining within the party itself, as thousands resigned their membership.

Glasnost and *perestroika* dramatically affected superpower relations as well. Gorbachev assumed office in 1985 during a diplomat's nightmare. He had inherited an endless guerrilla war in Afghanistan, a stalemate in arms control talks with the West, tension over the Horn of Africa, and world outrage that Moscow was persecuting dissidents and minorities. He understood that foreign and domestic goals were inextricably linked; that if he was to overhaul the Soviet economy he would also have to reduce external tensions and threats in order to push ahead with major domestic reforms. From the beginning he understood that the arms race had not really provided security for the Russian homeland.

The fundamental principle of the new political outlook is very simple:

> *nuclear war cannot be a means of achieving political, economic, ideological or any other goals* . . . nuclear war is senseless; it is irrational. There would be neither winners nor losers in a global nuclear conflict: world civilization would inevitably perish. It is a suicide.[7]

The arms race, he said, was an "absurdity" because its logic led to the destabilization of international relations and eventually to nuclear war. In the meantime it served to keep the country's enemies united and forced them to explore new technologies of warfare with which to challenge Soviet power. At the same time, the Soviet bloc countries had proven to be an onerous imperial burden and too much for the faltering Soviet economy to bear. To accomplish a major tailing back in the military establishment and to allow the satellites to stand on their own, he had to open direct negotiations with the United States and revive detente and peaceful coexistence. "New thinking" for Gorbachev meant that force was to be replaced by politics as a means of resolving interstate conflicts. It also called for the repudiation of the idea that the class struggle formed the basis of Russia's struggle with the capitalist West. With Gorbachev and his minister of foreign affairs, Edvard Shevardnadze, the "Two-Camps" doctrine was finally laid to rest once and for all, and the international system was now defined in terms of interdependence.

Gorbachev improved the negotiating climate between the two superpowers by removing impediments to it in the Soviet diplomatic corps. He not only removed the usually intransigent André Gromyko as foreign minister, but he also replaced ten of twelve deputy foreign ministers and nearly every important ambassador. Gromyko was replaced by Shevardnadze, a more flexible man, a close friend of Gorbachev, and a firm believer in reform. Reflecting on his years as foreign minister, he recalled:

> From the outset it was clear to all that the old methods of confrontation and the elevation of theology above politics and law were no longer suitable. By remaining stuck in the old positions, we would not stop the arms race which was bleeding our already anaemic country or reestablish cooperation with the West. . . . We had to build new relations with the Third World, to search for a new economic order, and to prevent the dangers of global crises.[8]

The change in Soviet foreign policy thinking met with a ready and positive response from the Reagan administration in the United States. This was quite remarkable since Reagan had come to office in 1980 as an implacable enemy of Soviet Communism. Viewing world politics in extremely Manichaean terms, Reagan believed that satanic forces drove Soviet behavior in the international arena. Until 1985, Reagan never stopped believing that the Soviet Union had deliberately chosen to promote civil wars, rebellions, and terrorism throughout the world in a malevolent attempt to construct an "evil empire."[9] A simple but level-headed man, Reagan ignored the previous U.S.-Soviet attempts at detente and thought more in terms of global containment and confrontation. He believed that with a huge arms buildup the weakening Soviet Union would have no choice but to negotiate on terms favorable to the United States. For this reason he launched the largest peacetime arms buildup in U.S. history. In spending more than two trillion dollars on new bombers, missiles, and ships, Reagan likened the arms race to "two westerners standing in a saloon aiming their guns at each others head—permanently. There had to be a better way."[10]

The foreign policy extension of this program was the so-called Reagan

Doctrine. The president made it clear that the United States would extend open military support to "freedom fighters" anywhere who struggled against Soviet-backed governments. Accordingly, crucial aid was extended to anti-communist insurgents in Afghanistan, Nicaragua, Angola, Cambodia, and Ethiopia. The policy did not call for any direct conflict on the part of the U.S. military, but instead committed the administration to local conflicts waged by allies and proxies. Not since the Eisenhower and Dulles years had an administration waged the Cold War in such an unabashed and evangelical way. Reagan sincerely believed that the United States was a chosen nation. "We have it in our power," he declared, "to begin the world over again."[11]

As part of the modernization of the U.S. military the administration introduced the Strategic Defense Initiative (SDI) in 1983. Nick-named "Star Wars" it was a vast defensive weapons system composed of laser beams designed to destroy enemy missiles targeted on the United States, and therefore it provided the United States with security from attack. According to Robert C. McFarlane, Reagan's assistant for national security affairs, SDI was basically a "bargaining chip," designed to intimidate the Soviet Union into an arms control agreement; almost all the original proponents of the program, he says, realized that it was too costly and too unreliable ever to be built.[12] Reagan, however, was the exception. He was so confident that this new technology would avoid a nuclear showdown that he offered to share its secrets with other nations. The Kremlin ignored the offer believing that the United States would never give away the secret to an advanced technology like SDI. Instead, it feared that SDI could easily be converted to offensive uses in an effort to carry out a first strike against the Soviet Union. Gorbachev inherited the fear that the United States might be preparing to fight a nuclear war it could win. He was very impressed with the potential of U.S. technology and he was worried that with any progress in SDI the United States would gain a decisive political and psychological advantage. This being the case, unless SDI was stopped Moscow would have to match the new system with a costly program of its own. This would deepen the Soviet economic problem and endanger *perestroika* and the modernization of the Soviet Union.

Was SDI and the larger U.S. military buildup the thing that convinced Gorbachev to end the Cold War? According to Robert Conquest it was. He points to a high-level conference on the Cold War held at Princeton University in February 1993 that brought together American and Soviet officials, including the former Soviet foreign minister, Alexsander Bessmertnykh. "The Soviet delegates," he writes, "insisted that Reagan's Strategic Defense Initiative was decisive in convincing Moscow that its attempt to match and outmatch the United States could not be sustained. This is still disputed in the West, though it is hard to see why."[13] There is some truth to this view that the Reagan arms race forced an end to the Cold War, but it is equally as legitimate to argue that it may actually have delayed its demise. Two historians have recently argued that SDI had little real impact on defense spending in Gorbachev's first four years in power; that his decision to end the Afghan War was made *despite* the U.S. arms buildup; and that Gorbachev was extremely put out by the SDI program because it made it more difficult to convince his officials and his conservative rivals that arms control was in the Soviet interest. They quote Alexander Yakovlev on this very point: "Star Wars was exploited by hardliners to complicate Gorbachev's attempt to end the Cold War."[14] This view is also held by Georgi Arbatov, who insists that the arms race not only undermined both the Soviet and U.S. economies but especially in the Soviet Union "it served to strengthen the positions of the Soviet military elite and the military-industrial complex, to boost the influence of militarism and Communist orthodoxy. By creating a hostile external environment, it frustrated the growth of internal contradictions, inherent in the system, as well as the courageous efforts of thousands and thousands of people who strove to free themselves from the totalitarian yoke."[15]

It is clear that the Reagan arms buildup complicated Gorbachev's drive to reform his country, but not to the exclusion of other more internal factors that argued for a termination of the Cold War. Gorbachev ended the Cold War because he was afraid that his country was fast becoming a second-rate power. SDI (and for that matter the Western advantage in personal computers, video recorders, etc.) demonstrated more than anything else that there existed between the two rivals an enormous technological gap, and that it was growing.

Gorbachev was no sooner in power than he announced that confrontation was an anomaly in Soviet-American relations. He also singled out the SDI program as the single most important impediment to a relaxation of tensions between the two countries. Seizing the initiative in April 1985 he unilaterally halted nuclear testing and ceased to deploy new intermediate-range nuclear missiles aimed at Western Europe. From November 19 to 21 Gorbachev and Reagan met for the first time at the Geneva Summit. The meeting on the whole was a positive one, although Gorbachev grew angry at Reagan's dogged commitment to SDI and his refusal to add his support to the nuclear testing ban. Reagan defended his program with passion: "It's not an offensive system. I am talking about a shield, not a spear." Gorbachev countered that "the reality is that SDI would open a new arms race."[16] Once the conference was over, Gorbachev proposed a major reduction of nuclear delivery systems and a limitation on the number of warheads, provided an agreement could be reached on "offensive space weapons." In January 1986 he dramatically proposed an eventual ban on all nuclear weapons by the year 2000. Gorbachev had not only seized the initiative but he shifted the moral onus for the continuance of the arms talks to Reagan.

On 11 and 12 October 1986, the two leaders met for the second time at Reykjavik, the capital of Iceland. The summit proved to be a debacle from the beginning. The U.S. delegation seemed unprepared for the sweeping Soviet proposals to reduce strategic weapons by 50 percent and had to scramble to catch up. The U.S. counterproposal called for the elimination of all strategic missiles in ten years, but the retention of defensive systems against long-range bombers and cruise missiles. Gorbachev then proposed abolishing all nuclear missiles over the next decade. Without consulting his advisors, Reagan replied positively to this. The two sides in the most euphoric moment of the conference agreed to cut their missile stockpiles in half by 1991, and eliminate them entirely by 1996. At the same time, Gorbachev demanded that SDI research be confined to the laboratory until that point. Reagan refused and the conference ended with nothing actually accomplished, and both sides blaming the other for the deadlock. When the two men said goodbye outside the conference building, Gorbachev bitterly said: "Mr. President, you have missed the unique chance of going down in history as a great president who paved the way for nuclear disarmament." Reagan replied, "that applies to both of us."[17] According to Donald Regan, the president was shattered. Anatoly Dobrynin, who participated in the conference, blamed both men for the failure of the summit; Reagan for being so stubborn on SDI, and Gorbachev for holding the program "hostage for the success of the meeting." He argues that substantial cuts could have been agreed to on a serious reduction of nuclear weapons and the whole matter of SDI should have been postponed for consideration at a future conference.

After the Reykjavik failure both leaders became absorbed in their own deepening domestic problems—Gorbachev with the chaotic progress of *perestroika* and Reagan with the Iran-Contra scandal that embarrassed the president and threatened to hurt his reputation.

By 1987 Gorbachev had reconsidered his view about SDI. The domestic situation was so bad that he tried to beef up his position by scoring successes on the international scene. He therefore pressed for urgent negotiations with Washington. In December 1987 the two sides agreed to the Intermediate Nuclear Forces Treaty (INF), which provided that both powers dismantle their medium-range and short-range nuclear missiles while talks on a Strategic Arms Reduction Treaty (START) to limit long-range missiles continued. The agreement also called for full on-site inspection and verification. INF was clearly a breakthrough: it was the first time in history that an agreement had been reached to abolish a whole category of weapons. In addition to these dramatic initiatives on arms control Gorbachev decided in early 1988 to pull out of the Afghan War. He apparently thought that the continued investment of Soviet resources in third world conflicts was an unneeded drain on the treasury and would achieve no tangible political advantages. When the evacuation of Soviet troops from Afghanistan was completed the following year, Shevardnadze formally apologized to the international community for his country's role in the war. In a remarkable speech before the U.N. General Assembly in December 1988, Gorbachev declared that war no longer could be considered an extension of politics and ideology had no place in international affairs. Force, he added, should be renounced as a mechanism for resolving international disputes. He then went on to propose a unilateral reduction in Soviet forces by 500,000 troops and 10,000 tanks, and its presence in Europe by 50,000 troops and 5,000 tanks. The domestic and foreign political effect of this reduction was quite positive, and Gorbachev certainly basked in the praise that came to him from the West. But as Anatoly Dobrynin points out, the Soviet government had failed to plan for the reintegration of so large a number of men into the civilian economy. Further large cuts in 1990 were made, which followed from a treaty between NATO and Warsaw Pact countries. The result was the mass withdrawal of Soviet forces from Central and Eastern Europe but with no place to house them in Russia. Because of it, "morale declined in the armed forces, and military and civilians alike wondered how the Soviet army, still seen as the European victors of World War II, could be rushed home as if it had simply been thrown out. This is an inglorious heritage of the Gorbachev era."[18]

When Gorbachev delivered his speech before the U.N. in 1988 there was every reason to believe that the Cold War was drawing to a close. But no one could predict under what circumstances it would take place.

Notes

1. Edvard Shevardnadze, *The Future Belongs to Freedom* (New York: The Free Press, 1991), 37.

2. Joel Kurtzman, "Of Perestroika, Prices and Pessimism," *New York Times*, 6 November 1988, 16-17.

3. Quoted in Michael R. Beschloss and Strobe Talbott, *At the Highest Levels: The Inside Story of the End of the Cold War* (Boston: Little, Brown and Company, 1993), 159.

4. Anatoly Dobrynin, *In Confidence* (New York: Random House, 1995), 625-26.

5. Robert V. Daniels, *The End of the Communist Revolution* (London: Routledge, 1993), 23.

6. Richard Pipes, *Times Literary Supplement* (October 8, 1993), 15.

7. Mikhail Gorbachev, *Perestroika: New Thinking for Our Country and the World* (New York: Harper and Row, 1988), 127.

8. Edvard Shevardnadze, *The Future Belongs to Freedom*, xi.

9. Quoted in Strobe Talbott, *The Russians and Reagan* (New York: Vintage, 1984), 32.

10. Ronald Reagan, *An American Life* (New York: Simon and Schuster, 1990), 547.

11. Quoted in *Department of State Bulletin* 84 (November 1984), 7.

12. Robert C. McFarlane, *Special Trust* (New York: Cabell and Davies, 1994).

13. Robert Conquest, "Red for Go. How Western Pundits Got the Wrong Signals about the USSR," *Times Literary Supplement* (9 July 1993), 4.

14. Quoted in Richard Ned LeBow and Janice Gross Stein, "Reagan and the Russians," *The Atlantic Monthly* (February 1994), 37.

15. Georgi Arbatov, *The System: An Insider's Life in Soviet Politics* (New York: Random House, 1993), 346.

16. Quoted in Dobrynin, *In Confidence*, 589.

17. Quoted in Dobrynin, *In Confidence*, 621.

18. Quoted in Dobrynin, *In Confidence*, 627.

23

The Collapse of the Soviet Union and the End of the Cold War

When Gorbachev originally sought a rapprochement with the West he had no thought of relinquishing control of Eastern Europe. He felt that the states of the region should be less of a burden on Moscow and this could only be accomplished if they were allowed to stand on their own feet. If they were a little more independent they would find it easier to duplicate the reforms associated with *perestroika* and *glasnost*. What he also seems to have misunderstood was that with the satellites so heavily in debt to the West a major renewal of detente might draw them even further away from Moscow's control. And this in a region replete with illegitimate regimes whose ultimate survival traditionally rested on Soviet tanks. With Gorbachev's belief that Soviet reforms could refurbish a moribund system, hope seemed to triumph over reality.

The reality, of course, was that declining rates of growth and technological stagnation led to a loss of confidence in central planning and to a widespread hatred of communist rule. The great debates about change throughout the Soviet bloc centered ultimately around the question whether a Western-style market economy might solve the problems of the region. More and more countries in the 1980s turned away from Moscow and looked to the capitalist West for their economic model.

The attempt to reform the Soviet Union by an indecisive and hesitant leadership sent a signal—originally encouraged by Gorbachev—to the reformers throughout the bloc that they could apply the same methods to similar problems. Until the collapse of the bloc in 1989, Gorbachev never really understood just how far his own reforming logic would take him. He believed that *glasnost*, even when extended to the full, was compatible with a Leninist socialist society. He wanted *glasnost* to sweep away the state institutions and bureaucrats that stood in the way of progressive change. But the peoples of Eastern Europe took *glasnost* to its logical conclusion by rebelling against communist rule and bringing a true end to the Cold War.

Once again, Poland was in the vanguard of change. For years General Jaruzelski had tried to revive the economy and failed miserably. The Communist

Party had been thoroughly discredited and in 1983 its general unpopularity was highlighted by Lech Walesa's winning of the Nobel Peace Prize. Events took a dramatic turn in the spring and summer of 1988 when a wave of strikes broke out throughout the country. It was fed by the general demoralization of the people and their demand for the legalization of Solidarity. The police failed to deal with it. The strike movement peaked in November with massive protests against the government's decision to close the Lenin shipyards in Gdansk.

Jaruzelski now elected to draw Solidarity into a cooperative effort to take responsibility for the country's economic future. Discussions were opened between the government, Solidarity, the Catholic Church, and other opposition groups in February 1989, and from them two things emerged: a shared belief that the old system was beyond salvation and that market solutions would in the future drive economic growth; and that Solidarity would once again be legalized and free elections held to a refurbished legislature of two houses—the Sejm, the lower house, and the Senate.

Elections to the legislature were held in June 1989 and they proved a major humiliation for the government. Solidarity won 80 percent of the popular vote, 99 out of 100 seats in the Senate, and dominated the Sejm. "Our defeat," Jaruzelski admitted, "is total." Before the year was out a Solidarity-led coalition was formed with the Solidarity editor and leading Catholic layman Tadeusz Mazowiecki as prime minister. Jaruzelski at first became the president to maintain the spirit of cooperation, but by early 1990 he was replaced by Lech Walesa, who then began Poland's rocky transition to a market economy. For the first time the Warsaw Pact included a non-communist government.[1]

Twenty years before, developments like these would have brought the wrath of Moscow down on Poland's head. But in 1989 Soviet intervention was not a consideration. In March 1989 Gennady Gerasimov, a spokesman for the Soviet foreign ministry, explained that the Brezhnev Doctrine had been replaced by what he called the "Sinatra Doctrine."[2] The reference was to the singer's popular song "My Way," and implied that Moscow would now allow Eastern European governments to develop their countries "their way." In June, other Soviet officials made similar statements and on a trip to France that summer, Gorbachev himself repudiated the Brezhnev Doctrine. He made it clear that the Soviet Union would no longer use force to keep the present Eastern European governments in power. In November 1989 he even went so far as to state that the Prague Spring of 1968 had been justified. Gorbachev threw his support to the reformers in Eastern Europe in the belief that he might rescue his own reform program, which in 1989 seemed to be going nowhere. At any rate, his repudiation of the Brezhnev Doctrine tolled the end to communist reforms in Eastern Europe. As it became evident that Moscow would not intervene in Poland, its most important satellite, the collapse of communism repeated itself in one country after another.

In Hungary, popular demands for liberalization spread from economics to politics at the beginning of the 1980s. In 1983 the government introduced a law that allowed for a choice of candidates in elections. They still had to proclaim their loyalty to the government but it was an encouraging step forward. In 1988 an even greater change was signalled when Janos Kadar was pressured into stepping down as general secretary of the Communist Party. Under the leadership of Karoly Grosz, party members themselves became forceful advocates of change. In early 1989, when Moscow began to withdraw Soviet troops from the country, Grosz announced constitutional changes designed to transform Hungary into a multiparty state—he legalized political parties, trade unions, and other non-communist organizations—and called for free elections for 1990. Critical journals appeared almost at once and the populace boycotted the traditional May Day parade. At the same time, under the pressure of events, the reformers within the Communist Party voted the party out of existence and subsequently reconstituted it as a Socialist Party. In June the government disinterred the remains of Imre Nagy and reburied the national hero of 1956 with great ceremonial before 300,000 people. The funeral took place a few weeks after the death of Janos Kadar. In the fall, the Hungarian parliament dismissed the Communist Party as the official ruling institution and people tore down communist symbols throughout the country. Nevertheless, more than any other East European state Hungary's transition to democracy was managed by the party.[3]

The events in Poland and Hungary produced a chain reaction throughout the bloc. In Czechoslovakia people watched the progress of events in the region expectantly. On January 16, 1989, a group of Czech students attempted to commemorate the death of Jan Palach, a young man who had immolated himself after the fall of the Prague Spring. Communism would not die easily in Czechoslovakia and the government, which fought change to the end, decided to ruthlessly suppress the demonstration and arrest Vaclav Havel. The repression was followed by mass demonstrations in all the major cities of the country. Reformists from all over the bloc criticized the Prague government's actions as well. Hungary's prime minister publicly voiced his disapproval, while political opposition leaders called for a hunger strike. Even in Bulgaria 100 intellectuals signed a petition for Havel's release. In the spring of 1989 a petition campaign within Czechoslovakia together with the pressure from outside the country was successful in securing Havel's release.

The events of early 1989 had produced an explosive situation—large public protests against an illegitimate government, a charismatic leader in Havel, and the necessary alliance between workers, students, and intellectuals. At the same time, East and West were preparing to declare an end to the Cold War and neither Washington nor Moscow would have tolerated the sustained use of force to maintain the Communist Party in power. Looking at the Czech situation on a visit to Prague that summer, Gorbachev emphasized that "minor repairs will not be enough. An overhaul is in order."[4]

In late October, large demonstrations broke out once again in Prague, this time in response to the marking of the seventy-first anniversary of the country's founding. The demonstration quickly turned into a massive protest for democracy and the government just as quickly cracked down. On November 19 the opposition group "Civic Forum" was formed which took the lead in organizing the demonstrations. Despite the violence of the police, the crowds soon grew larger and demanded an end to the regime. The turning point came on November 24, when the entire politburo resigned. The Communist Party put forward a new leader, Karel Urbanek, but the "Velvet Revolution" was not to be so easily defused. The new appointment produced only anger and a general strike and on the same day Alexander Dubcek and Vaclav Havel addressed huge crowds in Wenceslas Square where they called for the ouster of Stalinists from the government. The Communist Party now gave up its monopoly of power and its hard-line leader Milos Jakes and the rest of the politburo resigned capping the country's Velvet Revolution. In December Dubcek, still honored as a hero of 1968, became the president of the Czech parliament and Vaclav Havel, the country's most notorious dissident and its main symbol of resistance, became the president of Czechoslovakia. Czechoslovakia now proceeded to establish a pluralistic political system with a market economy. On December 4, 1989, following the Malta Summit, the Warsaw Pact took the unusual step of denouncing the 1968 invasion of Czechoslovakia. Indeed, Gorbachev went out of his way to say that the Prague Spring was "right at that time and . . . right now."[5]

The changes in Poland and Hungary worked to accelerate the pace of change elsewhere in the bloc, particularly in East Germany, Bulgaria, and Romania. A Slovak dissident writer noted that television played a major role in the spread of revolution.

> Isolation is now unthinkable with the existence of modern mass media. . . . Thirty or even twenty years ago, such parallel activities as ours would have been nipped in the bud, and nobody would have been the wiser, as indeed happened in the past.[6]

Although many East Germans hoped that Gorbachev's reforms would lead to change, Erich Honecker remained adamant in his resistance to reform as a matter of survival. He insisted that the GDR would not join a "march to anarchy." Honecker understood, as he nervously eyed developments elsewhere in the bloc, that East Germany was an artificial state and that one major gust of reform could topple his regime *and* sweep away his state. But the attempt to limit change in a country surrounded by democratic states or those in the process of democratizing was futile. This became clear in August 1989 when Poland, Hungary, and Czechoslovakia opened their borders and allowed East Germans to seek asylum in the West German embassies in their capitals. Because so many thousands of East Germans chose this option the embassies were forced to close, but in September Hungary decided to open its borders, thereby permitting the East German visitors to defect to the West via Austria without risk. The Berlin Wall, which was still standing, was thus rendered irrelevant. By October 1989 a flood of refugees soon reaching 225,000 made their way to the West. Their departure threatened to damage East Germany's economy even further. In early October 1989 Gorbachev paid a state visit to East Germany for celebrations to mark the fortieth anniversary of the GDR. While he was there he criticized Erich Honecker's failure to understand the popular mood in his country. Until this point, the Honecker regime had repressed popular dissent with the usual brutality. It had even banned Soviet journals from being sold in the GDR because they were deemed too liberal. But East Germans used the occasion of Gorbachev's visit to stage massive demonstrations against the regime, the largest seen in the country since 1953. On October 9, 1989, troops were deployed in Karl-Marx-Platz in Leipzig where the demonstrations were centered, and the local commander stated that he was ready to defend socialism "with weapon in hand."[7] Despite the fact that Gorbachev warned the regime privately not to expect Soviet help in putting down the protesters, Honecker issued a written order to crush the demonstration.[8] Much to his credit, Egon Krenz, recognized as Honecker's designated heir, countermanded the order and told local leaders to let the demonstrations proceed peacefully. Back in East Berlin Erich Mielke, the security chief, told Honecker, "Erich, we can't beat up hundreds of thousands of people."[9] On October 18 the Politburo compelled Honecker to resign and replaced him with his lieutenant, Egon Krenz. Gorbachev then sent a congratulatory telegram, which urged the new leadership to prove "sensitive to the demands of the time." He seems to have believed that reform communists would replace Stalinists in East Berlin and keep East Germany socialist. Krenz *did* make a concession to *perestroika* and *glasnost* by promising a program of economic and political reform and more openness in East German society. This was not enough, however, to stave off popular rage, and in the second week of November roughly one million protesters spilled into the streets determined to destroy the regime completely. These demonstrations accomplished one thing: the mass resignation of the East German government and its ruling politburo. With power slipping from his hands, Krenz announced on November 9 that citizens of the GDR would now have the unrestricted right to travel abroad and he opened the Berlin Wall. During the night of November 9-10 crowds of young people converged on the wall to physically destroy it. The wall was not just the quintessential symbol of the Cold War, it was also—like the Bastille of 1789 and the Winter Palace of 1917—the tyrannical symbol of a moribund autocracy. Attacking the wall with sledgehammers, the Berliners released years of frustration at their division and oppression. With the wall breached, some two million East Germans crossed briefly into the West exercising their new found freedom, and celebrating what had once again become a single city. By the end of 1989 leaders in both the East and the West declared that the Cold War was over and that a new and permanently peaceful relationship would take its place. The dismantling of the Berlin Wall was the most visible sign that the Cold War was indeed over.

Most of the changes in Eastern Europe in 1989 were accomplished with a minimum of blood spilled. In Bulgaria on November 10, 1989, for example, Todor Zhivkov, was ousted in a palace coup by Peter Mladenov, who promptly changed the name of the Communist Party and called for elections. The coup was swift and bloodless but in Romania it was not. At the beginning of 1989 the Ceausescu regime seemed to be as firmly as ever entrenched in power. Its leader was still the

Soviet bloc's harshest dictator. Ruling tsar-like, he destroyed hundreds of villages in the name of modernization and, despite the hatred of his people, felt secure behind the shield of a particularly ruthless and omnipresent secret police. That being the case, Ceausescu believed that his regime could be insulated against the dramatic events taking place elsewhere in Eastern Europe.

In December 1989 a Hungarian Protestant leader refused a deportation order to remove himself from the city of Timisoara. He had been actively defending the ethnic and religious rights of the persecuted Hungarian minority of Transylvania. The attempt to arrest him led to large demonstrations in the city and much bloodshed as the police fired on the crowd. Believing the situation stabilized, Ceausescu left the country to make a state visit to Iran. On his return on December 20 his attempt to address a large crowd in Bucharest backfired. The event turned into an anti-Ceausescu riot with the army this time refusing to fire on the crowd. Indeed, some military units even joined the demonstrators and marched on Communist Party headquarters. Fighting then broke out between the Romanian army and the secret police. With the army soon in control of the situation, some of its leaders, along with intellectuals and reform-minded communists, quickly formed a National Salvation Front and claimed to speak for the country. Meanwhile, Ceausescu and his wife were captured trying to flee the capital, tried secretly on charges of corruption and genocide, and—defiant to the end—executed.[10]

With every communist regime collapsing in Eastern Europe, it became apparent that Gorbachev was no longer the master of events but rather a helpless witness to history. This was particularly true of the German question.

The whole protest movement against the regime of the GDR was accompanied by the popular demand for reunification of the two Germanies. But the prospect of uniting Germany once again filled the Soviet leadership—as it did other Europeans—with dread. Up until the moment when the two Germanies were joined, the Soviet leadership maintained that the split was essential for maintaining the European balance of power. Nevertheless, Gorbachev was so helpless that he could not bring himself to use this reunification of Germany as a bargaining chip to extract important concessions. For example, Gorbachev had briefly flirted with the idea of accepting a united but neutral Germany, or even offering it simultaneous membership in both NATO and the Warsaw Pact. He at first understood that while reunficiation was inevitable, it should be integrated rationally into a completely new security structure for the continent, which merged East and West into a sensible whole. But according to Anatoly Dobrynin, Gorbachev yielded on all important points and the Western countries intensified their pressure and skilfully manipulated him, as the Soviet economy continued its downward spiral.[11]

It took the Bush administration until 1989 to appreciate the validity of the Gorbachev revolution. On December 2 and 3 while Eastern Europe was trampling on communism and charting its own destiny, Bush and Gorbachev held a summit on board a Soviet ship anchored off the coast of Malta. It was obvious from the start that Gorbachev approached Bush with his hat in hand. He admitted to Bush that his reform program was languishing and that if something was not done soon, his whole regime would likely fail. Bush responded by offering various proposals on arms control designed to end the pressure on the Soviet economy. The Malta summit reflected the new era of mutual trust and cooperation between two former rivals.

Chancellor Helmut Kohl of Germany seized the opportunity offered by the events of 1989 to speed up the process of unification. This process was facilitated when the East Germans, in their first free elections in March 1990 voted overwhelmingly for candidates who favored a unified Germany, and who elected as prime minister a Christian Democrat, the same party Kohl headed in West Germany. In July 1990 Kohl arranged for East German currency to be exchanged on a one-to-one basis with West German marks. With the economic foundations for unity in place, Kohl then agreed to make major economic concessions to the Russians in exchange for acquiescence to German unification. These included the extension of a five billion mark bank credit to Moscow and a promise to pay the cost of removing the Soviet army from East German soil.

By July 1990 Gorbachev dropped any conditions he might have made and accepted Germany's membership in NATO as a unified nation. According to Anatoly Dobrynin, Kohl was stunned by the capitulation. "I believe," Dobrynin concludes, "that Gorbachev never foresaw that the whole of Eastern Europe would fly out of the Soviet orbit within months or that the Warsaw Pact would crumble soon. He became the helpless witness to the consequences of his own policy."[12] Being helpless he precipitated the rout of communism everywhere and the Revolution of 89. Zbigniew Brezezinski has called Gorbachev's capitulation over a united Germany: "The functional equivalent of the act of capitulation in the railroad car in Compiègne in 1918 or on the U.S.S. *Missouri* in August 1945," and therefore the end of the Cold War.[13]

The Revolution of '89 occurred concurrently with the growing collapse of the Soviet Union. Economically speaking, Gorbachev's reforms in the final analysis failed to satisfy the demands for more radical change that the campaign for *perestroika* and *glasnost* seemed to promise. The Soviet people since 1985 had been asked to make greater sacrifices—to work harder and drink less—but they failed to see any immediate benefit from it. Unlike the Chinese whose memory of capitalism was more recent, the Russian worker was not used to the idea of working for profit, and he completely lacked market skills. The peasants, on the other hand, only wanted to concentrate on their private plots and as a consequence the supply of meat and dairy products fell. By 1988, as the system was becoming more democratized, the shortages became more acute and hundreds of convenience items began disappearing from the shelves. Barter became more common, ration cards were introduced in Moscow, and the black market flourished. Gorbachev, who was increasingly flattered by Western governments and their media for democratizing his country, became increasingly vulnerable at home.[14]

Economic distress brought about by the transition from socialism to capitalism contributed to the rise of nationalism and ethnic unrest within the Soviet Union's constituent republics. Gorbachev's regime became vulnerable to these changes, which increasingly weakened the bonds that held the country together. Whatever Marxism meant to intellectuals, it was nationalism and ethnic identity that stirred the masses of Europe in the twentieth century. Not understanding its power, Lenin had wrongly believed that nationalism would disappear under communism. As a consequence, since the 1920s Moscow had generally succeeded in ruthlessly suppressing ethnic politics but made only a half-hearted attempt to erase ethnic culture. But as the center of the Soviet empire unravelled in the 1980s, all the pent-up passions and hatreds erupted, culminating in demands for independence. This fragmentation of the Soviet Union was accelerated by Gorbachev's reforms. Because of *perestroika* and the attempt to break the resistance to it by reducing the power of the Communist Party, Moscow managed to loosen its "command-administrative methods" in the republics. At the same time, *glasnost* entailed talking about past grievances and injustices. Local party leaders, trying to maintain their balance and their jobs, increasingly threw in their lot with the nationalist forces in the regions. It now became politically popular for communist officials to publicly flout the Kremlin. Initially this movement was strongest in the Baltic republics where the elections of 1989 showed the strength of nationalist candidates.

Absorbed by the Soviet Union in 1940 the Baltic republics possessed peoples who felt culturally superior to their Russian masters, and who retained a strong sense of national identity. The desire to retain their own cultural integrity was just one of the factors in their drive for liberation from Moscow. Another important factor was their growing concern about the ecological damage done to their countries. Protests against this emerged in 1986 and 1987 and their success prompted nationalist groups to press for broader political action.

At the congress of June 1988, which dealt with democratization, the non-Russian delegates from the Baltic states demanded greater political autonomy. This was followed by the creation of popular fronts in all three republics to work for independence. In November 1988 the Estonian parliament adopted a "Declaration of Sovereignty," which asserted its right to veto laws passed by Moscow. Visiting Lithuania in January 1989 Gorbachev offered the Baltic peoples the creation of a new Soviet federation with increased autonomy for all. Denouncing his proposal as so much "trickery," the Baltic governments continued to press for complete independence. On March 11, 1990, the Lithuanian government took the major step of actually declaring its independence. This now appears to be the fateful moment in the breakup of the Soviet Union. Until 1990 no republic had seceded from the Soviet Union and few politicians had even seriously considered such a step. The Estonians declared their independence on March 30, and the Latvians followed suit on May 4. Over the following months Gorbachev reinforced the Soviet garrison in Lithuania and imposed an economic blockade on the country. He also ordered some 1,500 Lithuanian soldiers who had deserted from the Soviet army to return to their units. The Lithuanian president, Vyatautas Landsbergis, a former music teacher, urged the soldiers to disobey orders and seek sanctuary in churches. Like many nationalist politicians of the period, Landsbergis sensed that Gorbachev was unable to draw back from the political and moral consequences of his policies. The three Baltic states now began to coordinate their efforts and in May 1990 they renewed the Baltic Entente of 1934. When Gorbachev failed to punish Lithuania's apostasy—there was some harassment by Red army personnel, but there was no sustained use of military force—secession from the Soviet Union became a political option and the subject of daily discussion in the Soviet Union.[15]

Lenin once referred to the vast, polyglot Russian empire of the tsars as a "prison of nations." Three of the smallest of these nations had now declared their independence from the Soviet Union. Their success in achieving this encouraged other nationalist movements to grow in some of the largest of the nations, such as Russia and Ukraine.

On May 29, 1990, Boris Yeltsin, an outspoken reformer who had been dismissed from the party leadership after openly criticizing the slow pace of reform, was elected chairman of the Supreme Soviet of the Russian Republic. This made him the de facto president of the Russian Republic. A man whose whole outspoken and populist style seemed to clash with bureaucratic torpor, Yeltsin asserted that Russia had the right to control its own natural resources, establish its own citizenship, conduct its own foreign policy, and he declared that its laws took precedence over those of the Soviet Union. Containing a bit more than half the population of the Soviet Union, and by far the richest of all the republics, a secessionist Russia could have destroyed the unity of the entire country.

The resource-rich Ukraine, with a population second only to Russia's, took similar moves toward independence. It took control of its own internal and foreign affairs and it even took some initial steps toward the creation of a Ukrainian currency.

Independence movements were also in progress in Belorussia, Moldava, Georgia, Kazakhstan, Turkmenistan, Uzbekistan, and Tadzhikstan. From the initial defections from the country, and in a growing atmosphere of crisis, Gorbachev pinned his hopes on the republics seeing that there were clear economic advantages in maintaining links to some kind of union. In June 1991, in a desperate bid to hold the Soviet Union together, the Kremlin and nine republics negotiated a new "Union of Sovereign Soviet Republics," which was designed to turn the Soviet Union into a confederation. Under the agreement the Kremlin would maintain control of transportation, communications, and the military, while the republics retained the power to tax, control their own resources, and police themselves. The new arrangement alarmed the security organs, the military, and their hard-line supporters, and on August 19, 1991, the day before the agreement on the new union was to be signed, there was an attempt to arrest Gorbachev and seize control of the central government. The leadership of the coup was dominated by representatives of the traditional national security establishment. Nevertheless, the coup was poorly organized and led, and key units of the army and police refused to cooperate. While Gorbachev was detained by the KGB in his Crimean retreat, Boris Yeltsin led the resistance to the coup in Moscow. The leaders of the coup had no stomach for violence and neither did their soldiers, who quickly defected. The coup quickly unravelled and its leaders were arrested.

It was Boris Yeltsin who had determined the course of events—it was he who saved the day, and not Gorbachev whose authority received an irreparable blow. The voice of reform now belonged to Yeltsin. As a result of the coup local leaders all across the Soviet Union turned on the Communist Party, which had been so thoroughly discredited. They sealed the party's offices, confiscated its property, closed the special stores, and destroyed its outward symbols. Statues of Lenin were toppled all over the country.

On December 1, 1991, Russia, Ukraine, and Belarus (Belorussia) created a new Commonwealth of Independent States (CIS). They were subsequently joined by eight former Soviet republics. On December 25, 1991, in a final and dramatic television address to his nation, Gorbachev defended himself against the charge that he was responsible for the breakup of the Soviet Union. "All the halfhearted reforms—and there were a lot of them—fell through," he said, "one after another. This country was going nowhere, and one couldn't possibly live the way we had been living. We had to change everything." He then went on to thank those people who took his side in the debates of the previous six years, admitted having made a few mistakes, expressed his bitterness toward his rivals, and at the same time voiced his hope in the country's rebirth. He then resigned his office as president of the Soviet Union. The red flag, which was raised for the first time in 1917, was now lowered for the last time on Russian soil. The Soviet Union ceased to exist.

That evening President Bush made a television address of his own from the White House. In it he praised Gorbachev for allowing the transition to democracy to take place in the Soviet Union without bloodshed. Then turning to the Cold War he said that "for over forty years, the United States led the West in the struggle against communism and the threat it posed to our most precious values." "That confrontation," he concluded, "is over."

One month later in his State of the Union Address Bush was less cautious in his appraisal of Cold War history. He used this occasion, at the beginning of an election year, to trumpet the American role in postwar history by declaring that the United States had "won the Cold War." He then received thunderous applause from the joint session of Congress.[16]

Notes

1. Karen Dawisha, *Eastern Europe, Gorbachev and Reform: The Great Challenge*, 2nd ed. (Cambridge: Cambridge University Press, 1990), 179-82.

2. Quoted in Michael R. Beschloss and Strobe Talbott, *At the Highest Levels: The Inside Story of the End of the Cold War* (Boston: Little, Brown and Company, 1993), 134.

3. E. Abel, *The Shattered Bloc: Behind the Upheaval in Eastern Europe* (Boston: Houghton Mifflin, 1990).

4. Abel, *The Shattered Bloc*, 58.

5. Abel, *The Shattered Bloc*, 67.

6. Abel, *The Shattered Bloc*, 83.

7. Timothy Garton Ash, *The Uses of Adversity: Essays and the Fate of Central Europe* (New York: Random House, 1989), 67.

8. Abel, *The Shattered Bloc*, 115.

9. Quoted in Gale Stokes, ed., *From Stalinism to Pluralism: A Documentary History of Eastern Europe since 1945* (New York: Oxford University Press, 1991), 257.

10. Dawisha, *Eastern Europe*, 182-85.

11. Anatoly Dobrynin, *In Confidence* (New York: Random House, 1995), 629.

12. Dobrynin, *In Confidence*, 632.

13. Zbigniew Brzezinski, "The Cold War and Its Aftermath," *Foreign Affairs* 71, no. 4 (Fall 1992): 34.

14. Marshall I. Goldman, *What Went Wrong with Perestroika* (New York: W.W. Norton and Company, 1992).

15. Anatol Lieven, *The Baltic Revolution: Estonia, Latvia, Lithvania and the Path to Independence*, 2nd ed. (New Haven, Conn.: Yale University Press, 1994).

16. Quoted in Beschloss and Talbott, *At the Highest Levels*, 463-64.

Conclusion

After the war and revolutionary crisis of 1914-1918 there existed a deep suspicion between Washington and Moscow. But their relationship remained suspended for the next quarter century as the Soviet Union continued to consolidate the gains of the revolution and build "socialism in one country," and the United States retreated behind the walls of isolationism.

In 1941 both states were wrenched suddenly into the second global crisis of the twentieth century. The Cold War confrontation arose directly out of the diplomacy and national competition of the Second World War. In this sense, the Cold War was a natural clash between two great states that reached superpowerhood at the same historical moment. The confrontation was realized in the chaos of the war's aftermath when empires began to topple and when there was widespread destitution in key parts of the world.

The immediate cause of the Cold War was the Soviet Union's refusal to confine itself to its own borders, its intention to exploit the chaos left by collapsing empires, and its attempt to fill the vacuums left in the Eastern Mediterranean and the Middle East by the collapse of British power. For the first time since 1917, the Soviet Union had thrown down a world-historical challenge. The Cold War was then joined when the United States mobilized its considerable resources and responded to this clear geopolitical challenge.

The United States began the Cold War with a clear and overwhelming advantage. It emerged from the war an economic colossus while the other major countries, including the Soviet Union, concentrated their energies on rebuilding war-torn economies. Nevertheless, the United States relegated itself to an essentially passive diplomacy during the period of its greatest power. Instead of bringing its considerable assets into line with its will to use them to achieve a decisive breakthrough against its enemy, it chose to do several other things: first, it decided to maintain the balance of power by deliberately restraining itself and not abusing its preponderance of power. It accomplished this through the policy of "containing" the Soviet Union. In doing so, it tacitly acknowledged the existence of spheres of influence, the very thing that American presidents made a point of condemning. Second, realizing that Germany and Japan would be critical in any protracted geopolitical struggle, the United States rebuilt their economies and restored their previous power, albeit in a more benign form. Third, the United States responded to the immediate postwar crisis with the Truman Doctrine and the Marshall Plan, brilliant strategies that succeeded in denying critical areas of the world to the Soviet

Union and its allies. In doing so, it robbed the Soviet Union of any real chance to win the Cold War.

The strategic discrepancy between the United States and the Soviet Union—and the ever-present fear of the nuclear superiority of the United States—determined much in the Cold War from 1945 until the 1970s when Moscow pulled abreast. That discrepancy was decisive in preventing local crises from spilling over into general ones. This was why, even when Moscow appeared to achieve a breakthrough (like Suez, Angola, and Cuba) it nevertheless demonstrated its inability to decisively effect the outcome of events. It simply would not challenge U.S. nuclear superiority. By the 1980s when the Soviet Union was armed to the teeth, it no longer mattered. There was no confrontation crisis because the Soviet Union had already begun its fatal slide into chaos and collapse.

By the 1970s the Soviet problems of economy and state had reached crisis proportions. Ultimately, like the Austro-Hungarian empire, the Soviet Union became the victim of clashing nationalisms with a moribund imperial state. Like Francis Joseph I, the last emperor of the Habsburg Empire, Mikhail Gorbachev inherited an inefficient and corrupt empire in crisis. A man of reforming purpose, he could never build from strength. With *perestroika* failing and worried at the prospect of its country's demise, the Soviet leadership might have been tempted—as the Austrians were in 1914—to indulge itself in an overly aggressive foreign policy to reverse the decline at home, solve its domestic problems, and preserve national unity. This was potentially a very dangerous moment. Fortunately, the leadership lost its nerve and chose to retreat. Instead of setting off on an adventure into, for example, the Persian Gulf, Gorbachev elected to end the Cold War, relinquish the satellites, and allow the Soviet Union to split up peacefully.

The Cold War was as much a thought as it was a fact. In the long march to its conclusion people all over the world were involved emotionally as the struggle often inspired fear or enthusiasm, patriotism or self-deprecation. In both countries the Cold War gave a certain purpose to national life. In the Soviet Union it helped for decades to shore up the power of the Communist Party. In the United States, it fuelled the need to defend American freedom and values and, at its peak, it provided the inspiration of crusading.

Like the other power struggles of the past, the Cold War has passed from current events to history. This has been clearly recognized by both superpowers as is the fact that the balance of power has now disappeared as well. The whole postwar geopolitical order has come to an end.

Index

About the Author

ROBERT C. GROGIN was born in New York City in 1935. He did his undergraduate education at New York University where he received his B.A. in 1957. After graduation he served two years with the U.S. Army's Counter-Intelligence Corps in Stuttgart, Germany. He then returned to New York University where he received his Ph.D. in 1969. He has been teaching Modern European History at the University of Saskatchewan since 1966. Professor Grogin has written a previous book, *The Bergsonian Controversy in France, 1900-1914*, which appeared in 1988.